John Bromyard
on Church and State

JOHN BROMYARD

ON CHURCH AND STATE

The *Summa Predicantium*
and Early Fourteenth-Century England

A Dominican's Books and Guide for Preachers

Keith Walls

Published by Clayton-Thorpe Publications
37 Londesborough Road
Market Weighton
York YO43 3HR

ISBN 978-1-904446-11-8

Walls, Keith
John Bromyard on Church and State
The *Summa Predicantium* and early fourteenth-century England
A Dominican's books and guide for preachers
p.xii, 323 : cm25.
Includes bibliographical references and index.
1. Dominicans – Hereford and Southern Britain. 2. Books – Bible, Canon Law, Civil Law, classics.
3. Preaching. 4. Morality in Church and State – early fourteenth century. 5. Christians, Muslims and Jews.
6. Italy – fourteenth century.

Bound by Smith Settle of Yeadon
Designed by Mandy O'Sullivan
Typeset and printed by
Quacks the Printers
7 Grape Lane
York YO1 7HU

DEDICATION

This modest study has a triple dedication:

to the scholar-publisher Johann Amerbach of Basel, who read enough of the *Summa* in manuscript to realize its importance, then took the financial gamble to issue a text of Brobdingnagian scale:

to his team of skilled compositors – tireless and able Latinists – and printers who worked those long hours in 1484 which ensured the text's widespread transmission throughout Europe, and survival:

and to the imperishable memory of the fearless, upright, God-fearing Dominican who has been my daily companion for the best part of five years.

ACKNOWLEDGEMENTS

It is a pleasure to declare the debts I owe to the generosity of both individuals and institutions, and to express my thanks.

My indebtedness to the two great libraries of York is profound. Of the two hundred or so books listed in Abbreviations 55 were borrowed from the University of York library, while 38 were loaned from or consulted in York Minster Library. Without the access to such a wealth of learning I could hardly have embarked on this modest enterprise. I am particularly grateful to John Powell, the Minster librarian, for rescuing for me from Conservation a volume of the Calendar of Patent Rolls.

The great privilege of consulting the Peterhouse manuscript of the *Summa Predicantium*, as well as the manuscript of Bromyard's *Exhortationes*, I owe to the kindness of Dr Patrick Zutshi and Cambridge University Library.

Throughout the writing of successive versions of each one of the chapters I have been buoyed up by the steadfast encouragement of my two readers, and have readily profited from their sage advice: Deirdre Mortimer, former Rare Books Consultant at York Minster Library: and Peter Young, Archivist at York Minster Library and Archives.

For the tracing of three quotations whose sources puzzled me I am extremely grateful to Ian Andrews of Pocklington School. I am heartened too by the generous encouragement given me by Professor Nicholas Orme of the University of Exeter. The probing questions posed by Lydia Harris have prompted me to consider afresh several key points in my later chapters. For his patient and lucid explications of the evolution and workings of the Common Law of England I am deeply beholden to David Stather.

A special accolade is due Christine Harbisher. From the untidy Urschrift of attempts on early chapters and the jumbled paragraphs and scorings out disfiguring longer sections of the later texts she has cheerfully brought neatness, order and clarity through her immaculate skills on the word processor, and has expertly handled far more passages of medieval Latin than I dared prepare her for.

Finally I own my huge obligations to a galaxy of scholars, past and present, whose studies have so richly illuminated a fascinating period in English and continental history. Of specific value to me have been the writings of A. T. Bannister, Peter Binkley, the greatly missed Leonard Boyle, the several editors of the CBMLC, C. R. Cheney, Wendy R. Childs, Natalie Fryde, Bernard Guillemain, R. M. Haines, W. A. Hinnebusch, Norman Housley, William C. Jordan, Ian Kershaw, F. M. Powicke, H. E. Salter, Sylvia Schein, Norman P. Tanner and Paget Toynbee. To modify Bromyard's comment on modern clerics: 'non [sum]..nisi gnanus exaltatus super scapulas gigantis..' (S.4.8)

Corpus Christi 2007

CONTENTS

LIST OF TABLES

PART II

NOTE

The use, for emphasis, of italics and upper case in translations of Bromyard's text
was determined by the translator, who also supplied the insertions between square
brackets.

PREFACE

I chanced upon the *Summa Predicantium* in late 2002. The Prologue alone persuaded me that I was encountering a text worthy of deeper acquaintance. Quite soon I became intrigued by the author's punctilious referencing of his multifarious sources and imagined it might throw a modest light upon his library resources to record and categorize these references. Table 3.1 is the outcome of this endeavour. It slowly became apparent to me that Bromyard's access to some sources was mediated through other texts and that I could not recreate on paper the Hereford Dominicans' library of the early fourteenth century. But my interest in what he read remained: and Part I of this little study attempts, through a series of tables within the brief chapters 1 to 20, to quantify the author's dependence on his texts. The short comments accompanying these tables are not designed to evaluate those texts but to indicate Bromyard's access to, interest in, and use of, the texts.

As I read further into the *Summa* certain concerns and engagements of the author forced themselves upon me. These I explore and assess in, I am aware, a rather perfunctory manner, in chapters 21 to 30 of Part II. Central to one's understanding of the focus and nature of Bromyard's views on the Church and society in general is the question of the date of composition to be assigned to the *Summa*. Scholars of the generation of G. R. Owst, A. Miller and G. G. Coulton accepted a date of c.1390. Then in 1927 J. Th. Welter dated it to 1360-1368. G. Mifsud's 1953 study proved that the *Summa* could not postdate 1354: and Sister M. A. Devlin's 1954 edition of Thomas Brinton's *Sermones* made clear that the *Summa* must have been written at least by 1352. That date had already been established as a *terminus ad quem* by the publication in 1912 of J. H. Parry's edition of the Register of John Trillek, which recorded Bromyard's replacement in October 1352 by another friar from the Hereford convent. L. E. Boyle's 1973 essay, sanctioned by Peter Binkley in 1995 and 2004, makes the case for c.1328 to 1348. These dates will be challenged in chapter 24 and, intermittently, elsewhere in Part II. The matter of which period of English history Bromyard's comments should be seen as illuminating is clearly of fundamental importance. The remarks prized by the social or political historian are, however, not always those at the heart of Bromyard's concerns. These are essentially focused on the Dominicans' rôle, by means of a vigorous and unremitting campaign of preaching, to turn the men and women of England, from the highest rank to the lowest, away from subjection to sin towards a life lived by the Laws of God.

INTRODUCTION

'A preacher's life, S.Gregorius tells us[1], reverberates and blazes. It reverberates with the Word: it blazes with desire. An ignited preaching, then, is white-hot bronze. But from white-hot bronze come sparks: since from his encouragement issue forth to the ears of his audience words on fire. It's right that a preacher's words are called sparks: because those he touches at heart are set on fire. And just as sparks fly out to those standing back, so the preacher should not only inflame the present generation with the sparks of his words but also, as much as he can, he should benefit future generations and far-off peoples through the examples given by the scriptures. And so Cassiodorus stated[2] 'Let the age to come take its place with an innovation that is worthwhile.'…

Much still remains to be done and much will remain: no one born one hundred thousand years from now will be denied the chance of adding something yet to this task. We all, you see, must live not just for ourselves or our own time but for succeeding generations too. For this we have guide, example and authority. Our *guide* is nature. The sun and all the stars give their light, as best they can, to all: not just for the present generation but for our descendants too their light will shine. Our *example*, Iustinianus tells us[3], is the life of eminent men. 'Of Our own free will', he declared, 'We take on drudgery to pave the way for others to have peace'… 'All Our days and nights', the emperor adds, 'it falls to Our lot to pass in thought of how something useful and pleasing to God should be rendered through Our gifts..' Our *authority*, the wise. For the wise men of antiquity did not consider anyone lived unless he or she lived for the benefit of their fellow men: as Seneca observes[4] 'The man who lives for no one does not live for himself..' Cicero agrees[5]: 'The condition of my country after my death is of no less concern to me than its condition today.'

It was Cicero too who said[6] Plato made the admirable remark 'It's not only for ourselves we are born: part of our origin is claimed by our homeland, part by our friends': and, as the Stoics have it, whatever is created on earth, all of it, is brought into being for the use of man, but men were born for the sake of humanity so that they could help each other in mutual relationships. With this sentiment the civil law too is in agreement: stating that man is born for the common weal.[7] Aristoteles is of like mind[8]: he teaches that the general good has a greater element in it of the divine… That's what S.Paul says too[9]: 'No one lives for himself', etc. And Ecclesiasticus[10] also: 'See that I did not toil for myself alone, but for all who seek guidance.' '[11]

This extract from the Prologue to the *Summa* neatly introduces us to Bromyard the preacher as well as to one of the major principles driving him: namely, that one should live one's life not for oneself but for others. That idea, though praiseworthy, is not unusual. What takes this declaration into remarkable territory is his belief that our distant descendants too must be in the forefront of our thoughts and that the mode of our living and the decisions we make now should encompass the needs of future generations. The observation Cicero attributes to Laelius is selected and used by Bromyard to emphasize this central point: 'The condition of my country after my death is of no less concern to me than its condition today.'

The *Summa Predicantium* is a guide for preachers. The immediate readership John Bromyard had in mind was his fellows at the Dominican convent in Hereford, which was securely established at its Frog Lane site in 1322, after lengthy disputes.[12]

1

The *Summa* is not a technical manual offering instruction on the composition of sermons, although advice is found here and there on matters such as selection and honing of themes. Bromyard was freed from the need to proffer such counsel since training in the techniques of public speaking was carried out inside the convent.[13]

What the *Summa* does offer is a largeness of outlook on the proper conduct of human life lived under God's law. It achieves this through the breadth of material developed in its 189 capitula. Other books, both preceding and roughly contemporary with the *Summa*, employed the same alphabetic format and dealt, in encyclopedic fashion, with issues similar to those Bromyard addressed. What distinguishes *his* greatest book from those others is the depth of treatment he accords his subjects. The 189 chapters have an average length of some 5,250 words, but it is not the wordage alone which marks out the *Summa*. The evidence of a wide reading is apparent, attested by his 14,000 citations: more telling is the unmistakable presence of a powerful and well-organized intellect which has chosen its extracts judiciously, has appraised them and controlled their use, subsuming them into the mainstream of its own argument. It is not swamped by them. There is no impression of the pudding being overegged as there is in, for example, the *Communiloquium* of John of Wales. The relative importance to Bromyard of his subject matter may be gauged by the length of the individual capitula, presented in Table 0.1:

TABLE 0.1 : THE 20 LONGEST CAPITULA

1.	MORS	98.00
2.	ORDO CLERICALIS	61.33
3.	RELIGIO	59.00
4.	PENITENTIA	54.33
5.	PRELATIO	49.33
6.	TRIBULATIO	47.00
7.	VISITATIO	37.25
8.	AVARICIA	33.50
9.	FALSITAS	32.75
10.	EUCHARISTIA	32.00
11.	PASSIO CHRISTI	31.75
12.	FIDES	31.33
13.	CONFESSIO	29.50
13.	LUXURIA	29.50
15.	RAPINA	29.25
16.	PREDICATIO	28.50
17.	ACQUISITIO	27.50
17.	ELEMOSINA	27.50
17.	BELLUM	27.50
20.	MISERICORDIA	26.50

The figures represent the number of columns each capitulum occupies in the first printed edition [Goff J-260]. The average length of each of the 189 capitula is 13.62 columns, some 5,250 words. MORS runs to an extraordinary 37,000 words.

The significance of these figures is that they reveal which topics most closely engaged Bromyard's interest, and/or which seemed in need of a lengthier development, and/or which he thought would be of the greatest concern to his readers, present and future. We know he took the long view.[14]

The 14,000 citations have been classified and assigned to their several categories, as displayed in Table 0.2:

TABLE 0.2 : THE *SUMMA* : BROMYARD'S CITATIONS BY CATEGORIES

	NUMBER OF CITATIONS	% OF TOTAL
BIBLIA SACRA	10,566	74.28
PATRISTIC AGE	1,230	8.65
CANON LAW	904	6.36
CLASSICAL	442	3.11
CIVIL LAW	384	2.70
CHRISTIANS 1100 – c.1330	373	2.62
SCHOLASTICS	140	0.98
HAGIOGRAPHA	66	0.46
CHRISTIANS 700 – c.1080	42	0.30
HISTORICA	36	0.25
MUSLIMS	13	0.09
OTHER LIVES	9	0.06
FEUDAL LAW	9	0.06
ENGLISH LAW	3	0.02
JEWS	3	0.02
ROMANCIAE	3	0.02
LITURGICA	1	0.01
unplaced*	1	0.01
TOTAL	14,225	

The six leading categories furnish 97.71% of Bromyard's citations.
*There is one citation, of Melchebron at M.11.72, which I cannot place in any category.

All seventeen categories of citations are examined separately in chapters 2, 4 to 19 of Part I, largely for the light they cast on Bromyard's access to, interest in, and use of, his texts. These chapters are flanked by chapter 1, which analyses the structure of the *Summa* and places it within the frame of the other works in his oeuvre, and by chapter 20, which considers how he might have planned the *Summa*. Of the ten chapters in Part II nine are devoted to treating of matters whose importance to Bromyard emerges from a multitude of references within the work, while chapter 24 assesses the currently accepted dating for the *Summa*.

Someone, somewhere, taught young John Bromyard his ABC. He may have learnt from a hornbook at home or a parish priest may have helped. A classroom, however, is suggested by his recollection of school punishments:

'..if a schoolboy takes pride in being able to give a [good] account of his reading to avoid a beating..'[15]

Provided we accept that John was christened at S.Peter's Bromyard,[16] and that he grew up in the village, then we *may* look to either Worcester, 17 miles east,[17] or Leominster, 12 miles west,[18] as possible sites for his schooling. His parents may have been quite well-to-do since he writes of the cost of maintaining a son at school (or, in the schools) as three or four silver pennies per week.[19] We are still in the dark in respect of his higher studies, even though he displays some knowledge of university life (in a passage prompted by citations of Isaiah 8.[1] and Apocalypse 21.[27] – 'nisi qui scripti sunt in libro vite agni'):

'This [usefulness] is evidenced by means of the magisterial rolls of the university in which are inscribed the names of the scholars: on account of which inscription they are safeguarded in many aspects and enjoy the privileges of the university denied to others whose names are not inserted.' He goes on to detail the funeral honours accorded such scholars.[20]

He is familiar too with attendance figures in lecture halls: '..where other masters have a hundred students a master in theology will not have twenty.'[21] And 'the school of civil lawyers has a hundred or two hundred students whereas the school of theology perhaps can't muster five.'[22]

The pressures of copying a *pecia* text late into the night by the flickering light of a single candle will explain some students' fatigue: Bromyard contents himself with censuring their behaviour during lectures. His discourse was triggered by the verse he cites from Matthew 20.[16] of the Vulgate, 'multi sunt enim vocati pauci autem electi',[23] on which he tersely and accurately comments 'take away free will and hell will not exist.'[24] As an example of this freedom of choice we enjoy – to choose good or evil – he instances university students. His numbers ('many thousands') are grossly inflated for contemporary Oxford: he may have in mind Paris or Bologna:[25] but his reproach is for their non-attendance at lectures: '..or they come, certainly, but they sleep and turn a deaf ear, and want to carry away from the lecture nothing of value..'[26] The direct speech – 'I wouldn't give a halfpenny to such [a bad priest] to celebrate mass for a year for my soul or my father's' – attributed to a professor of theology in his lecture room[27] reinforces the impression conveyed by the above quotations from three different capitula that these remarks are those of an eyewitness. He is, moreover, aware of brawls in university towns, brawls leading to manslaughters, occasioned by exuberant behaviour on saints' days.[28]

How can we account for Bromyard's deep and wide familiarity with both canon and civil law? No evidence links him to the University of Oxford (or to Cambridge). Courtenay observes that Oxford was, until the second decade of the fourteenth century, the only official 'studium generale' for the Dominicans in England. 'Some ninety friars were resident in the Oxford convent in 1317.. The actual selection of students sent to Oxford or Cambridge was made by the provincial and the provincial chapter.. those selected had to have completed their training in logic and philosophy and to have spent two years in a provincial school of theology attending lectures on the 'Sentences', the Bible, and various treatises of Thomas Aquinas.' Courtenay also states that the English province occasionally sent Dominicans to Paris, Cologne or Bologna: they rarely, if ever, completed their studies there, he adds.[29]

The Dominican house at Oxford had among its many members Nicholas Trevet (c.1258-1334) who twice held the post of regent master in theology, author of surviving works in three main fields: history, literature and theology.[30] A classicist of distinction, his commentary on the 'De consolatione philosophiae' of Boethius is attested in over a hundred manuscripts.[31] He lectured in Paris, at St Jacques, from 1307 to 1314.

Residence, then, at the Oxford convent might have afforded Bromyard opportunities of access to the core texts of both the learned laws. There are also tantalizing references within the *Summa* to France and Italy which invite speculation about foreign travel. But wherever the centre of study was, Bromyard read his canon and civil law, and read voraciously and retentively.

Bromyard's Italian experiences form the subject of chapter 29. Travel in Italy implies the lengthy journey through France to the lodestone of Avignon and beyond. His frequent references to ships and sailors are therefore not unexpected. He watched the operation of the rudder:[32] admired the alacrity with which the crew carried out a captain's commands:[33] felt the odd sensation that people on dry land were moving when the ship entered or left port:[34] he noted the use of rafts for river transport[35] [on the Rhône?] and of ship's biscuit for voyages to the Holy Land.[36] His most striking comment is that 'some sailors are more willing to carry robbers than decent men of religion.'[37] The robbers were perhaps abjuring the realm and glad to secure a passage whereas mendicants might have begged their passage and would be giving no tips.

Several remarks found in eight different capitula of the *Summa* point to Bromyard's familiarity with the papal court at Avignon. His journeys in Italy, evidenced in chapter 29, would have made Avignon a natural staging post, quite apart from its attraction as the new centre of the Catholic Church. Bromyard would presumably have stayed at the Dominican convent:[38] luckier than the Aragonese ambassadors who in 1316 had to go outside the town to find accommodation.[39] Memories of his sojourn in Avignon were exploited to add force to comments and arguments, such as the obligation for silent reverence in the papal presence,[40] and a recollection of attending a mass celebrated by Iohannes XXII was used to make a telling point in MORS. '..when the pope enters a church to celebrate a solemn mass a candle is lit as an acolyte calls out 'Sic transit gloria mundi.' '[41]

He recalls the badges worn by the paupers maintained by papal charity, which distinguished them from non-approved beggars:[42] and a grim humour marks his comparison of the queues of supplicants for prebends and numerous other preferments to the perseverance of the good Christian cited by S.Gregorius who will endure a whipping in the expectation and knowledge of reward in heaven.[43] He is aware of the examinations in reading, chanting and writing which some candidates are put through.[44] He may even have been inside the papal chancery.[45] But the lasting memory he took from Avignon was of the lavish mode of life indulged in by the great princes of the Church, so repugnant to a man of his simple tastes.[46] Elsewhere he decries the maintenance of large stables as a factor contributing to the decline and even ruin of a monastic property:[47] the streets and alleys of Avignon must have been covered in horse-manure, amply provided by the mounts of resident cardinals and visiting bishops alike. In HONOR he writes:

'..for take away the burdensome legion of cardinals and the excessive multitudes of horses and household-attendants and the inordinate family-ties of their kin and the proud vanity of their total hierarchy – and the need for the monstrous taxes [supporting them] will wither away..'[48]

The refrain denouncing the prevalence of simony in Church affairs is also levelled against the papal court, both cardinals and pope. Guillemain calculates the minimum figures for the support staff of Iohannes XXII as 460, the maximum as 538.[49] Add the minor courts retained by each of the cardinals[50] and Bromyard's complaint and suggestion seems eminently reasonable. Lateran III had allowed 20 to 25 horses for each cardinal, 20 to 30 for each bishop.[51] Even these numbers were exceeded: Adam Orleton set out for Avignon in 1327 accompanied by 70 men and 46 horses.[52]

Jews had been expelled from England in 1290. In Avignon, however, they were present in substantial numbers: the Jewry, moreover, was only some 600 m from the Dominican convent.[53] Despite several references, usually favourable, to Jews throughout the *Summa* Bromyard gives no hint of personal contacts: his French, in a Provençal-speaking town, may have been partly inadequate for street conversations.[54]

To most of us the remark seems unbearably, shockingly hard-hearted, yet Bromyard quotes it with no hint of disapproval:

'And so Bernard states that a man who has taken religious vows should be, like Melchisedech, without father and mother: that is, with no memory of his parents.'[55]

Such was the Cistercian ideal, freeing the mind for devotion to God and His purposes. Bromyard evidently met few instances of disinterested love shown to parents:

'..nowadays love for a father [expressed] by a son, or by a daughter for her mother..is a scarce commodity, except as a fly [loves] a bowl of milk or honey, or dogs a bone.'[56]

Bromyard was absent on 1 February 1326 when, at S.Lawrence's in Lechlade, his superiors had intended him to receive a licence to preach and to hear confession in the diocese of Hereford.[57] The only reasons which suggest themselves are his own illness, grave illness or death of a parent, or even more pressing external business. There is, however, a curious and unsettling account of a deathbed scene at which he was present, linked by extremely close ties to the dying man (he writes, not 'quem *bene* novi', not 'quem *optime* novi', but 'quem *peroptime* novi').

'But Lady Greed does not allow her loyal slave at death either to know God or to bind his soul to Him but to focus entirely on *her*: as was made clear in the case of the man whom I knew not just very well but supremely well. He'd been stricken with paralysis and had lost the power of speech. The friars who were standing round his bed, seeing that death was stealing upon him, began urging him to thoughts of his soul and to receiving the eucharist, and began shouting, their lips close to his ears, that if he was agreeable to receive the sacrament he should at least make some sign either by nodding or by [moving] his hand, his tongue or his expression. When they could get no sign from him one colleague said 'I'll soon get a sign from him', and laid his hand on the chest at the foot of his bed which held his money, his heart, and his treasure, as though he intended to prise it open or make off with it. Immediately, as if he'd been wakened from sleep and was striving to lift his head he showed the dismal sign of life with his voice and expression: the same man who, while [the friars] were speaking of God and the salvation of his soul, lay as if dead: [thus] showing himself more concerned about Lady Avarice than about God. For she so gripped him by the throat that she allowed him to make no sign about *any* god. On seeing this a certain friend who loved him with special affection left the room in embarrassment.'[58]

Was the dying man Bromyard's father? Was the 'certain friend' Bromyard himself? He is certainly distinct from the friars, not one of them. Presumably the deathbed scene predated Bromyard's taking religious vows. Apart from the light thrown by this passage on an incident from his younger days there is also the insight into his code of values granted by his disapprobation of the dying man's impulse to protect his life savings. Unhappily, instances of defrauding the very elderly and infirm are not uncommon in the England of today. They range from the physical removal of valuable objects to the forging of signatures on cheques. Now bank accounts may be transferred at the click of a mouse: few of us would remain impassive were we to see our pension funds raided and all that safeguarded our families and us from the humiliations of beggary ruthlessly taken away before our eyes, as befell this poor creature. There are other distasteful elements in this story too, of which the harassing of the dying man is the more apparent to us moderns: another is the failure of either Bromyard himself or the 'certain friend' (if they are not one and the same) to intervene and interpret the pressure of a finger as the wish to receive the sacrament. For the friars and for Bromyard, however, it was of the utmost import that the man should himself declare his desire to receive Christ.

Bromyard, as a confessor, had been in attendance at many deathbeds. His familiarity with the final frailties of the human condition is evidenced in the clinical description which yet has the capacity to move:

'..before death he scarcely has the power to move his feet for carrying out his natural and private needs or to lift his hands to put food or drink in his mouth, or to brush flies from his lips: and he lacks the strength to turn from side to side in his bed..'[59]

The generation which witnessed the fall of Acre to the Muslim armies in 1291 continued to be exercised by the question of an appropriate response and the crusade for the recovery of the Holy Land was one of the three major issues dominating the Council of Vienne in 1311-1312. A good part of the *Summa* is devoted to this problem and Bromyard's stance is explored in chapter 26. He certainly looks favourably upon the crusading enterprise, and also champions the cause of converting Muslims to Christianity.[60] He must not, however, be categorized as a chauvinist, as can be deduced from the cautious note he sounds in sections of BELLUM, where he makes plain his approval of Charlemagne's subjecting himself to questioning by his confessor on his reasons for going to war: and of king Edward's pilgrimage and consultations before undertaking war.[61] He shows awareness too of the horrifying nature of bodily injuries and mutilations resulting from war: and of the appalling damage to the spirit of men who have both executed and witnessed the barbarities of evisceration and disembowelling of soldiers and horses alike. Bitterest of all for Bromyard is the knowledge that men killed in battle would often die

'unhousel'd, disappointed, unanel'd.'[62]

In the second of the eleven articuli of BELLUM under which he discusses war Bromyard finds 27 areas in which physical and spiritual war may fittingly be compared. 'There are revealed, then, twenty-seven similarities and concurrences between physical and spiritual war.'[63] In the 23rd of these points he cites, between several Old Testament instances of war being undertaken (by heroes such as Jonathan Maccabaeus and David) and the example set by 'the saintliest emperor Charlemagne' in going to confession before starting out for war, the example of 'the noble king Edward: whose custom it was before war to make pilgrimages in person: and to take the advice of men eminent in wisdom in both laws, of God and of the world. Because, as Seneca testifies in letter 14, weapons abroad are worth little if sensible counsel is lacking at home. And if examples were deficient then reason would suffice, which informs us that where greater danger threatens one should proceed with greater caution. In physical war there is the greatest danger both to bodies and souls: in war there is not only physical but spiritual death of thousands upon thousands because of the hatred which envelops people: not just of two men but of two kingdoms: and through the other sins in which they are enmeshed when they are killed.'[64]

Bromyard has only contempt for men ennobled in name only.

'..that nobles – noble in title, not in reality - are often punished in their descendants is evident from the fact that, quite often, they either have children who turn out bad or are altogether childless, just as ordinary folk. This is thought to befall them through the fair justice of God, so that those who often cause trouble for God's children should themselves have trouble from [their] stupid children: and that's as it should be, that those who deprive multitudes of their children by murders and illicit wars should themselves have their children die..'[65]

From these brief extracts it is clear that Bromyard conceives of circumstances wherein a decision to go to war is appropriate. We note that such a decision is to be taken only after a wide consultation not only with scholars learned in the moral law of the Church but also with sober interpreters of that depth and width of human experience shaped by centuries of judicial commentaries encompassed within the vast bulk of the Roman civil law. Furthermore the leaders who are then to make that decision must precede it with a rigorous examination of their motives conducted by an upright confessor. Lastly, dangers are to be foreseen: the watchword is 'caution'.

We must remember that Bromyard wrote both on BELLUM and on PAX. The views expressed in the following passage are certainly controversial. It may be objected, for instance, that making concessions and displaying humility will always be perceived as weakness driven by fear and, moreover, will not be reciprocated by enemies in the tradition of an honour culture where the saving of face is more important than doing right. But Bromyard belongs to a different tradition, expressed in all its glory in Jesus' words 'Love your enemies: do good to them that hate you.'[66]

'Since Bromyard refers his readers to three other passages they too are translated since they complete his argument.

'The fourth point: what is required is that in establishing agreement and restoring peace between the warring parties reparations that are sought should not be too severe, not just for the reason I touched on previously, at D.10.14* but also so that their aim and effort should not be seen to be more centred on acquisitiveness than on peace. And peace made on such terms will never endure as was made clear at B.2.55[†]: for if the party brought to terms of agreement in such a manner were to dare to open his heart he would say, not that he had been given peace but had been pushed into it, on the grounds that he had bought peace at too dear a price, or had yielded, out of fear, too much of his own rights to the other party. As a consequence, when the time seems opportune, he will reveal that never, in the intervening months or years, had true peace existed. The person, therefore, who wants true peace should carry out three steps rather than be deprived of it. First, he should adopt a humbler posture in the face of his adversary… Second, he should make concessions from his own domain, as is clear from both the moral example and the authority cited at D.9.11.[‡] Third, he should at some point give way on his own right and accept some loss or even pain.'[67]

*'Again they say 'I seek only the justice which he deserved.' But such men should note that the rigour of justice is not always to be sought: for two reasons. First, because peace founded on heavy or excessive reparations or the full rigour of justice will be neither sincere nor stable: the proof is at P.4.20. Second: in the throes of dying or in other necessity you don't seek the rigour of justice from God, bur *mercy*: and what you

want to squeeze out of God you are to offer to the next man. On this point see section 5 in the same chapter [P.4]. Note too M.9.30.'[68]

†'The second reason is that a dominion acquired through war is less stable: for although the purpose of war [or, the result of war] is peace, yet it would be more secure to obtain peace, and dominion, without war, after the parties had been brought to agreement, because those subjects who are gained by war and brought into subjection are obedient through fear rather than from affection. They ever await the time when, at some opportunity, they can avenge themselves and members of their families slaughtered in war.'[69]

‡'Third: love your enemies: not just because they bring advantage to you, and for the reward the text mentions: but so that they, in return for the love and kindness shown them, may be recalled to a life well lived and to friendship, with God *and* with you.'[70]

Of the five longest capitula in the *Summa* three – ORDO CLERICALIS, RELIGIO and PRELATIO – are devoted to an examination of the duties, conditions, qualities and performances of those men who have chosen as their life's work the service of God and His church. A good number of Bromyard's objective comments on these matters form the subject of chapter 22: a few passages, however, allow us to sense his frustration over an unfairness which overvalues others' worth and may hint at a personal rebuff. Of several such examples an extract from RELIGIO may serve as representative. His target is men who have taken religious vows.
'..who eagerly hanker after offices and dignities..'[71]
A pithy jingle sums up his exasperation ('anni multi actus stulti'):
'..men are promoted for growing old, even though they have no learning: their years aplenty, acts inane: they snatch the master's chair and the deserving are shamefully pushed to the back... They end up there where they begin, in possession of a sufficient ignorance and illiteracy..'[72]
The charlatans he has encountered on his travels hawking their wares under a religious guise receive the sharp edge of Bromyard's tongue:
'These are they who have renounced the world – in speech only, not in action: they live in a worldly way and conceal their vices under the empty promise of a better life, and under the cloak of the image and name of religion take up the reputation of virtues: they preach great things and do nothing, they lambast vices but don't give them up, they pretend in public to despise what they commit in private, they study to appear great men yet not be such, they eagerly set themselves to collect the fragments and relics of saints left to them yet not their moral standards: like the men who go about with indulgences: everything they preach and undergo is for profit NOW..'[73]
Such a polar opposition of appearance and reality is a strong motif in the *Summa*. He vivifies this with an image familiar to all church-goers:
'..just as carved statues of the saints have gilded accoutrements in beard and vestments, skilfully executed, and on the inside, quite often, are rotten and worm-eaten. In themselves, however, while they were alive the saints possessed the opposite characteristics: they were most handsomely adorned internally in their soul yet meagrely in their physical presence.'[74]
The passage also serves to remind us of Bromyard's indifference to the physical trappings with which devotion to the divine may be encompassed.

The third longest of Bromyard's 189 capitula, RELIGIO, is arranged in 24 articles, of which articles 16 to 19 lay bare the condition of those who fall short in their religious life as regards their desires or ambitions: their actions: their consumption of food, and their dress: and their sense of their own superiority. The following extract from article 19 begins with a criticism of the expenditure on celebrations of inceptions at university ('multi ad cenam vocantur inceptoris') and goes on to level far harsher charges against such clerics:

'But when they're assembled for the divine offices the depth of their negligence is revealed since only a meagre handful of them even deign to be present for the sacred vigils and seem to congregate for the holy solemnities of the masses rather for gaming, laughing and guffawing than for singing the psalms. The matters, I maintain, that the corrupt and dissolute find amusing make the devout weep.. the depths they sink to in their banquets and drunken bouts in their bedrooms – I won't say *in their shamelessness* – amount to this, that now gatherings of clerics have gained a reputation as brothels of the lascivious and conventicles of fairground entertainers in that with them slackening of standards is styled sociability: prodigality is called openhandedness: garrulousness is affability, guffawing and making fun of others is jollity, effeminacy and high fashion in dress are called 'keeping up the appropriate dignity.' '[75]

Unseemly conduct in church also, predictably earned Bromyard's disapproval. The behaviour takes the form of late arrival: chatter and exchange of gossip with neighbours: sleeping: or the reading, composing or sealing of letters – this last charge directed at priests present at a mass but not celebrating. Those who have followed services in *some* Italian and Greek churches will recognize one or two of Bromyard's complaints.

'Nor when the priest rings the bell for mass does he get up. If he is a man of some importance he reckons the priest will wait for him. If he's poor he thinks it's enough just to be present for the elevation of the host.'[76]

'For every one who prays with devotion in a procession or in church there are many who chatter away quite nonchalantly – and damagingly.'[77]

'..in church they're willing to pray only when they can't find someone to gossip with.'[78]

More seriously for the health of the Church Bromyard has observed the rapid deterioration in the attitude of many priests towards the obligations of their office. This same fecklessness reveals how lukewarm is their personal faith.

'They scarcely manage to attend one mass: they never celebrate one, not even those [priests] who, before their preferment, used to say mass: and when they attend mass it's not about saying the litanies they busy themselves but with reading or composing or sealing letters.'[79]

Extravagance may be difficult to define: what was otiose for Diogenes the Cynic philosopher, naked in his barrel, is absolutely essential for most of us moderns. For Bromyard it manifested itself in a lavish mode of life particularly to be censured in men who had taken holy orders. Dress was one of several forms in which flamboyance was expressed and the following passage from RELIGIO is all the more powerful for being focused on precise details.

'They seek for their vestments not what is found more serviceable but something flimsier or more eye-catching: not what can keep out the cold but what leads to arrogance: which soothes and caresses with its soft touch and by its colouring attracts the eyes of onlookers: not what can be seen as more functional but what can be shown off as more charming, vainer. It wasn't with such ornamentation that He is said to have been dressed: He whom they are supposed to declare in their speech and in their life: Christ, I mean, the supreme shepherd, of whose flock they should be the guardians: nor did He ride on horseback, nor was He accompanied by a man-servant carrying His cloak-bag... that habit which once was the special mark of religious vows they now flaunt as a symbol of their pride. Knight and monk on the same footing share the cloak and the military boot with such insignia of Christ. They preach humility, they talk of God's justices: they extend their hoods and phylacteries, they enlarge their fringes, they tighten their sleeves, they pull up their tunics, they pleat their cloaks, they embroider their flanks, they bring forward their lace-like jewels, they flourish their kerchiefs and signet-rings, and while in this fashion they race to their chapters it is more the aspiration for advancement at the meeting which wears out the threshwood than any feeling of devotion. 'But', they say, 'what has God to do with vestments? Isn't *morality* His concern? And religion doesn't subsist in *clothing*.' But in their heart and the outward form of their vestments lies the proof of a deformity of mind and morals.'[80]

The tensions and rivalries which existed between secular clergy and mendicants were paralleled by those between mendicants and the old settled orders such as the Benedictines. Of men who have taken vows of poverty, chastity and obedience he handsomely concedes that 'all good men praise God': but goes on to delineate a crucial difference:

'Some [religious] [are] established on the land of possessions and riches, as the possessioners. Others lifted up from the earth as though into the heights through their willingness to be poor, all wealth left behind: who can the more devote themselves to praises of God the less they concern themselves with earthly matters.'[81]

'There was an apposite riposte from a member of a mendicant order to one from an order of possessioners who was wondering how they [sc. mendicants] could be better preachers than members of *his* order, since they had more books. The mendicant replied 'King Henry [III] is the richest man in the whole realm of England in terms of timber and masonry: yet a poor workman is better able to build a house than the king is.''[82]

Bromyard observes a diminution in support for monasteries. This he links to their failure to offer condign hospitality to the poor, though it *is* provided for the wealthy 'so that good relations in this world be preserved between men of power and the Church and among neighbours too to avoid, in case they are corrupt, any harm at their hands.' He continues: 'So if you see monasteries being impoverished and their granges being mortgaged and their inner houses in ruins look outside the gate for the reason where you will see the paupers' lodging, previously a spacious building, deserted and in disrepair. You may conclude that this is the cause: for as long as Christ was fed Christ fed them, and enriched them: while the opposite, the opposite.'[83]

'For in the Old Law fruitfulness was considered a woman's fulfilled state: but in the New it is considered to be virginity.'[84]

The stark contrast Bromyard paints here between the ideal woman under the Law of Moses, as the married mother of several children, and the Christian goal of chastity so fervently advocated by S.Paul[85] should alert us to expect a formidable chasm separating Bromyard's views from those held by modern liberals. The organs of procreation are stained by vice: '..the belly and genitals are close together so that from the closeness of the members may be understood the confederation of vices.'[86] The philosopher Diogenes and S.Bernard of Clairvaux are invoked in two quotations in PULCHRITUDO, each as mean and disgusting as the other: 'A beautiful woman is a temple built over a sewer'[87] and 'Beauty is nothing but a cover for obscenity'.[88] Bromyard condemns, of course, the abandoning of the controls which check impurity of thought, in a striking image: '..when a dissolute man or woman lets his/her heart *bathe* in fantasies of fornication..'[89] and reminds his readers – and through them, the congregations they preached to – of the discolouring effects of a candle burning next to a white sheet or the interior wall of a house, so as to lead them to contemplate a *moral* blemish: '..because if such thoughts, or a woman's company, stay with thee for long enough it will be with thee just as with a wall or a white sheet: since in the same way that a candle tarnishes a wall so *she* [will tarnish] thy mind, however pure and white it was before.'[90]

It is not only a woman's looks and fashionable clothing but her voice too, and conversation, which will corrupt men, turning their thoughts to foul lust: '..for one silly woman, dressed up to the height of fashion, will sooner turn, by her looks and her talk, one hundred men to evil concupiscence than the best man in the world, by his preaching, [will turn] twenty to wholesome desires and the abandonment of evil.'[91]

Bromyard confessed women as well as men. However, he warns his readers – his fellow Dominicans will have been uppermost in his mind – to avoid private conversations with women in secluded places: '..and shun..withdrawn and hole-and-corner chats with them [sc. women]..'[92] From the austerity and maddening landscapes of the Egyptian semi-desert arose the heroic self-denials which germinated much of the material for the Vitas Patrum, a collection of lives Bromyard knew well. An anecdote of an unnamed recluse exemplified the perils attending contact with women: '..or who would risk touching a woman from outside his family, when the holy hermit, carrying his own mother over the stream would not venture to touch her bare hands, saying 'A woman's flesh never ceases to be *fire*.' '[93]

Even excessive, immoderate love within marriage was dangerous, and sinful. Of the married state he writes 'It is safeguarded with purity when they make use of matrimony in such a way that all libido is restrained.'[94] Citing S.Gregorius he concludes 'so the married state is the midway point between inordinate fleshly desires, which all are required to abjure, and the mount of self-restraint or chastity to which whoever, from weakness, cannot ascend may save himself/herself in Segor, i.e. in marriage. And this is what S.Paul declares in I Corinthians 7: 'But if they cannot contain, let them marry: for it is better to marry than to burn.' '[95]

For the young woman's conduct Bromyard finds no better guide than Augustinus. 'The young woman who belongs to the Lord most of all should shun the public gaze and avoid frequenting the piazzas. Sitting at home she should devote herself to carding and spinning wool or reading the Bible.'[96]

Bromyard's anger at men who abuse their status and power is one of the recurrent notes sounded throughout the *Summa*. He occasionally harnesses his disgust to a rhetorical device so as to give additional force to the feelings he needs to express. In this case it is epanalepsis he employs to drive home his denunciation of the ungodly with repeated hammer-blows of details:

'..where are the ungodly lovers of [this] world who lived shortly before our time: where are the ungodly princes of [this] world, the kings, earls and other lords of the earth who lived in pride and lavish state, a host of horses in their stables: who maintained large kennels and a huge, ungodly household: who owned great palaces and a multitude of manors, broad acres bringing in vast revenues: and maintained their persons in the gratifications and pleasures of gluttony and lust: who for the maintenance of such a lifestyle subjected their underlings to a harsh and cruel control which flayed the skin off them: where, too, are the deceitful experts of [this] world, the judges, assessors, lawyers, jurors and perjured foremen leading the jury to hell: who, in return for 'gifts' sold God and the Kingdom of Heaven, and bought damnation: where, again, are the usurers, skilled in turning a halfpenny into a penny and making eleven become twelve and from a bushel of wheat, or its equivalent, making two, or three: and the fraudulent dealers, adroit at looking a man in the face even as they cheat him..?'[97]

In several places throughout the *Summa* we hear the voice of the countryman. He remarks that infirmity in a sheep's eye is a sign of inner disease:[98] and that a shepherd will eject a diseased sheep from the fold.[99] He also maintains that a ewe is hard to pull from a burning shed and will return to it unless held back.[100] He tells us we don't expect to water thirsty animals till the end of Lent: perhaps relying on 'February fill-dyke'.[101] To illustrate incompetence he presents the picture of a man who can't control three geese.[102] Herefordshire is a county of mixed farming but has enough arable for Bromyard to mention the practice of burning stubble after harvest.[103] He notes too the weightier matter of the pressure of an expanding population on the resources of land,[104] and mentions, perhaps after many conversations with farmers and farmworkers, a decline in the fertility of the soil and the yield from orchards.[105]

Scenes from daily and holiday life are here too. Bromyard has stood in marketplaces on feast days and watched as countrymen and townspeople have been cozened by fraudsters practising a version of the three-card trick: 'a trickster..with three dice lets his victim win something at first but in the end takes all his money..'[106] A variant of this was the use of weighted dice: again the same lure and the same result.[107] Altogether nastier, and a common sight on these holidays, was bear-baiting. The dogs hurling themselves at the muzzled and chained bear, urged on by their owners, are presented by Bromyard as an image of the demons men and women allow to assault their souls as they lower their standards in festal merriment, in the same way as the bearward, for a fee, lets owners test the mettle of their hounds.[108]

English excess in drinking has often been viewed tolerantly, but Bromyard was undoubtedly aware of the consequences for the dependent family of the man 'who spends on a feast day for his own pleasure and gratification the whole sum of what he earns in the week.'[109] His 'drink's in, wit's out' neatly expresses proverbial wisdom.[110] In the country these drunks would, as Autolycus, 'but look upon the hedge':[111] in towns precautions were taken: '..[hypocrites] are to be compared to a house: inside it has perhaps not a single cross but plenty of filth: outside, however, there are lots of crosses imprinted so that passers-by are deterred from urinating on it..'[112] Not everyone took to English ale: Bromyard has watched Italians pulling a face as they sipped the national drink. 'Just as those brought up in Italy, before becoming used to it, take no pleasure in the English drink, however good it may be in itself.'[113] This is the sole reference attesting the presence of Italian Dominicans in at least one institution where Bromyard resided: the clause 'before they become used to it' betokening some length of time. Their familiarity with travel routes will undoubtedly have smoothed Bromyard's journeys. There is reason to believe, however, that his own palate will have informed him that 'wine is better for growing on higher and stony ground.'[114]

Through Bromyard's eyes we also glimpse a series of mundane events: a cow overturning the pail as she is milked in her byre:[115] buckets on a pulley at a building site, one going up, the other coming down:[116] and his own discomfort at being shaved with a blunt or serrated razor without a preliminary moisturizing of the cheeks.[117] We may imagine too the human tragedy which lies behind the secretive abandonment of babies at the door of a hospital or church:[118] and the instinctive fear of infection at the approach of lepers.[119] We see an almoner waiting for a quorum before dispensing food to beggars:[120] and are taken to an age when glass windows[121] and gargoyles[122] were relatively rare.

13

Some young women earn a precious coin or two by the sacrifice of cutting off their long hair, to be acquired by wealthier (older?) women: Bromyard mentions too that thick, long hair was cut from newly dead (young) women: and condemns the vanity of the purchasers, and the fashion for wearing 'horns'.[123] We meet Bromyard at a bishop's dinner table when the conversation had turned to the question of which bodily member caused the greatest expense.[124] The odd and seemingly enduring fantasy – visited on women more than on men, according to Bromyard – of being carried off by alien creatures for flights on horseback is firmly dismissed as an illusion in an early encounter by an English writer with this belief.[125] More prosaically, he feels the need to explain how computations were performed on an abacus:[126] but I leave to the last the universal and most heart-warming picture Bromyard gives us, that of a mother opening her arms to catch her young child as he takes his first tottering steps towards the security of her breast.[127]

Bromyard was not musical.[128] He reveals this in a rather involved passage on the different degrees of pleasure experienced by the greatest and the least of the saints resulting from the different intensity of their visions of God.[129] (Bromyard elsewhere rejects the Greek Orthodox position that the sight of God is only to be granted after the Last Judgement).[130] Although he recognizes that 'many willingly listen to and appreciate beauty in the voices of singers'[131] he is distrustful of the worth of descants and flourishes, exemplifying his distaste: '..as some were singing in high voices a voice from heaven gave the response that an old woman praying in a corner [of the church] sang better.'[132] He adds that 'a low [humble?] chant, with devotion, pleases God more than a formal chant [sung] without concentration and *with* self-conceit.'[133]

Whether in England or France or Italy he does not tell us, but in some churches he has taken note of painters studiously scrutinizing pictures with the aim of learning from their outstanding beauty and from the treatment of the subject matter.[134] Just possibly he might have stood behind Duccio, Giotto or Simone Martini, and seen some of their work when paint and gold leaf had been freshly applied.

The power of paintings to move and to direct those who respond fully to the images they take to heart is demonstrated in a story Bromyard tells of two brothers, one lettered, the other a layman. Both took religious vows. A year later the cleric considered abandoning his undertaking, only to be strengthened in his new status by his lay brother. Asked where his reasoning came from he replied: 'I have a book in which I have learnt all the good I know.' The cleric yearned to see this book: his brother led him to an image of Christ crucified saying '*This* is my book.' Bromyard comments on the appropriateness of calling this image a book: '..for the laws of the Church say the same: that statues and pictures are the books and the scriptures of the laity.'[135]

The power of simple interrogatives to help unlock the secrets of stubborn hearts was known and used by Bromyard in his métier as confessor. He lists them in a neat hexameter:

Quis quid ubi quociens per quos cur quomodo quando (Who? what? where? how often? through whom? why? how? when?).[136]

He notes that 'wine and confession reveal everything'[137] and his insights into the inner life of married couples will have come not only from his astute observation of the marital state but from face-to-face confessions.[138] His assertions that 'those who live together out of wedlock in the most passionate love, after being joined in marriage cool off'[139] and that 'an adulterous woman who has been beaten by her paramour does not leave him, but if beaten by her husband she does leave him'[140] must derive from confessional revelations.

The licensing of friars to hear confessions, to grant absolutions and to impose salutary penances issued from a constitution of Bonifacius VIII,[141] and at least from 1318 was combined with the licence to deliver sermons, as may be instanced from the commission of Adam Orleton of 26 April 1318.[142]

Maturity of judgement will have been sought by a prior in the candidates he selected for presentation to a bishop, as well as a sound grasp of theology and canon law, and these qualifications would need to be allied to personal probity of life.[143] There were, after all, potential dangers to the confessor in being exposed to disclosures which might open *his* eyes to the temptation of sins he could not have imagined. (Equally, the confessor had to exercise caution by not suggesting modes of sin the confessant had no notion of). The dangers are expressed in VITA:

'But, they will say, in the active [as opposed to the contemplative] life many are the temptations and contingencies of sins which occur from what is seen and heard in confession for those who wend their way through the world to preach and hear confession. Many too are the burdens of bodily weariness.. But one must never cease from these.'[144]

Bromyard will have been thorough in probing the conscience – and memory – of his confessants and rigorous in his imposition of penance. PENITENTIA is the fourth longest of his 189 capitula at some 21,000 words and Bromyard approaches this subject from twenty different aspects. The 14th articulus, for example, is headed 'The danger of tardy or doubtful penitence in that they expose themselves to the chance of losing everything.' Bromyard reinforces the necessity of penitence for sin with 34 *exempla* (see chapter 23 *exemplum* no.4). Grief over the commission of the sin must be followed by the determination not to commit it again. This is *contrition*. Next comes *confession*, whereupon the priest will assign a form of *penance*. The final step, especially if another has been wronged, is *satisfaction*: e.g. the return of something stolen, or compensation in case it cannot be returned. Remorse by itself is not enough.[145] Yet his compassion for human frailty shines out. We began this introduction with his own vision of the preacher: to end, let us hear Bromyard the confessor.

'But to set against the shame which could arise from the confessor's hearing [our] sins God has provided several remedies, one of which is that He has not ordained that we should confess to *angels* – that would make us afraid, and blush to reveal our impurities to such pure creatures – but to a *human being*: someone beset with weakness just like others: who also experiences the wars of temptations within himself: who from his own feebleness and frailty has the material for bestowing sympathy on the frail, not for despising or loathing them.'[146]

1   Third homily on Ezechiel. The image is followed by an unacknowledged echo of S.Paul, I Corinthians 13.1.

2   Book II ep.22.

3   Bromyard here quotes from the *Authentica* or *Novellae constitutiones* of Iustinianus, from the preface of the second titulus (Novella number VIII). His text, however, differs somewhat from the received text (on which the translation is based), viz.

        'Omnes nobis dies ac noctes contingit cum omni lucubratione et cogitatione degere semper volentibus ut aliquid utile et placens Deo a nobis collatoribus praebeatur..'

4   Ep.58.

5   De amicitia 43. The compositor has misread the manuscript contraction as 'anima'. I owe the sourcing of the quotation to Mr Ian Andrews.

6   Bromyard's text of *De officiis* differs slightly from that of modern editions (which also place this extract in chapter 7) which give:

        'Sed quoniam (ut praeclare scriptum est a Platone) non nobis solum nati fuimus, sed ortus nostri partem patria, partem parentes vendicant, partem amici: atque (ut placet Stoicis) quae in terris gignuntur, ad usum hominum omnia creari, homines autem hominum causa esse generatos, ut ipsi inter se alii aliis prodesse possent..'

My translation is of Bromyard's text. His earlier 'ducem habemus naturam' seems an unacknowledged, perhaps unconscious, debt to Cicero, as this passage continues

        'in hoc naturam debemus ducem sequi, et communes utilitates in medium afferre, mutatione officiorum, dando, accipiendo, tum artibus, tum facultatibus devincire hominum inter homines societatem.'

        [In this we should take nature as our guide and bring into the common use the shared interests and advantages of taking it in turns to perform services, by giving by receiving, by our skills, by our enterprise, and by so doing bind together our human society.]

7   Digestum novum lib.xi.tit.xv.lex.xix. 'De captivis et postliminio reversis et redemptis ab hostibus': (Bromyard follows the later medieval practice of a tripartite division of the Digesta into vetus, infortiatum and novum: his reference is now expressed as Dig.49.15.19). He quotes the opinion of Iulius Paulus, an eminent jurist under the emperors Septimius Severus (193-211) and Aurelius Severus Alexander (222-235). 'Postliminium' is the resumption of civic rights on one's return from exile or capture, so defined by Paulus in this lex. It is the lead words of the seventh paragraph which Bromyard cites:

        'Filius quoque familias transfuga': which continue: 'non potest postliminio reverti, neque vivo patre: quia pater sic illum amisit quemadmodum patria, et quia disciplina castrorum antiquior fuit parentibus Romanis quam caritas liberorum.' [A son under the authority of his father who deserts to the enemy can not be returned to the resumption of his civic rights, nor at any time during the life of his father, because his father has lost him just as his country has, and because the discipline of the military camps had a longer ancestry for Roman parents than had the love for their children.]

This is a rather recherché judgement from the civil law for Bromyard to cite in support of his tenet that one should live not just for oneself but for others: for others, moreover, of both present and future generations. It certainly demonstrates his wide acquaintance with the Roman law: the old adage comes to mind: 'legista sine canonibus parum valet: canonista autem sine legibus nihil valet.'

8   Nichomachean Ethics, book 1.

9   Romans chapter 14 [verse 7] 'Nemo enim nostrum sibi vivit..'

10   Bromyard's quotation of Ecclesiasticus (Liber Iesu Filii Sirach) 33.18 reveals (1) dependence on a manuscript tradition differing from that of our preferred reading: and (2) an undoubted recall from memory. The Weber-Fischer edition of the Biblia sacra (Stuttgart 1983) explains Bromyard's 'solum mihi' as deriving from the group of manuscripts represented by C whereas the preferred

16

'mihi soli' is owed to AMPhic. His 'Videte' (for respicite') lacks manuscript authority and so indicates his easy familiarity with his Vulgate: he has no need to check . Underlying Cicero's moral treatise in books I and II, and unknown to Bromyard, is the 'Peri kathekontos' of the Rhodian Stoic Panaitios (c.185-109 BC).

The textual variations noted in the quotations from both Iustinianus and Cicero may be explained by Bromyard's dependence upon a different manuscript tradition: or – and this would be impressive – a reliance upon the capacious memory of a scholar who could not always, in the England of the troubled reign of Edward II and the early years of Edward III, command access to the books he needed.

[11] Predicantium vita secundum beatum Gregorium super ezech. omelia tercia. Sonat et ardet. Sonat verbo Ardet desiderio. Es ergo candens est predicatio accensa. Sed de candenti ere scintille prodeunt: quia de eorum exhortatione verba flammancia ad aures audientium procedunt. Recte ergo predicatorum verba appellata sunt scintille: quia eos quos in corde tetigerint incendunt. Et sicut scintille ad distantes volant: ita predicatores non solum inflammare debent presentes scintillis verborum sed etiam posteris et distantibus quantum possibile est proficere debent exemplis scripturarum. Unde Cassiodorus libro secundo epistola.xxii. Sequens, inquit, etas cum aliqua opinabili novitate succedat..multum adhuc restat multumque restabit nec ulli nato post mille secula precludetur occasio aliquid adhuc adiicendi. Cuilibet ergo non solum sibi vel suo tempori sed etiam posteris vivendum est. Ad hoc habemus ducem, exemplum, et auctoritatem Ducem habemus naturam. Sol enim et omnia luminaria quantum possibile est omnibus lucent, non solum presentibus sed etiam posteris nostris lucebunt. Exemplum, illustrium virorum vitam dicit Imperator: voluntarios, inquit, labores appetimus ut quietem aliis preparemus Ut in autentica: ut divine iussiones in principio Collatione secunda. Item dicit imperator Omnes, inquit, dies ac noctes contingit cum cogitatione degerere ut aliquid placens deo et amabile nostris collationibus prebeamus.. Auctoritatem sapientum. Antiqui enim sapientes non estimabant aliquos vivere nisi viverent ad aliorum utilitatem. Unde seneca ad lucillum epistola. lviii. Non sibi vivit qui nemini vivit... Sic etiam loquitur tullius libro de anima capitulo. vi. Non, inquit, minoris cure est mihi qualis post mortem meam respublica fuerit quam qualis hodie. Idem de officiis li.i.c.vi. preclare, inquit, scriptum est a platone non solum nobis nati sumus ortusque nostri partem patria vendicat, partem amici, atque ut placet stoicis que in terris gignuntur ad usum hominum omnia creari, homines vero hominum causa esse generatos ut ipsi inter se alii aliis prodesse possent. Sic etiam loquitur lex civilis dicens quod homo nascitur rei publice. ff.de capti. et. postli. reversis. l. postliminium. §. filius quoque fa. transfuga. in digesto novo. li. xi. Quibus concordat philosophus primo Ethicorum docens quod bonum universale divinius est.. Sic etiam loquitur paulus ad Ro.xiiii. Nemo, inquit, sibi vivit etc. Et sapiens in ecclesiastico. xxxiii. Videte, inquit, quoniam non solum mihi laboravi sed omnibus exquirentibus disciplinam. (Prologus)

[12] Binkley, Hereford pp.259-260: Orleton pp.220-221, 249-250.

[13] Hinnebusch, EEFP pp.282-287.

[14] His Prologue makes this plain.

[15] ..si scolaris gloriatur de hoc quod scit rationem reddere de lectione sua ne verberetur..(G.2.2)

[16] The font is Norman, of tub shape. (Pevsner, Herefordshire p.92)

[17] 'City (Archdeacon's) School. School, 1266-94; grammar school, 1312 [onwards, until after the year 1530]'. Orme p.370.

[18] 'School, probably of grammar, early 14th century..' ibid. p.358.

[19] Si enim ad exhibendum filium suum in scholis omni septimana tres vel quattuor denarios expenderet.. (R.6.2)
Bromyard's figures are probably meant to indicate the total cost to the parents as they seem too high for tuition fees alone. Orme states (p.132) that Merton College paid 4d a *term* for boys in the college to attend a grammar school in Oxford in 1277. He cites statutes of 1384 allowing holidays of a fortnight at Christmas and at Easter, a week at Whitsuntide and six weeks in summer from

Lammas to 14 September, giving schooling just over 40 weeks in 4 terms (ibid. p.155). Board and lodging would usually be with the schoolmaster: the same Merton boys in 1277 cost the college 8d a week in board (ibid. p.133). Orme's figures for Oxford in 1277 come to £1-6s-8d (2 marks) for board and 1s 4d for tuition: in all, 28 shillings. Bromyard's lower figure adds up to 10s a year, his higher figure to 13s 4d (1 mark). Doubtless some boys will have found cheaper lodgings near their school, perhaps with a widow or a labourer's family, or even with relatives. A grammar book, perhaps the *Ars minor* of Donatus, would be a further cost.

For many country families living far enough from a town which sustained a grammar school even Bromyard's lower figure of 10 shillings a year would have been a heavy burden: they would, furthermore, have lost for 40 weeks of the year the useful services which lads of twelve or thirteen would have performed for the family. Townsmen, of course, would have had only tuition fees to meet.

Elsewhere Bromyard writes that a man in possession of a carrucate of land worth more or less 10 marks a year could not only keep a wife and family but support two or three sons at school and marry off his daughters in a [fitting] marriage: '..se et uxorem et familiam exhibet in domo, et filios duos vel tres in scolis, et filias nuptui tradit: pro cuius terra vel redditibus vix inveniret qui ei daret. x. marcas per annum..' (P.13.25)

A glimpse into a school, from later in the century, is allowed us by Chaucer's Prioress:

> This litel child, his litel book lernynge,
> As he sat in the scole at his prymer,
> He Alma redemptoris herde synge,
> As children lerned hire anthiphoner;
> And, as he dorste, he drough hym ner and ner,
> And herkned ay the wordes and the noote,
> Til he the firste vers koude al by rote.
>
> Noght wiste he what this Latyn was to seye
> For he so yong and tendre was of age…
>   (Chaucer, The Prioresses Tale 29-37)

[20] Exemplis hoc ostenditur per rotulos magistrorum universitatis in quibus scolarium nomina scribuntur: ob quam scripturam in multis defenduntur et universitatis gaudent privilegiis quod non faciunt alii quorum nomina inserta non sunt… Huius etiam utilitas in morte patet *tam* per predictum exemplum de rotulo universitatis: quia sicut ad illum honorandum et pro ipso orandum et ad terram et ecclesiam deportandum cuius nomen in rotulo alicuius magistri invenitur omnes concurrunt magistri..*quam** per similitudinem libri hospitaliorum sancti Iohannis.. (L.4.15, 16)
        *57 words separate 'tam'from 'quam'.

[21] ..ubi alii magistri habent centum auditores: magister in theologia non habebit viginti. (S.4.4)

[22] ..scola legistarum habet centum vel ducentos auditores: ubi scola theologorum non habet forte quinque. (A.14.30)

[23] V.9.12 Rejected by Codex Sinaiticus and other manuscripts as a doublet of Matthew 22.14.

[24] ..aufer propriam voluntatem et infernus non erit. (V.9.14)

[25] Precise figures are lacking for the early fourteenth century, but Rashdall's chapter on numbers (with Powicke and Emden's comments) suggests 1,500 to 3,000 for Oxford, 3,500 for Paris and c.5,000 for Bologna. Rashdall vol.III pp.325-338.

[26] ..causa tante paucitatis electorum propria est voluntas: quia aufer propriam voluntatem et infernus non erit. Nullus ergo deo imputare poterit quod pauci salvantur: quod si fecerit exemplo docetur sensibili quomodo errat. Multis milibus scolarium in una universitate existentibus et magistris bene docentibus in scolis illa que ad instructionem pertinent morum quod multi sunt qui in utrisque deficiunt quibus imputatur nonne scolaribus vel qui ad scolas vel lectiones non veniant vel veniunt quidem sed dormiunt et faciunt surdam aurem et nihil boni inde asportare volunt.. (V.9.14)

27   quidam valens sacre theologie professor in cathedra sua legens dixit quod maluit unum bonum sacerdotem pro ipso celebrantem quam mille malos.. Tali ergo obolum non darem ut pro anima mea vel patris mei per annum celebraret.. (M.10.3, 4)

28   ..et sero in universitatibus et villis communiter plura inveniuntur homicidia et pugne: ita quod melius esset pro salute talium quod nullum festum esset. (F.3.6). Bromyard may have had in mind the extremely serious 'town and gown' battle of 1298. (Rashdall p.328).

29   Courtenay pp.63-64.

30   Clark, Trevet in ODNB vol.55 pp.349-351.

31   Sharpe p.395 quoting Kaeppeli, T., Scriptores Ordinis praedicatorum medii aevi (1970-93), no.3143.

32   ..sicut boni navis gubernatores qui stantes in ultima navis parte navem ad bonum dirigunt portum. (M.11.149)

33   ..more nautarum seu marinariorum qui in his que ad navis pertinent gubernationem precepto naucleri cum maxima obediunt celeritate. (O.1.11)

34   ..sicut moto in navi, videntur in terra stantes moveri. (E.7.13)

35   ..Sicut patet in aliquibus partibus in quibus homines super huiusmodi ligna per flumina descendunt. (P.7.40)

36   Sicut ergo volentes per mare ad terram sanctam vel ad patriam propriam transire secum panem bis coctum pro viatico accipiunt quia illius auxilio melius in mari sustentantur et ad portum perducuntur quia non cito putrescit.. (E.6.17)

37   Nonnulli namque marinarii libentius secum in mari latrones quam bonos ducerent religiosos.. (I.10.5)

38   It was sited just inside the western perimeter wall, near La Porte des Dominicains, some 500 m from Le Palais des Papes. (Guillemain, Carte 2: Avignon Pontificale, after p.810). It had been established by 1231. Iohannes XXII resided here until the Papal Palace was ready for him. (ODP p.214).

39   Mollat p.280.

40   ..quod si in presentia regis terreni anglie vel francie vel pape homines honeste et silenter se haberent.. (D.4.11)

41   ..quando papa ecclesiam intrat missam solemniter celebraturus stupa accenditur uno clamante sic transit gloria mundi. (M.11.93)

42   ..et sicut a numero pauperum quos papa pascit excluduntur qui signum non portant, ita de ovili dei excludentur.. (I.11.21)

43   ..consideratio premii minuit vim flagelli: sicut patet de expectante promotionem in curia pape. (P.9.11)

44   Quia sicut in curia pape non sufficit promovendo per graciam quod bene legat et cantet sed etiam quod bene construat de his tribus examinabitur ita in proposito non sufficit quod bene legat et cantet nisi bene componat in opere que legit et cantat. (F.3.5)

45   ..bulle vero papales signate sunt plumbo et chorda quandoque de serico pendente.. (X.1.8) This is confirmed by Mollat. 'So that the illiterate sealers could tell which [letters] had to be sealed on silken strings and which on hempen, the scribes of the chancery filled in with red or left

unilluminated the initial letter of the reigning pope's name. The leaden seal, or *bulla*, .. was attached to the rescript.' (Mollat pp.292-293)

[46] Item papa et cardinales videant specula sua quomodo munera refutare deberent. Item destruat symoniam et usuram in curia. (Tabula Realis s.v.Papa). The author of the 'Vita' makes the same complaint: Quid dicam de clericis qui hiis diebus accedunt ad curiam, et multa refusa pecunia tanquam in foro venali dignitates emunt et prebendas? Si dicamus simoniam committi, ipse papa non poterit excusari, quia simonia ultro citroque est obligatoria; sicut enim ementem ligat sic et vendentem condempnat. (Vita p.82, of the year 1313).

[47] 'Nor are these aforesaid vanities contented to walk.. It appears to be worse because of the money spent on horses and feasts..' (Ex equorum et festorum expensis..) 'For because of the payment for those riding to general and provincial chapters exactions and levying of taxes rise to such an amount, and communities are taxed so highly, and because of feasts for those incepting books are pawned or sold, so that communities will not be able to safguard or roof buildings or maintain the number of persons as was customary. The consequence is the imminent collapse of houses, the pawning or alienation of books or the impoverishment of libraries, the meagre maintenance of revenues and the indebtedness of [religious] houses.' (P.3.26) See also A.24.15.

[48] ..subtractis namque cardinalium onerosa numerositate et equorum et familie nimia multitudine et parentele inordinata affectione et totius apparatus superba vanitate tantarum necessitas cessabit collectarum.. (H.4.16)

[49] He divides the papal staff thus (giving minimum and maximum numbers): (Guillemain p.443):

Services administratifs	252 - 270
Entourage du pape	29 - 36
Offices domestiques	48 - 58
Corps du garde et d'honneur	131 – 174

figures which are roughly in line with those he calculates for Clemens V, of 447 to 579.

[50] In 1314, at the death of Clemens V, there were 24 cardinals. By 1327, in four promotions, Iohannes XXII had chosen 26 new cardinals, the four Italians among the cohort of the southern French rejoicing in names of considerable resonance: Giovanni Caetani Orsini, Annibale Caetani da Ceccano, Matteo Orsini, Giovanni Orsini. He added two others, but, in spite of this influx, at the 1334 conclave to elect a successor to Iohannes XXII the number of cardinals was still 24.

The retinue of Matteo Orsini was probably exceptional: he maintained, to house his aides and servants, seven entire buildings and individual rooms in 23 other houses (Guillemain pp.272-273). Besides these dependants – such as cooks, butlers, barbers, porters, grooms and secretaries – retained by each cardinal there was also a large group in the service of the score of cardinals which, at the most conservative estimate, comprised 500 clerics and perhaps 300 laymen. Guillemain succinctly conveys the impact on Avignon of these twenty or so minor courts: 'Les cardinaux, leurs parents, leurs familiers imposaient leur encombrante présence.' (ibid p.272).

[51] ..cardinales vero viginti vel viginti quinque non excedant, episcopi viginti vel triginta nequaquam excedant.. (Tanner p.213). The clerics were also, in this fourth canon, forbidden to set out with hounds for the hunt and falcons.

[52] See chapter 27 note 18.

[53] Even after the ravages of the Black Death there were in the census of 1358 no fewer than 209 Jewish heads of families living in Avignon, from which Guillemain estimates a population of 1,000 to 1,200. In 1341 in Aix-en-Provence there were 203 Jewish householders, over 1,200 people all told. (Guillemain pp.646-647). The Avignon synagogue, in the heart of the Juiverie, stood some 30 m west of the Commanderie des Hospitaliers de Saint-Jean and 250 m south-east of the papal palace. (Op.cit., Carte 2, after p.810).

[54] There are at least thirteen sentence-length quotations of French in the *Summa* as well as numerous words and phrases, usually in proverbial form, such as

On ne doit avoir pite de lui qui ne la [l'a] daltrui [d'altrui]. (P.10.5)

Bromyard also translates several French proverbs into Latin, such as

> gallice dicitur: qui non habet argentum non habebit amicum. (A.12.32)
>
> in gallico proverbium est: quod cor non desiderat quod oculus non videt . (A.13.14)

We have to wait 300 years for the earliest English version of this proverb, in 1620. (ODEP[2] p.183).

55   Ideo dicit bernhardus quod religiosus debet esse sicut melchisedech sine patre et matre: id est sine parentum memoria. (A.12.26)

56   Quia vix modo diligit filius patrem: vel filia matrem..nisi sicut musca vas lactis vel mellis: et sicut canes os. (D.9.22)

57   Orleton pp.350-351: '..admissione dicti fratris Johannis de Bromyerd propter eius absenciam personalem dilata.'

58   Sed domina avaricia non permittit servum suum fidelem in morte nec deum quidem cognoscere nec animam suam ei ligare sed sibi totaliter intendere: sicut patuit de illo quem peroptime novi. Hic paralisi percussus loquelam amisit,   religiosi vero cicumstantes videntes eum morti appropinquare eum hortabantur ad cogitandum de   anima et ad receptionem euckaristie et clamabant in auribus eius ut* si placeret sacramentum recipere saltem aliquod signum vel nutu manu lingua vel vultu faceret, et cum nullum signum ab eo habere possent quidam socius ait ego cito habebo ab eo signum, et apposuit manum ad cistam que erat ad pedes eius in qua erat pecunia sua et cor suum et thesaurus suus, quasi volens eam aperire vel asportare et statim quasi expergefactus et quasi nitens caput erigere et voce et vultu triste signum vite ostendit, qui dum de deo et anime salute loquebantur quasi mortuus iacebat ostendens se plus de domina avaricia quam de deo sollicitari. Hec enim ita eum per guttur tenebat quod de aliquo deo signum facere non permisit: hoc cum vidisset quidam amicus qui eum cum speciali affectione dilexit erubescens recessit. (A.27.18)

> *reading 'ut' for the compositor's 'et'.

59   ..ante mortem vix potest pedes movere ad exquisita et secreta nature facienda: vel manus levare ut cibum vel potum in ore ponat: vel ut muscas de ore abigat: nec fortitudinem habet ut se in lecto suo de latere in latus vertat.. (M.11.144)

60   See chapter 26 and especially notes 27 to 34.

61   Edward [then the Lord Edward] had taken the cross at the Northampton parliament of 1268: admiration for S.Louis may have influenced his decision. (Prestwich pp.67-68). He was out of England from, probably, 20 August 1270 to 2 August 1274 (ibid. pp.73, 85). For Edward's piety see Prestwich pp.111-114. He notes Edward's veneration for the shrine of the Virgin at Walsingham and that of Becket at Canterbury. He also despatched clerks to make offerings at the shrines of S.Denis in Paris, of the Three Kings in Cologne and of S.James at Compostella.

62   Hamlet 1.5.77. The Ghost's lines go on

> No reck'ning made, but sent to my account
>
> with all my imperfections on my head..

63   Patent ergo ex iam dictis vigintiseptem similitudines et convenientie inter bellum corporale et spirituale. (B.2.29)

64   Exemplo etiam nobilis regis Edwardi: cuius consuetudo erat ante bellum peregrinationes facere personaliter: et personas in utroque iure dei et mundi sapientissimos consulere. Quia teste Seneca epistola.xiiii. parva sunt arma foris: si non sit consilium domi. Et si exempla deessent, ratio sufficeret: qua scitur quod ubi maius imminet periculum cautius est agendum. Sed in bello corporali maximum est periculum, et corporum et animarum: quia ibi non solum moriuntur corporaliter sed etiam spiritualiter multa milia propter generale odium: non solum duorum hominum sed duorum regnorum: et propter alia peccata in quibus sunt quando occiduntur. (B.2.23)

65   ..quod nobiles nomine et non re frequenter in prole puniuntur patet quia frequentius vel prolem habent malam vel omnino sine prole sunt quam simplices: quod ideo eis iusto dei iudicio evenire creditur: ut qui dei filiis frequenter tedium faciunt ipsi quoque de stultis filiis suis tedium habeant: et de bona congruitate: qui multos bellis illicitis et homicidiis filiis privant ipsorum filii moriantur. (N.3.14)

66   Luke 6.27: diligite inimicos vestros benefacite his qui vos oderunt.
Jesus' innovative command is all the more startling when it is set against a more traditional stance such as is found in the Quran: 'Fight those who believe not in Allah nor the Last Day, nor hold that forbidden which hath been forbidden by Allah and His Messenger, nor acknowledge the Religion of Truth, from among the People of the Book, until they pay the *Jizyah** with willing submission, and feel themselves subdued.' (Quran 9.29)
       *a poll tax

67   Quartum quod requiritur est quod in concordia facienda et pacem inter discordantes reformanda non nimis graves petantur emende, non tantum propter causam pretactam. D.x.xiiii.* verum etiam ne illorum intentio et nisus potius videatur esse circa cupiditatem quam pacem. Et pax que tali fit pacto nunquam erit durabilis, sicut ostensum est. B.ii.lv.† quia si sic concordatus auderet cor ostendere non diceret se pacificatum sed provocatum quia nimis care pacem emit vel nimis de iure suo parti timore dimisit. Et ideo tempore viso oportuno ostendet quod nunquam in medio tempore vera pax fuerat. Qui ergo veram desiderat pacem tria potius facere deberet quam illa frauderetur. Primo namque deberet se potius humiliare adversario suo… Secundo deberet potius de suo dare: sicut patet per exemplum et auctoritatem. D.ix.xi.‡ Tertio deberet aliquando iuri suo cedere et iniuriam vel etiam gravia pati. (P.4.20)

68   *Iterum dicunt nihil peto nisi iusticiam quam meruit. Sed advertant tales quod iusticie rigor non semper est petendus propter duo. Primo quia pax fundata super nimia vel gravi emenda vel iusticie rigore non erit sincera nec stabilis. Sicut patet. P.iiii.xx. Secundo quia in mortis articulo vel alia necessitate non petis a deo iusticie rigorem sed misericordiam et quod vis a deo exigere alteri facias. Sicut patet supra eodem capitulo. v. Nota M.ix.xxx. (D.10.14)

69   †Secunda [causa] quia dominium bello acquisitum est minus stabile licet enim finis belli sit pax tamen securius esset partibus concordatis pacem obtinere sine bello et dominium quia illi qui bello obtinentur et subiiciuntur potius timore quam amore serviunt: semper tempus expectantes quando se et suos in bello occisos aliqua occasione inventa vindicent. (B.2.55)

70   ‡Tercio diligite inimicos non solum quia vobis prosunt et propter mercedem ut dictum est: sed ut ipsi pro dilectione et benivolentia eis ostensa ad bonam vitam et amiciciam dei et vestram revocentur.. (D.9.11)

71   ..qui multum anhelant ad officia et dignitates.. (R.5.48)

72   ..surgunt annosi indocti: quorum anni multi actus stulti: et cathedram rapiunt magistralem et digni turpiter postponuntur.. qui ibi videlicet desinunt ubi incipiunt, pro principio medio et fine ignorantiam et sufficientem illiteraturam habentes. (R.5.50)

73   Hi sunt qui sermone tantum non opere seculo renunciaverunt seculariter vivunt et vitia sua sub inani professione melioris vite abscondunt ac religionis imagine et nomine palliati opinionem virtutum suscipiunt, predicant magna nec faciunt, accusant vitia nec deponunt, publice despicere simulant quod occulte committunt, magni student videri nec tamen fieri tales, bene volunt colligere fragmenta et reliquias sanctorum eis dimissas sed non mores: sicut illi qui vadunt cum indulgentiis: qui omnia predicant et sustinent propter lucrum temporale.. (R.5.5)

74   ..sicut imagines sanctorum apparatum habent deauratum in barba et vestimentis et curiose factum: et interius ut frequenter sunt putride et a vermibus comeste. Sancti vero in se dum vixerunt contrarias habuerunt virtutes qui fuerunt pulcerrime ornati interius in anima et exiliter in corpore. (S.2.7)

Ipsis vero congregatis in divinis officiis quanta sit negligentia patet cum sacris vigiliis paucissimi vix interesse dignentur et ad sacra missarum solennia ad ludendum, ad ridendum et ad cachinnam magis quam ad psallendum congregari videantur: dicam de quo mali seu dissoluti rident devoti lugent: dicam inquam plane ut dolens: sed amans amens tamen magis videar: sed ei qui non amat et qui vim non sentit amoris: si tamen dici libeat quo defluunt in comesationibus et ebrietatibus in cubilibus non dicam in impudicitiis ut iam cetus clericorum putentur   prostibula lascivorum et conciliabulum histrionum: quia ibi remissio societas, effusio liberalitas, loquacitas affabilitas, cachinnatio et derisio iocunditas, mollicies et nitor vestimentorum honestas vocatur et nuncupatur.. (R.5.53)

Expenditure on feasts for members of religious communities who were incepting as university teachers was in Bromyard's eyes wasteful. The money would be better spent on the maintenance of the fabric of buildings or to obviate the need to pawn or sell books. (R.5.54). In 1363-4 Roger Thurston, sacrist of the cathedral priory at Norwich, paid 'pro inceptione domini Ade de Eston et domini Thome de Brynton XXX sol.' [360 silver pennies]. Both Easton and Brinton were at Gloucester College, the principal Benedictine foundation at Oxford. (Brinton p.xii).

..nec sacerdote ad missam pulsante surgit: quia si magnus sit cogitat quod sacerdos ipsum expectabit: si pauper sit cogitat quod sufficit quod veniat ad elevationem sacramenti. (P.6.18)

..quia contra unum qui in processione et ecclesia devote orat sunt multi qui ociose et nocive garrulant. (O.5.26)

..in ecclesia volunt orare quando non inveniunt cum quo non poterunt garrulare. (P.7.13)
..ita magni tyranni divites et potentes et magni peccatores vel ad predicationem non veniunt vel si venerint dormiunt vel garrulant.. (P.12.6)

..Et quod vix unam audiunt missam nullam vero dicunt missam: etiam illi qui non promoti dicere solebant, in qua cum audiunt non circa letanias dicendas sed circa litteras legendas vel conficiendas vel sigillandas occupantur. (S.8.9)

..queritur ad induendum: non quod utilius sed quod subtilius [et]* nitidiusve invenitur: non quod frigus repellat sed quod superbire compellat: quod per mollem tactum mulceat et per colores oculos attrahat intuentium: non quod utilius potest observari sed quod venustius et vanius ostentari. Non enim ille quem ore et vita ostendere deberent id est christus summus pastor: cuius gregis custodes esse deberent: talibus legitur fuisse indutus ornamentis: nec vectus equo vel stipatus baiulo manticam portante... quia illum habitum qui religionis signum quondam fuit speciale: nunc in signum gestant superbie: miles et monachus ex eodem sibi partiuntur capam et caligam cum talibus insigniis christi: humilitatem predicant: dei iusticias enarrant: ecclesie testamentum assumunt dilatant capucia et philateria, magnificant fimbrias, stringunt manicas, trahunt tunicas, rugant capas ornant latera produnt laqueata iocalia ostentant sudariola et munuscula et dum sic currunt ad capitula plus loci illius ambitio quam devotio terit limina. Sed inquiunt numquid de vestibus cura est deo: et non magis de moribus nec in habitu est religio: sed in corde ac forma hec vestium deformitatis mentium et morum est indicium. (R.5.52)
    *I reject 'et'.

Cuncti tamen boni deum laudant. Aliqui [religiosi] super terram posessionum et divitiarum fundati sicut possessionati. Alii quasi in altum a terra per paupertatem voluntariam et divitiis derelictis elevati qui eo plus divinis laudibus intendere possunt quo minus circa terrena occupantur. (R.5.29)

..congrue respondit quidam de ordine mendicantium cuidam de ordine possessionatorum admiranti quomodo illi possent esse meliores predicatores quam ipsi cum plures haberent libros Cui ille Rex Henricus est ditior homo totius regni anglie in lignis et meremio: et tamen unus pauper operarius melius scivit facere domum quam ipse. (S.4.10)

..ut amor in hoc mundo inter potentes et ecclesiam et etiam inter vicinos conservetur: ut si mali sint ne noceant.. Si ergo videris monasteria depauperari et grangias impignorari et domus interiores esse dirutas: vide causam extra portam ubi domum pauperum quam in principio orationis habebant longam videbis desertam et dirutam: et intelligas hanc esse causam: Nam dum christus pascebatur christus eos pascebat et ditabat: Dum econverso econverso. (V.8.50)

84
..in veteri namque lege mulieris perfecta conditio reputabatur fecunditas. In nova vero reputatur virginitas. (M.3.21)

85
E.g. bonum est homini mulierem non tangere. (I Corinthians 7.1)

86
..venter et genitalia sibimet vicina sunt ut ex vicinitate membrorum intelligatur confederatio viciorum. (G.5.5)

87
Mulier pulchra: templum est edificatum super cloacam. (P.14.2)

88
Pulchritudo non est nisi velamen turpitudinis. (P.14.2)

89
..quando solutus vel soluta cor in cogitatione fornicationis balneat.. (L.7.4)

90
Quia si cogitatio talis vel mulieris societas tecum diu moretur erit de te sicut de pariete vel panno albo: quia sicut candela parietem maculat ita illa mentem tuam quantumcunque fuerit prius munda et alba. (L.7.42)

91
Una namque fatua mulier decorata suo aspectu et loquela citius centum ad concupiscentiam malam convertet quam optimus homo sua predicatione viginti ad concupiscentiam bonam et desertionem mali.. (S.10.7)

92
Et fuge.. secreta et angularia illarum [sc. mulierum] colloquia.. (M.12.9)

93
Aut quis mulierem tangere auderet extraneam cum sanctus heremita matrem propriam ultra aquam portando manus eius nudas tangere non auderet, dicens: caro mulieris semper ignis est. (O.7.17)

94
Munde custoditur quando sic utuntur matrimonio quod omnis refrenatur libido. (M.4.1)

95
Ita status matrimonii medium est inter desideria carnalia inordinata: de quibus fugere tenentur omnes: et montem continentie seu castitatis ad quem qui ascendere ex vecordia non potest salvet se in segori.i. in matrimonio. Et hoc est quod ait apostolus.i.Cor.vii. Si non continent, nubant. Melius est enim nubere quam uri etc. (M.4.3)

96
Ideo dicit Augustinus libro ad sacras virgines quod dominica virgo primitus vitare debet publicos conspectus et platearum frequentiam devitare, atque in domo posita operi lanifico insistere vel lectioni divine. (M.12.10)

97
..ubi sunt mali mundi amatores qui parum ante nos fuerunt: ubi sunt mali mundi principes reges comites et alii terrarum domini qui cum superbia et magno apparatu et equitatu vixerunt qui canes multos et multam et malam familiam nutriebant, qui magna palatia et maneria multa et terras latas cum multis redditibus possidebant: et corpora sua in deliciis et voluptatibus gule et luxurie nutriebant: qui subditos pro predictis nutriendis dure et crudeliter regebant et excoriabant: ubi insuper sunt falsi mundi sapientes, iudices, assessores, advocati et iuratores atque periuri patrie ad infernum ductores: qui pro muneribus deum et regnum celorum vendebant et infernum emebant, ubi iterum sunt usurarii qui sciebant de obolo denarium et de undecim duodecim: et de modio frumenti vel eius valore duos vel tres facere: et falsi mercatores qui hominem in facie decipere sciebant.. (G.2.41)

98
..sicut infirmitas corporalis in oculo ovis apparens signum est interioris infirmitatis.. (L.7.42)

99
..sicut pastor ovem scabiosam ab ovili [subtrahit] ne alias inficiat. (P.6.1)

100
..ovis de domo que ardet vix eiici potest: et si eiecta fuerit nisi vi teneatur in ignem recurrit. (R.2.4). This suggests an unusual circumstance which, presumably, Bromyard had experienced,

possibly at lambing time when a brazier may have been overturned. A ewe may have been reluctant to leave her lamb.

101 Sicut animalia sitibunda non expectatis adaquare usque ad finem quadragesime.. (V.9.2) A good milking cow will give upwards of five gallons a day and in summer will drink more than ten gallons of water daily. Sheep, on the other hand, were and are often left to fend for themselves, getting enough liquid intake from grass and fodder: but they will drink when water is provided for them. (I profited from conversations on these two points with Mr David Milne.)

102 ..qui tres anseres nescit gubernare.. (P.13.12)

103 ..si quis tempore ventoso ignem in stipula propria ponit sicut moris est in aliquibus partibus ubi post messiones statim stipulam comburunt.. (O.6.54). The benefit derives from nitrogen fixation.

104 in mundi nanque principio cum terra seu terrena possessio esset habitatoribus amplior: quia habitatores habuit pauciores..terra ita ampla erat quod plus erat sufficiens pro paucis tunc quam pro multis nunc.. Moderno vero tempore cum sicut terrarum termini et possessiones artantur quia possessores et habitatores multiplicantur, quibus terra vix sufficit.. (M.11.90)
McEvedy and Jones put the population of England and Wales in 1300 at 3.75 million: this figure, more than double that of c.1100, 'seems to have been well over the optimum for the agricultural technology of the time, for, as more and more marginal land was brought into use, both productivity and standards of living fell. Since the norm was little better than subsistence, the nutritional state of the population declined dangerously. By 1300 the population was having difficulty maintaining itself..' (WPH pp.41-42). Postan too writes of a growing pressure of population against land. (CEHE II p.216).

105 ..quia tempore moderno nec terra vel arbores vel aque tante sunt fertilitatis sicut esse solebant. (M.13.2)

106 ..lusor aliquando cum tribus taxillis alium qui forte aliquid in principio lucratus est finaliter depauperat. (T.1.4)

107 ..sicut de falso lusore qui falsos habet decios cum quibus primo permittit socium suum lucrari ut ad ludendum eum provocet: sed in fine totum amittet. (P.5.6)

108 ..nisi sicut magister vel ductor ursi servit urso qui in diebus solemnibus ursum suum quibus canibus exponit lacerandum ita quod quanto melior dies tanto urso peior: quia a pluribus laceratur canibus. (F.3.6)
..sicut ursus in maioribus et festis melioribus plus a canibus laceratur.. (I.6.9)
The artists of the Luttrell Psalter, at 161 recto, depict a muzzled brown bear chained to a stake being set on by four dogs. The three owners encourage them while the bearward taps the nose of a mastiff which has seized on the bear's right ear.

109 ..qui de lucro totius septimane in festo inebriatur.. (F.3.21)
..qui totum quod in septimana lucratur in die festo voluptuose expendit. (O.4.10)

110 ..intrat potus exit sensus. (E.1.4). This may be the earliest recorded use of this proverb by an English writer. (The Oxford Dictionary of English Proverbs[2] cites nothing comparable till 1555 and 1612-15). It is not only labouring men whom Bromyard berates for drunkenness but men called to parliament too. (N.3.15)

111 The Winter's Tale 4.4.827.

112 ..[hypocrites] domui assimilantur que interius forte nullam habet crucem sed multas sordes: sed exterius cruces imprimuntur multe ne transeuntes super illam urinent sed propter cruces domum illam quodammodo in reverentia habeant. (I.7.3)

25

113 ..sicut nutriti in ytalia antequam sint assueti non delectantur in potu anglicano quantumcunque sit in se bonus. (E.6.20) See also the reference at A.5.6 (sicut italici de cervisia..) They are in for a surprise.

114 ..sicut vinum melius est quod crescit in alto loco et petroso.. (A.24.9)

115 ..ad modum vacce que totum lac prius datum in fine pede evertit.. (P.1.5)

116 ..sicut de duabus situlis quarum una descendente alia ascendit.. (O.1.21)

117 ..sicut est grave et penale radi a rasore malo et cum novacula obtusa vel dentata vel ubi non precedit debita madefactio.. (O.1.4)
Bromyard uses this image of the clumsy barber and blunt razor to compare the pain such shaving causes with that generated by an unskilled (or malicious: 'malo') superior, who fails to smooth his 'correctiones mordaces et contentiosas' with the 'moisturizing of kindliness and sympathy and pleasantness.' This extract thus provides two insights into his personal experience.

118 ..sicut qui ponunt infantes suos ante ostium hospitalis vel ecclesie ut de hospitali nutriantur quos ipsi nutrire nolunt. (O.6.48)

119 Sicut enim leprosorum fugeres societatem ne corpus inficerent.. (R.2.14)

120 ..sicut.. elemosynarius qui non dat uni ad portam petenti, sed expectat quousque multi fuerint simul congregati. (O.5.20)

121 ..similis fenestre vitree que lumen recipit et tempestates excludit.. (P.12.36)

122 Tales revera imaginibus assimilantur que gallice garrule vocantur: que in istis magnis edificiis os quasi flendo aperiunt et vultum tristem quasi onus impositum ferre non possent se ostendunt. (O.1.11, 12)
[He uses 'gargoules' at B.2.5, closer to the modern French *gargouille[s]*: 'garrule' may well be a compositor's error.]

123 Et quando de proprio illam grossam et longam [sc. capillaturam] sicut optant habere non possunt ut ex illa cornua faciant in quibus niti videntur ut diabolo assimilentur qui cum cornibus depingitur ab aliis vivis vel mortuis crines muto accipiunt.. (O.7.5)
Bromyard recounts an incident which took place in Paris: an elderly woman 'who had cut off the beautiful hair of a young woman recently dead' had her hairpiece snatched from her head during a procession near Notre Dame (in medio civitatis) by a monkey [and became the talk of the town, no doubt]. (O.7.5)

124 ..cum in mensa cuiusdam prelati questio mota fuisset quod membrum corporis magis sumptuosum esset*..quidam sapiens inter eos quid ipse de hoc sentiebat requisitus dixit quod oculus fuit.. (N.3.13)
          *correcting the compositor's dittographic 'fuisset'.

125 'There is shown the deception of those people who claim they are kidnapped, by day or by night, by a beautiful people, or speak or fly with them..' (S.11.0) 'Deception' could have an active or a passive sense: that it is the latter is clear from the following extract:
Hac insuper illusione decepte* sunt mulieres, que in hac parte magis inveniuntur culpabiles quam viri, que dicunt se rapi a quodam populo et duci ad loca quedam pulcra et ignota: que etiam dicunt se cum eis equitare per multa terrarum spacia intempeste noctis silentio.. (S.11.8)
          *my reading for 'decepti'of the text.
'Deceived by this illusion moreover are the women – who in this aspect are found more blameworthy than men – who assert they are carried off by a certain people and taken to certain beautiful, unknown places: who also claim they ride with them over many expanses of lands in the silence of the dead of night.. and that whatever places are locked they leave and enter at will.'
Bromyard quotes the Decretum of Gratianus, Secunda pars, Causa XXVI Quaestio V, 'Episcopi eorumque ministri.' This text had been collected by Regino the Benedictine abbot of Prüm in the

diocese of Trier about 906 and later incorporated into the Decretum. (For Regino see Tritheim 295 and Chevalier 3917-3918).

'That also is not to be passed over that certain wicked women perverted to follow Satan, seduced by illusions and fantasies of demons, believe and profess that in the company of Diana goddess of pagans in the nocturnal hours, or with Herodias or with an uncountable multitude of women they ride on certain beasts, and in the silence of the dead of night traverse the expanses of many lands and submit to her commands as to their mistress.'

See 'Witchcraft'pp.74-77 and, on Transvection, pp.511-514. Bromyard, it must be stressed, accepts Church teaching that such night-flights are indeed flights of fancy, dreams inspired by the devil.

126   'For [merchants (as opposed to money-changers)] in their calculations are readier to use copper denarii than gold, nor do they consider what value the denarius has but the position it occupies: in that if a copper [denarius] is placed in a higher position and a gold [denarius] in a lower one the copper [denarius] stands for a hundred times or a thousand times the value of the gold [denarius]..' (S.13.5)

127   ..ad modum matris que filium ad se venientem et cadere incipientem apprehendit.. (V.9.9)

128   Sicut ergo simul stant quod ego sciam quot notas musice alius scit: et quod gaudeam quod tot scit: que tamen ego in illa arte ignarus nescio.. (G.1.13, 14)

129   Four sermons of Iohannes XXII which ventured into the field of this doctrine involved him in considerable controversy. 'While traditional doctrine held that the souls of the saints are in paradise already enjoying the full vision of God, John taught that this would be delayed for them until after the final judgement; until then they would contemplate only the humanity of Christ.' (ODP p.215). The sermons had been delivered in the winter of 1331-32. This thesis was sharply condemned by the theologians of the University of Paris in 1333: and Bromyard's omission of any mention of the polemics thus engendered is yet another pointer to his having completed the *Summa* by 1330. (On this see chapter 24).

130   ..contra grecos et alios incredulos qui dicunt animas bonorum et malorum penas et premia usque ad diem expectare iudicii. Cuius contrarium quantum ad malos per predictum patet divitem. (P.8.10)

131   ..sicut multi libenter audiunt et appreciantur pulchritudinem in voce cantantium.. (P.14.9)

132   ..sicut patet per illud quod quibusdam alte cantantibus voce celitus emissa responsum dicitur fuisse quandam vetulam illuc in quodam angulo orantem melius cantare. (O.5.15)

133   ..plus placet deo humilis cantus cum devotione quam solemnis sine attentione et mentis vanitate. (O.5.15)

There are other musical references at E.4.3 and T.5.46, 47.

134   ..conditiones consequamur pictorum qui pulcras imagines diligenter considerant ut consimiles faciant. Et unam excellentem pulcritudinem vel *tractum* colligunt de una imagine et aliam de alia ut omnes illas excellentias in una imagine ponant et pulcerrimam faciant. (E.7.7)

I translate 'tractus'as 'treatment.' If my translation is correct this would seem to be its first such use by an English writer. Other references to pictures occur at G.4.9, H.1.1, I.7.2, M.13.3, M.13.5, P.2.20 and P.14.2. They include a mention of a depiction of the Wheel of Fortune, which he has seen on several walls (M.13.3): and of paintings of the Crucifixion.

135   Et congrue imaginem crucifixi librum dixit: Nam idem dicunt iura ecclesie quod videlicet imagines et picture sunt libri et scripture laicorum.. (P.2.20)

136   C.6.11. The police structure their investigations of serious crimes using the same concepts: motive: means: opportunity.

137   ..vinum et confessio omnia revelant. (E.1.4)

138 The Luttrell Psalter, at 74 recto, depicts a kneeling nun receiving absolution from a kneeling friar who places his right hand on her covered hair (below the verse from psalm 37.11, cor meum conturbatum est.).

139 ..quod qui peccando in ferventissimo amore convivunt: postquam fuerint matrimonio copulati tepescunt. (A.17.5)

140 ..quia sicut adultera a leccatore verberata ab eo non recedit: verberata vero a marito ab eo recedit. (M.13.23)

141 '*Super cathedram* of February 1300 required that they [sc. friars] must obtain episcopal authority for hearing confessions.. Nothing in the bull contradicted the earlier decision as to the annual confession to the parish priest.' (Boase p.191) This latter point had been affirmed in canon 21 of Lateran IV:
'Omnis utriusque sexus fidelis, postquam ad annos discretionis pervenerit, omnia sua solus peccata confiteatur fideliter, saltem semel in anno *proprio sacerdoti*..' (Tanner p.245). The text is notable for its advocacy of caution in a confessor's questioning, using the words 'discretus', 'cautus', 'diligenter', 'prudenter', 'caveat', etc.

142 Adam, etc., ..salutem, etc. Quia nos religiosos viros, fratres Johannem de Rectham [and five others], ordinis Predicatorum, nunc de Conventu Salopsire, ad confessiones audiendas, absoluciones impendendas, et salutares penitencias injungendas *ac sermones populo faciendos*, secundum tenorem constitucionis felicis recordacionis domini Bonifacii Pape octavi edite.. vobis mandamus..quatinus cum eosdem fratres ad ecclesias vobis subjectas contigerit declinare, eos ad premissa curetis graciose admittere.. (Orleton pp.70-71)
Orleton gave this commission to the six Dominicans at Monnington on Wye on 26 April 1318. Unfortunately resentment at what was perceived by many parish priests as an intrusion into their rôle was widespread: Bromyard writes of 'envy gnawing at them over others who preach correctly..' (ne rector ecclesie dum soli sibi ius predicationis vendicat etiam aliis recte predicantibus invidia se mordente contradicat.) (P.12.8)

143 So John of Bristol described his two candidates (Hugh of Ledbury and John of Bromyard) for admission to the licence to hear confessions, [impose penances and deliver sermons] as 'viros probate vite et doctrine..' (Orleton p.350).

144 Sed dicent in vita activa multe sunt temptationes et peccatorum occasiones que occurrunt ex visis et auditis in confessione, quantum ad illos qui per mundum discurrunt ad predicandum et confitendum. Sunt etiam multa tedia corporalia.. Nec tamen est ab his cessandum. (V.7.2). One may suppose that Bromyard did *not* cease from shouldering the burden of his calling till his death, some three years after the ravages of the Black Death, in 1352. This date may be inferred from the entry for 27 October 1352 in bishop Trillek's *Registrum*: '..apud Sugwas, admissus fuit frater Willelmus le Wyte de conventu fratrum predicatorum Herefordie, *loco fratris Johannis de Bromyard* ad confessiones audiendas in comitatu Herefordie..' (Trillek p.20). Previous admissions had been granted on 31 August 1351, 14 December 1351, 9 October 1352 and 18 October 1352.

145 P.7.17, P.7.31. Bromyard calls these 'steps on the ladder of penitence'.

146 Contra verecundiam vero que posset evenire ex hoc quod confessor audit peccata: deus plura remedia providit: quorum unum est quod non ordinavit quod confiteremur angelis: ne timeremus vel erubesceremus tam mundis creaturis immundicias nostras ostendere. Sed homini: qui circumdatus infirmitate sicut alii: qui etiam temptationum bella in seipso experitur: qui ex propria debilitate et fragilitate potius habet materiam fragilibus compati: quam contemnere vel abhominare. (C.6.59)

PART I

Modern books are not as truthful as those of long ago..[1]

For if a papal bull carries great authority and credence, how much more do the supremely true words of God, which can in no way be false.[2]

I say that a yearning for wealth is the reason why advocates study the civil law and their stratagems… And this is the reason..why the school of civil lawyers has a hundred or two hundred students whereas the school of theology perhaps can't muster five.[3]

Philosophy has now consumed virtually the whole of theology..the truth of the matter is that theology, which has as its duty the clarification and application of God's commandments to contemporary behaviour, is being emptied of content...[4]

---

[1]   Novi libri non sunt ita veraces sicut antiqui.. (V.8.12)

[2]   Si enim bulla pape magne sit autoritatis et credibilitatis: quanto magis verba dei verissima: que nullo modo falsa esse possunt. (V.2.1)

[3]   Dico quod amor diviciarum est causa quare advocati leges et cautelas addiscunt… Et hec causa est..quare scola legistarum habet centum vel ducentos auditores: ubi scola theologorum non habet forte quinque. (A.14.30)

[4]   Ita iam philosophia quasi totam theologiam consumpsit..sic in rei veritate theologia que mandata dei ad mores declarare et trahere deberet evacuatur.. (S.4.15)

1

THE *SUMMA*: AND ITS RELATIONSHIP TO OTHER WORKS WITHIN BROMYARD'S OEUVRE

The references between one book in Bromyard's oeuvre and another – both the four surviving books and the five lost ones - are lucidly presented by Binkley in the appendix to his 1995 study[1] on which I base the following summary in tabular form.

Surviving
1. Opus trivium
    called by Binkley his first work[2]: it is not cited in the surviving three works, nor does it cite any others in the corpus.
2. Distinctiones
    has one reference to the *Registrum*.
3. Summa predicantium
    refers to i Sermones ii Collationes (and, Binkley found in the Peterhouse Manuscript, 'added..by an early corrector'[3] iii Additiones).
4. Exhortationes
    contains references to i Summa predicantium ii Distinctiones iii Sermones iv Persuasiones. Binkley comments that this appears therefore, to be Bromyard's last work.[4]

Lost
5. Sermones
    cited by i Summa ii Exhortationes.
6. Collationes
    cited by i Summa ('in its later revisions').[5]
7. Additiones
    cited by i Summa (see 3 above).[6]
8. Registrum
    cited by i Distinctiones.
9. Persuasiones
    cited by i Exhortationes.

The relative order of composition of these nine works cannot be established in entirety, but certain deductions seem safe: e.g. that the *Sermones* precedes the *Summa* which in turn precedes the *Exhortationes*. The *Sermones*, moreover, may well have been a sizeable compilation. We know from Bromyard's own cross-referencing that there were at least 148 sermons in this collection.[7]

The order of composition has important implications for the absolute dating of Bromyard's works. Binkley's statement[8] that the *Distinctiones* includes a sermon-outline for the feast of St Thomas Cantilupe (bishop of Hereford 1275-1282) may well push back this part at least of the work to a time between 17 April 1320 – the date of Cantilupe's canonization[9] – and 2 October 1320, the very first celebration of his feast-day.[10] Furthermore, if we accept that the citation of the *Registrum* by the *Distinctiones* implies the precedence of the *Registrum* then we may perhaps guess a date of 1319 or earlier for the *Registrum*. It is worth remembering that we do not know when, or where, Bromyard joined the Dominican order: nor do we know whether he joined as a young or mature man, with his studying days behind him.

A brief outline follows of the four surviving works.

Bromyard's *Opus Trivium* is so styled from its three-fold source:

'Here begins the *Opus Trivium* of materials supremely useful for preaching elegantly assembled in alphabetic order from laws sacred, canon and civil.'[11]

Its first capitulum is ABBAS, followed by AB INFANTIA, ABSOLUTIO, ABSTINENTIA, ABUSIO, ACCEPTIO, ACCIDIA, ACCUSATIO and so on through the alphabet: ending with VOTUM, USURA, XRISTIANORUM PRIMA LEX and XRISTUS. His ABBAS begins

'Abbas non potest in duobus monasteriis possidere nec monachus in diversis monasteriis locum habere per decretalem...'

It entered the printing age not after 1473 in Ulrich Zel's edition[12] in which it has 297 folio-size leaves with 36 lines in double column to each page: a large work.

Bromyard's *Distinctiones* is ably described by Wenzel.[13] 'This is a series of 155 sermon outlines for all Sundays and feast days of the church year, in exact chronological order. The title *Distinctiones* is quite accurate, because all the pieces begin by dividing their respective thema from the day's lection into four parts, which are then briefly developed with biblical and other authorities, similes, and occasional stories that are often homely and include references to contemporary Wales. All sermons bear indications of the occasion for which they were intended. These include 26 Trinity and the feast of the Crown of Thorns, as well as the feasts of major Franciscan and Dominican saints and of saints David, Chad, Cuthbert, Richard of Chichester and Thomas of Hereford, whose cult has otherwise left few if any traces in the surviving sermon literature..'[14] Wenzel's note 8 states that sermons for saints Stephen, John, Innocents, Thomas of Canterbury and Silvester [26-31 December] occur in both the temporal and saints' cycles and that sermons for Christmas, Circumcision, Epiphany and the Sunday after Epiphany appear in both cycles.

In addition to his citations of three of his own works (i.e. the *Sermones,* the *Collationes* and the *Additiones*) Bromyard deploys a system of massive cross-referencing within the gigantic *Summa*. Peter Binkley draws attention to this achievement: 'The pragmatic intent of all his literary work is illustrated by his providing each of his books with a detailed alphabetical index and an efficient system of cross-reference, at a time when it was still a relative novelty for an author to index his own works.'[15]

The cross-referencing may be exemplified from four of his 189 capitula:

F.5.23	to	F.3.14, 15: E.5.4, 5: G.4.21, P.2. art.8
P.9.8	to	O.4.15
P.9.14	to	T.5.35, T.5.39, T.5.50, T.5.64, R.5.11, S.5.6
P.13.56	to	S.3.7, G.4.6
P.13.59	to	D.12.32, R.1.37
R.5.60	to	O.4.15, M.9.15 and P.13.43, O.8.4

Hundreds of man-hours must have been expended on this laborious task, whose effect was – and is – to ensure easy and rapid access to kindred themes and their treatment. He may well have been helped in this huge undertaking by colleagues at Hereford. It is legitimate to wonder whether Bromyard had planned in advance the numerous articuli in his 189 capitula. But what is illegitimate is to assume that Bromyard *wrote* his capitula in alphabetical order. He had before him a previously written work whose structure he could use, emend and augment in whatever sequence suited his and his fellow-Dominicans' needs.

'Informed therefore by their example I have emended and augmented in this book the compilation previously put together by me, placing particular materials under letters fixed in alphabetical order..'[16] ('Their example' refers to Aristoteles, S. Paul, Ecclesiasticus and other authorities urging one to work not for the individual but the common good.)

The 'compilation previously put together' is generally assumed to be the *Tractatus iuris canonici et civilis* (often styled the *Opus trivium*), which Binkley's biographical sketch[17] calls his first book. *Iudicium divinum,* in which (at I.11.3) his dating of 1330 appears, may have been written as the first or the last of his 189 capitula or in any other position. The sentence which provides this date may even have been added on completion of the whole work.

The alphabetical index to the *Summa* mentioned by Binkley is found in the *Tabula Realis*. This contains 321 headwords the vast majority of which are keyed to related words.

They begin with
    Ab infantia
    Absolutio
    Abstinentia
    Abusio
and end with
    Votum
    Usurarii
    Christus
    Christiani mali
    Christiani boni
Most of these headwords are linked to two or three others: e.g.

Adulterium	to	Luxuria. Matrimonium
Advocati	to	Falsitas. Lex. Sapientia
Divitie	to	Divites. Abundantia. Prosperitas
Gulosi	to	Abstinentia. Ebrietas. Ieiunium
Ornatus	to	Mulier. Novitas. Pulcritudo. Superbia

A few have none or just one: e.g.

Beginagium	to	Mulier
Cor	to	Mundicia
Peccare	to	Misericordia
Resurrectio	to	-

A few more are heavily laden with references: eg.

Executores	to	Avaricia. Cupiditas. Fidelitas. Furtum. Ingratitudo. Iusticia. Mors

Prelati   to   Ambitio. Dispensatio. Episcopi. Clerici. Hospitalitas.
Elemosyna. Misericordia. Papa. Patroni. Reges.
Sacerdotium. Ecclesiastici. Ordo. Symonia

This outline, however, gives only the skeleton of the *Tabula realis*. The entries contain greater riches. One example must suffice:

SACERDOTES in sacra scriptura vocantur dii et angeli. S.1.1.
Et reges. S.1.2
Inter quos tamen multi sunt insufficientes: et causa quare. C.5.18, 19
Talium periculum. C.18.4. cum sequentibus
Quod requirunt decimas [tithes] plus quam animas. D.2.12
Quod multi illorum damnantur. L.7.18
Quod multas mulieres seducunt. L.7.4, 9
Quomodo serviunt deo in mensa [i.e. the Lord's table]. M.8.6
Malos sacerdotes conducentes peccant. M.10.4
Contra illos qui post mortem tantum induuntur vestibus sacris. O.6.75, 76
Tales faciunt contra nominis sui interpretationem. S.1.3
Et contra vestimentorum significationem. S.1.5
Et sunt ingrati deo et ecclesie ipsos honorantibus. S.1.6
Et decipiunt illos de quibus vivunt: vel pro quibus celebrant. S.1.4
Et immundi [the unclean] inter illos sunt pessimi inter omnes homines. S.1.7
Quam scientiam habere tenentur: et quod studium est eis necessarium. S.1.8
Sacerdotes christianorum assimilantur sacerdotibus iudeorum. S.1.9
Quod ditiores missas dicunt pauciores. S.1.10
Penam habebunt in inferno aliis maiorem. S.1.11
Quia ad supremum gradum male veniunt: et peius in eo vivunt. S.1.12
Et quia multos super se cespitare [stumble] et cadere faciunt. S.1.13
Quere [look up, see] clerici: cum concordantiis suis. Item scandalum: communio

The Tabula realis occupies 67 folio-size pages, in double-column format, in the first printed edition.[18] It is flanked by a Tabula vocalis which lists the 189 headwords of the capitula: and by a second Tabula vocalis which is notable for including in its 201 entries a large number of names of animals with keys to the text: e.g. (giving the English names):

Spider	I.6.8
Hawk	A.14.6, O.6.31, P.13.49, R.1.35
Bee	E.7.16, L.6.28, M.3.15, N.3.11, R.4.8, R.5.30
Eagle	A.25.8, 29, 30: D.6.30, N.4.4, O.6.4,P.2.13, R.1.6, 7: S.3.15
Swallow	H.6.25
Barnacle-goose	E.7.3
Owl	E.2.4, R.1.32
Toad	I.8.7, V.12.5
Beaver	M.14.4
Crab	O.6.55
Swan	I.7.4
Cuckoo	D.6.17, S.9.6, S.11.4

'Dog' has 15 references, 'Wolf' 18 and 'Fox' 18. In all 60 creatures of the animal kingdom are listed here, as well as the mythological basilisk and the fire-dwelling salamander. They would doubtlessly provide a leaven to a sermon, whether preached in church or outdoors, and are within a well-established European tradition of deriving instructive conclusions from animal behaviour: whose literary antecedents go back to the Fables of Aesopus: beyond them to Hesiodos and his fable of the Hawk and the Nightingale in *Erga kai Hēmerai* (*Works and Days*).

TABLE 1.1 : ALL CREATURES LISTED IN THE TABULA VOCALIS

Spider	[Dove]	Ewe
Boar	Cuckoo	Peacock
Hawk	Dragon	Panther
Bee	Horse	Partridge
Asp	Falcon	Nightingale
Ass	Ant	Fish
Eagle	Hen	Frog
Lamb		
Basilisk	Crane	King of the birds
Barnacle-goose	Hedgehog	(Sicut dicitur in
Owl (eagle-owl)	Lion	fabulis de avi qui
Toad	[Lion]	gallice vocatur reistel)
Locust (pre-flight)	Lioness	Salamander
Chameleon	Hare	Serpent
Dog	Lynx	Monkey
Beaver	Locust	Stork
Crab	Wolf	Scorpion
Swan	Kite	Ostrich
Cicada	Fly	Tortoise
Dove	Weasel	Bat
Snake	Mouse	Viper
Crow	Glow-worm	Fox
Raven	Little owl	Vulture

(There are one or two omissions: e.g. the stag of an *exemplum* at T.3.5).

His *Exhortationes* too is designed for the maximum ease of reference for his readers. In this work he follows the course of the liturgical year, from the first Sunday in Advent to All Saints': in all, 76 exhortations[19] or sermons.[20] There then follows a *Tabula realis* –

yncipit tabula realis sermonum precedentium et cetera –

which lists 211 headwords, each of which is keyed in to the relevant sections of the 76 sermons. So

CLERICI is keyed to sermons 22c: 41f: 40: and the reader is advised to look at ORDO SACERDOTUM

DIABOLUS to 8c: 29b and 41h: 29f: 31b: 68h

GULA to 57: 65a: 65c: 69c [quere supra in abstinentia]

TRIBULATIO to 4a: 14h: 18e: 24d: 27a: 31b, c: 41a: 42e: 43f: 41g: 43c: 68a, b: 70d: 70f: 73b.

The concepts under which this preacher of prodigious energies organized his thoughts and directed his zeal may be better demonstrated through particulars, not generalities. Tabulated below, side by side for comparison, are the headwords from (a) the *Exhortationes* and (b) the *Summa*.

TABLE 1.2: HEADWORDS OF THE *EXHORTATIONES* AND THE *SUMMA*

EXHORTATIONES		SUMMA
A		
AB INFANTIA	A1	ABIECTIO
ABSCONDERE	A2	ABIICERE
ABSTINENTIA	A3	AB INFANTIA
ABUSIO	A4	ABSTINENTIA
ACCIDIA	A5	ABSCONSIO
ADQUISITORES	A6	ABUSIO
ADVENTUS	A7	ABSOLUTIO
ADVERSITAS	A8	ACCIDIA
ADULATOR	A9	ACCEDERE
ADULTERIUM	A10	ACCIPERE
AMICITIA	A11	ACCUSATIO
AMOR	A12	ACQUISITIO
ANGELI	A13	ADVENTUS
ANIMA	A14	ADVOCATI
ARMA	A15	ADULATIO
AVARUS	A16	ADORATIO
AUDIRE	A17	ADULTERIUM
	A18	ADVERSITAS
	A19	AMBULATIO
	A20	AMOR
	A21	AMICITIA
	A22	ANGELUS
	A23	ANIMA
	A24	ARMA
	A25	ASCENDERE
	A26	AUDIRE
	A27	AVARICIA
B		
BALLIVI	B1	BEATITUDO
BELLUM	B2	BELLUM
BENEDICTIO	B3	BENEFACERE
BONA	B4	BONITAS

C
CARTA
CARITAS
CARO
CELUM
CLAMANDI
CLERICI
COGITATIO
COMMUNIO
CONCORDIA
CONDITIO
CONFESSIO
CONFESSIONIS
   FREQUENTIA
   UTILITAS
   STABILITAS
-I INIUNGAT
   IMPEDIMENTUM
CONSTANTIA
CONCILIUM ANIME ET MUNDI
CONSULENDO
CONTRITIO
CONVERTI
COR
CORPUS
CORRECTIO
CREDUNT
CRUX
CUPIDITAS
CUSTODIA

C1	CARITAS
C2	CARO
C3	CASTITAS
C4	CIVITAS
C5	CONTRITIO
C6	CONFESSIO
C7	CONSCIENTIA
C8	CONSUETUDO
C9	CONCORDIA
C10	COGITATIO
C11	CONSILIUM
C12	COMPASSIO
C13	CONVERSATIO
C14	COR
C15	CHOREA
C16	CORRECTIO
C17	CRUX
C18	CUSTODIA

D
DAMNATUS
DAMNATIO
DAT DEUS bona
   nature bonis et malis
DEDICATIO
DECIMA
DILECTIO
DESPERATIO
DETRACTOR est
   malus iudex
DEUS
DIABOLUS
DILIGERE
DIMITTERE
DISCORDIA
DIVITES
DOCTRINA
DOMINI sunt stulti qui

D1	DAMNATIO
D2	DESPERATIO
D3	DECIME
D4	DEDICATIO
D5	DELECTATIO
D6	DETRACTIO
D7	DISCRETIO
D8	DISCORDIA
D9	DILECTIO
D10	DIMITTERE
D11	DIVICIE
D12	DOMINATIO

E

EBRIETAS	E1	EBRIETAS
ECCLESIA	E2	ELECTIO
ECCLESIASTICI	E3	ELEMOSINA
ELECTIO	E4	EQUITAS
ELEMOSYNA	E5	ERUBESCENTIA
EUKARISTIA	E6	EUCHARISTIA
EXECUTORES	E7	EXEMPLUM
EXEMPLA	E8	EXECUTOR
	E9	EXCOMMUNICATIO

F

FAMA	F1	FALSITAS
FIDELITAS	F2	FAMA
FIDES	F3	FERIE
FILIUS	F4	FIDES
FORTITUDO	F5	FILIATIO
FORTITUDO CORDIS	F6	FORTITUDO
FORTUNA	F7	FRATERNITAS
FURTUM	F8	FURTUM

G

GAUDIUM	G1	GAUDIUM
GLORIA	G2	GLORIA
GLORIA MUNDANA	G3	GRATIA
GRATIA	G4	GRATITUDO
GRATIARUM ACTIO	G5	GULA
GULA		

H

[H]ABUNDANTIA terrenorum	H1	HOMO
HABERE	H2	HOMICIDIUM
HEREDITAS	H3	HONESTAS
HOMO	H4	HONOR
HOSTES	H5	HOSPITALITAS
HONOR	H6	HUMILITAS
HUMILITAS		

I
IACTANTIA
IEIUNIUM
INCONSTANTIA
INFIRMUS
INFIRMITAS
INGRATITUDO
IMMUNDICIA
INOBEDIENS
INTENTIO MALA
INVIDIA mortificat
   bona opera
IUDEX
IUDICIUM
IUDICIUM HUMANUM
IURAMENTUM
IUSTICIA
INVENTUS EST DEO

I1   IEIUNIUM
I2   INCONSTANTIA
I3   INFIRMITAS
I4   INOBEDIENTIA
I5   INTENTIO
I6   INVIDIA
I7   YPOCRISIS
I8   IRA
I9   IUDICES
I10 IUDICIUM HUMANUM
I11 IUDICIUM DIVINUM
I12 IURAMENTUM
I13 IUSTICIA

L
LABOR
LIBER VITE
LINGUA
LOQUELA
LUXURIA

L1   LABOR
L2   LAUS
L3   LEX
L4   LIBER
L5   LOCUTIO
L6   LUDUS
L7   LUXURIA

M
MAGISTRATUS
MALEFACTORES
MANDATA
MARIA
MARTIRES
MATRIMONIUM
MERCATIO
MILICIA
MINISTRI MALI
MISERCORDIA
MALI MALEFACTORIS
   adiutor filius est diaboli
MORS
MULIERES
MUNDICIA
MUNDUS
MUNERA

M1   MALEDICTIO
M2   MANDATA
M3   MARIA
M4   MATRIMONIUM
M5   MENDACIUM
M6   MERCATIO
M7   MILITIA
M8   MINISTRATIO
M9   MISERICORDIA
M10 MISSA
M11 MORS
M12 MUNDICIA
M13 MUNDUS
M14 MUNUS

N
NATIVITAS
NOBILITAS
NOCENS

N1	NATIVITAS
N2	NEGLIGENTIA
N3	NOBILITAS
N4	NOCUMENTUM

O
OBEDIENTIA
OCIOSI
ODIUM
OPERA
ORATIO
ORDO
ORNATUS
ONUS

O1	OBEDIENTIA
O2	OCIUM
O3	ODIUM
O4	OPERATIO
O5	ORATIO
O6	ORDO CLERICALIS
O7	ORNATUS
O8	OSTENSIO

P
PATIENCIA
PASCHA
PASSIO
PARTICIPATIO
PAUPERTAS
PREDESTINATIO
PREDICATIO
PRELATI
PRESUMPTIO
PROFICERE
PROVIDENTIA
PROSPERITAS
PRUDENTIA
PULCRITUDO
PURGATOR
PURGATORIUM est locus
   satisfactionis

P1	PATIENTIA
P2	PASSIO CHRISTI
P3	PAUPERTAS
P4	PAX
P5	PECCATUM
P6	PECCATOR
P7	PENITENTIA
P8	PENA
P9	PERSEVERANTIA
P10	PIETAS
P11	PREDESTINATIO
P12	PREDICATIO
P13	PRELATIO
P14	PULCHRITUDO

Q
QUADRAGESIMA est tempus
   spiritualis laboris
QUERERE debemus
   celestia et non terrena
QUESTIO

Q1	QUERERE

R
RATIO
RAPINA
RESIDIVA
REDDERE
REDIMERE
RESURRECTIO CHRISTI
RESTITUTIO
REGES

R1   RAPINA
R2   RECIDIVUM
R3   REDDITIO
R4   REGIMEN
R5   RELIGIO
R6   RESTITUTIO
R7   RESURRECTIO

S
SACERDOS MALUS
SALVATIO
SANCTI
SAPIENTIA
SATISFACTIO
SCIENTIA
SENEX
SENSUS
SEQUI non debemus
    multitudinem ad malum
SERVITURI DEO faciunt
    que impediunt servitium
    domini terreni
SERVITUS hostibus anime
SIGNA
SIMONIACI
SOCIETAS
SORTILEGIUM
SPES facit vitam
    bonorum delectabilem
SPES SANCTA
SUPERBIA

S1   SACERDOTIUM
S2   SANCTITAS
S3   SAPIENTIA
S4   SCIENTIA
S5   SENECTUS
S6   SENSUS
S7   SEQUI
S8   SERVIRE
S9   SYMONIA
S10   SOCIETAS
S11   SORTILEGIUM
S12   SPES
S13   SPIRITUSSANCTUS
S14   SUPERBIA

T
TABERNA
TENTATIONES
TEMPORALIA
TIMOR
TESTAMENTUM
TIRANNUS
TRINITAS
TRIBULATIO

T1   TEMPTATIO
T2   TESTIMONIUM
T3   TIMOR
T4   TRINITAS
T5   TRIBULATIO

V
VENDERE
VENIRE
VERBA
VIA
VITIA
VIDERE
VINDICTA
VIRTUS
VISITATIO
VITA
VERITAS
VOCAT nos Christus
VOLUNTAS
USURA

V1   VERITAS
V2   VERBUM
V3   VIA
V4   VISUS
V5   VINDICTA
V6   VIRTUS
V7   VITA
V8   VISITATIO
V9   VOCATIO
V10   VOLUNTAS
V11   VOTUM
V12   USURA

X
Xpc [CHRISTUS]
CHRISTIANUS

X1   XPS [CHRISTUS]

If we are not persuaded that Bromyard followed an alphabetic order in composing the *Summa*, can we propose an alternative mode in which he set about his enormous undertaking?

Already to hand lay his *Opus trivium perutilium materiarum predicabilium, ordine alphabetico e divina, canonica civilique legibus contextum*. This large work was organized following the pattern under which compilations known as *Distinctiones* were written, a pattern which rendered access easy for readers, that by which our dictionaries and encyclopedias are arranged, namely the alphabetic: it began with AB INFANCIA. His *Exhortationes* was laid out on the same principle too.

I am suggesting that a great deal of detailed planning will have preceded the writing of the *Summa*[21]: and that not only will the headwords have been set down but also that the 1200 articuli into which the 189 capitula are divided will have been adumbrated. If this supposition is granted I can see no reason why he should not have written his articuli without any deference to the order of the letters of the alphabet.

[1] Binkley, Hereford p.264.

[2] Binkley, ODNB vol.7 p.830.

[3] Binkley, Hereford p.264: Peterhouse MSS 24, 25.

[4] ibid. p.259 n.11.

[5] ibid. p.258, 264.

[6] ibid. pp.258, 264.

[7] See chapter 8, Table 8.2.

[8] ibid. p.262.

[9] Orleton p.xviii: Saints pp.507-508.

[10] Orleton pp.139-140, 142-143. We should not underestimate the significance of this event for both the diocese of Hereford and the English church as a whole. Bromyard could not have failed to respond to the occasion since canonizations of English saints in the post-conquest centuries were exceedingly rare. In the century and a half after the canonization of Thomas Becket in 1173 only five Englishmen were sainted: Gilbert of Sempringham (d.1189, canonized 1202): Wulfstan of Worcester (d.1095 canonized 1203): Hugh of Lincoln (d.1200 canonized 1220): Edmund of Abingdon (d.1240 canonized 1246): and Thomas Cantilupe (d.1282 canonized 1320). (Saints[3] p.xxi).

[11] Incipit opus trivium perutilium materiarum predicabilium ordine alphabetico e divina canonica civilique legibus eleganter contextum..

[12] Goff J-258.

[13] Wenzel pp.137-138. His description is of the one surviving copy: Bodleian Library, MS Bodley 859, folios 60-225 verso, completed on 14 February 1410.

[14] Wenzel goes on to illustrate the use of the *Distinctiones* by Bromyard's earliest named reader, John Sheppey, bishop of Rochester (d.19 October 1360) who cited Dist.55, on Welsh thieves being led to the gallows: and Dist.97, which declares that anyone who helps a sinner to commit a sin or to conceal it shares himself in that sin. (Wenzel pp.28-29, 322-323: BRUO p.1683).

[15] Binkley, ODNB vol.7 p.830.

[16] Istorum ergo informatus exemplo compilationem a me prius collectam in isto libello ad meam et aliorum utilitatem emendavi et augmentavi ponendo certas materias sub determinatis literis secundum ordinem alphabeti. (Prologus)

[17] Binkley, ODNB vol.7 p.830.

[18] Goff J-260 [not after 1484].

[19] CUL MS Kk.iv.24.

[20] Occupying folios 1 recto to 114 verso (in modern foliation: the late medieval foliation goes wrong at 42, jumping to 45). The Tabula realis and Tabula vocabulorum take up leaves 115 recto to 120 verso.

[21] On this see chapter 20.

2

BIBLIA SACRA

TABLE 2.1 : CITATIONS OF THE OLD TESTAMENT: THE NEW TESTAMENT:
THE BIBLIA SACRA: AND THE GLOSSES

	CITATIONS
OT TOTAL	6,881
glossa ordinaria	30
glossa interlinearis	4
TOTAL	6,915
NT TOTAL	3,624
Glossa ordinaria	27
TOTAL	3,651
BIBLIA SACRA	10,505
glossa ordinaria	57
glossa interlinearis	4
TOTAL	10,566

OT citations make up 65.45% of all biblical citations.

NT citations make up 34.55% of all biblical citations.

Biblical citations make up 74.27% of all 14,225 citations.

The pre-eminence of the Bible over all other texts engaging Bromyard's study and thoughts is plain to see. Moreover, its authority is immeasurably greater than that of any earthly legislator. 'For if a bull of the pope has great authority and credibility, how much more have the supremely truthful words of God, which can in no way be false..'[1]

TABLE 2.2 : CITATIONS OF THE BIBLIA SACRA BY INDIVIDUAL BOOKS:
THEIR LENGTHS AND THEIR CITATIONS AS PERCENTAGES

		Citations	% of length of OT	% of Citations
GENESIS		266	4.19	3.84
EXODUS		168	3.29	2.43
LEVITICUS		82	2.63	1.18
NUMERUS		95	3.79	1.38
	glo. ord.	1		
DEUTERONOMIUM		183	3.33	2.64
IOSUE liber		37	2.05	0.53
IUDICUM liber		91	2.12	1.31
RUTH		3	0.28	0.04
I. REGUM [I SAMUEL]		139	2.77	2.01
II REGUM [II SAMUEL]		96	2.50	1.40
	glo. ord.	1		
III REGUM [I KINGS]		139	2.70	2.01
IV REGUM [II KINGS		105	2.63	1.52
I PARALIPOMENON [1 CHRON.]		16	2.56	0.23
II PARALIPOMENON [II CHRON.]		61	3.12	0.89
	glo. ord.	1		
I ESDRAE [EZRA]		12	0.90	0.17
II ESDRAE/NEHEMIAE liber		31	1.35	0.45
III ESDRAE [I ESDRAS]		1	1.25	0.01
TOBIAE liber		76	1.01	1.10
JUDITH liber		37	1.18	0.53
HESTER liber*		42	0.65	0.60
IOB		309	3.74	4.47
PSALMORUM liber		1,333	9.39	19.36
	glo. ord.	6		
PROVERBIORUM liber		561	3.00	8.11
ECCLESIASTES		159	0.62	2.30
CANTICUM CANTICORUM		69	0.60	1.01
	glo. ord.	1		
SAPIENTIAE liber		241	1.23	3.48
ECCLESIASTICUS		629	5.48	9.12
	glo. ord.	2		
ESAIAS		641	6.94	9.33
	glo. ord.	3		
	glo. inter.	1		
IEREMIAS		291	6.28	4.22
	glo. ord.	1		
THRENI		64	0.83	0.92
BARUCH		34	0.35	0.49

		Citations	% of length of OT	% of Citations
EZECHIEL		184	4.65	2.66
DANIEL[†]		109	1.90	1.60
	glo. ord.	2		
OSEAS		90	1.04	1.33
	glo. inter.	1		
	glo. ord.	1		
IOHEL		24	0.42	0.35
AMOS		44	0.83	0.67
	glo. ord.	2		
ABDIAS		6	0.14	0.10
	glo. inter.	1		
IONAS		14	0.16	0.20
MICHEAS		57	0.63	0.87
	glo. inter.	1		
	glo. ord.	2		
NAUM		23	0.24	0.33
ABACHUC		33	0.31	0.48
SOPHONIAS		20	0.27	0.29
AGGAEUS		6	0.10	0.09
ZACHARIAS		53	0.79	0.82
	glo. ord.	4		
MALACHIAS		39	0.22	0.61
	glo. ord.	3		
I MACHABAEORUM		88	2.84	1.27
II MACHABAEORUM		80	2.05	1.15
		Citations	% of length of NT	% of Citations
MATTHAEUS		605	12.85	16.76
	glo. ord.	7		
MARCUS		93	8.01	2.57
	glo. ord.	1		
LUCAS		507	13.74	14.00
	glo. ord.	4		
IOHANNES		416	10.43	11.42
	glo. ord.	1		
ACTUS APOSTOLORUM		130	13.74	3.59
	glo. ord	1		

		Citations	% of length of NT	% of Citations
AD ROMANOS		287	5.34	7.91
	glo. ord	2		
AD CORINTHIOS I		245	5.09	6.79
	glo. ord.	3		
AD CORINTHIOS II		114	3.56	3.12
AD GALATAS		105	1.78	2.90
	glo. ord.	1		
AD EPHESIOS		105	1.78	3.01
	glo. ord.	5		
AD PHILIPPENSES		73	1.27	2.00
AD COLOSSENSES		36	1.14	0.98
AD THESSALONICENSES I		42	1.14	1.15
AD THESSALONICENSES II		21	0.64	0.57
AD TIMOTHEUM I		73	1.27	2.00
AD TIMOTHEUM II		43	1.02	1.18
AD TITUM		16	0.57	0.44
AD PHILEMONEM		1	0.25	0.03
AD HEBRAEOS		138	3.94	3.78
EPISTULA IACOBI		148	1.33	4.08
	glo. ord.	1		
EPISTULA PETRI I		90	1.40	2.46
EPISTULA PETRI II		41	0.89	1.12
EPISTULA IOHANNIS I		65	1.34	1.78
EPISTULA IOHANNIS II		7	0.15	0.19
EPISTULA IOHANNIS III		2	0.13	0.05
EPISTULA IUDAE		9	0.38	0.25
APOCALYPSIS		203	6.61	5.59
	glo. ord.	1		
Apostolus [Paulus] unspecified		9		0.25

*   Chapters 1-10.3 are placed in Protestant Bibles between Nehemiah and Job: and the remnant, to chapter 16.24, is placed in the Apocrypha.

†   Including the sections which Protestant Bibles distinguish as i The Song of the Three ii Daniel and Susanna iii Daniel, Bel, and the Snake.

TABLE 2.3

BOOKS WITH FEWER THAN HALF OF THE CITATIONS THE CRITERION OF
LENGTH ALONE WOULD CLAIM

LEVITICUS	MARK
NUMBERS	ACTS
JOSHUA	Philemon
Ruth	John 3
1 CHRONICLES	
2 CHRONICLES	
1 ESDRAS [EZRA]	
2 ESDRAS [NEHEMIAH]	
3 ESDRAS [1 ESDRAS]*	
JUDITH	
1 MACCABEES	

> *This is the text beginning 'Et egit Iosias pascha in Hierosolymis' which
> the third Stuttgart edition of the Vulgate prints as the second text of the
> Ordo Librorum Appendicis under the title of 'Liber Ezrae Tertius'. In the
> NEB it is included in the Apocrypha as 'The First Book of Esdras.'

TABLE 2.4

BOOKS WITH MORE THAN DOUBLE THE NUMBER OF CITATIONS IN
PROPORTION TO THEIR LENGTH

PSALMS	LETTER OF JAMES
PROVERBS	
Ecclesiastes	
WISDOM	
Malachi	

(The shorter books are shown in lower case.)

The Bible is cited more than 10,500 times, making up some 74% of the total number, (over 14,000), of his citations. If we ask in what form he read it it seems safe to assume that it was in separately bound groups of related, and glossed, books. He cites the glossa ordinaria to 25 books and the glossa interlinearis to 3 books (Oseas and Micheas are cited in both glosses).

He cites the glosses to six of the twelve minor prophets: he may well have accessed these books in a separate volume: other groupings, such as the Pentateuch, I-IV Kings and the Pauline letters suggest themselves. Hereford Cathedral for example, held volumes of such groupings: their modern shelf marks are[2]

O.IV.4	Numeri, Deuteronomium Glo	(s.xii²)
O.IV.7	Ezcchicl ct Daniel Glo	(s.xii²)
O.V.8	Actus, Epistulae Canonicae, Apocalypsis Glo	(s.xii²)

While Lincoln Cathedral held a volume with the modern shelf mark[3]

MS 28 (B.1.5)	I-IV Regum, I-II Macc., I-II Paral., I Esdras Glo	(s.xii¹)

A good part of his exposure to the Bible will have been aural. The lectiones of the daily and weekly office were made up of excerpts from the Fathers but mainly from the biblical books. He will have heard these not only within the Dominican chapel at Hereford but also in the refectory during meals. The weekly recitation of the 150 psalms will have ensured that he knew them by heart: they form 12.62% of his total Bible citations and 9.37% of the complete citations.

The Dominicans were, supremely, a preaching order. The Bible was subjected to a rigorously painstaking scrutiny which mined it for texts to be exploited for their impact upon their audiences in their central task of salvation of souls. Surviving Bibles, especially from the 13th century, reveal how Dominican scholars prepared themselves for their preaching missions.

However meagre the resources of the Hereford Dominicans – firmly secure in their house only from 1322[4] – they will have possessed at least one Bible complete within two covers. So whether he worked from several discrete units of biblical books supplied with the standard gloss or whether he used a portable one-volume Bible as a working copy, he certainly had access to the prologues of S.Hieronymus. The standard set has 64[5] and Bromyard cites Hieronymus 17 times from his prologues and comments on the Bible books.

He makes no direct reference to the 'Interpretationes Nominum Hebraicorum' but he does often give etymologies and meanings. These vary in accuracy, as do those of Hieronymus: e.g. Arab = occidentalis vel insidie: (from 'Joshua'): Appolonius = miraculum vel mirabilis vel congregans eos (from the second book of Maccabees).

He numbers his psalms consistently. De Hamel observes 'The 150 Psalms in a thirteenth-century Bible were never numbered, and they would be cited instead from their opening words.'[6] Numeration, however, had its advantages. Saenger observes: 'While the tradition of psalm numbering in the waning centuries of the Middle Ages was weak, it had not perished.'[7] When, therefore, Bromyard's practice breaks down, at T.5.43, and he quotes psalms without their number, the inference may be drawn that the copy he worked from had to be ceded to a colleague or to other demands. From T.5.43, then, to the end of the *Summa* he cites 48 psalms by number, 61 without: for the twelve capitula of V and the one of X the disparity is greater: 38 numbered, 59 unnumbered: a striking departure from his usual meticulous habit in giving references. One of the unnumbered psalms he does cite by its opening words.

Writing on the standard Paris Bible of the 1230s and onwards De Hamel[8] comments on the benefits which the ease of reference brought by its apparatus of chapter numbers and headings. He observes: 'The Dominicans in the convent of St-Jacques in Paris under the supervision of Hugh St-Cher (d.1263) devised a vast verbal concordance of the Bible which was apparently in use by 1239. Each word is referred to a biblical book and chapter number.. The Dominicans had produced two further versions of their concordance by the 1280s.' Hinnebusch[9] dates this first Concordance to c.1230, and the expanded version, known as the 'Concordantiae Anglicanae', of John of Darlington, Richard of Stavensby and Hugh of Croydon to 1250-52.

It is worth noting that Hereford Cathedral[10] possessed a copy of the earliest version, the St-Jacques concordance of the 1230s. Its present shelfmark in the library is O.III.14: the Concordantiae Bibliorum de S.Iacobo, of the 13th century.

Bromyard undoubtedly profited from these heroic endeavours and was aware of his generation's debt to the labour of its predecessors:

'Modern clerics have no great occasion to boast of their learning..unless it's as a dwarf hoisted up on the shoulders of a giant.'[11]

In this image, which he will owe to John of Salisbury, he chooses to write 'habent' and 'sua' rather than 'habemus' and 'nostra'!

Bromyard cited the glossa ordinaria to the Bible 57 times and the glossa interlinearis 4 times. These 61 citations from 26 different books reveal the format of the biblical texts from which much of his reading was carried out. Teresa Webber[12] emphasizes the potency for scholarship developed by the masters of the sacred page of the twelfth century. 'It was the schools at Paris that popularized a new reference tool for the study of the Bible, the 'Glossa ordinaria', in which the biblical text was written in a narrow column, with commentary drawn largely from the inherited wisdom of the Fathers and the early medieval commentators, written in smaller script as glosses in the margins and between the lines.' Among these commentators are Hieronymus, Augustinus, Cassiodorus, Beda and Hrabanus Maurus. De Hamel names Anselm of Laon (d.1117) as the principal compiler of the gloss, with help from his younger brother Ralph (d.1133) and a collaborator from the schools in Auxerre, Gilbert the Universal (d.1134)[13]. In this ascription he follows Tritheim, who notes of Anselmus

'novo expositionis genere utriusque testamenti scripturas glosa interlineari et marginali ex patrum scriptis explanavit.'[14]

To this erudition Bromyard was heir.

The one-volume Bible, dated to the 1220s by Christie's, whose description is given in their catalogue for the King Street London sale of 8 June 2005, lot 21, furnishes evidence of the detailed examination to which biblical texts were subjected for the purpose of providing material for sermons governed by a single motif.

The book is written on vellum: its dimensions are 217 x 140mm. Leaves 2-317 verso are occupied by the vulgate text. Further texts follow, dated by Christie's to the second half of the thirteenth century: the last of which, on leaves 336 to 340, are texts for sermons grouped under seventy-six headings. The cataloguers suggest that these will have been added for a cleric who expected to be an active preacher, possibly a French Dominican. Under 76 headings there are over 1,600 references to biblical texts, from which I list a few examples.

1.   Contra linguam dissolutam

                              [42 references are given]

        Math.xii   De omni verbo ocioso
        Prov.xiii   qui custodite os suum
        Iudic.xii   Occupaverunt galadite

2.   Contra eos qui secreta revelant

                              [4 references]

        Ecci.xxvii   qui denudant archana

3.   De confessione peccatorum et fructu eius

                              [39 references]

        ps.   dixi confitebor
        ysa.xliii   narra si quid habes
        Act.xix   multique credentium
        Iudic.i.   ait iudas simoni
        Ysa.xxvi   in die illa cantabitur
        Iere.iii   convertimini filii israel

4.   De habenda memoria peccatorum

                              [30 references]

        Iob.x   iudica mihi cur me ita iudices

5.   Quod dominus ex gratia flagellat ex ira parcit

                              [7 references]

        Osee.iiii   Non fornicabuntur

6.   De discretione loquendi

                              [29 references]

        Ia.i   sit omnis homo
        Iob.iiii   de mane usque ad

7.   Quod prelatus debet habere scientiam in verbum in corde per intellectum

                              [24 references]

        Zach.xi   si pastor et ydolum

8.   De constantia et securitate et fortitudine predicatoris

                              [19 references]

        luc.ix   Dum complerentur dies

9.   Quod per fidelem predicationem augetur virtus et gratia predicandi

                              [8 references]

        ps.c.xviii   os meum aperui

10.   De efficacia verbi dei

                              [28 references]

        Iere.v   negaverunt deum et dixerunt

11.   Quales et qualiter instituendi sunt

                                [17 references]
            Gen.xli   pharao ad ioseph quia est
            Iere.iii   introducam vos

12.   Contra taciturnitatem prelatorum

                                [11 references]
            Ysa.lviii   Clama ne cesses
            Eze.xi   O pastor

13.   Contra acceptores munerum

                                [28 references]
            Gen.xiii   Levo manum meam
            Deut.x   Deus magnus potens et terribilis
            Act.xx   Argentum et aurum nullum

14.   Contra gulam

                                [? references]
            Gen.iii   vidit mulier quod bonum esset
            Exodi xvi   utinam mortui essemus
            Hester I   vasti regina

        The few words keying the reader into the text do not always correspond exactly with that text: e.g. the 'Iustum deduxit' of Sap.x is a composite from 'et reddidit *iustis* mercedem laborum suorum et *deduxit* illos in via mirabili.'

        In addition to the texts suggested for addressing specific themes the compiler also provided texts for sermons of the Temporale, e.g.

15.   Dominica prima in adventum domini
            Ep. ad Rom.xiii   Scientes quia hora est

16.   In vigilia Iohannis baptiste
            Iere.i   Priusquam te formarem

        Credence is lent to the cataloguers' view that these five leaves were written for a Dominican by the bearing of the 2nd, 3rd, 4th, 8th and 9th of these headings: while one would perhaps not expect the 7th and 12th headings to have been chosen for a secular cleric. Bromyard holds forth on many of the 76 themes: of this 16-strong selection on numbers 1, 3, 4, 5, 6, 7, 10, 12, 13 and 14.
        We cannot know whether Bromyard's task was rendered easier by access to such a powerful tool as this index with its 1600-odd references which functioned as a basis on which a sermon could be constructed.

A second example – though not from the Bible – of meticulous preparation of texts for preaching purposes by Dominicans is preserved in a mid-thirteenth century Florilegium.[15] The cataloguers note:

'Perhaps written in the Dominican convent in Oxford.. This is a quarry book for a preacher, probably a Dominican, with sample sermons and wide-ranging extracts from texts which might be useful in preaching, especially on natural history. It is massively referenced with the sections, pages, columns and even line numbers noted.'

A remarkable series of interlocking brackets (giving the appearance of a flow chart) diagrammatically leading in each case from a single headword to double, triple, even septuple development continued through four or five stages illustrates the care and minute attention to detail which was lavished on this book.

Bromyard's *Tabula vocalis* to his *Summa* referenced the occurrences in his text, mostly in *exempla*, of members of the animal kingdom. Here too in this Sotheby's florilegium appear in Latin alphabetical order the eagle, goose, bee, silkworm, cicada, gnat, swan, owl, dove, ant, crow, the fabulous caladrius, falcon, hen, ibis, peacock, partridge, sparrow, pelican, ostrich, hoopoe, vulture et al: creatures, for the most part familiar to a rural society, from which to point a moral and adorn a tale.

[1] Si enim bulla pape magne sit autoritatis et credibilitatis: quanto magis verba dei verissima: que nullo modo falsa esse possunt..que dicit Ioh.xiiii. Ego sum via veritas (V.2.1). The supremacy of the text of the Bible over any ruling by any pope is thus asserted by Bromyard.

[2] Hereford pp.26-27: 27-28: 34-35.

[3] Lincoln pp.20-21.

[4] Binkley, Hereford p.260.

[5] Ker vol. 1 p.96.

[6] De Hamel, The Book p.128.

[7] Saenger p.41.

[8] De Hamel, The Book p.133.

[9] EEFP pp.298-299.

[10] Hereford pp.24, 25.

[11] Moderni clerici non habent de scientia sua magnam superbiendi occasionem quia non sunt in his que de scripturis vident nisi sicut gnanus exaltatus super scapulas gigantis..(S.4.8)

[12] Cambridge Illuminations p.78.

[13] De Hamel p.108.

[14] Tritheim 362.

[15] Lot 50 in Sotheby's sale catalogue of 5 July 2005 in London.

3

BROMYARD'S AUTHORITIES

TABLE 3.1 : NON-BIBLICAL AUTHORITIES CITED BY BROMYARD IN THE *SUMMA* : TOGETHER WITH THE NUMBER OF CITATIONS OF EACH OF THEIR WORKS

A

1. ACCURSIUS (1185-1263)
    Glossa in Digestum Vetus 1

2. AESOPUS (s.vi BC)
    Fabulae 10

3. ALANUS DE INSULIS (c.1128-1203)
    De planctu naturae 1

4. ALBERTUS MAGNUS (1193-1280)
    Comm. In Aristotelis Meteora (Super libros meteororum) 1
    Super Lucam 2
    Super quartum sententiarum 1
    unspec. 1

5. ALBUMASAR (ABU MA'SHAR JA'FAR) (d.886)
    De magnis coniunctionibus 1

6. ALEXANDER CANTUARIENSIS (fl.1120)
    De similitudinibus 1

7. ALEXANDER NEQUAM (1157-1217)
    De naturis rerum 3
    unspec. 1

8. ALFARABIUS (MUHAMMAD ABU NASR AL-FARABI) (c.873-950)
    De diffinitione philosophiae 1

9. ALPHONSUS X SAPIENS (1221-1284) (REX CASTELLAE ET
    LEGIONIS 1252-1284)
    Liber 5

10. 'AMBROSIASTER' (fl.370)
    Comm. in Epistulas Pauli 4

11. AMBROSIUS AUTPERTUS (d.781)
    De conflictu vitiorum et virtutum 2

12. AMBROSIUS MEDIOLANENSIS (c.339-397)
    Comm. in Lucam 2
    Comm. in Matthaeum 1
    Comm. in Psalmos 1
    De bono mortis 1
    De Helia 1
    De officiis 16

12. AMBROSIUS MEDIOLANENSIS (c.339-397) (cont.)
De quadragesima   1
Hexaemeron   3
Homilia   2
unspec.   8

13. ANASTASIUS BIBLIOTHECARIUS (d.886)
(as translator) $\longrightarrow$ LEONTIUS NEAPOLITANUS

14. ANAXAGORAS (c.500-c.428 BC)
unspec.   1

15. ANNIANUS (s. v. in.)
(as translator) $\longrightarrow$ IOHANNES CHRYSOSTOMUS

16. ANSELMUS CANTUARIENSIS (c.1033-1109)
De casu diaboli   2
De incarnatione verbi   2
in quadam epistula   1
unspec.   8

17. ARISTOTELES (384-322 BC)
Categoriae (Praedicamenta) (tr. Boethius)   2
De anima   1
De caelo et mundo   1
Ethica (tr. Robertus Grosseteste)   40
Libri de animalibus (tr. Michael Scot)   5
Metaphysica   4
Meteora   1
Physica   4
Politica   3
Regula   1
unspec.   23
[pseud.]
De vegetabilibus (tr. Alfredus de Shareshill fl. 1200)   1
Secretum secretorum (tr. Iohannes Hispalensis)   3

18. ATHANASIUS (c.296-373)
Symbolum   1

19. AUGUSTINUS HIPPONENSIS (354-430)
Ad sacras virgines   2
Ad Bonifacium de correctione   1
Confessiones   11
De benedictionibus Esau et Iacob   1
De cathezizandis rudibus   1
De civitate dei   93
De communi sermone clericorum   2
De doctrina christiana   15

19. AUGUSTINUS HIPPONENSIS (354-430) (cont.)

De Genesi ad litteram	2
De Genesi contra Manichaeos	3
De gratia et libero arbitrio	4
De incarnatione contra Iudaeos	1
De quantitate animae	1
De regula religiosorum	2
De sancta viduitate	1
De sancta virginitate	1
De sermone Domini in monte	5
De trinitate	8
De vera religione	1
De vita et moribus clericorum suorum	17
Enarrationes in Psalmos	14
Enchiridion	2
Epistula ad Hieronymum	1
Epistula ad Macedonium	1
Epistula ad Marcellinum	1
Epistula ad Vincentium	2
Epistulae (unspec.)	4
Sermo ad religiosos	1
Sermo de decem chordis	2
Sermo de decimis	1
Sermo de decollatione Iohannis baptistae	1
Sermo de pastoribus	1
Sermo de puero centurionis	2
Sermo de sancto Laurentio	1
Sermones de verbis Domini	17
Sermones (unspec.)	15
Soliloquia	1
Super epistulam ad Galatas	3
Super Iohannem	8
Super Matthaeum	3
unspec.	51

[pseud.]

De visitatione infirmorum	1
Speculum clericorum	6

20. AULUS GELLIUS (c.130-c.180)

Noctes atticae	1

21. AVERROES (IBN RUSHD) (1126-1198)   1

22. AVICENNA (ABU 'ALI AL-HUSAIN IBN 'ABDALLAH IBN SINA) (980-1037)

De venenis (from 'Canon medicinae' (?), tr. Gerardus Cremonensis)	1
Philosphia sua	3
unspec.	1

B

1. BARTHOLOMAEUS BRIXIENSIS (d.1258)
   Glossa ordinaria in Decretum Gratiani   44

2. BASILIUS MAGNUS (c.330-379)
   Hexaemeron (tr. Eustathius)   1
   Homiliae (tr. Rufinus)   1

3. BEDA VENERABILIS (c.673-735)
   Comm. in Epistulas canonicas   2
   Comm. in Proverbia   1
   De luxuria super Matthaeum   1
   Historia ecclesiastica gentis Anglorum   9
   unspec.   2

4. BENEDICTUS CASINENSIS (d. post 547)
   Regula   1

5. BERNARDUS CLARAEVALLENSIS (1090-1153)
   Ad milites Templi   1
   Apologia   7
   De consideratione   22
   De hypocritarum pena   1
   De libero arbitrio   1
   De praecepto et dispensatione   2
   Epistula ad Cluniacenses   1
   Epistula ad dominum abbatem   1
   Epistula ad ducem Aquitaniae   2
   Epistula ad episcopum Senosensem   2
   Epistulae   3
   Expositio regula S.Benedicti   1
   In glossa   1
   Sermo de divinis   1
   Sermo de labore messis   1
   Sermo de trinitate   1
   Sermo de via vitae   2
   Sermo 35   1
   Sermo 38   1
   Sermo 89   1
   Sermones   14
   Sermones de angelis   4
   Sermones quadragesimae   2
   Super Cantica canticorum   14
   Super Marcum   1
   Super Matthaeum   1
   Super Missus est   1

5. BERNARDUS CLARAEVALLENSIS (1090-1153) (cont.)
      Super Psalmos   1
      unspec.   59

      [pseud.]
        Meditationes   2

6. BERNARDUS PARMENSIS (d.1266)
      Glossa ordinaria in Decretales   25

7. BOETHIUS, ANICIUS MANLIUS SEVERINUS (c.480-524)
      De consolatione philosophiae   10
      De institutione musica   1
      unspec.   1

      [pseud.]
      De disciplina scholarium   5

      [app.]
      Commentator super Boethium, De disciplina scholarium   1

8. BONIFACIUS VIII (1235-1303 : sedit 1294-1303)
      Constitutio   2
      Liber Sextus   39

9. BREVE REGIS 'TARDE VENIT'   2

C
1. CAESARIUS ARELATENSIS (c.470-542)
      Sermo de resurrectione (Ammonitio)   2
      unspec.   6

2. CASSIODORUS SENATOR (c.485-580)
      Epistulae   2
      Expositio Psalmorum   9
      Historia ecclesiastica tripartita   15
      unspec.   3

3. CATO Ps. (s.iii/iv)
      Disticha Catonis   3

4. CHARTA (MAGNA CARTA)
      1

5. CICERO, M. TULLIUS (106-43 BC)
      De amicitia   4
      De legibus   1
      De officiis   9
      De senectute   1
      Epistulae   1

5.   CICERO, M. TULLIUS (106-43 BC) (cont.)
        Paradoxa stoicorum   4
        Tusculanae quaestiones   5
        unspec.   5

6.   CLAUDIANUS, CLAUDIUS (d. post 404)
        unspec.   2

7.   CLEMENS V PAPA (1264-1314 : sedit 1305-1314)
        Constitutiones Clementinae   21

8.   CORNIFICIUS RHETOR (s.i. BC)
        Rhetorica   2

9.   Q. CURTIUS RUFUS (s.i.) ? or
    Ps. CALLISTHENES (s.iii) ?
        Historia Alexandri (Gesta Alexandri magni)   3

10.   CYPRIANUS CARTHAGINENSIS (c.200-258)
        De disciplina et habitu virginum   1
        Epistula contra haereticos   1
        Sermo de virginitate   1
        unspec.   3

    [pseud.]
        De XII abusivis saeculi   6
        De singularitate clericorum   2

D
1.   DIOGENES PHILOSOPHUS (fl.440 BC)   1

2.   DIONYSIUS AREOPAGITA Ps. (fl. c.500 ?)
        Assignatio   1
        De caelesti hierarchia   3

3.   DONATUS GRAMMATICUS, AELIUS (s.iv)
        unspec.   1

E
1.   'EUSEBIUS GALLICANUS'
        Homiliae X ad monachos   4

2.   EUSEBIUS VERCELLENSIS (d.371)
        De trinitate   1

3.   EUSTATHIUS (d. c.1194)
        (as translator) ⟶   BASILIUS MAGNUS

F

1.   FRONTINUS, SEXTUS IULIUS (c.30-104)
        Strategemata (De scientia rei militaris)   7

2.   FULGENTIUS MYTHOGRAPHUS (fl.500)
        Mitologiae   1

3.   FULGENTIUS RUSPENSIS (d. c.532)
        Super Matthaeum   1

G

1.   GENNADIUS MASSILIENSIS (fl.470/480)
        Diffinitio rectae fidei   1

2.   GERARDUS CREMONENSIS (1114-1187)
        (as translator) ⟶   AVICENNA
                  ⟶   ISAAC
                  ⟶   PTOLEMAEUS

3.   GIRALDUS CAMBRENSIS (1146-1226)
        Itinerarium Kambriae   6

4.   GRATIANUS (d. ante 1160)
        Decretum   558

5.   GREGORIUS I PAPA (c.540-604: sedit 590-604)
        De animarum (   )   1
        De cura pastorali   33
        Dialogi   84
        Homilia de angelis   2
        Homilia de discipulis   1
        Homilia de Maria   3
        Homilia 'Ductus est Iesus in desertum'   1
        Homilia 'Duo ex discipulis Iesu ibant   1
        Homilia 'Multi sunt vocati'   1
        Homilia Pentecostes   1
        Homiliae (unspec.)   26
        Homiliae de Spiritu Sancto   3
        Homiliae in Ezechielem   18
        Homiliae in Matthaeum   1
        Homiliae XL in evangelia   10
        Moralia in Iob   97
        Registrum   7
        Super Proverbia   1
        unspec.   97

    [dub.]
        Expositiones super Psalterium   1

6.	GREGORIUS IX PAPA (c.1148-1241: sedit 1227-1241)	
	Decretales	153
7.	GREGORIUS X PAPA (1210-1276: sedit 1271-1276)	
	Statuta in Concilio Lugdunensi	3
8.	GREGORIUS NAZIANZENUS (329-389)	
	Apologeticus (tr. Rufinus)	1
	unspec.	2
9.	GUIDO DE BAYSIO (d.1313)	
	Apparatus ad Sextum	1

H

1.	H. SALTERIENSIS (s.xii ex.)	
	De purgatorio S. Patricii	1
2.	HAIMO ALTISSIODORENSIS (fl.840-865)	
	Comm. in Epistulas Pauli	2
3.	HELINANDUS DE FRIGIDO MONTE (d. post 1229)	
	Chronica	2
	unspec.	1
4.	HENRICUS DE SEGUSIO (HOSTIENSIS) (c.1200-1270)	
	Summa super titulis Decretalium	7
	Super Codicem	2
	unspec.	10
5.	HIERONYMUS (c.342-420)	
	Contra Pelagianos	1
	Contra Vigilantium	1
	Epistula ad Aletham	1
	Epistula ad Augustinum	1
	Epistula ad Damasum papam	1
	Epistula ad Furiam	1
	Epistula ad Heliodorum	3
	Epistula ad Marcellam	1
	Epistula ad Monachos	1
	Epistula ad Nepotianum	2
	Epistula ad Pammachium	1
	Epistula ad Paulinum	1
	Epistula ad Rusticum de penitentia	3
	Epistula ad Theodorum	1
	Epistula ad Tirasium	3
	Epistula contra Helvidium	1
	Epistula contra Iovinianum	4
	Epistula de viduitate servanda ad Eustochium	2

5.   HIERONYMUS (c.342-420) cont.

Epistulae	21
Prologus totius sacrae scripturae	2
Prologus in Abdiam prophetam	1
Prologus ad Naum	1
Super Epistulam ad Ephesios	1
Super Ezechielem	1
Super Isaiam	2
Super librum Actuum	1
Super Matthaeum	5
Super Osee	4
Super Psalmos	2
unspec.	31

(as translator)   ⟶   BIBLIA SACRA

6.   Q. HORATIUS FLACCUS (65-8 BC)

Ars Poetica	2
Carmina	1
Epistulae	4

7.   HRABANUS MAURUS (d.856)

Comm. in Matthaeum	3

8.   HUGO DE FOLIETO (d.1172/3)

De claustro animae	4

9.   HUGO DE S.VICTORE (c.1096-1141)

De anima	3
De sacramentis [christianae fidei?]	1
De vanitate mundi	2
Didascalicon de studio legendi	2
Epistula ad quendam nobilem nubere volentem	1
Soliloquium de arra animae	2
Super librum Psalmorum	1
unspec.	7

10.   HUGUTIO PISANUS (d.1210)

unspec.	1

11.   HUMBERTUS DE ROMANIS (d.1277)

Liber de dono timoris (Tractatus de abundantia exemplorum)	3

I

1.	IACOBUS DE VITRIACO (c.1170-1240)	
	unspec.	4

2.	IACOBUS DE VORAGINE (c.1230-1298)	
	Legenda Sanctorum	16

3.	INNOCENTIUS III PAPA (1160-1216: sedit 1198-1216)	
	De vilitate conditionis humanae	6

4.	INNOCENTIUS IV PAPA (sedit 1243-1254)	
	Apparatus in quinque libros Decretalium	7
	Super Liber Sextum	5

5.	IOHANNES ANDREAE (c.1270-1348)	
	Apparatus ad Clementinas (glossa ordinaria)	7
	Apparatus ad Sextum (glossa ordinaria)	2
	Gradus consanguinitatis vel affinitatis	2

6.	IOHANNES DE BROMYARD (d.1352?)	
	Collationes	4
	Sermones	69

7.	IOHANNES CASSIANUS (c.360-435)	
	Collationes patrum	11

8.	IOHANNES CHRYSOSTOMUS (c.347-407)	
	De compunctione cordis (tr. ?Annianus)	1
	De dignitate sacerdotali	1
	De eo quod nullus laeditur nisi a semet ipso	1
	De reparatione lapsi	1
	De symbolo	3
	Epistula (unspec.)	1
	Homilia de fatuis virginibus	1
	Homiliae	6
	In dialogo suo	1
	Super Epistulam ad Hebraeos (tr. Mutianus)	3
	Super Epistulam ad Timotheum	2
	Super Epistulam ad Titum	1
	Super Iohannem	33
	Super Lucam	1
	Super Matthaeum	53
	Super Videns arborem fici	2
	unspec.	22

[pseud.]
    Opus imperfectum in Matthaeum   4

9. IOHANNES DAMASCENUS (c.675-749)
    unspec. 3

    [pseud.]
        Liber Barlaam et Iosaphat 9

10. IOHANNES FRIBURGENSIS (d.1314)
    Summa confessorum 22

11. IOHANNES HISPALENSIS (fl.1140-1150)
    (as translator) ———> Ps. ARISTOTELES, Secretum secretorum

12. IOHANNES MONACHUS (d.1313)
    Glossa super bullam Benedicti 1
    Super Constitutionem 1

13. IOHANNES SARISBURIENSIS (c.1115-1180)
    Policraticus 11

14. [IOSEPHUS FLAVIUS (d. post 100)]

15. ISAAC IUDAEUS (ISHAQ IBN SULEIMAN) (s.ix)
    De diffinitionibus (tr. from Arabic into Latin by 1
    Gerardus Cremonenis)

16. ISIDORUS HISPALENSIS (d.636)
    Ethica 1
    Etymologiae 3
    Epistulae 1
    In libros veteris et novi testamenti prooemia 1
    Sententiae (De summo bono) 4
    Synonyma (Soliloquia) 1
    unspec. 8

17. IULIANUS POMERIUS (s.vi in.)
    De vita contemplativa 2

18. IULIUS VALERIUS ALEXANDER POLEMIUS (s.iii-iv)
    Historia Alexandri magni 1

19. IUSTINIANUS (483-565: imperator 527-565)
    Codex 130 + 13
    Digestum Vetus 81 + 7
        Infortiatum 32
        Novum 81 + 7
    Institutiones 7 + 1
    Novellae Constitutiones (Authenticum) 22

20.   IUSTINUS, M.IUNIANUS (s.iii)
        Epitome (of Pompeius Trogus' lost Historiae Philippicae)   4

21.   IUVENALIS, D. IUNIUS (c.60-c.130)
        Saturae   6

L
1.   LEGENDA COMMUNIS (LECTIONARIUS ?)
                                                                          1

2.   LEO I PAPA (sedit 440-461)
        Apologia   1
        Sermo [in Breviarium, first Sunday in Lent]   1
        unspec.   1

3.   LEONTIUS NEAPOLITANUS (fl.650)
        Vita S.Iohannis Eleemosynarii (tr. Anastasius Bibliothecarius)   4

M
1.   MACROBIUS, AMBROSIUS THEODOSIUS (fl.400)
        Saturnalia   1

2.   MARTINUS BRACARENSIS (d.580)
        Formula vitae honestae (De quattuor virtutibus cardinalibus)   1

3.   MELCHEBRON
        Liber   1

4.   MICHAEL SCOT (d.1234)
        (as translator) ⟶ ARISTOTELES

5.   MUHAMMAD (c.570-c.632)
        Alcoranum (al-Quran) (tr. Robertus de Ketton)   5

6.   MUTIANUS (s.vi)
        (as translator) ⟶ IOHANNES CHRYSOSTOMUS

O
1.   ODO DE SOLIACO (episcopus Parisiensis) (d.1208)
        Sermones   1
        Tractatus de quadam muliere   1

2.   ORIGENES (c.185-254)
        Homiliae in Exodum (tr. Rufinus)   1
        Homiliae in Leviticum (tr. Rufinus)   1
        unspec.   6

3.   OROSIUS, PAULUS (d. post 418)
          unspec.   1

4.   OTTOBONUS FIESCHI (later HADRIANUS V PAPA: d.1276)
          Constitutiones   1

5.   P. OVIDIUS NASO (43 BC – AD 17/18)
          unspec.   3

P

1.   PAPIAS GRAMMATICUS (fl.1050)
          unspec.   1

2.   PASSIONARIUM (Liber Passionarius)

                                            1

3.   PAULINUS AQUILEIENSIS (c.750-802)
          Liber exhortationis   3

4.   PELAGIUS (c.350-post 423)
          Epistula ad Demetriadem   2
          Liber de vita christiana   2

5.   C. (or T.) PETRONIUS ARBITER (d.66)
          Satyricon   1

6.   PETRUS BLESENSIS, BATHONIENSIS ARCHIDIAC. (c.1135-1212)
          Epistulae   3

7.   PETRUS CHRYSOLOGUS (RAVENNAS) (s.v.)
          in quadam epistula   5
          Sermo super Matthaeum   1
          unspec.   6

8.   PETRUS COMESTOR (d.1179)
          Historia scholastica   42

9.   PETRUS DAMIANI (1007-1072)
          Historia Petri Damiani   1
          unspec.   2

10.   PETRUS TARENTASIENSIS (later INNOCENTIUS V PAPA (d.1276))
          Comm. in Petri Lombardi Sententias   4

11.   C. PLINIUS CAECILIUS SECUNDUS (c.61-114)
          Epistula ad Ursum   1

12. C. PLINIUS SECUNDUS (23-79)
    Historia naturalis   4

13. POSSIDIUS (s.v.)
    Vita S.Augustini   2

14. PROSPER AQUITANUS (c.390-c.463)
    De vitiis et virtutibus   1

15. PTOLEMAEUS, CLAUDIUS (fl.127-148)
    Prologus Almagesti (tr. Gerardus Cremonensis)   3

16. PUBLILIUS SYRUS (s.i. BC)
    Sententiae (Proverbia)   4

Q
1. QUINTILIANUS, M. FABIUS (d. c.100)
    Institutio oratoria   1

2. QUODVULTDEUS CARTHAGINENSIS EP. (sedit 437-453)
    Sermo adversus quinque haereses   2

R
1. REMIGIUS ALTISSIODORENSIS (841-908)
    unspec.   1

2. RICHARDUS [DE S. VICTORE ?] (d.1173)
    unspec.   1

3. ROBERTUS DE KETTON (d.post 1150)
    (as translator) ⟶ MUHAMMAD

4. ROBERTUS GROSSETESTE (c.1175-1253)
    Epistula ad Innocentium IV   1
    Sermo papae et cardinalibus traditus   2
    Super Dionysiii De caelesti hierarchia   2

    (as translator) ⟶ ARISTOTELES, Ethica

5.   RUFINUS, TYRANNIUS (c.345-410)

(as translator) $\longrightarrow$ BASILIUS

$\longrightarrow$ GREGORIUS NAZIANZENUS

$\longrightarrow$ PS. HIERONYMUS

$\longrightarrow$ ORIGENES

$\longrightarrow$ PTOLEMAEUS

$\longrightarrow$ VITAS PATRUM

S

1.   C. SALLUSTIUS CRISPUS (86-c.34 BC)
      Catilina   2

2.   SAPIENS QUIDAM
      Liber de sacerdote   1

3.   SECUNDUS PHILOSOPHUS Ps.
      Vita et sententiae (tr. Willelmus medicus)   1

4.   SENECA, L. ANNAEUS (4 BC – AD 65)
            De avaritia   1
            De beata vita   1
            De beneficiis   13
            De clementia   5
            De constantia sapientis   3
            De contemptu mortis   1
            De ira   5
            De moribus   4
            De providentia   2
            De senectute   1
            De tranquillitate animi   2
            Epistulae (unspec.)   5
            Epistulae morales   73
            Libellus ad Marciam   1
            Naturales Quaestiones   4
            Otium sine litteris   1
            Tragoediae   1
            unspec.   31

      [pseud.]
            De musica   1
            De remediis fortuitorum   3
            Epistulae ad Paulum   4

5. SENECA, L. ANNAEUS RHETOR (c.55 BC – AD c.40)
 Declamationes 8

6. SEPTUAGINTA INTERPRETES (s.iii BC)

 1

7. SIDONIUS, APOLLINARIS (d.488)
 Epistulare 1

8. SOCRATES (469-399 BC)
 Sententiae 2

9. SOLINUS, C. IULIUS (fl.260)
 Collectanea rerum mirabilium (De mirabilibus mundi) 4

10. SUETONIUS, C. TRANQUILLUS (c.69-c.140)
 De XII Caesaribus 2

T
1. TALMUD (s.iv – vi)

 1

2. P. TERENTIUS AFER (d.159 BC)
 Andria 1

3. THOMAS AQUINAS (c.1225-1274)
 Epistula ad ducissam Lotharingiae 2
 Quaestiones quodlibetales 2
 Scriptum super secundum Sententiarum 2
 Scriptum super quartum Sententiarum 5
 Summa contra gentiles 1
 Summa theologica
  Prima pars 6
  Prima secundae 10
  Secunda secundae 36
  Tertia pars 6
 unspec. 2

4. THOMAS CANTIPRATENSIS (1201-c.1270)
 Bonum universale de proprietatibus apum (Liber de apibus) 18

U

1. URBANUS II PAPA (sedit 1088-1099)
   Rescriptum   1

V

1. VALERIUS MAXIMUS (fl. c.31)
   Facta et dicta memorabilia   46

2. F. VEGETIUS RENATUS (s.iv ex.)
   De re militari   7

3. P. VERGILIUS MARO (70-19 BC)
   Aeneis   3

4. VICTORINUS, C. MARIUS (c.275-post 363)
       1

5. VINCENTIUS BELLOVACENSIS (1189/94-c.1264)
   De eruditione regalium filiorum   6
   Speculum historiale   8
   Speculum naturale   2

6. VITAE SANCTORUM
   (the saints whose Lives are cited are:-)
   Ambrosius Mediolanensis   2
   Bartholomaeus   2
   Basilius   1
   Beatrix virgo   1
   Bernardus   3
   Dominicus O.P.   2
   Eadmundus rex Angliae   1
   Edmundus archiepiscopus   3
   Edwardus rex Angliae   1
   Furseus   1
   Gangolphus   1
   Germanus Altissiodorensis   3
   Gregorius   11
   Hieronymus   2
   Iohannes Eleemosynarius   4
   Iohannes evangelista   1
   Leo I papa   1
   Lodovicus rex Franciae   5
   Lucia   1
   Lupus Trecensis   1
   Marcus evangelista   1
   Martha   1
   Maria Magdalena   1

6.　　VITAE SANCTORUM (cont.)
　　　(the saints whose Lives are cited are:-)
　　　　　Martinus　　　　　　　　　　　　　　　　　4
　　　　　Matre dei, Historia apocrypha de　　　　　　3
　　　　　Nicolaus　　　　　　　　　　　　　　　　　1
　　　　　Sanctorum, in aliquibus gestis　　　　　　　1
　　　　　Sebastianus　　　　　　　　　　　　　　　1
　　　　　Silvester　　　　　　　　　　　　　　　　3
　　　　　Stephanus　　　　　　　　　　　　　　　　1
　　　　　Thomas apostolus　　　　　　　　　　　　1
　　　　　Thomas Cantuarensis　　　　　　　　　　1

7.　　VITAE
　　　　　Alexander III papa　　　　　　　　　　　1
　　　　　Fratres mendicantes　　　　　　　　　　　2
　　　　　Hugo de S.Victore　　　　　　　　　　　2
　　　　　Karolus magnus　　　　　　　　　　　　4

8.　　VITAS PATRUM
　　　　　　　　　　　　　　　　　　　　　　　112

W

1.　　WALTERUS MAP (c.1140-1210)
　　　　　Epistula Valerii ad Rufinum ne ducat uxorem　　　1

2.　　WILLELMUS DE MONTE LAUDUNO (d.1343)
　　　　　Glossa in Decretales　　　　　　　　　　1
　　　　　Glossa in Librum Sextum　　　　　　　　2
　　　　　Lectura super Clementinas　　　　　　　2

3.　　WILLELMUS MEDICUS
　　　　(as translator) ⟶ Ps. SECUNDUS

TABLE 3.2 : NON-BIBLICAL AUTHORITIES CITED MORE THAN 20 TIMES

A1	ACCURSIUS*	29
A12	AMBROSIUS	36
A17	ARISTOTELES	85
A19	AUGUSTINUS	304
B1	BARTHOLOMAEUS BRIXIENSIS	44
B5	BERNARDUS CLARAEVALLENSIS	150
B6	BERNARDUS PARMENSIS	25
B8	BONIFACIUS VIII	41
C2	CASSIODORUS	29
C5	CICERO	30
C7	CLEMENS V	21
G4	GRATIANUS	558
G5	GREGORIUS I	388
G6	GREGORIUS IX	153
H5	HIERONYMUS	101
I6	IOHANNES DE BROMYARD	73
I8	IOHANNES CHRYSOSTOMUS	133
I10	IOHANNES FRIBURGENSIS	22
I19	IUSTINIANUS	353
P7	PETRUS COMESTOR	42

S4	SENECA	154
T3	THOMAS AQUINAS	73
V1	VALERIUS MAXIMUS	46
V6	VITAE SANCTORUM	66
V8	VITAS PATRUM	112

*Accursius is named only once: but his gloss to the Corpus Iuris Civilis is cited a further 28 times

TABLE 3.3 : INDIVIDUAL NON-BIBLICAL WORKS CITED MORE THAN 20 TIMES

A17	ARISTOTELES Ethica	40
A19	AUGUSTINUS De civitate dei	93
B1	BARTHOLOMAEUS Glossa ordinaria In Decretum	44
B5	BERNARDUS CLARAEVALLENSIS De consideratione	22
B6	BERNARDUS PARMENSIS Glossa ordinaria in Decretales	25
B8	BONIFACIUS VIII Liber Sextus	39
C7	CLEMENS V Constitutiones Clementinae	21
G4	GRATIANUS Decretum	558

G5	GREGORIUS I	
	De cura pastorali	33
	Dialogi	84
	Homiliae	68
	Moralia in Iob	97
G6	GREGORIUS IX	
	Decretales	153
H5	HIERONYMUS	
	Epistulae	21
I6	IOHANNES DE BROMYARD	
	Sermones	69
I8	IOHANNES CHRYSOSTOMUS	
	Super Iohannem	33
	Super Matthaeum	53
I10	IOHANNES FRIBURGENSIS	
	Summa confessorum	22
I19	IUSTINIANUS	
	Codex	130
	Digesta	194
	Novellae Constitutiones	22
P8	PETRUS COMESTOR	
	Historia scholastica	42
S4	SENECA	
	Epistulae morales	73
T3	THOMAS AQUINAS	
	Summa theologica	58
V1	VALERIUS MAXIMUS	
	Facta ac dicta memorabilia	46
V8	various authors	
	Vitas patrum	112

Twenty authors produce 26 works cited more than twenty times. When we subtract the works of canon and civil law we are left with thirteen authors of 17 works, the writings, apart from the Bible and the learned laws, which Bromyard knew most thoroughly and was most deeply indebted to.

TABLE 3.4 : THE 17 INDIVIDUAL WORKS CITED MORE THAN 20 TIMES
(EXCLUDING BIBLICAL BOOKS AND WORKS OF CANON AND CIVIL LAW)

V8	various authors	
	Vitas patrum	112
G5	GREGORIUS I	
	Moralia in Iob	97
A19	AUGUSTINUS	
	De civitate dei	93
G5	GREGORIUS I	
	Dialogi	84
S4	SENECA	
	Epistulae morales	73
I6	IOHANNES DE BROMYARD	
	Sermones	69
G5	GREGORIUS I	
	Homiliae	68
T3	THOMAS AQUINAS	
	Summa theologica	58
I8	IOHANNES CHRYSOSTOMUS	
	Super Matthaeum	53
V1	VALERIUS MAXIMUS	
	Facta ac dicta memorabilia	46
P8	PETRUS COMESTOR	
	Historia scholastica	42
A17	ARISTOTELES	
	Ethica	40
G5	GREGORIUS I	
	De cura pastorali	33
I8	IOHANNES CHYSOSTOMUS	
	Super Iohannem	33
B5	BERNARDUS CLARAEVALLENSIS	
	De consideratione	22

I10	IOHANNES FRIBURGENSIS	
	Summa confessorum	22
H5	HIERONYMUS	
	Epistulae	21

Total citations of the 17 works		966
Of all citations		6.79%
Of non-biblical citations		26.40%
Of all citations except those of the Bible and the learned laws		40.74%

TABLE 3.5 : BROMYARD'S RELIANCE UPON THE BIBLE, THE TWO LEARNED LAWS AND THE 17 WORKS

Citations of the Bible, Canon and Civil Law		11,854
Of all citations		83.33%
Citations of the Bible, the learned laws and the 17 key works		12,820
Of all citations		90.12%

The long list of entries in Table 3.1, if we omit the translators but include the pseudonymous writers, runs to some 151 names: an impressive collection. Quite a few of these authors, however, will have been accessed through Bromyard's core texts.[1] The conclusion to which the above data impel us is that the great edifice of the *Summa* is firmly grounded upon the secure foundations provided by Bromyard's discerning reading of, and pondering on, a relatively few but hugely important texts.

[1] This proposition is explored in several of the succeeding chapters: e.g. in the short entries on D. Iuvenalis and C. Sallustius in chapter 6. An instance of this practice is encountered too in his one citation of P. Terentius: Bromyard quotes the line from the *Andria* [67/68]

hoc tempore
Obsequium amicos, veritas odium parit.

one of two lines of Terentius quoted by Laelius in Cicero's dialogue *De amicitia*. Bromyard *does* source the line to the *Andria*: but he will have learnt this from Laelius' speech, as the *De amicitia* was familiar to him.

4

CHURCH FATHERS : CHRISTIAN WRITERS OF THE PATRISTIC AGE (to 700)

TABLE 4.1 : THE FOUR GREATER DOCTORS OF THE WESTERN CHURCH:
AND EASTERN CONTEMPORARIES

A12	Ambrosius	36
A19	Augustinus	304
G5	Gregorius I	388
H5	Hieronymus	101
I8	Iohannes Chrysostomus	133
V8	Vitas patrum	112
	Total	1,074

Of all citations	7.55%
Of non-biblical citations	29.35%

TABLE 4.2 : NUMBER AND PERCENTAGE OF UNSPECIFIED CITATIONS

A12	Ambrosius	8 of 36	22.22%
A19	Augustinus	51 of 304	16.78%
G5	Gregorius I	97 of 388	25.00%
H5	Hieronymus	31 of 101	30.70%
I8	Iohannes Chrysostomus	22 of 133	16.54%
V8	Vitas patrum	0 of 112	-

This high incidence of unspecified citations is in marked contrast to Bromyard's practice of always giving precise references when citing texts of canon and civil law. The inference must be that he enjoyed unbroken access to *these* texts: whereas he was either often deprived of texts of the five major patristic writers or felt confident he could rely on his retentive memory when quoting. It is worth recalling here Bromyard's own admission:

secundum philosophum in politicis (si bene recordor).[1]
[according to Aristoteles in the *Politics* (if my memory serves me well).]

A comparable pattern of high incidence of unreferenced citations is also to be observed in three other heavily-cited sources. These are

A17	Aristoteles	23 of 86	26.74%
B5	Bernardus	59 of 150	39.33%
S4	Seneca	31 of 154	20.13%

Had the appropriate volume been to hand he would surely have transcribed from the text: one must admire his capacity for near-verbatim recall.

TABLE 4.3 : 30 OTHER CHRISTIAN WRITERS OF THE PATRISTIC AGE
(TO THE YEAR 700)

A10	Ambrosiaster	4
A18	Athanasius	1
A19b	Ps. Augustinus	7
B2	Basilius	2
B4	Benedictus	1
C1	Caesarius	8
C2	Cassiodorus	29
I8b	Ps. Chrysostomus	4
C10	Cyprianus	6
D2	Ps. Dionysius Areopag.	4
E1	Eusebius Gallicanus	4
E2	Eusebius Vercellensis	1
F3	Fulgentius Ruspensis	1
G1	Gennadius	1
G8	Gregorius Nazianzenus	3
I7	Iohannes Cassianus	11
I16	Isidorus	19
I17	Iulianus Pomerius	2
L2	Leo I	3
L3	Leontius	4
M2	Martinus Bracar.	1
O2	Origenes	8
O3	Orosius	1
P4	Pelagius	4
P7	Petrus Chrysologus	12
P13	Possidius	2
P14	Prosper	1
Q2	Quodvultdeus	2
S7	Sidonius	1
V4	Victorinus	1

Total	156

Of all citations	1.10%

26 of the 30 writers of Table 4.3
are cited fewer than ten times

Total of Patristic Age	1,230

Of all citations	8.65%

Of non-biblical citations	33.62%

A19   Thirty percent of Bromyard's citations of Augustinus are from the *De civitate dei.* This was one of his core texts and a major gateway for him into the classical world.

B7   Boethius is omitted on the grounds that the two works cited are not specifically Christian.

C2   The Historia ecclesiastica tripartita, compiled by Cassiodorus from the church histories of Sokrates, Sozomenos and Theodoretos (translated by Epiphanios bishop of Salamis), was one of the essential texts which Humbertus de Romanis urged Dominican librarians to provide.[2]

D2   Ps. Dionysius Areopagita is included in this group despite the caveat of A. W. Lintott[3]. ('Scholars are divided as to whether Dionysius' allegiance is fundamentally pagan and Neoplatonic or authentically Christian'). On this relationship Louth is unequivocal: 'Denys' writings are *explicitly* Christian. It is the Christian Scriptures that he seeks to interpret in his writings, not the works of Plato or the Chaldaean Oracles.. When he quotes, he quotes from the Scriptures. He never ascribes any authority to (pagan) Greek philosophical sources.'
        However a caveat is needed on Louth's use of 'quotes'. He continues: 'If he never quotes from Plato and the Neoplatonists, he frequently *alludes* to them. In DN II.7 [Divine Names, peri theiōn onomatōn] on love of the beautiful, he reproduces word for word part of Diotima's speech to Socrates from the Symposium (211A-B). It is not a quotation only because he does not say where it comes from.'[4] His treatises were first cited in 532. The *De caelesti hierarchia* is characterized by Louth as an account of the workings of the divine economy through angelic agency.

E1   *Eusebius Gallicanus* is included here although dating is uncertain. Clarke[5] notes that his homilies normally accompany those of Caesarius in English manuscripts.

G5   Apart from seven books of the Bible and Gratianus' *Decretum* Bromyard's single largest source of citations is the oeuvre of S.Gregorius. His is the very first work to be cited (the third homily on Ezechiel). Bromyard adds:
        'Whatever in this little study is considered to be deserving of reproof should be attributed to my deficiency: but whatever is useful should be ascribed to the clemency of the Saviour and of the perpetual Virgin and to the auspices of the most blessed doctor Gregorius and of our father blessed Dominicus..'[6]
        It is notable too that of the 32 saints whose individual 'Lives' are cited only S.Louis of France (Louis IX) with five citations comes anywhere near to S.Gregorius' eleven.

H5   S.Hieronymus' original contributions to the *Vitas Patrum* (e.g. Lives of Paula and Eustochium) have not been catalogued separately. Bromyard may have thought of him as the author or at least the editor of the whole compilation but nowhere links him with the work: his references are usually in the form 'in vi. pa.' (in vitis patrum). The original *Life* in the Vitas Patrum was of S.Antonius and written by Athanasios. This was translated from Greek into Latin by Evagrius. Three *Lives* written by S. Hieronymus, including that of S.Hilarion, made up the basis of a collection which was added to by others, among them Dionysius Exiguus who contributed the Life of S.Pachomius. Then probably in the sixth and seventh centuries were added numerous biographies of female penitents such as the *Vita S.Mariae Aegyptiacae*. The popularity of the assemblage ensured its continuing growth: the seventh-century *Vita S.Iohannis Elemosynarii* by Leontius of Naples translated by Anastasius Bibliothecarius in the ninth century joined the collection at this late stage.[7]

P4   The heretic Pelagius is cited four times. Bromyard thought his *De vita christiana* was Augustinus' work, and his *Epistula ad Demetriadem* he assigned to S.Hieronymus.

V4   Victorinus, late in life, became Christian. It seems likelier that Bromyard would have had access to one of his Christian writings than to his Neo-Platonic studies: he came across Victorinus through Cornificius, the author of the *Rhetorica ad Herennium* (falsely attributed to Cicero at S.3.8). 'The marriage between knowledge and virtue is a delight: intelligence without virtue prompts one to defend one's own sins and scorn one's critics.'[8] Augustinus had read Plotinos in his fellow-African's translations.

---

[1]   B.2.10.

[2]   Humbertus vol.II p.265.

[3]   OCD^3 p.478.

[4]   Louth p.21.

[5]   CBMLC 10 p.17.

[6]   quicquid vero utile salvatoris et perpetue virginis attribuatur clemencie et beatissimi doctoris Gregorii ac patris nostri beati Dominici auxiliis.. (Prologus).

[7]   Berschin pp.57-58.

[8]   Dulce est matrimonium inter scientiam et virtutem: quia sapientia sine virtute facit propria peccata defendere redarguentesque contemnere. (S.3.8)

5

CANON LAWYERS

TABLE 5.1 : CITATIONS OF CANON LAWYERS

-	Anon. glo. interlin. in Decretum	8
B1	Bartholomaeus Brixiensis	44
B6	Bernardus Parmensis	25
B8	Bonifacius VIII	41
C7	Clemens V	21
G4	Gratianus	558
G6	Gregorius IX	153
G7	Gregorius X	3
G9	Guido de Baysio	1
H4	Henricus (Hostiensis)	17
I 4	Innocentius IV	12
I 5	Iohannes Andreae	9
(I 5)	id. as unnamed gloss. to Lib. VI + Clem.	3
I 12	Iohannes Monachus	2
O4	Ottobonus	1
U1	Urbanus II	1
W2	Willelmus de Monte Laud.	5
	TOTAL	904

Of all citations	6.36%
Of non-biblical citations	24.71%

Bromyard's familiarity with the enormous range of the corpus of canon law was demonstrated in his *Opus trivium*: and amply confirmed in the *Summa* by the ease and appropriateness of the multitude of his citations of both the original texts and of the standard glosses.

He shows a much smaller reliance upon the later commentators: 49 citations in all from the apparatuses of Guido de Baysio, Hostiensis, Innocentius IV, Iohannes Andreae, Iohannes Monachus (Jean LeMoine) and Willelmus de Monte Lauduno: only 5.42% of this sub-total.

Iohannes Andreae's *Apparatus ad Clementinas* (the glossa ordinaria), completed in 1322 (not 1326)[1], must have been among the very latest works to come into Bromyard's hands.

He does not cite the *Extravagantes* of Iohannes XXII, a collection of 20 decretales assembled between 1325 and 1327 by Zenzelinus de Cassanis (d.1354), who also wrote glosses on it.[2]

Bromyard's citations of the major texts of the *Corpus Iuris Canonici* reveal his debt to them. They are the texts which, after the Bible, and together with the *Corpus Iuris Civilis*, honed his intellectual and moral development and guided his judgement.

The *Decretum* or *Concordia discordantium canonum* of Gratianus is dated to c.1140: the *Decretales*, commissioned by Gregorius IX, to 1234: the *Liber Sextus* of 1298 was promulgated by Bonifacius VIII: and the *Clementinae* were issued in 1317 by Iohannes XXII.[3] None of these texts can be dissociated from their apparatuses or bodies of glosses and commentaries to which Bromyard will have accorded equal respect: the 44 citations of Bartholomaeus' *glossa ordinaria* to the *Decretum*, the 25 of Bernardus' gloss to the *Decretales* and Iohannes Andreae's 3 glosses to the two later works constitute one whole. The four texts alone yield 23.26% of Bromyard's non-biblical citations.

TABLE 5.2 : THE FOUR MAJOR TEXTS

DECRETUM	558
glo. ord.	44
glo. inter.	8
DECRETALES	153
glo. ord.	25
LIBER SEXTUS	39
glo. ord.	2
CLEMENTINAE	21
glo. ord.	1
TOTAL	851

H4 The growing interdependence of the civil and the canon law from the end of the twelfth century onwards is the main theme of Brundage's study 'Universities and the "ius commune" in Medieval Europe'. He notes that Hostiensis declared in the prologue to his *Summa aurea* that he proposed to draw his material from both Roman civil law and canon law, since the two laws complemented one another 'and neither was complete without the other'. Brundage quotes the proverb 'Legista sine canonibus parum valet, canonista sine legibus nihil.'[4] Charles Lefebvre quotes Rolandino da Padova, who describes him as 'theologiae scientia plenum..doctissimum in scientia naturali, in Veteri et in Novo Testamento, peritum *utique in iure canonico et civili.*'[5] Lefebvre points to the admiration Hostiensis evinces for the subtleties and the rigour in the interpretation of Roman law displayed by Azo in his 'Summa': 'il la cite plus fréquemment qu' aucune autre oeuvre de légiste.'[6]

W2 Willelmus de Monte Lauduno (d.1343) glossed three of the constitutions of Iohannes XXII which were then glossed by Zenzelinus[7], along with 17 others, and, as a collection, became known as the *Extravagantes*. G. Mollat, in his article on the *Clementinae*, attributes to Willelmus [Guillaume de Montlauzun] the earliest of the commentaries on this text, his Apparatus of 1319[8]. Mollat dates

Zenzelinus' Apparatus on the *Clementinae* to 7 September 1323[9]. Willelmus is cited by Bromyard but Zenzelinus is not. Kuttner corrected Mollat's dating of Iohannes Andreae's *glossa ordinaria* on the *Clementinae* (cited 7 times by Bromyard) of 1326 to 1322.[10]

[1]   Makowski p.10: citing Stephan Kuttner *The Apostillae of Johannes Andreae on the Clementines* p.198.

[2]   Brundage, MCL p.199.

[3]   ibid. pp.190-198. (This book, and especially pp.190-202 and pp.206-230, is a clear introduction to the subject.)

[4]   Brundage, Profession pp.244, 245: and 242 note 23.

[5]   DDC vol.5 col.1211.

[6]   ibid. col.1218.

[7]   DDC vol.4 cols.640-641.

[8]   ibid. col.639.

[9]   ibid. col.639.

[10]   Makowski p.10: citing Stephan Kuttner (vide supra).

6

CLASSICAL AUTHORS

TABLE 6.1: FORTY GREEK AND ROMAN WRITERS

A2	Aesopus	10
A14	Anaxagoras	1
A17	Aristoteles	85
A17b	Ps. Aristoteles	4
A20	Aulus Gellius	1
B7	Boethius	12
B7b	Ps. Boethius	5
B7c	Commentator ad Boethium	1
C3	Ps. Cato	3
C5	Cicero	30
C6	Claudianus	2
C8	Cornificius	2
C9	Q. Curtius Rufus	3
D1	Diogenes	1
D3	Donatus	1
F1	Frontinus	7
F2	Fulgentius Mytho.	1
H6	Q. Horatius	7
I 18	I.V.A. Polemius	1
I 20	Iustinus	4
I 21	D. Iuvenalis	6
M1	Macrobius	1
O5	P. Ovidius	3
P5	Petronius	1
P11	Plinius (iunior)	1
P12	Plinius (senior)	4
P15	Ptolemaeus	3
P16	Publilius Syrus	4
Q1	Quintilianus	1
S1	C. Sallustius	2
S4	Seneca	154
S4b	Ps. Seneca	8
S5	Seneca rhetor	8
S8	Socrates	2
S9	Solinus	4
S10	Suetonius	2
T2	P. Terentius	1
V1	Valerius Maximus	46
V2	Vegetius	7
V3	P. Vergilius	3
	Total	442

Of all citations	3.12%
Of non-Biblical citations	12.08%

TABLE 6.2 : FOUR CLASSICAL AUTHORS

A17	Aristoteles	85
C5	Cicero	30
S4	Seneca	154
V1	Valerius Maximus	46
	Total	315
	Of classical citations	71.27%
	Of non-biblical citations	8.61%

The 40 writers here listed range in date from the 6th century BC to the 6th century AD: from Aesopus to Boethius. 'Classical' is used here as a convenient portmanteau word to embrace pre- and non-Christian writers in Greek and Latin up to late antiquity rather than as a period term referring to literature of 5th and 4th century BC Athens and of late republican and Augustan Rome. (Boethius could easily fit into another category).

Twelve of the 40 sources in this group are cited only once: and a further ten merely twice or three times. These 22 primary sources may well have been accessed by Bromyard through the mediation of the core texts which he had at his disposal in the Hereford convent. The same working hypothesis will inform this little study for the lightly cited authorities in the other groups. Bromyard was also well-travelled and will have stayed at several other Dominican houses[1], perhaps too at foundations of other orders[2]: one may assume that a learned and bookish man will not have missed an opportunity to consult the holdings of their libraries. Furthermore the Dominicans are known to have been generous with inter-house loans.

A17 Bromyard had no Greek. In INTENTIO he writes:
'..in order that the book of our life should be perfect it is a requirement that it be written internally with a good intention: and outside with approved work: because a book written externally with beautiful manners and not on the inside with a good intention: is a book of hypocrites and cheats formed like an antique book: which is not in use: or which on the inside is all mildewed or written in the Hebrew or Greek script or any other deformed [writing]: in as much as it cannot be of help..'[3]
His reading of Aristoteles, then, and pre-eminently the *Ethica,* cited 40 times, was undoubtedly of Aristoteles latinus. The *Ethica* he will have read in Grosseteste's version: the *De Vegetalibus* perhaps in Alfred of Sarashel's translation from the Arabic: and it may have been William of Moerbeke's versions from the Greek of the *Politica* (c.1260) and of the *Metaphysica* that he studied[4]. He had not always a text to hand: in BELLUM he had to quote from memory:
'..according to Aristoteles in the *Politica* (if my memory serves me well').[5]

A14 The three Greek philosophers who make four appearances between them
D1 (Anaxagoras, Diogenes and Socrates) perhaps were accessed from a compilation
S8 such as the Reading-Leominster tract B75.316 *Diversorum philosophorum epistole et sententie* in CBMLC 4. The enormous gulf between Bromyard's and

modern sensibilities is illustrated by his seeming approval of the view he quotes of Diogenes:

'A beautiful woman is a temple built over a sewer.'[6]

He reinforces this judgement by quoting S.Bernardus: 'Beauty is nothing but a cover for impurity.'[7] He, however, might well consider many of us Laodicean.

Socrates is quoted each time with approval.

'No one can be judged strong/brave unless he shows foresight too. For manliness devoid of intelligence is foolhardiness, and dangerous.'[8]

He declared that the height of common sense was this: the ability to tell the difference between good and bad: so that one can know to censure the bad and choose the good.[9]

A20   Aulus Gellius is cited at I.7.7 (*Agellius* to Bromyard, as to the York Austin Friars 519e: 'excerpta ex libro Agelii noxium Atticarum'): but at O.7.17 his text is accessed through Vincentius Bellovacensis: 'Liber noctuum atticarum et habetur prima parte speculi historialis. li.iii. c.xxxii.'

C6   The two citations of Claudius Claudianus are unreferenced and clearly derive from another source. The second is even a prose rendering of his verse: '..that remark of Claudianus about those who had no knowledge of God, and yet were diligent in liberal studies..'[10]

C9   The four editors of CBMLC 4 index the 5 copies of *Gesta Alexandri/chronicon*
or   *de Alexandro magno/historia Alexandri* in four Benedictine libraries under
I 18   Q. Curtius Rufus: but note in the text at each entry 'Probably *Historia Alexandri magni*, tr. Julius Valerius..'

A strong candidate for original authorship must be Ps. Callisthenes. L. J. Engels observes[11]: 'The medieval picture of Alexander rests above all on the late-classical, pseudo-historical Greek narrative of Alexander, probably written in Alexandria towards the end of the 3rd century. Since then this text has been constantly rewritten, with new traditions continually being incorporated into it.'

A. B. Bosworth notes[12]: 'It is popular fiction, a pseudo-historical narrative interspersed with an 'epistolary novel'..' Engels remarks that one version of the Ps. Callisthenes romance was reworked around 310 by Iulius Valerius Alexander Polemius: and he goes on to record its complex progress through the medieval period.

Bromyard names no author in his citations of *Gesta Alexandri.*

H6   There are seven quotations from the poems of Q. Horatius Flaccus of which three only are attributed to him, and for these Bromyard gives but a general reference.

Ad idem (the subject is AVARICIA) Oracius libro carminum: Crescentem sequitur cura pecuniam maiorque fames: multa petentibus desunt multa.[13]

Bromyard has combined lines from two separate stanzas, Carmina 3.16.17-18 with 3.16.42-43. The metre is not sustained by his misquoting 'maiorque' for 'maiorumque', although the sense is. It is a neat dovetailing which he may have come across in some commonplace book or florilegium.

In CONSILIUM he writes:

dicit Oratius in libro epistularum
dulcis inexpertis cultura potentis amici est.
Expertus vero metuit.[14]

89

Epistularum 1.18.86-87 is the source of his quotation. His intrusive 'vero' spoils the metre (though the equally intrusive 'est' would not).

In FIDES we read
..sicut fabule habent de quodam qui
minabatur se montem vel leonem producturum:
et produxit murem..[15]
This is a mangled recollection of Ars Poetica 139:
parturient montes, nascetur ridiculus mus.
The mountain/s and the mouse are Horatian: not, however, the fabulous lion.

Capitulum I.2 deals with INCONSTANTIA: it is in the second articulus which treats of its causes that Bromyard quotes from the Epistulae, but without reference or attribution.
..quia celum et non animum mutat.[16]
The Horatian verse is
caelum non animum mutant qui trans mare currunt
(Epistularum 1.11.27)
(It is their surroundings that travellers from overseas change, not their mindset).

IUSTICIA is the subject of I.13. The third articulus examines 'the difference between divine and earthly justice, or between true and apparent'. In this context he raises the issue of the poor and their animals being incarcerated 'even perhaps up to death' by their lords: perhaps justly, perhaps unjustly. The innocent, on their release, are awarded no compensation for the loss inflicted on them:
nullam de damno eis illato reportant emendam.
22 words more, then he quotes
quidquid delirant reges plectuntur achivi. (Epist. 1.2.14)
(Whatever madness seizes the kings it's the Achaeans – [i.e. the common soldiers] – who suffer).
and adds
because it's always *they* who sustain the maltreatment either from their lords or for their lords: but don't share the gains.[17]
Yet again Bromyard's choice and use of his classical quotations is totally apposite and telling.

RECIDIVUM (i.e. relapse, especially into sin) is the theme of R.2. The fourth articulus deals with
ingratitudo: pena et periculum.
Bromyard fastens on the finely observed cameo of the restless millionaire, never satisfied with his latest purchase or building, ever changing:
Quod petiit sprevit repetit quod nuper omisit
Estuat et vite disconvenit ordine toto
Diruit edificat mutat quadrata rotundis..[18]
Apart from the medieval e for ae this is an exact transcription of Epistularum 1.1.98-100, acknowledged as Oratius libro epistolarum.

In SENECTUS Bromyard quotes, without attribution to Horatius :
multa senem circumveniunt incommoda..[19]
(Ars Poetica 169).

The incomplete line is introduced simply by 'Audi poetam.' Here a 46-word quotation is acknowledged as deriving from 'Innocentius libro i de vilitate conditionis humane' (and more exactly, from I.9 *De incommodis senectutis*). This strongly suggests that between writing capitula I13 and S5 he accessed a complete text of at least book one of *De miseria* and that therefore S5 was written after I13. Another deduction of interest is that, since Bromyard omits the words
'set non tardus ad iram'
omitted also by MS C[18] (described by the editor R. E. Lewis as English of the 14th century) he *may* have used this very copy[20]: or its parent or sibling.

It seems clear, from these seven citations, that Bromyard did not have access to a text of Q. Horatius' poems: but that he selected his quotations partly from an oral culture (possibly even from his early schooling) and partly from florilegia. That he used florilegia he himself declares:
'..in the book *The clash of the vices*: claimed by some for S.Gregorius..the noteworthy elements from that book are incorporated in the *Flowers of S.Gregorius*.'[21]

I 21   Bromyard's six quotations from the *Saturae* of D. Iunius Iuvenalis perhaps allow us a revealing glimpse into his library access.
In the capitulum AVARICIA he quotes
'Cantabit vacuus coram latrone viator': [22]
(Sat.10.22)
a line apposite for a mendicant preacher for whom a wayside robber may have been more than a literary reality.

He remembers, and uses, the same line to bolster an argument in the capitulum PAUPERTAS. In neither case does he name the author of the verse, which is contrary to his usual meticulous practice. This *may* suggest a retentive memory for an oral culture prevailing at the Hereford convent or possibly a quip thrown out in conversation at the episcopal table in Llandaff.

In GLORIA he both quotes and names the satirist:
'quia dicit Iuvenalis quod omne animi vicium tanto conspectius est in se: quanto maior est qui peccat.'[23]
This gives the core of the poet's aphorism, but the two lines are slightly misquoted: they should read:
'Omne animi vitium tanto conspectius in se
crimen habet: quanto maior qui peccat habetur'.
(Sat. 8.140-141)
Clearly he had no copy of the *Saturae* before him as he wrote. This misquoting may indicate an impressive recall from memory of an earlier reading: and very possibly from a florilegium rather than from a complete text, for D. Iuvenalis is rarely found in monastic or mendicant libraries. Of the 62 Benedictine houses examined in CBMLC 4 only four are known to have held copies (Bury St Edmunds, Evesham, Reading and Whitby): the louche underworld so clinically and memorably dissected will not have commended the poet to many religious librarians and heads of houses.

In the same capitulum GLORIA we meet
> 'illud Iuvenalis. Malo inquit pater tibi sit
> torclices: dummodo tu sis eacidi similis:
> vulcanaque arma capescas: quam te terclite
> similem producat achilles.'

The lines should run:
> 'Malo pater tibi sit Thersites: dummodo tu sis
> Aeacidae similis: vulcaniaque arma capessas:
> quam te Thersitae similem producat Achilles.'[24]
> (Sat.8.269-271)

This time, apart from the mangling of the personal names by a copyist, the lines are almost perfect and, moreover, scan (if one allows no elision at 'vulcanaque arma').

In LUDUS we meet a quotation which smacks of the florilegium:
> 'ut ait Satiricus: Citius nos corrumpunt
> vitiosorum exempla: magnorum cum subeunt
> animos auctorum.'

This is a prosaic redaction of the verses
> 'velocius et citius nos
> corrumpunt vitiorum exempla domestica, magnis
> cum subeant animos auctoribus.'[25]
> (Sat.14.31-33)

Again the meat of the observation is preserved: but the marked divergence from the text suggests either an imperfect recollection of the lines or a correct transcription of his own or a colleague's entry, in semi-verse semi-prose form, in a commonplace book.

Articulus 8 of capitulum 14, COR, has as its theme 'malorum cordium periculum.' On the 'cor..nimis cupidum' he quotes from Hugo de S.Victore (De anima, li.iii): and ends
> 'et totus mundus ei non sufficit'[26]
> 'the world is not enough'

which is a dim memory of D.Iuvenalis on Alexander the Great:
> 'unus Pellaeo iuveni non sufficit orbis.'
> (Sat.10.168)

Bromyard's failure to recognize the original source can only mean that the magnificent tenth satire was to him a closed book.

S1 Sallustius also was accessed through Bromyard's core texts. In BELLUM he quotes an extract from section 52 of the *Bellum Catilinae* of C. Sallustius Crispus. The 71 words assigned to M. Porcius Cato differ slightly from those of the received text of Sallustius (e.g. 'veritatis' for 'virtutis', 'noxius' for 'obnoxius'): but contain several forceful utterances which attracted Bromyard's attention, such as

'Pro quibus [sc.virtutibus] nos habemus luxuriam et avariciam: publice egestatem: privatim opulentiam...' (instead of which we have luxury and greed: public need and private opulence..)

Bromyard cites Augustinus as his source (i.e. makes no claim to have read

C. Sallustius directly): giving the reference de ci. dei li.v.c.xiii (in modern editions of *De civitate Dei* it is 5.12): though he knew from Augustinus (Qui audit haec Catonis verba sive Sallustii..) what the original source was.[27]

Bromyard uses C. Sallustius again in the capitulum INCONSTANTIA to instance, for the fourth articulus, the signs or marks of inconstancy. He writes:

> Ad idem Augustinus quem allegat decretum di.xli.c.vlti.dicens:
> incompositio enim corporis ut Augustinus ait qualitatem mentis
> indicat. Unde hystoriographus glosa id est poeta. Salustius.
> Cum eius scilicet cantilene mutabilitatem describeret..

(On the same point Augustinus, quoted by the *Decretum*, distinction 41 the final chapter, which says:

> 'The disarray of the body according to Augustinus reveals
> the mental state. And so the historian – the gloss has 'the
> poet Sallustius' – when describing his (that is, Catilina's)
> changeability…')

Distinction 41 deals with the qualities needed for the priesthood (Ecce quibus oporteat sacerdotem esse ornatum moribus.) The glossa ordinaria of Bartholomaeus Brixiensis makes two identifications in this quoted section: of the 'hystoriographus' as Sallustius and of 'eius' as Catilina. It is Bromyard himself who erroneously calls Sallustius a poet.[28]

We see, then, that Bromyard comes to Sallustius not through accessing a text of his *Bellum Catilinae* but through (1) Augustinus' *De civitate dei* and (2) the *Decretum* of Gratianus amplified by the gloss apparatus of Bartholomaeus. For Bromyard the *De civitate dei* was a window onto an antique world: he cites it 93 times.

S4   Bromyard, it should be remembered, may well have considered Seneca as a Christian (Tritheim places him third in his catalogue of ecclesiastical writers: 'vir vitae continentissimae fuit. Quem testimonio beati Hieronymi celebratum, in catalogo Ecclesiasticorum Scriptorum idcirco posui, quoniam et Paulo apostolo amicissimus extitit, et ad institutionem moralis vitae multa eleganter composuit.')[29] Bromyard ever quotes Seneca with approval. The 14 letters in the correspondence of S. Paul and Seneca he will have believed authentic.
M. R. James remarks that it existed in the fourth century 'for Jerome mentions it, says it was 'read by many', and is led by it to insert Seneca in his catalogue of Christian authors.'[30]

V1   The *Facta ac dicta memorabilia* of Valerius Maximus is written in a gossipy and anecdotal style and furnishes Bromyard with a host of *exempla*. The book is divided into sections on moral and philosophical themes, with headings such as

De simulata religione	patientia
superstitionibus	constantia
miraculis	pudicitia
maiestate	felicitate
fortitudine	mutatione morum aut fortunae

a format which, together with the interest of the content, would make it doubly attractive to the preacher. Bromyard, moreover, is quite open on his use of sources emanating from differing perspectives. In the Prologus to the *Summa* he writes:

'In this little treatise it does not seem worthless to insert sayings and *exempla* from diverse branches of study.'[31]

He goes on to quote Petrus Blesensis that whatever the branch of study from which words originate the criterion for use is that they provide a building-block towards salvation: 'dummodo edificent ad salutem.' Bromyard continues: 'For from the morality of pagan fables sometimes the pattern of wisdom is drawn out.'[32]

One or more manuscripts from which the early printed editions of compilations such as the *Flores poetarum* derive will almost certainly have furnished Bromyard with material useful for many topics. The 1490 Johann Koelhoff edition of the *Flores*[33] is divided into nine books, viz.

1. de superbia	6. de gula
2. de bona fama	7. de luxuria
3. de invidia	8. de remediis luxurie
4. de ira	9. de donis sancti spiritus
5. de avaricia	(sive de virtutibus)

and puts under contribution no fewer than 45 authors, more than a third of whom belong to the 'classical' age and late antiquity, namely:

Arator	Everhardus	Persius
Aurora	Ganfridus	Pamphilus
Avianus	Geta	Prosper
Alexander	Gilbertinus	Prudentius
Alda	Henricus	Querulus
Alanus	Horacius	Rapularius
Boecius	Isengrinus	Susanna
Bernardus	Iuvenalis	Sedulius
Silvester	Lucanus	Speculum Mundi
Bernardus	Mahumeth	Tobias
Palpanista	Marcianus	Virgilius
Cato	Maximus	Stacius
Claudius	Maximianus	Theodulus
Clericus	Matheus	Thais
Dares	Otto	Zozimus.
Esopus	Ovidius	

1 Dominican houses en route from Hereford to Dover for the sea-crossing to France lay at Gloucester, Oxford, King's Langley, London and Canterbury. Worcester priory was not founded till 1347: but Brecon (1269) and Cardiff (1241) were close to Llandaff whose scholarly bishop John of Monmouth (sedit 1294-1323) he knew and admired.

2 The Hereford Franciscans, for example, held a text of the *De caelesti hierarchia* of Ps. Dionysius Areopagita (translated by Iohannes Scottus Eriugena?) as the first tract of a multi-tract volume of the mid-thirteenth century now in Hereford CL under shelf-mark P.V.10. Bromyard cites this text three times.

An example of hospitality between the two major mendicant orders is seen in Moorman's account of the arrival in England of the first Franciscans, in September 1224. 'Their passage paid for them by the friendly monks of Fécamp, the friars landed at Dover and made their way to Canterbury where they stayed for two days either as guests of the monks of Christ Church, or perhaps of the Dominicans. The party then divided, five remaining in Canterbury..while the other four went on to London.

Arriving in the capital they were received by the Dominicans, who kept them as their guests for fifteen days. ..But before the end of October, the two Richards had gone on to Oxford. Again they were received by the Dominicans and lived for a week with them..' (Moorman pp.72-73).

3 (..formatus ad modum libri antiqui: qui non est in usu: vel qui est intus totus putridus *vel litteris scriptus iudeorum vel grecorum vel quibuscunque aliis deformatis: intantum quod iuvare non potest..*) (I.5.8)

At S.1.3 his etymology for 'presbyter' betrays his ignorance of Greek: 'Presbyter etiam dicitur: quasi prebens iter.' At S.3.5 he attempts to write, in Roman letters, the Greek apothegm *gnothi seauton*. The compositors of the first printed edition struggled with their manuscript reading, producing 'nochis elycon. i. scitote ipsum' which may be a debased version of a manuscript 'nothi seauton' [id est] scito teipsum'. He cites it from the *Policraticus* book 3 chapter 2.

4 William, a confrère of Thomas Aquinas in his Viterbo years, was a Dominican who had lived in Greece for several years. His version of the *Politica* is rather opaque. (Bolgar p.229). There is a Leipzig edition of 1872. The *De vegetalibus* (also titled *De vegetabilibus*) is attributed to Nicholaus Damascenus (born 64 BC). Alfred of Shareshill's translation was made in about 1200. (Cambridge pp.506, 803, 849).

5 ..secundum philosophum in politicis (si bene recordor). (B.2.10)

6 Mulier pulchra: templum est edificatum super cloacam. (P.14.2)

7 Pulchritudo non est nisi velamen turpitudinis. (P.14.2)

8 Fortis nemo potest iudicari nisi et prudens fuerit. Virtus enim sine sapientia temeritas periculosa est. (S.3.11)

9 hanc summam dixit esse sapientiam: bona malaque distinguere: ut sciat reprobare malum et eligere bonum (S.4.5)

10 ..illud Claudiani 'Mobile mutatur semper cum principe vulgus' (E.7.5): and '..per hoc quod dicit Claudianus de his qui dei cognitionem non habuerunt: et tamen in liberalibus studiis diligentes fuerunt.' (S.4.12)

11 Engels p.16.

12 Bosworth in OCD^3 p.1270.

13 A.27.6.

14 C.11.9.

[15]   F.4.19.

[16]   I.2.6.

[17]   quia iniurias vel a dominis vel pro dominis semper sustinent: et cum illis lucra non participant. (I.13.12). The line of Horatius is quoted by Lotario dei Segni, *De miseria condicionis humane* I.15 but since Lotario is not named the immediate source will be a commonplace book (even though Bromyard used the text at least of book one of *De miseria*). The same may be said of Bromyard's 'Experto crede magistro' at A.26.29 which he owes to *De miseria* I.13. A line from D. Iuvenalis (Sat.14.139) 'crescit amor nummi, quantum ipsa pecunia crescit' would have been apposite for any of his several attacks on avarice. It is quoted by Lotario (De miseria II.6). Bromyard's failure to use the line is another indicator that he had not read book two.

[18]   R.2.9.

[19]   S.5.4.

[20]   The MS is CUL Dd.1.21 ff 147v-151v.

[21]   ..in libro de conflictu vitiorum: quem quidam dicunt esse beati Gregorii..que quidem notabilia de illo libro ponuntur inter flores beati Gregorii. (P.5.12)

[22]   A.27.48. The line is quoted again at P.3.6.

[23]   Since, as Iuvenalis observes, the greater the sinner the more subjected to public scrutiny is every failing of his character. (G.2.37)

[24]   I'd rather your father were Thersites [taken as a type of a rabble-rouser, lacking personal courage] provided *you* were like Achilles and took up the weapons of Vulcan, than that you had Achilles for your father but were like Thersites. (G.2.37)

[25]   Examples of vice in the home corrupt us more quickly whenever they penetrate our minds with the warrant of high authority. (L.6.8)

[26]   C.14.24.

[27]   B.2.51.

[28]   I.2.10.

[29]   Tritheim 3.

[30]   James, Apocryphal NT p.480.

[31]   In hoc enim opusculo non videtur vanum dicta et exempla inserere de diversis facultatibus. (Prologus).

[32]   Nam de fabularum gentilium moralitate forma quandoque eruditionis elicitur. (Prologus).

[33]   Goff F-223, GW 10074.

7

CIVIL LAWYERS

TABLE 7.1 : CIVIL LAW TEXTS

A1	Accursius	1
[A1]	glossator in Corpus Iuris	28
H4	Henricus (Hostiensis)	2
I 19	Iustinianus	353
	Total	384

Of all citations	2.70%
Of non-Biblical citations	10.49%

A1   Accursius is named once only: but it is his gloss to the Corpus Iuris Civilis that
[A1] Bromyard will have used c.1330 and earlier. As Tritheim observes of Accursius,
'primus totum ius civile glosavit.'[1]

H4   Hostiensis is renowned as a canonist: but Bromyard attributes to him a
commentary on the Codex. Brundage notes that he studied civil law under
Jacobus Balduinus and Homobono.[2]

I 19   The 353 citations assigned to Iustinianus:

TABLE 7.2 : IUSTINIANUS

Codex	130
Digesta	194
Institutiones	7
Novellae	22

Bromyard follows the later medieval triple division of the Digesta, namely:

TABLE 7.3 : DIVISIONS OF THE DIGESTA

Digestum Vetus	books I-XXIV.2	81
Infortiatum	books XXIV.3 – XXXVIII	32
Novum	book XXXIX – L	81

A commission headed by a non-lawyer, Iohannes of Cappadocia, had been set up
to prepare a comprehensive collection of imperial laws: and in April 529 Iustinianus'
initiative was rewarded with the promulgation in 12 books of the *Codex Iustinianus*. It is
the second edition, of 534, which survives.

He put in place a second commission, headed by Tribonianus, which condensed the contents of some 1,500 books into the work aptly named the *Digesta*, in 50 sections or books. This was promulgated in December 533.

The *Institutiones* was also issued in December 533 to be used as a text book in the law schools of Beirut and Constantinople.[3]

The *Novellae* (known also as the *Authenticum* or *Liber Authenticorum*) consist of 168 laws promulgated between 535 and 545 and collected during the reign of Tiberius II (578-582). In the Latin West, from the 11th century, glossators used a version of the *Authenticum* in which 96 of the *Novellae* were grouped into nine *collationes*.[4]

It is this rich heritage, one of the major civilizing forces of the high and late medieval West, in which Bromyard was steeped, which was one of the principal bases underpinning his intellectual fabric and grounding his view of the world.[5] He was, nonetheless, fully aware that the praiseworthy incentive to the study of the civil law could, in many cases, be driven by ignoble motives. 'I say that a yearning for wealth is the reason why advocates study the civil law and their stratagems... And this is the reason why such huge numbers, pretty well everyone, want to become students of the lucrative laws..why the school of civil lawyers has a hundred or two hundred students whereas the school of theology perhaps can't muster five.'[6]

TABLE 7.4 : BROMYARD'S CITATIONS FOR XI, CHRISTUS

	CITATIONS	% OF TOTAL
New Testament	73	48.67
Old Testament	34	22.67
Civil Law	36	24.00
Canon Law	5	3.33
Augustinus	2	1.33
TOTAL	150	

[1]   Tritheim 529.

[2]   Brundage, MCL p.214.

[3]   Honoré, Tony: articles on Justinian's codification and on Tribonianus in OCD[3].

[4]   Brundage, MCL p.204.

[5]   To illustrate this point Bromyard's 150 citations for XI (Christus) are of interest.

[6]   See Bromyard's caustic observation in full at p.246 in chapter 30.

8

CHRISTIAN WRITERS 1100 – c.1330
(excluding scholastic theologians, canonists and civil lawyers)

TABLE 8.1 : 23 CHRISTIAN WRITERS 1100-c.1330

A6	Alexander Cantuar.	1
A7	Alexander Nequam	4
A9	Alphonsus X	5
B5	Bernardus Claraevall.	150
B5b	ps. Bernardus	2
G3	Giraldus Cambrensis	6
H1	H. Salteriensis	1
H3	Helinandus	3
H8	Hugo de Folieto	4
H10	Hugutio Pisanus	1
H11	Humbertus de Romanis	3
I 1	Iacobus de Vitriaco	4
I 2	Iacobus de Voragine	16
I 4	Innocentius III	6
I 6	Iohannes de Bromyard	73
I 13	Iohannes Sarisburiensis	11
O1	Odo de Soliaco	2
P6	Petrus Blesensis	3
P8	Petrus Comestor	42
R2	Richardus [de S.Victore?]	1
T4	Thomas Cantipratensis	18
V5	Vincentius Bellovac.	16
W1	Walterus Map	1
	Total	373

Of all citations	2.62%
Of non-Biblical citations	10.19%

B5 The Cistercian monk Bernardus bestrides this group like a colossus. The 59 unreferenced citations perhaps indicate a reliance on memory of texts once read and studied but no longer to hand. Rather surprisingly it is the relatively slender tract of the five books of 'De consideratione' – occupying only 9½ leaves of the 322 devoted to his collected works in Jean Petit's edition of 1513 – which Bromyard seems to know best, cited 22 times: : the 86 sermons on the *Cantica canticorum* are cited only 14 times, although they take up 60 leaves in Petit's edition.

H11 The *Liber de dono timoris* of Humbertus de Romanis is to be distinguished from the book of the same title by his fellow-Dominican Stephanus de Borbone (Etienne de Bourbon) who died 16 years before Humbertus in 1261. This is packed with *exempla*[1] often introduced in conversational style as at 1.IV.896 'On the bathing of an adulterer and adulteress in a fiery vat' which begins 'Quidam homo bone uite et deuotus mihi dixit quod..'[2] Hinnebusch observes that Humbertus compiled a similar work.[3]

Bromyard quotes from Humbertus at M.11.121, M.11.145 and R.3.7.

To illustrate the emptiness and vanity of beauty (in his longest capitulum, MORS) he writes:

 'This is demonstrated by the story taken from the *Liber de dono timoris* about Isabella the daughter of S.Louis king of France, onetime queen of Navarre: who, struck low by a serious illness and rendered ugly, summoned her family to her and showed them how ugly she was, adding 'Look how ugly I've become, and deformed: they used to call me beautiful: so see in me how deceptive is charm, how empty is beauty'.'[4]

Bromyard assigns Isabella's final seven words to Proverbs 31 [verse 30]: she does not complete the verse, which would establish a more hopeful tone. The NEB translates the whole verse:

 'Charm is a delusion and beauty fleeting; it is the God-fearing woman who is honoured.'[5]

Isabella is styled here 'filia sancti Ludovici regis francie: quondam regina navarre.' Either Humbertus or Bromyard has confused her dynastic alliance. Isabella (1243-1271) was the daughter of Jaime I king of Aragon and Yolante of Hungary. In 1262 she married Philip dauphin of France and son of Louis IX (S.Louis). When Louis died in 1270 she became queen of France. Her son by Philip III (king of France 1270-1285) in 1284 married Joan, daughter of Henry I king of Navarre and thus became king of Navarre: there styled Philip I. (In 1285 his father died and so as king of France he was styled Philip IV)[6.]

I 1 Iacobus de Vitriaco (Jacques de Vitry, Latin bishop of Acre 1216-1228: cardinal-bishop of Tusculum (1228-1240)) is cited only four times: twice in CRUX, each time for an *exemplum*. The first tells of the sinking of a ship carrying both crusaders and merchants to the Holy Land. When the bodies were recovered a crimson cross was found on the bodies of the crusaders but nothing similar on the merchants or the crew. Iacobus attributes the account to 'a certain archbishop of great authority.'[7]

 The second *exemplum* is set at the time of the Albigensian crusade which followed the assassination in 1208 of Pierre de Castelnau the papal legate. A young man who had fought outstandingly well for his term of forty days was persuaded, for the sake of his father's soul, by 'a certain bishop' to serve a second forty days. This he did: and was rewarded by the appearance of his previously dead father 'more splendid than the sun' who thanked him for his liberation from the flames of purgatory.[8]

Bromyard uses both these *exempla* to illustrate the benefits of taking the cross. He does not give a precise reference for either *exemplum* but they are not from the *Historia occidentalis*.[9] Bromyard may have met them in Vincentius' *Speculum historiale*.

I 2 Bromyard never names Iacobus de Voragine. His citations sometimes take a form such as 'in legenda sanctorum in festo assumpcionis'[10]. At other times they take a form such as 'in legenda sancti Andree' as at M.4.12:

Andreas dixit: Merito hec pat[e]ris: quia male nupsisti

where the words correspond with de Voragine's text.

At other points he does not name his source, as at P.11.2:

..frustra videretur Laurentius dixisse: Ianuas tuas ingredi merui.

Since the words come from the *Legenda sanctorum* this citation was awarded to the archbishop of Genoa.

At M.11.56, however, 'in vita sancti Thome cantuariensis', the story does not derive from the *Legenda sanctorum* and so joins the group of 32 entries under VITAE SANCTORUM (V6).

I 6 'The third point is that there is frequent reference to the 'Sermones' on the ground of being material similar or more briefly arranged.'[11]   (Bromyard, the last sentence of his Prologue to the *Summa*).

Bromyard makes 69 references to 46 of his own, now lost, *Sermones*: 63 in the 27 capitula of A: the remaining six come at widely spaced intervals.[12]

The sermons cited (a few twice or three times) are:

TABLE 8.2 : BROMYARD'S CITATIONS OF HIS OWN *SERMONES*

1	16	49^2	74^2	107
5^3	17	50^2	77^3	112
6	22^2	51^4	80^2	129
7	22^3	52	83	130
10	24	53	84	135
11^2	28	57	86	141
12^2	30	58	100^2	142
13	31	69	104	144
15^3	33^2	71^2	105^2	147
				148

At E.7.6 the reference is unspecified: 'in sermonibus' followed by a blank space. At A.8.18 Bromyard allows us to recover the subject matter of one section of sermon 71: 'An *exemplum* of how such people are dispossessed of their celestial inheritance we see in sermon 71.7 in the case of two neighbours, both of them merchants: one of whom is canny, eager for profit and diligent in his dealings, the other negligent.   The former little by little supplanted the other in his inheritance..'

His referencing is, as usual, precise. Of the 63 references from A2 to A25 in 61 cases he gives the section number of the sermon (e.g. 51.3, 58.9, 147.12). The highest section number is 16, in sermon 142. At A.2.4 and A.22.20 he cites the opening words of the relevant section: 'a porticu sensuum' and 'Qualia etiam sunt opera.'

Bromyard's *Collationes* is also a lost text. There are references to this work at P.5.1 (Coll.10.4), P.13.56 (Coll.46), R.5.22 (Coll.36.5) and V.12.13 (Coll.54). However, I may well have missed others if they were cited as C (rather than Col. or Coll.) with a following number of 18 or under: (there are 18 capitula beginning with C, from C.1 CARITAS to C18 CUSTODIA.)   Binkley summarizes references from one work to another in Bromyard's oeuvre.[13]

P8   Petrus Comestor's *Historia scholastica,* a hugely popular work, skilfully dovetails biblical history with secular and gave Bromyard access to Iosephus. This is another of his core texts.

R2   The Richardus of S.3.7 could be any one of several of this name: his aphorism is 'Knowledge stands outside where love enters': 'Scientia foris stat ubi amor intrat.'

T4   The *Liber de apibus* of Bromyard's fellow-Dominican Thomas Cantipratensis furnishes him with numerous *exempla*. It was not well known: none of the 62 Benedictine houses of CBMLC 4 is known to have held a copy: and at Cambridge only the University library certainly had a copy:[14] nor is it recorded among the libraries of the Friars, of the Cistercians etc., at Dover Priory, or in the Registrum Anglie. It did survive into the printing age.[15]

The 352 *exempla* in Thomas' book are exploited by Murray as a keyhole into the secrets of the confessional. 'No fewer than ten of Thomas's stories certainly, and another seven probably, come directly from what he has been told in confession.'[16] Several of his acquaintances were confessors too, including a bishop of Lausanne (whom he met in Paris): another six of his anecdotes appear to derive from their revelations of confessions.[17]

Murray's analysis of the 352 *exempla* reveals that of their characters secular and regular clerics form the larger part: 58.50% as against 41.50% for the laity. The male-female proportion is 75% to 25%.[18]

One story Bromyard takes from Thomas is used to illustrate difficulties of obtaining justice in a lower court, whereupon a plaintiff will appeal to a higher court:

'Such an appeal was made by a certain abbot of whom an account is given in the *Liber de apibus*. Since he could obtain redress in no court for a wrong done to him by a certain lord he told the lord 'Let us both appear in God's court.' Some thirty days later the abbot fell ill and died. The lord was in his bath at the time, heard the bells and learnt from his servants the reason for the ringing was the death of this very abbot. 'Woe is me' he said: 'this means *my* death: I shall have to answer before God's tribunal on the matter in dispute between me and that abbot': as in fact happened.'[19]

[1] His *Tractatus de diversis materiis predicabilibus* contains, according to Little p.192, just under 2,900 *exempla*.

[2] Stephani Tractatus p.99.

[3] Hinnebusch EEFP pp.299-301.

[4] Hoc namque ostendit historia assumpta de libro de dono timoris de Isabella filia sancti Ludovici regis francie, quondam regina navarre, que gravi infirmitate percussa et turpis effecta ad se familiam convocavit et quam turpis fuit eis ostendit, dicens: Ecce quam turpis sum et deformis quam pulcram vocare solebant: videte ergo in me quam fallax gratia et vana est pulcritudo. (M.11.145).

[5] fallax gratia et vana est pulchritudo
mulier timens Dominum ipsa laudabitur (Proverbiorum 31.30)

[6] Louda, Tables 46, 65, 66.

[7] Unde quidam magne auctoritatis archiepiscopus predicavit quod quedam navis in qua erant cruce signati et alii mercatores in mari fuit submersa cum omnibus in ea contentis, in carne vero cruce signatorum inventa est una crux rubea miraculose facta: cum corpora in litore inventa sunt in aliis vero nihil tale* apparuit: hoc refert Iacobus de vitriaco. (C.17.7)
*for 'tali' of text

[8] Unde Iacobus de vitriaco refert quod cum exercitus cruce signatorum esset in terra albiensium circa hereticorum expugnationem quidam iuvenis pro se et fratre suo quadraginta dies ibi egregie dimicavit. Et cum de exercitu recedere vellet, rogatus a quodam episcopo pro anima patris sui stetit aliis quadraginta diebus et in fine pater prius mortuus apparuit ei sole splendidior et benedicendo ei regraciabatur quod eum de purgatorii incendio liberaverat. (C.17.7)

[9] I accessed this only in the French translation of Gaston Duchet-Suchaux (Paris 1997).

[10] He treats *legenda* as a feminine singular, not as a neuter plural.

[11] Tercium est quod frequenter fit missio ad sermones tanquam ad materiam similem vel brevius ordinatam.

[12] At E.6.40 to sermon 5: at E.7.6 'Item nota de ista materia in sermonibus [Here a blank is left, with no full stop: perhaps an omission by Bromyard or an inability of the compositor to read the manuscript figures.] At G.3.26 to sermon 84.6: at H.2.14 to sermon 141.5: at M.13.8 to sermon 144.3: and at P.4.16 to sermon 83.5 (Vide plura de istis impedimentis pacis: sermone lxxxiii.v).

[13] Binkley, Hereford p.264.

[14] There is a doubt over the second folio 'uel mitra' of the copy at Queens'.

[15] Goff T-346 to 348.

[16] Murray p.289.

[17] ibid. p.290.

[18] ibid. p.293.

[19] ..qui iusticiam obtinere non possunt in inferiori curia: clamant appellando ad superiorem. Sicut clamavit quidam abbas de quo scribitur in libro de apibus quod cum de iniuria sibi a quodam domino facta in nulla curia iusticiam obtinere posset: ait domino compareamus coram deo, et circa tricesimum diem sequentem abbas infirmatus mortuus est. Dominus vero ille tunc in balneo existens: audiensque campanas: et intelligens a ministris pulsationis causam esse quia abbas talis mortuus fuit. Dixit: ve mihi quia statim oportet me mori: ut respondeam ante tribunal dei de causa que vertitur inter me et abbatem illum quod et factum est. (D.12.37)

9

SCHOLASTIC THEOLOGIANS

TABLE 9.1 : SEVEN SCHOLASTICS

A4	Albertus Magnus, OP	5
A16	Anselmus Cantuar.	13
H9	Hugo de S.Victore	19
I 10	Iohannes Friburgensis	22
P10	Petrus Tarentas., OP	4
R4	Robertus Grosseteste	5
T3	Thomas Aquinas, OP	73
	Total	140

Of all citations	0.98%
Of non-Biblical citations	3.83%

What is noteworthy is the number of scholastic theologians he does *not* cite: which includes

Petrus Abelardus	(1079-1142)
Theodoricus Carnotensis (Thierry de Chartres)	(d.post 1151)
Gilbertus Porretanus	(1076-1154)
Petrus Lombardus	(c.1100-1160)
Robertus Melodunensis (Robert of Melun)	(d.1167)
Alexander de Hales	(c.1185-1245)
Willelmus de Alvernia	(1180-1249)
Richardus de Mediavilla	(1245 - ante 1308)

Furthermore, of Iohannes Sarisburiensis it is only the *Policraticus* he cites, not the *Metalogicon*.[1] His one citation of Averroes (at P.14.2) gives an anecdote of Aristoteles dissuading his students from being lured by woman's beauty. Alanus de Insulis he cites once, but from *De planctu naturae*, not from *De maximis theologiae*. Of his five citations of Grossesteste two only are of his commentary on the *De caelesti hierarchia*.

A4   Bromyard cites Albertus Magnus in the capitulum SANCTITAS:
     '..fire from on high, lightning, that is, or a flash of light sometimes consumes gold and silver in a purse, as Albertus shows [in his commentary] on the book *Meteora* [of Aristoteles], and leaves the purse undamaged..'[2]
     In YPOCRISIS there is another reference to the *Meteora*, although here Bromyard does not state whether this is Aristoteles' work or Albertus' commentary. The presence, however, of the Arabic plural shhb[3] [meteors], transliterated as *assub*, reveals this as a quotation from Albertus. He seizes on meteors, comparing hypocrites to the deceitful nature of meteors, to their brevity of duration and to their fall.

'First they have the condition and likeness of falling stars, which in the book *Meteora* are called assub: they are like these in two respects. First, in that they seem to be in the sky of the number of other stars, and they are not..'[4]

The lack of a precise reference here leads one to doubt whether he had access to a complete text of Albertus, Commentarii super [IV] libris metheororum. The tractatus dealing with meteors or 'assub' are numbers 19-23 of book I, although in the table of tractates on folia 25 recto to 27 recto of the exemplar I inspected[5] 'comets' was the heading: e.g. tractatus 20 was titled 'De errore dicentium cometem esse coniunctionem plurium stellarum.' The presence of citations by Albertus of the views of Avicenna and Algazel in tractatus 23, and of Albumasar in tractatus 23 and 29 (where 'assub' and 'comete' are distinguished) makes it likelier than not that it was through Albertus, and perhaps from a florilegium of his writings, that Bromyard encountered the three writers in Arabic whom he cites once only.

I 10 Iohannes Friburgensis is included. Although his *Summa confessorum* is characterized by L. E. Boyle as 'the most influential work of pastoral theology in the two hundred years before the Reformation'[6] its huge scope merits its place in this group. Boyle characterizes this *Summa* as a mixture of practical theology and canon law. 'Like the *Summa copiosa* of the canonist Hostiensis (d.1271), upon which John [of Freiburg] draws extensively, the *Summa* is in question and answer form, each question being answered "according to" one or other of John's main authorities: Raymond [of Peñafort], William of Rennes' *Apparatus*, Hostiensis, Geoffrey of Trani, William Durandus the Elder..the *glossa ordinaria* on the Decretals, Albert, Aquinas, Peter of Tarentaise, Ulrich of Strasbourg.'[7]

P10 At S.9.1 Bromyard cites Petrus [Tarentasiensis] and Albertus [Magnus]:
Et Petrus et Albertus in scriptis[8] super quarto: dis. XXV…
This reference to the two Dominicans' commentaries on the *Sententiae* of Petrus Lombardus (Book IV Distinctio 25, *De ordinatis ab hereticis*) is shown by Boyle to have been lifted from Iohannes Friburgensis without acknowledgement. Boyle notes another instance of such unacknowledged borrowing at R.6.2.[9]

T3 Of Thomas' 73 citations 36 are of the *Secunda secundae*: the text which Bromyard knew best and which held the greatest interest for him: the 'detailed account of the virtues and corresponding vices of the moral agent using reason and under grace.'[10]

Bromyard's slight reliance on the oeuvre of the scholastic theologians may be understood by a reading of his comments on their concerns which he expresses in three of his capitula in the *Summa*.

In ARMA (A.24) he deals with the issue of
'How against those weapons of the devil the soul is armed with the weapons of God.'
Here (A.24.12-15) he inveighs against those who receive gifts from God but fail to use and exercise them for the general good. He scrutinizes those who have entered the priestly order: those who have taken monastic or mendicant vows: and the holders of ecclesiastical benefices.

His strictures are directed towards three categories of these recipients of God's grace: those who
1. are lazy and do not work after receiving these [weapons]
2. do not expend them usefully
3. clothe themselves with them [these weapons] so as to evade the spiritual war.
Of this second category he writes:
>'The second group, while they do not work in the grace which they have received and do not expend it as they ought, rather abuse it than use it: like those who occupy their minds on fields of knowledge and unprofitable 'quaestiones', who exercise their order with the purpose of living the temporal life..'[11]

The lengthy capitulum PREDICATIO (P.12) has as its fourth articulus
>Qualiter oportet quod predicatores discant antequam doceant.
(Here one may note that although many Christians held offices which include preaching as a duty the word 'predicatores' will carry a special resonance for Dominicans.)
He quotes S.Paul (ad Romanos 10.17):
>'ergo fides ex auditu: auditus autem per verbum Christi'.
(The New English Bible translates, from the Greek:
>'We conclude that faith is awakened by the message, and the
>message that awakens it comes through the word of Christ.')
Bromyard continues:
>'How are they to preach the faith who have scarcely ever heard one word about Christ or the faith in the schools of theology?'[12]

The third relevant passages occur in the capitulum SCIENTIA (S.4).
In his introduction to 'Scientia' he presents the eight sections in which he will treat of this topic:
>'Second: how much usefulness the study of the scriptures confers.
>Sixth: how one ought to study in philosophy and other secular
>fields of knowledge and understand holy scripture.
>Seventh: denunciations are to be levelled against those who study
>in these subjects with different attitudes.'[14]
In the second article his intense concern for the primacy of scripture studies is made clear:
>'Other studies enable one to know or distinguish between what is fitting and unfitting, as does the study of grammar/language: or between the true and the false, as does logic: and the same holds good for other studies: but *this* [i.e. the study of the scriptures] is clearer and has a wider capacity for making things plain: in that it makes plain and enables one to know God, in the sight of whom consists life everlasting.'[15]
In dismay, however, he quantifies attendances in university lecture halls:
>'..where other masters have a hundred listeners a master in
>Theology will not manage twenty.'[16]
Further on he cites Augustinus in a letter to Hieronymus. Augustinus tells of a man who'd fallen into a well. A passer-by questioned him on how he'd contrived to fall in and what he was doing. Reasonably enough the man in the well felt these weren't the most relevant questions and considered the focus of the enquiry

should be on how to get him out! 'The same can be said to those who conduct daily disputations about the means by which the soul is instilled into the body: or by what means it is present there as the sole essence or the corporeal essence together with other elements: these and suchlike are the problems they propose. Of much greater use it would be to find out and put forward in debate how to be freed from this bodily prison and achieve salvation.....than to learn and direct their attention to all the attributes and affinities of God and the conditions of the soul and miss out on the reward, already mentioned, of everlasting happiness.'[17]

He comes to his sixth section at S.4.12.

Here it is proper to draw attention to the curious case of the text Bromyard does *not* cite: the *De vita regulari* of Humbertus de Romanis, the fifth Master General of the Order of Preachers. (Bromyard cites Humbertus only three times, from his *De dono timoris*). It is difficult to imagine how Bromyard could not have had access to a treatise of such importance for the Dominicans. In the Prologus to his *Expositio super constitutiones fratrum praedicatorum*[18] capitulum XIII, Utrum possimus studere in philosophia, Humbertus debates the relevance of philosophical studies to the preacher's task perspicaciously and reasonably fully.

He states the position of those opposed to the study of philosophy:

'But again it seems from this (i.e. that here it is said that we should study on account of the usefulness for souls) that the brothers ought not to study in philosophical studies, which confer little benefit to souls: but only in the Scriptures, which contribute to the edification of faith or morals, or are of value for giving salutary counsel and similar help.

My reply is: Many impugn and will impugn the catholic faith by means of philosophy, and so it is expedient for certain things to be known in the hands of philosophers so that faith may better be defended, just as it is expedient to know heresies for this purpose.'

He continues under seven more heads in his advocacy of the need for philosophy to be in the Dominican armoury: among them two shorter points:

'Item, there are many things in the divine books, as in *Job* and many others, and in the glosses, and in the writings of the saints, which can not be understood without the philosophical sciences.

Item, through these kinds of sciences the intellect is honed for the better penetration of the divine [writings].'

Humbertus' conclusion is:

'Therefore the philosophical sciences are of value for the defence of the faith, for the demolition of errors, for the understanding of the sacred scriptures, for the sharpening of the intellect, for the buttressing of faith, for the moving of hearts, for the avoidance of contempt for the Order for [its] contempt of those sciences. For these reasons they are not at all to be contemned.'[19]

This is a magisterial handling of the question. Bromyard's is a thinner treatment: but he too admits philosophy to the curriculum, though in a secondary rôle.

'It has already been stated that the principal emphasis and object of study is of the science/knowledge of achieving salvation. Now it has to be seen, first, how one may properly consider other fields of knowledge which are not of themselves immediately directed towards the salvation of the soul, such as philosophy, the civil law and suchlike: second, how, in general, we should understand holy scripture in places where it is obscure.'[20]

(Here 'scientiam de salute' is contrasted with 'alias scientias'.)

Bromyard then uses the analogy of offering hors d'oeuvres before a main course, and salt before drinks, to place the pursuit of philosophy: as an appetizer to serve theology.

'In the same way we [should offer] philosophy and other sciences so as to have a better sense of taste [discernment?] and clearer understanding in theology.'[21] He backs up his judgement with a quotation from Proverbs 1.4:

'ut detur..adolescenti scientia et intellectus.'

In his seventh section he assembles authorities berating those who make different uses of books of philosophy and secular literature.[22]

He cites Isaiah 1.22

argentum tuum versum est in scoriam

vinum tuum mixtum est aqua

enlisting Hieronymus to justify the equivalence of 'scoria' (defined by the Oxford Latin Dictionary as 'the waste obtained in smelting metals, slag') to 'rubigo' (rust).[23] He continues

'..rust: which very well conveys the meaning of the emptiness of philosophy: since, just as rust eats up metal: in the same way philosophy has now consumed the whole of theology..'

Bromyard here enters on his severest condemnation of the scholastic theology of his age in a passage which needs to be quoted at some length.

'In the same way philosophy has now consumed the whole of theology: since what are the 'quaestiones' or disputations or determinations of theologians but the empty opinions and unprofitable subtleties of the philosophers and commentators? It is not the case now of the Egyptians being robbed and the Hebrews being thereby enriched: since philosophy is not being drawn to theology but instead, on the contrary, it's theology which is being drawn to philosophy. As a result the truth of the matter is that theology, which has as its duty the clarification and application of God's commandments to [contemporary] behaviour, is being emptied of content: 'You however have made God's law null and void out of respect for your tradition': Matthew 15. As a consequence 'Thy wine is mixed with water.' To such an extent, that is, that in several schools of theology the wine of holy scripture is mixed with the water of emptiness and triviality..'[24]

He then quotes Petrus Chrysologus 'in quodam sermone':

'Nothing is more hateful than subtlety where there is nothing but subtlety: for what is the benefit of spending one's days on matters which are beneficial neither at home nor on military service nor in commerce nor in the cloister nor at court nor in church nor anywhere except in the one case – the schools?'[25]

1   The Metalogicon seems to have been somewhat of a rarity in medieval libraries: the Queens' copy the only one recorded at Cambridge: none in the lesser Benedictine libraries. Its content would not have been of interest to Bromyard: e.g. 2.13 'Quantae utilitatis sit scientia probabilium..': 3.9 'Quid sensus, et quomodo omnis philosophiae species ex ipso convalescat per imaginationem'.

2   ..ignis de excelso fulgur videlicet seu coruscatio quandoque aurum et argentum in bursa consumit sicut ostendit Albertus super librum metheororum, et bursam illesam derelinquit.. (S.2.7)

3   shháb is the singular form.

4   ..primo conditionem habent et similitudinem stellarum cadentium que in libro Metheororum assub vocantur: istis in duobus assimilantur. Primo quia videntur [for 'videtur' of text] in celo de numero esse aliarum stellarum et non sunt, sed sunt inferius in aere in superiori parte ab igne ad quem multum appropinquant inflammante.. secundo, quia sicut lumen illarum est breve, quia cito cadunt, ita gaudium hypocrite..' (I.7.1)

5   Albertus, Commentarii super libris de generatione et corruptione et [super IV libris] metheororum: a late 13th century manuscript from southern France, described in Sotheby's catalogue of Western Manuscripts and Miniatures offered for auction in London on 6 July 2006, as lot 56.

6   Boyle, Freiburg p.258.

7   ibid. p.249.

8   I read the abbreviation thus in preference to Boyle's 'scripto'.

9   Boyle, Freiburg p.265.

10   Kerr p.216.

11   Secundi dum in gracia accepta non laborant: nec expendunt ut deberent: ea pocius abutuntur: quam utuntur: sicut sunt qui intellectum occupant circa scientias et questiones inutiles qui ordinem exercent ut temporaliter vivant.. (A.24.14)

12   Quomodo illi fidem predicabunt: qui vix unquam unum verbum de christo vel fide in scolis theologie audierunt? (P.12.12)

13   The relation between philosophy and theology and the contribution the former can make to the latter (raised here by Bromyard) is explored by Gilson in his chapter on Aquinas: 'The question is often asked why a historian of philosophical doctrines should take an interest in the works of a theologian? One of the answers is that he should not, because theological speculation presupposes faith in revelation which the philosopher has not to take into account in his reasoning. Another answer is that he should, because, in the particular case of Thomas Aquinas, we are meeting a theologian so careful to distinguish between faith and reason that the philosophical elements included in his theology can be extracted from it and considered apart without undergoing any modification in nature or in content.' (Gilson p.366).

14   Secundo quantam utilitatem studium conferat scripturarum..
Sexto qualiter quis in philosophia et aliis mundi scientiis
studere et sacram scripturam debeat intelligere.
Septimo contra aliter in istis studentes faciende sunt invectiones.
(S.4.0)

15   ..alie [i.e. scientie] faciunt cognoscere vel discernere inter congruum et incongruum sicut grammatica: vel inter verum et falsum sicut logica: et sic de aliis: hec vero clarior est et ampliorem habet manifestationem: quia manifestat et cognoscere facit ipsum deum: in cuius visione vita consistit eterna. (S.4.3)

16   ..ubi alii magistri habent centum auditores: magister in theologia non habebit viginti. (S.4.4.)

Sic dici poterit illis qui quotidie disputant quomodo anima corpori infunditur vel quomodo ibi sit tanquam forma sola vel cum aliis sit corporis forma: et his similes querunt questiones: multo utilius esset discere et disputare quomodo de corporis carcere poterit ad salutem liberari.....quam scire et conferre de omnibus deo attributis et relationibus et anime condicionibus et predicto fructu carere eterne felicitatis. (S.4.4.)

18

Written, according to his editor Fr. J. J. Berthier (vol. I p.XXI), 'in ultimis auctoris annis': i.e. by 1277. Humbertus had enjoyed enormous respect in his Mastership of the Order (1254-1263).

19

Humbertus vol.II pp.42-43

20

Sed quia predictum est: quod circa scientiam de salute est principaliter insistendum et studendum Videndum est primo quomodo alias scientias licite respicere licet: que de se non ordinantur ad salutem anime directe: ut philosophiam leges et huiusmodi Secundo quomodo in generali ipsam sacram scripturam ubi obscure loquitur intelligere debeamus. (S.4.12)

21

Sic nos philosophiam et alias scientias: ut meliorem saporem et clariorem intellectum habeamus in theologia. (S.4.13)

22

Contra illos vero: qui aliter philosophorum vel litterarum secularium respiciunt libros: multe in diversis scripturarum locis invectiones sunt.. (S.4.14)

23

..rubigo: que optime significat philosophicam vanitatem: quia sicut rubigo metallum consumit: Ita iam philosophia quasi totam theologiam consumpsit.. (S.4.15)

24

Ita iam philosophia quasi totam theologiam consumpsit: quia que sunt questiones vel disputationes vel determinationes theologorum: nisi vane opiniones et inutiles philosophorum et commentatorum subtilitates? ita quod non iam spoliantur* egyptii: ut ditentur hebrei: quia non philosophia ad theologiam trahitur sed potius econverso theologia ad philosophiam trahitur. Et sic in rei veritate theologia que mandata dei ad mores declarare et trahere deberet evacuatur: vos autem irritum fecistis mandatum dei: propter traditiones vestras[†] Matth.XV. Sequitur Vinum tuum mixtum est aqua.[††] Intantum nanque in nonnullis scholis theologie vinum sacre scripture mixtum est aqua vanitatis et levitatis.. (S.4.15)

> [*] 'spoliantur egyptii' is a reference to Exodus 12.36 'et spoliaverunt Aegyptios'
> and the preceding verse 'et petierunt ab Aegyptiis vasa argentea et aurea vestemque
> plurimam.'
>
> [†] The quotation from Matthew 15 is a compressed version of verses 5 and 6. The
> plural 'traditiones vestras' for the singular of the received text (translating *ten
> paradosin* of the Greek) may reflect Bromyard's own text of Matthew or may
> indicate, together with the compression of verses 5 and 6, a quotation from memory.
>
> [††] He follows this with a second citation of Isaiah I.22

25

Odibilius nihil est subtilitate: ubi est sola subtilitas.[*] Quid enim prodest in illis expendere dies suos: qui nec domi nec militie nec in foro nec in claustro nec in curia nec in ecclesia nec alicubi prosunt: nisi dumtaxat in scholis. (S.4.15)

> [*] The double occurrence of 'subtilitas' in the Petrus Chrysologus citation reinforces
> the impact of 'commentatorum subtilitates' above. Iohannes Duns Scotus died in
> 1308: the accolade of 'doctor subtilis' bestowed on the Franciscan may well have
> been in Bromyard's mind when, c.1330, he so brusquely dismissed the proponents
> of scholasticism as both unproductive and leading to a dead end.

10

HAGIOGRAPHA

TABLE 10.1 : SAINTS WHOSE *LIVES* ARE CITED

Ambrosius Mediolanensis	2
Bartholomaeus	2
Basilius	1
Beatrix virgo	1
Bernardus	3
Dominicus O.P.	2
Eadmundus rex Angliae	1
Edmundus archiepiscopus	3
Edwardus rex Angliae	1
Furseus	1
Gangolphus	1
Germanus Altissiodorensis	3
Gregorius	11
Hieronymus	2
Iohannes Eleemosynarius	4
Iohannes evangelista	1
Leo I papa	1
Lodovicus rex Franciae	5
Lucia	1
Lupus Trecensis	1
Marcus evangelista	1
Martha	1
Maria Magdalena	1
Martinus	4
Matre dei, Historia apocrypha de	3
Nicolaus	1
Sanctorum, in aliquibus gestis	1
Sebastianus	1
Silvester	3
Stephanus	1
Thomas apostolus	1
Thomas Cantuarensis	1
Total	66
Of non-Biblical citations	1.80%

The *Vitas Patrum* might well be placed under 'Hagiographa': but seems of a genre somewhat different

The veneration Bromyard displayed in his relatively frequent citations of the Life of S.Gregorius is foreshadowed in the Prologus: '..whatever is useful [in the *Summa*] should be ascribed to the clemency of the Saviour and of the perpetual Virgin and to the auspices of the most blessed doctor Gregorius and of our father blessed Dominicus ..'[1]

His admiration for S.Ludovicus (Louis IX of France) is also strongly evident. His canonization by Bonifacius VIII in 1297 will have been remembered by the middle-aged and elderly whom Bromyard met in his travels in France. Two 'Lives' of S.Louis, as material providing evidence towards his canonization, were written by the king's confessor and his chaplain. Four other 'Lives' followed shortly after 9 August 1297 including that by queen Margaret's confessor William of St. Pathus.[2] (Only the five citations of the 'Gesta Lodovici' are counted in table 10.1. Several other stories, however, are scattered throughout the *Summa* which centre on S.Louis, all in praise of his rectitude. Some of these are examined in the later chapter on Bromyard's references to events in France.)

---

[1] quicquid vero utile salvatoris et perpetue virginis attribuatur clemencie et beatissimi doctoris Gregorii ac patris nostri beati Dominici auxiliis..

[2] Richard/Lloyd p.333.

11

CHRISTIAN WRITERS 700 – c.1080

TABLE 11.1 : TEN CHRISTIAN WRITERS 700-c.1080

A11	Ambrosius Autpertus	2
B3	Beda	15
H2	Haimo Altissiodor.	2
H7	Hrabanus Maurus	3
I 9	Iohannes Damascenus	3
I 9b	ps. Ioh. Dam. (Liber Barlaam)	9
P1	Papias	1
P3	Paulinus Aquileiensis	3
P9	Petrus Damiani	3
R1	Remigius Altissiodor.	1
Total		42
Of non-Biblical citations		1.15%

B3   Beda's European repute was founded on his commentaries on biblical books, to which he brought his knowledge of the writings of the more than a hundred authors held in the libraries at Wearmouth and Jarrow.[1] It is the church history of the English people which Bromyard cites most often (9 times): but he will also have encountered Beda's comments embedded in the *glossa ordinaria* to the Bible.

H7   Hrabanus was archbishop of Mainz 847-856. His comments too are found in the *glossa ordinaria* and were also used by Bartholomaeus Brixiensis for his apparatus on the *Decretum*.

I9b   L. J. Engels comments: 'Opinions are still divided on the identity of the author of the most widespread Greek version (oldest known manuscript, 1021). For a long time the theologian John of Damascus (c.650-750) was generally regarded as the author; however, since the early modern period the work has been ascribed to any number of others. Apart from John of Damascus, the Georgian Abbot Euthumios (d.1028) of the Iviron monastery on Mount Athos is the most serious candidate for the authorship.'[2]

---

[1]   Ward p.60.

[2]   Engels, Barlaam and Josaphat p.49.

12

HISTORICA

TABLE 12.1 : HISTORIES AND CHRONICLES

Chronica Pontificum Romanorum	1
Chronica Quaedam	6
Chronica Romanorum Imperatorum	3
Gesta Augustini Cantuariensis	1
Gesta Iuliani Apostatae	1
Gesta Saracenorum	1
Gesta Traiani Imperatoris	3
Historia Antiochena	4
Historia Gallicorum	2
Historia Inventionis Verae Crucis	1
Historia Quaedam Apocrypha	4
Historiae	4
Historiae Romanorum	3
Total	36

Fourteen of Bromyard's 36 references to *Chronica* and *Historiae* are too vague to place with certainty. His citations of the *Historia Antiochena* – the account known to us as the *Gesta Francorum et aliorum Hierosolimitanorum* – betray two major lapses which may indicate a distance in time and space from the text which modern scholars are spared. I instance his story emanating from the *Gesta Francorum* of the decisive battle of 28 June 1098 which secured Antioch and the surrounding region: which Bromyard assigns to the siege of Jerusalem. He follows a citation of 2 Maccabees 10 and 11 (the heavenly assistance of 'viri quinque in equis frenis aureis decori' for Judas Maccabaeus) with this:

'A similar event is recorded in the *Historia Antiochena* in the siege of Jerusalem by the Christian army when they had slipped back after their assault and as if in despair were retreating. Suddenly there appeared, in noble apparel, a knight brandishing, it seemed, the arms of saint George and drove all to return to the onslaught. And on that very day the city was taken, in defiance of the Muslims.'[1]

Antioch had already been captured, on the third of June, as recorded in the *Gesta*.[2] Bromyard also omits S.George's comrades SS.Mercurius and Demetrius, and the innumerable battalions they led.[3] It is strange too that he does not conflate this success with the discovery of the lance with which Christ was wounded.[4] All in all it is clear that Bromyard is much more interested in drawing conclusions which may be exploited for the making of moral judgements than in presenting a historical narrative. He also chooses to simplify his memory of the account in the *Gesta*: one example of this being his use of *saraceni* for the forces opposing the crusaders, whereas the *Gesta* distinguishes between the [Seljuk] Turks[5] and the Arabs.

Bromyard sees the eventual loss of the Holy Land as stemming from early discord within Christian ranks:

'What destroyed the Christian army in the Holy Land when Jerusalem was captured by Godfrey of Bouillon duke of Brabant and other leaders and nobles of France but the quarrel which arose out of the desire and lust of domination among the clergy over the army and soldiery [knights?] as is openly stated in the *Historia Antiochena*?'[6]

The treachery to which Bromyard assigns the utter defeat of the Christian army at the Horns of Hattin on 4 July 1187 (and the capture of Jerusalem by Saleh ed-Din's troops on 2 October) probably derives from the breakthrough of the knights commanded by Raymond of Tripoli, Balian of Ibelin and Reynald of Sidon. The unwise decision of Guy de Lusignan to abandon the well-watered defences of Sepphoris did not present itself to Bromyard as an explanation for the catastrophe.[7]

The *Historia Gallicorum* cited here *may* be the French translation, with a continuation, of William of Tyre's history known as the *Estoire d'Eracles*.[8]

'What destroyed the Christian army in that land in the time of Guy [de Lusignan] but betrayal, as the *Historia Gallicorum* relates? Because, that is, certain great men from [that] land were unwilling for Guy to reign over them they despatched an embassy to the Sultan stating 'We do not want this man to rule over us'. This was [done] covertly, however: they pretended they wanted to be on Guy's side, but in the war they turned against him.'[9]

He links these moral delinquencies (cupiditate, libidine dominandi: proditio:) with two major vices, superbia and invidia, in his reference – in this same passage – to the Third Crusade, led in its latter stages by Richard I and Philippe II.

'What destroyed the Christian army in the time of Richard in the Holy Land but pride and jealousy? Since each king wanted to ascribe the victory to himself.'[10]

A further reference to the eastern crusades shows Bromyard's willingness to puncture the braggadocio of certain Christians. (Interestingly he chooses to lead on to Peter's[11] failure of nerve in the High Priest's cold courtyard.)

'In the same way [as the timorous house-martin] sitting and lolling in their homelands they boast that they want to kill loads of Muslims and do wonderful things. They say 'They're dogs: one Christian against twenty of those dogs!' But when they've come to the point they're afraid of a paltry charge*. Just like Peter: all prepared: saying he would go to the death with Christ: but at a paltry charge*, i.e. the challenge of a maid-servant, he denied Him.'[12]

The *Gesta Saracenorum* is cited once only in the *Summa*, and that for a remarkable passage for knowledge of which Bromyard may be indebted ultimately to reports brought back to Europe by returning crusaders.

'Assassins is the popular name for a secret order of the Ismailite sect of Muslims. The order was founded in the late 11th century, in Persia, by Hasan ibn-al-Sabbah. In 1090, Hasan seized the fortress of Alamut, near Kazvin, Persia, to use as a base for his operations. His followers supposedly were aroused by use of the drug hashish to commit murder in the name of religion.. Crusaders in the 1100's encountered the order in the Holy Land..'[13] A different explanation for the use of hashish is offered by Bernard Lewis: '..the sectaries were believed to use [it] in order to induce ecstatic visions of paradise and thereby fortify themselves to face martyrdom.' He adds: 'The stories told by Marco Polo' [who returned to Venice in 1295] 'and other eastern and western sources of the "gardens of paradise" into which the drugged devotees were introduced to receive a foretaste of the eternal bliss that awaited them after the successful completion of their missions are not confirmed by any known Ismāᶜīlite source.'

Bromyard places his account in AVARICIA, as one of his 1217 *exempla*. He uses the story to illustrate the folly of men greedy for rewards available to them, after their unlawful killings, in an afterlife promised them by their unscrupulous manipulators.

'And so..wretched fools are duped. Like those of whom one reads in certain books of *Deeds of the Saracens* where [this story] is contained. A certain powerful Muslim created a luxurious garden full of a multiplicity of delights. He arranged for strong young men to be carried into the garden, practically sedated and by means of certain potions in a condition resembling drunkenness. Whenever they awoke and asked where they were they were told they were in paradise – which Muhammad in the Quran promises to his loyal followers – a place, that is, of bliss, full to the brim of bodily delights where abound fountains of olive oil, honey and wine: [paradise] which he mendaciously promises them: and when they yearned to be there for ever they were assured that if they wanted to be there for ever they should go and kill such and such a man: they would carry out any atrocity (it was for this, after all, that he'd put them there): and that they were not to fear death – that was their gateway to arrive at that everlasting place [paradise]..'[14]

The *Chronica Romanorum Imperatorum* has as its subject the Holy Roman emperors: Conrad IV (1250-1254) and his boyhood promise of a bishopric – in return for the present gratification of a silver [musical] pipe – makes for an *exemplum* in the capitulum SYMONIA.[15]

The defeat by the Christian emperor Theodosius I of the pagan Eugenius and the *magister militum* Arbogastes in September 394 dates the subject-matter of the *Historiae Romanorum*: Bromyard may have accessed this source in any later epitome.[16]

---

[1] Simile etiam habetur in hystoria antiochena in obsidione ierusalem ab exercitu christianorum cum essent lapsi de insultu quem fecerant et quasi desperati recederent: subito apparuit quidam* eques in nobili apparatu habens quasi arma sancti Georgii et omnes ad insultum redire fecit. Et eodem die capta fuit civitas contra saracenos. (B.2.41)
    *for 'quidem' of text.

[2] Haec omnia gesta sunt tertia die intrante mense Iunio.. Nullus vero poterat ire per semitam civitatis, nisi super cadauera mortuorum. (p.48)

[3] Exibant quoque de montaneis innumerabiles exercitus...cuius ductores fuerunt sancti, Georgius, Mercurius et Demetrius. (p.69)

[4] pp.59, 60. He chooses instead to use the episode to illustrate how God especially helps those who fight against infidels.
    'Idem [sc. God's help] apparet ex hystoria anthiochena in qua continetur quod cum essent circa sexaginta milia saracenorum in obsidione civitatis anthiochie et circa decem cristianorum infra civitatem obsessam, et multi vellent civitatem reddere. Consilio episcopi portantis lanceam qua cristus in cruce perforatus erat exierunt et voce terribili in aere audita omnes infideles in fugam conversi sunt.' (C.17.6)
    (When some 60,000 Muslims were besieging Antioch, with about 10,000 Christians inside the city, many of whom wanted to surrender it 'by the advice of the bishop who brandished the spear with which Christ on the cross has been run through they made a sortie and, as a fearsome cry was heard from the sky, all the infidels turned in flight.')

[5] The Turks had captured Antioch in 1085. See 'Warfare' p.89 for details of the campaign of 1097-98.

6   Quid destruxit exercitum cristianorum in terra sancta quando capta fuit ierusalem a godefrido de boylando duce brabancie et aliis proceribus et nobilibus francie nisi briga orta ex cupiditate et libidine dominandi inter clerum de exercitu et milicia sicut expresse in hystoria continetur antiochena? (B.2.50).

7   Runciman vol.II pp.448-460: Atlas pp.60-61.

8   Runciman vol.II p.477 (The *Estoire* would then be the sole source for Bromyard written in French.)

9   Quid destruxit exercitum christianorum in terra illa tempore regis guidonis nisi proditio: secundum quod gallicorum narrat hystoria: quia videlicet aliqui magni de terra noluerunt guidonem super eos regnare miserunt legationem ad soldanum dicentes: Nolumus hunc regnare super nos: occulte tamen simulantes se velle esse ex parte guidonis: sed in bello verterunt se contra eum. (B.2.50).

10   Quid destruxit exercitum cristianorum tempore regis Richardi in terra sancta nisi superbia et invidia: quia uterque‡ rex voluit sibi ascribere victoriam. (B.2.50).
       ‡for 'ubique' of text.

11   Nowhere in the *Summa* does Bromyard accord Peter the honorific 'sanctus'.

12   Ita multi in terra sua sedentes et iacentes iactant se velle multos saracenos occidere et mirabilia facere, dicentes canes sunt: unus cristianus contra viginti de canibus illis: sed cum ad punctum venerint timent parvum insultum. Sicut Petrus paratus fuit et dixit se cum cristo in mortem ire: quem tamen ad parvum insultum id est ad vocem ancille negavit. (C.17.12).
       *I seize upon the ambiguity of 'charge' (a military onslaught *or* an accusation) as a way of resolving my doubt over Bromyard's meaning in his use of 'insultus'. In classical Latin 'insultare' may mean 'to mock': and in medieval Latin 'insultus' often means a military attack.

13   Encyclopedia Americana vol.2 p.524. Lewis pp.108-109.

14   Et sic patet quod in omnibus fortunis miseri decipiuntur. Sicut illi de quibus legitur in quibusdam libris de gestis saracenorum. Ubi continetur quod quidam magnus saracenus fecit ortum delicatum ubi erant multe delicie et fortes iuvenes quasi soporatos et quibusdam potibus quasi inebriatos fecit portari in ortum illum. et cum evigilarent et quererent ubi essent: dictum fuit eis quod essent in paradiso quem machometus in alcorano suis fidelibus promittit: locum videlicet amenum deliciis corporalibus plenum: ubi sunt fontes olei mellis et vini: quem eis mendaciter promittit et cum desiderabant ibi semper esse dictum fuit ab eis: quod si semper vellent ibi esse quod irent et talem et talem ociderent: †aliquod maleficium facerent propter hoc enim eos ibi posuit et quod mortem non timerent per quam ad illum locum sempiternum venirent.. (A.27.63)
       †I suspect the omission of 'et'.

15   S.9.9.

16   C.17.18.

13

MUSLIM WRITERS

TABLE 13.1 : MUSLIM WRITERS

A5	Albumasar	1
A8	Alfarabius	1
A21	Averroes	1
A22	Avicenna	5
M5	Muhammad	5
	Total	13

A5 Albumasar is cited in NATIVITAS: 'the tide is at its strongest at the conjunction of the sun with the moon.' The quotation is unreferenced but may well come from his *Liber de magnis coniunctionibus*: probably through the mediation of Albertus Magnus who frequently cites the Turkestani astronomer.[1]

A8 On the proposition that happiness may be achieved by way of self-knowledge – he has just quoted, from the *Policraticus*, the Delphic oracle's 'know thyself' – he cites Alfarabius, allegedly quoting Plato: 'Philosophia est tedium et cura et studium et sollicitudo mortis.' Bromyard goes on to comment 'By disquiet over death he means the mortification of vices, depraved desires and carnal pleasures'[2]: which seems to stretch the Turkic philosopher's aphorism rather far. Alfarabius too is often cited by Albertus.

A21 Averroes is cited as 'the commentator on Aristoteles' rather than by name and solely for the anecdote of the Greek polymath dissuading his students from the lure of feminine beauty.[3] His commentary had been translated by Michael Scot before 1250.

Bromyard gives general, not specific, references to his first two sources and none to the third: which, together with the extreme rarity of these citations, strongly suggests that he encountered them either in some compilation, or through Albertus Magnus.

A22 Avicenna (Ibn Sina) was born in Bukhara and wrote in both Arabic and his native Persian/Farsi. His most influential work, the *Canon Medicinae*, was not germane to Bromyard's purposes: unless it is from this that his unreferenced citation comes, in the capitulum GULA:

> 'And according to Avicenna more people die by food [food poisoning? overeating?] than by the sword.'[4]

Civil society and the protection of the citizen by the government cannot exist, Bromyard argues (C.4.10, 11), without a body of laws and sound doctrine to instruct/influence those who conform and coerce those who dissent.[5] It is in this context he has recourse to Avicenna's support:

'There should exist no one in the State of use who is not able to hold some respectable status, and from each individual there should proceed some service to society. And so (according to Avicenna) the legislator should forbid inactivity and idling. There should be no lack of obedience. Those who refuse to be so bound should be deported: it is because of such laziness that estates come to be sold up. He [the legislator] should also ban the presence in the State of gamesters and gamblers, ban too pursuits and undertakings contrary to the interests of the State such as theft, kidnapping [extortion? abduction?] and fornication.'[6]

In the capitulum LUDUS, at L.6.2, he directs his readers back to this passage.

He quotes from Avicenna's tract *De venenis* at I.6.6. to the effect that snakes inhabiting woodlands have deadlier poisons than those of the meadowland snakes.

M5   Although I have grouped together these five Muslims this may well be a categorization which would not have occurred to Bromyard to make. Albumasar, Alfarabius, Averroes and Avicenna are undoubtedly perceived as comfortably belonging to the fellowship of international scholarship.[7] Muhammad, however, is inextricably bound up with the core text of Islam, the Quran, and Bromyard's stance vis-à-vis both the text (to whatever degree of immediacy or mediation he accesses it) and the beliefs and practices of a competitor religion will, therefore, be briefly scrutinized as a whole in chapter 26.

---

[1]   fluxus maris est fortissimus: in coniunctione solis cum luna. (N.1.9)
His *De Magnis coniunctionibus* is catalogued by Thorndike and Kibre (615, 1172, 1402-3, 1581) and survived to be printed in Augsburg, 31 March 1489 (Hain *611) with woodcuts.

[2]   per sollicitudinem mortis volens intelligere mortificationem vitiorum: et pravorum desideriorum et carnalium voluptatum. (S.3.5)

[3]   P.14.2.

[4]   Et teste avicenna plures moriuntur cibo quam gladio. (G.5.22)

[5]   Sed quia iste conditiones predicte congrue haberi non possunt sine legibus et statutis et sana doctrina: que volentes informent nolentes coerceant. (C.4.11)

[6]   ..nullus sit in civitate utilis qui non habeat aliquem statum laudabilem et ab unoquoque proveniat aliqua utilitas civitati. Et ideo inquit prohibeat legislator ociositatem et vacationem nec sit aliquis qui non obediat alicui: qui autem compesci nolunt expellendi sunt extra civitatem: propter enim talia ocia venduntur hereditates. Prohibeat etiam inquit quod non sit in civitate luctator vel aleator: prohibeat etiam studia et opera contraria utilitatibus civitatis sicut furtum rapinam fornicationem. (C.4.11, 12)

This widely held perception is given expression by Dante, who places Avicenna and Averroes amid the host of virtuous non-Christians

genti di molto valore
Conobbi, che in quel limbo eran sospesi
(Inferno 4.44, 45)

who included Lucretia, Saleh ad-Din, Cicero, Seneca and Hippokrates. Their abode is the first circle of Hell, where Dante finds the souls of those who have lived upright lives but have not been baptized.

Moran Cruz also fastens on a divergence between what she discerns as intolerant attitudes and restrictive practices towards Muslims within Christian territories and 'the degree of toleration western intellectuals extended to Arabic writings, commentaries, and translations.' (p.67)

14

LIVES OF NON-CANONIZED

TABLE 14.1 : FOUR LIVES

Alexander III papa	1
Fratres mendicantes	2
Hugo de S.Victore	2
Karolus magnus	4
Total	9

The authorship of the *Vitae fratrum* is assigned in the bibliographies to Gerardus de Fracheto O.P. (1205-1271). However, in his 2001 study[1] Tugwell reveals the part played by Humbertus de Romanis in the complicated evolution of this text from Gerardus' first draft, compiled between c.1247 to 1252, to the non-completed edition undertaken by Humbertus, supplemented by additions made at the general chapter of 1260 at Strassburg. There never existed a definitive version[2]: Bromyard may have used any of several texts from different stages of its composition.

Charlemagne is accorded great reverence by Bromyard: for instance, he is styled 'sanctissimus imperator.'[3] He is also linked with the Roland of the battle of Roncevaux ('gesta de Karolo et Rolando.')[4] Although he is not admitted to the Martyrologium Romanum of 1757 of Benedictus XIV there is a strong tradition of his saintliness to which Bromyard clearly subscribes. Dr H.van Dijk sees the *Historia Karoli Magni et Rotholandi*, written in France as early as the first half of the 12th century, as the basis for the *Vita Sancti Karoli*, compiled in 1165 "when the great emperor was canonized."[5] This event led to the inclusion of a chapter on Charlemagne in the *Legenda sanctorum* of c.1270: not *in* the book but *of* the book: Johann Zainer's Ulm edition of not after 1478 follows its 177 entries with 'Finiunt capitula super librum de legendis sanctorum feliciter': then 'Sequuntur festivitates et legende adiuncte post historie lombardice finem' in which the 13th of 16 entries is 'De historia Karoli magni', an account of some 2,500 words[6].

Praising those rulers who chose learned and wise men as their advisers Bromyard finds exemplars among the pagans of Nero, whose mentor was Seneca, and Traianus, who had Ploutarchos. Among the Christians it is only Charlemagne he instances, whose realm benefited by his selection of Alcuin of York and Petrus the Spaniard as his teachers.[7]

In the National Gallery, London, picture 4092 in the numeration of the Illustrated General Catalogue of 1973 is titled Charlemagne, and the Meeting of SS.Joachim and Anne at the Golden Gate, which depicts the instant of the Immaculate Conception of the BVM. The authors of this catalogue observe of Charlemagne: 'He was never canonized but often appears in art treated as a saint.' (They attribute the painting to the Studio of the Master of Moulins, dating it shortly after 1500[8]: others date it slightly before 1500 and are content to assign it to 'The Master of Moulins.')[9]

[1]   Tugwell pp.415-418.

[2]   ibid. p.417: '..il n'a jamais existé aucun texte definitif.. Ce que l'on trouve dans les manuscrits de la tradition <<vulgate>>, à part la contribution, consciente ou non, des copistes, est un mélange de plusieurs tentatives de rédaction et des suggestions, des corrections et des commentaires proposés par les lecteurs auxquels Humbert avait confié le texte.'

[3]   B.2.23.

[4]   F.4.23.

[5]   Van Dijk p.75.

[6]   Goff J-91.

[7]   In christianis patet in karolo magno qui in theologia doctorem habuit albinum cognomento alquinum: in grammatica dialectica et astrologia petrum hispanum: Unde tunc respublice bene gubernabantur quando doctos habuerunt rectores. (S.4.12).

[8]   National Gallery p.440.

[9]   Longmuir & Lynton p.481.

15

FEUDAL LAW

TABLE 15.1 : FEUDAL LAW CITATIONS

Libri Feudorum	4
glossa in libros feudorum	5
Total	9

In the Middle Age this compilation was attributed to he shadowy figures of either Gerardus Niger or Obertus de Horto, according to GW 7751.

Book I begins abruptly with Titulus I:

'De his qui feudum dare possunt et qui non: et qualiter acquiratur et retineatur.' [Of those who can grant a fief and who cannot: and in what manner it may be acquired and retained.] It contains 28 tituli.

Book II begins with the address of Obertus de Horto. 'Of the court-cases whose cognizance is frequently committed to us, some are determined by Roman law, others by the laws of the Lombards, others yet according to the custom of the kingdom..' is his exordium to Titulus I.[1] He adds 'The authority of the Roman laws is not to be despised: but it does not extend its force to such a degree as to overcome use or inherited practice.'[2] The 58 tituli run to three times the length of Book I.

Brundage well observes that multiple legal systems coexisted and overlapped within the same town or region, each with its own complex rules and conventions as well as its own system of courts that applied them.[3] In his chapter 'IUDICIUM DIVINUM' Bromyard comments: '..there has never been a people so uncivilized as not to punish the wicked and reward the upright. For this is the purpose of the laws of kings and emperors, the decrees of the popes, the canons of the Fathers, the statutes of States, the customs of the regions.'[4]

Bromyard nowhere cites the Libri Feudorum by name. Four times, however, he cites Collatio.x. of the Authentica (G.4.21, P.4.25 (bis), R.4.14): e.g.

'in autentica[5] quibus modis feodum amittitur. col.x.§.i.ibi enim habetur quod vasallus propter ingratitudinem amittit feodum'.[6]

Now there are only nine collationes in the Authentica/Novellae. The tituli which Bromyard cites are actually in the Libri Feudorum. The Libri Feudorum, then, in some usage – to which Bromyard subscribes – is the tenth Collatio.

The Lyon printing (GW 7770) of Iustinianus contains these texts:
1. Authentica/Novellae Constitutiones
2. Codicis libri X-XII
3. Libri II Feudorum
4. Extravagantes duae Henrici Septimi [Holy Roman Emperor 1308-1313: crowned 1312] 'quas nonnulli. xi. collationem appellant.'

The York Minster Library copy[7] of GW 7770 is bound after the *Institutiones* of Iustinianus (GW 7622): this combination is known as the *Parvum Volumen*: Hereford Cathedral's P.VIII.8 is such a book, although it lacks the *Extravagantes.*

The multiplicity of legal systems and traditions of law each jostling for influence in Bromyard's England, together with their potential for conflict, is acknowledged in at least three passages in the *Summa.*

'However, sons of a concubine do not succeed in their paternal inheritance unless they are legitimized. However, one method of legitimizing according to the laws is that the man accept for his wife the woman who previously was his concubine, as is clear from the canon law[8].. and in the civil law[9].. although the custom of England is opposed [to this].'

On this very clash Maitland writes, referring to the Statute of Merton of 1236: 'Among its other noticeable clauses, we come across the famous declaration of the barons that they will not change the laws of England. They have been asked by the clergy to consent that children born before the marriage of their parents should be deemed legitimate:- their reply is '*Nolumus leges angliae mutare*'.'[10]

The large temporal claims asserted by Innocentius III as against the powers of the Emperor were maintained by Gregorius IX and Innocentius IV in their contention with Frederick II. A memory of this may underlie Bromyard's observation at X.I.3, which is difficult to divorce from a contemporary application to the deposition of Edward II in 1326/27. The first part of the charge, however, 'negligence in extirpating heresy', *may* be a suppressed reference to the crusade bulls launched by Iohannes XXII at the end of 1321 (reaching their targets in early 1322) against Matteo Visconti in Milan and the Estensi in Ferrara.[11] The passage reads:

'..if a negligent prince or king on account of his negligence in extirpating heresy or also whensoever [he be] useless and dissolute and negligent vis- à-vis his kingdom and the observing of justice will be able to be deposed from the kingdom he acquired by the vicar of Christ on earth.. a fortiori Christ will be able to depose and will depose those [who are] negligent in spiritual governance..'[12]

Maitland comments: 'The idea current in the thirteenth century is not so much that of a power to try your king and punish him, as that of a right of revolt, a right to make war upon your king. It is a feudal idea and a dangerous one; the vassal who cannot get justice out of his lord may renounce his fealty and his homage..'[13]

'Quod principi placuit legis habet vigorem.' This opinion of Ulpianus[14] represents an extreme position which received later modification in the late fourth century under the names of Theodosius I and Valentinianus II. They are quoted by Bromyard in support of his own stance. They state:

'It is an utterance worthy of the majesty of the Ruler that the Prince profess himself bound by the laws..'[15]

Buttressed by this imperial declaration Bromyard roundly declares: 'From which it is patent that all empires and kingdoms and emperors and kings should be governed by *laws* and not by *use* or *personal whim*.'[16] This too could not have been written – or read – without the rule of Edward II being in the writer's, and reader's, mind.

1 Causarum, quarum cognitio frequenter nobis committitur, aliae dirimuntur iure Romano: aliae legibus Longobardorum, aliae autem secundum regni consuetudinem.. (CIC p.729)

2 Legum autem Romanarum non est vilis authoritas: sed non adeo vim suam extendunt ut usum vincant aut mores. (ibid. p.729).

3 Brundage MCL p.2. Maitland (pp.105-106) lists five kinds: (1) the shire and hundred courts (2) the feudal courts (3) the king's own central courts (4) the courts held by the king's itinerant justices (5) the ecclesiastical courts.

4 ..nunquam fuerat gens tam barbara que non puniret malos et premiaret bonos. Ad hoc enim sunt leges regum et principum, decreta pontificum, canones patrum, statuta civitatum, consuetudines regionum. (I.11.15) The 'consuetudines' include feudal law.

5 Bromyard treats 'Authentica' as a fem sg., whereas it should be neut. pl. It is also styled 'Authenticum'. Brundage writes (p.204): 'The *Novellae leges* consist of 168 laws promulgated between 535 and 545 and collected during the reign of Tiberius II (578-82).. Medieval lawyers in the West cited the *Novels* from another collection, the *Authenticum* or *Liber authenticorum*. This collection comprises 134 of the *Novellae leges*.. presented in a Latin translation. From the eleventh century, Western glossators were accustomed to use a version of the *Authenticum* in which 96 of the *Novellae* were grouped into nine *collationes*..'

6 In the Authentica, in which ways a fief is lost: collatio x § i.: for there it is stated that a vassal on account of ingratitude loses the fief. (Liber feudorum II titulus xxiii: CIC p.733).

7 Inc. XV.A.14(2).

8 ..filii autem concubine in paterna non succedunt hereditate nisi legitimentur. Unus autem modus legitimandi secundum iura est quod vir accipiat in uxorem illam que prius erat concubina: sicut patet de iure canonico extra libro iiii titulo qui filii sint legitimi capitulo tanta. (S.13.3)

9 Et in iure civili in Autenticis quibus modis naturales filii efficiantur legitimi collatione vi circa principium [Auth. Coll. VI Tit. iii cap. i] licet consuetudo anglie sit contraria. (S.13.3)

10 Maitland p.16.

11 The lengthy campaigns proclaimed by Innocentius III against the Cathars in 1208 directed at three temporal lords (Raymond Roger of Trencavel, Raymond VI and his son Raymond VII) might seem suitable examples to cite: but Bromyard does not refer to these in the *Summa*. He *does* treat of the crusades against Milan and Ferrara at L.7.10 The omission here in X.1.3 of any reference to Matteo Visconti and the Este family *may* be an indication that the capitulum XI XPISTUS was written *before* 1322 (whereas L7 must have been written in or after 1322). A contrary reading which sees a reference here to Edward II would date the passage to 1327 or later. (For Milan and Ferrara see Housley pp.26-27).

12 ..si princeps seu rex negligens propter suam negligentiam contra heresim extirpandam vel etiam quandocumque inutilis et dissolutus et negligens contra regnum et iusticiam observandam de regno adepto deponi poterit per christi vicarium in terris... A fortiori ratione christus deponere poterit et deponet negligentes in regimine spirituali.. (X.1.3)

13 Maitland p.103.

14 Digesta I.4.1. Ulpianus (d.223) provided over 40% of the material used for the Digesta (Honoré p.493).

15   Digna vox est maiestate Regnantis legibus alligatum se Principem profiteri: adeo de auctoritate iuris nostra pendet auctoritas.. (Codicis Liber I.14.4).

16   Ex quibus patet quod omnia imperia et regna et imperatores et reges legibus et non ab usu vel propria voluntate deberent gubernari. (X.1.9)

16

ENGLISH LAW

TABLE 16.1 : ENGLISH LAW

Breve Regis	2
Magna Carta	1
Total	3

The writ is known as 'Tarde venit': but under which king it was issued I cannot say. Bromyard cites this writ under ORDO CLERICALIS[1] and PENITENTIA where he writes:

> per breve regis: quod vocatur: Tarde venit. Que quidem veniendi mora
> sicut facit multos in curiis regum causas suas: et res de quibus agitur:
> amittere. Ita etiam in curia dei.[2] (By a royal writ titled 'Tarde venit'.
> Just as this delay in attending causes many to lose in the kings' courts
> both their cases and the matters being raised, so also in God's court.)

From the context the writ seems to pertain to court cases. Perhaps not all such writs were recorded. Prestwich notes that writs of summons to parliaments and councils were rarely enrolled and that there are few records of proceedings that survive.[3]

In NOBILITAS we read:

> ..in nova charta latam. In qua continentur quod wardam cum disperagio maritare
> non debent.[4]

This corresponds with clause 6 of the Great Charter of Henry III (3rd revision, issued 11 Feb. 1225):

> Heredes maritentur absque disparagatione. (Heirs are to be married without
> disparagement).

Presumably it will have been the confirmation of 1300 that Bromyard saw. Powicke writes: 'The royal charter of liberties, well and clearly written, was to be affixed in a public place within every cathedral and collegiate church and a new copy was to be substituted for the existing copy at the end of the year on the vigil of Easter.'[5]

---

[1] O.6.75.

[2] P.7.51.

[3] Prestwich p.441.

[4] N.3.16.

[5] Powicke p.473.

17

JEWISH WRITERS (EXCLUDING THE HEBREW BIBLE AND NT)

TABLE 17.1 : JEWISH WRITERS

I 14	Iosephus	
I 15	Isaac Iudaeus	1
S6	LXX	1
T1	Talmud	1
TOTAL		3

I 14 Iosephus is named 4 or 5 times (e.g. at F.5.21): but it is clear that Bromyard's knowledge of his work derives from Petrus Comestor's *Historia scholastica*: 'exemplo Iohannis hircani: de quo verba recitantur Iosephi in fine hystorie. i.Mach.i.quod Ptholomeum...'

I 15 In SAPIENTIA Bromyard observes:
..The height of philosophy is to know oneself, since, as Isaac remarks in his *De definitionibus* philosophy is self-knowledge.[1]
Isaac's essay was written in Arabic and translated into Latin by Gerardus of Cremona in Toledo and earlier by Constantinus Africanus (c.1015-1087). Thorndike and Kibre (233, 1054, 1159) list surviving manuscripts.

S6 In REGIMEN we read:
..through the example of [Ptolemaios II] Philadelphos king of Egypt, of whom the Master [Petrus Comestor] relates in the *Historia scholastica* that although he had twenty thousand books, on the advice of Demetrios the curator of his library he sent a message to the Jews in order to acquire the Law of God and translators to translate it. We call them the Seventy Interpreters [the Septuagint].[2]

T1 In the capitulum ORDO CLERICALIS:
..in the Talmud of the Jews it is written, and by them believed, that a corpse sprinkled even with a tiny handful of sacred earth brought from the Holy Land will not rot.[3]
One source of this reference to the Talmud may have been either the writings or the oral tradition emanating from Jewish converts to Christianity such as Nicholas Donin[4], in Paris in 1240, and Paul the Christian. Paul joined the Dominicans and it was he who engaged in debate with Moses ben Nahman[5] in the Barcelona disputation of 1263, of which accounts survive, in Hebrew and in Latin[6].
Ramon Martí (d.1285/90), after graduating from one of the language academies, produced his *Dagger of Faith*,[7] 'a massive study of the Jewish texts, in which he sought to distinguish what he regarded as the 'true' and the 'false' traditions of the Jews, talking

of certain traditions he had found in the Talmud and other books..'[8] Abulafia writes of the extraordinary care he had taken to study his texts, ensuring accuracy in his translations.

The apparently neutral observation at O.6.76 is preceded, however, by references to the gap between appearance and reality in quotations adapted from I Maccabees 6.43-46,[9] 3 Kings 22.30[10], Philippians 2.6-7[11]: interspersed with a cross-reference to S.1.5 which treats of the significance borne by difference in clothing: and Leviticus 10. 1-2[12]. Mixed in with these is also an allusion to the fable of the wolf in sheep's clothing[13]:

'and after he has been captured his garments and his sacred ornaments will no more save him from damnation/condemnation than the holy earth/land [will save] the Jews from corruption or than their holy vestments [saved] their priests Nadab and Abiu from combustion.[14] For in the Talmud of the Jews it is written, and by them believed, that a corpse sprinkled even with a tiny handful of sacred earth brought from the Holy Land will not rot.' (O.6.76)

All five of these extracts used by Bromyard end with deaths, albeit of different natures. Even without a direct contradiction of the belief he ascribes to an unnamed tractate of the Talmud his rejection of the conviction is clear. (He also links the Nadab/Abiu account to a denunciation of those in holy orders who, 'in place of the divine fire, i.e. charity, devotion, and divine love which should ever burn on the altar of the heart...place an alien fire, that is of greed, carnality and such kind of hellish fire of sinners..')[15]

This citing of the Talmud is tantalizing by its brevity and uniqueness. Was Bromyard aware that in 1299 Philip IV ordered the extermination of copies of the Talmud: and that in 1309 three cartloads of Jewish books – among which must have been many copies of the Talmud – were burned in Paris? Grayzel quotes from a letter of Iohannes XXII to the archbishop of Bourges (some 125 miles due south of Paris, on the Loire), dated 4 September 1320 from Avignon. 'You are to see to it that as a complete collection should be handed over to you the law or the foresaid book which they call the Talmud and all other of their books with their additions and commentaries/scholia' for examination by the archbishop and by some Franciscans and Dominicans and other theologians. Any books found to contain blasphemies, errors, falsehoods and curses were to be burned.[16]

---

[1] Summa ergo philosophia est seipsum cognoscere: quia ut ait Isaac de diffinitionibus. Philosophia est cognitio suiipsius. (S.3.5)

[2] ...per exemplum Philadelphi regis egypti: de quo recitat magister in historia scholastica: quod licet haberet virginti milia librorum: de consilio tamen demetri prefecti bibliothece sue misit ad iudeos ad habendum legem dei et translatores: qui eam transferrent: quos nos vocamus septuaginta interpretes. (R.4.6)

[3] ..in iudeorum namque talmuth scribitur et ab eis creditur quod corpus mortuum et aliqua portiuncula terre sancte de terra sancta portata aspersum non putrescet. (O.6.76.)

[4] Donin helped focus Christian attention on the Talmud, parts of whose contents he had made known. (Abulafia p.91).

[5] A substantial figure, whose commentary on the Pentateuch was sufficiently esteemed to survive into the printing age: his Perush ha-Tora was printed in Rome [1469-72], Lisbon 1489 (302 leaves, folio) and Naples 1490 [Goff Heb-86 to 88, Oates 4222].

[6] Abulafia 93-94, 102: Grayzel pp.9-11.

[7] A possible debased offspring of this may be the slight work *Obiectiones in dicta Talmut seductoris iudeorum* (Hain *15229 to 15234), whose tenor may be gauged by its final lines

Cum ergo iudei sepissime peccata grandia et maxima commiserint per idolatriam et cetera multa et tamen nunquam tam acriter passi sunt ergo patet quod grande peccatum commiserunt quod christum verum regem occiderunt etc.

Since therefore the Jews have very frequently committed huge and enormous sins through idolatry and many other things, and yet have never suffered so bitterly [as Christ] it is therefore evident that they committed an enormous sin in that they slew Christ/the Messiah, the true king, etc.

[8] Abulafia p.94.

[9] et vidit Eleazar filius Saura unam de bestiis loricatam loricis regis...et ivit sub pedes elefanti.. et occidit eum et cecidit in terram super ipsum et mortuus est illic..
(Bromyard has 'bestia loricata loricis regis').

[10] porro rex Israhel mutavit habitum et ingressus est bellum..
(Bromyard has 'Achab malus in armis alienis': Ahab, despite his change of clothes to render himself less conspicuous, is killed by a man who 'drew a bow at a venture').

[11] qui cum in forma Dei esset .. semet ipsum exinanivit formam servi accipiens .. et habitu inventus ut homo..

[12] arreptisque Nadab et Abiu filii Aaron turibulis posuerunt ignem et incensum desuper offerentes coram Domino ignem alienum quod eis praeceptum non erat egressusque ignis a Domino devoravit eos et mortui sunt coram Domino..

[13] Et lupus timore ad ovile fugiens ovium pelle indutus ovina.. (Number 376 in Halm's Teubner edition of 1852 of the fables: the wolf's disguise led to his death).

[14] Quo deprehenso non plus salvabunt eum vestimenta et ornamenta sancta a damnatione quam iudeos terra sancta a corruptione vel quam sacerdotes illorum Nadab et Abiu. Levit.x. vestes sancte a combustione. (O.6.76)

[15] ... loco ignis divini.i.caritatis, devotionis et divini amoris qui in altari cordis semper ardere deberet...ignem imponunt alienum: scilicet cupiditatis carnalitatis et huiusmodi ignem peccatorum infernalem.. (O.6.76)

[16] ..legem seu librum quem talmutz predictum [for Grayzel's 'predicitur'] vocant omnesque alios ipsorum libros cum additionibus et expositionibus eorundem faciatis vobis integraliter assignari.. (Grayzel pp.316-319).

18

ROMANCIAE[1]

TABLE 18.1 : ROMANCE

Gesta Romanorum	3
Total	3

Bromyard cites the *Gesta Romanorum* at A.27.59, F.1.33 and P.3.37: but clearly from a compilation different from our familiar and popular collection[2] as none of his citations accords with any of the tales in the copy I read, the Paris edition of 1503.[3] He *does* retail as an *exemplum* story XXIX of the Paris edition, the account of a judge compelled to dispense justice from a seat covered with the skin of a corrupt judge, his own father,[4] but he does not source this from the *Gesta*.

Although Bromyard makes free use of moral tales and fables he sternly sets his face against the incorporation of romances into the curricula for the education of princes. 'A king should study or listen to the laws of God and *not* to romances, fables and lies.'[5]

---

[1] The first occurrence of 'romancia' (fem.sing.) by British or Irish writers is dated by Latham to 1390. Bromyard, writing c.1330, uses the word four times: at A.26.9, F.3.5, F.4.23 and R.4.7. His meaning is well illustrated at F.4.23 in FIDES:
      '..credimus narranti: etiam de antiquis regibus vel legentibus cronicas
      vel romancias seu gesta de Karolo et Rolando et huiusmodi credimus
      que tamen nunquam vidimus.'

[2] Engels notes: 'The success of this collection of exempla [the *Gesta Romanorum*] (dating from the beginning of the 14th century) had led to the production and circulation of many different collections of stories, each entitled *Gesta Romanorum*..' (Engels, Apollonius p.30). The three brief tales Bromyard uses have as their content (1) a lens [speculum] which enables enemies to be detected afar off (2) the rejection by C. Fabricius of the offer by Pyrrhus' doctor to poison the king (3) a debate in the Roman senate on whether to deify Christ.

[3] Gesta romanorum. Cum applicationibus. STC France p.378: 1456. a.3.

[4] Sedebis super pellem patris tui ut iudices populum meum. Si vero aliquis affert tibi donum ut declines a via recta ad pellem patris tui respice ne tibi hoc idem contingat. (I.9.36) This is an exceedingly rare case of a misattribution of a source. The tale comes not from Cicero but from Valerius Maximus VI.3 [De Severitate] ext.3:
      'Iam Cambyses inusitatae severitatis, qui mali cuiusdam iudicis e corpore pellem detractam sellae intendi in eaque filium eius iudicaturum considere iussit..'
Bromyard has rehearsed the essence of the story without having the text before him: his neater 'excoriari' captures Valerius' 'e corpore pellem detractam': 'intendi' becomes 'extendi': 'sellae' changes to 'cathedram.'

[5] ..studere vel audire deberet [sc. rex] legem divinam et non romantias nec fabulas et mendacia. (R.4.7) By 'romances' Bromyard probably had in mind the cycles of the Arthurian and Charlemagne romances: the matter of antiquity (Troy, Alexander, Thebes): and courtly romance.

19

LITURGICA

TABLE 19.1 : LITURGY

Liber passionarius	1
Total	1

Usually 'a book containing the narratives of our Lord's Passion from the four Gospels.'[1]
The sybil's presence here suggests the incorporation of extraneous material:

> 'Furthermore, the emperor Augustus – a pagan – shunned vainglory to such
> an extent, as one can read in the *Passionarium*, in the account of Christ's
> nativity, that after he had been informed by the Sibyl of Christ's nativity he
> forbade the addressing of himself as 'Lord'.'[2]

---

[1]   ODCC[1] p.1022.

[2]   Octavianus etiam imperator homo saracenus intantum vanam gloriam fugit sicut legitur in
passionario in hystoria nativitatis cristi: quod postquam a sibylla de cristi nativitate informatus
fuit: dominum se vocari prohibuit. (G.2.46)

20

HOW DID BROMYARD PREPARE FOR THE *SUMMA*?

We should not picture Bromyard sitting in a carrel with ready access to many scores of volumes. The data in tables 3.4 and 3.5 of chapter 3 demonstrate that 90% of his more than 14,000 citations are derived from the Bible, the two learned laws and 17 key works. The precision of the biblical and legal quotations leads one to conclude that he had as constant companions the Bible and the corpus of the civil law and canon law. The same precision of referencing reveals that the autograph copy of his own *Sermones* was at his side constantly during the composition of the 27 capitula of A (it may have been removed for copying thereafter).

A good number, however, of his important sources are cited without specific reference, as is shown in table 4.2. This is so for 25% of his citations of Gregorius I: for S.Bernardus 39%. This strongly suggests he did not have these authors at all times within arm's reach. He must often have relied upon his capacious and retentive memory when quoting from books he knew well.

But even a retentive, trained memory may benefit from props. The over 10,500 citations of the Bible are given with their chapter numbers: perhaps one should not imagine Bromyard flicking through his well-thumbed copy for each reference. Chapter 2, in its exploration of a Bible of the 1220s, shows how the sacred text was mined for specific themes useful for the preacher and confessor: 39 references had been assembled, for example, on 'Confession of sins and its benefits.' It is not unlikely that Bromyard had access to such a finding device. A disciplined reader such as he will almost certainly have compiled his own index of useful passages, and this practice will surely have extended to his non-biblical, non-legal texts. He will then, if this view is correct, have marshalled a huge topic-index from which he could withdraw quotations at will: an alphabetic disposition would further his ease of access. Several years of assiduous reading and note-taking doubtlessly preceded his embarking on the daunting venture of the writing of the *Summa*, but these notes, and his topic-index, will have rendered his writing less troublesome. Evidence of this meticulous planning is to be seen both in his extensive cross-referencing and in the alphabetical indexing of the *Tabula realis*, a matter touched on in chapter 1.

The structure of the *Summa* seems modelled upon that of the *Opus trivium*, rather as the *Summa* itself served as a model for his later *Exhortationes* (their interrelationships were examined in chapter 1). The reasons dictating the choice of many of the subjects of his capitula are considered in the opening paragraphs of chapter 30.

PART II

Error which is not resisted is given the seal of approval.[1]

The men who, by their office, should be leading the assault on the devil and the vices are now become the devil's proctors and promoters of vice.[2]

..bishops..who mete out punishment and impose silence: others who contrive that silence and a muzzling of his preaching be imposed on the man who speaks out against the arrogance and vanity of the powerful.[3]

..Westminster Hall, the virtual head and fount of all falsity: for there the law is torn to shreds and the ungodly prevails against the just.[4]

How can it stand or agree with reason that one man, in heavy labour and sweat day and night, scrapes a meagre living: and another, who leads a lazy, lustful and luxurious life, lusting in bed till nine o'clock, sating his desire, can take away that living: that one man can live enjoying every pleasure and another – who is made in the image of God and serves God – can scarcely eke out a miserable existence?[5]

[1] P.13.50 : p.274.
[2] M.13.12 : p.160.
[3] V.1.8 : p.216.
[4] I.9.21 : p.245.
[5] R.1.20 : p.250.

21

BROMYARD THE PREACHER

The capitulum PREDICATIO Bromyard divides into twelve sections [articuli], namely:

1.   The duty of the preacher of the word of God is described.
2.   What kind of intention should precede the exercise of so great a duty.
3.   What kind of praying should precede the act of studying and preaching.
4.   How it is necessary that preachers learn before they teach.
5.   How it is necessary that they fulfil by their actions what they learn and teach: and otherwise, in what manner in evil matters they resemble several conditions.
6.   How it is necessary that they display and continue good examples in their exterior life.
7.   How it is necessary for them to teach persistently, frequently and perseveringly.
8.   What method in their preaching they will have of railing against specific vices.
9.   It will be shown that that method is more useful and more productive.
10.   What hinders the office of preaching.
11.   The reward of preaching well, and the peril of those refusing to preach will be made clear.
12.   Of what attitude of mind the hearers of preaching should be. (P.12.0)

Bromyard introduces articulus viii with a reference to Jonah ordered to go and preach in Nineveh. A translation of most of the first quarter of this articulus follows.

'Preach, he said, avoiding long themes, because just as it is tedious that a guitar-player in a hall takes a long time tuning his guitar, so etc.   And straightaway getting down to the essential core [quiditatem],[1] launching attacks specifically against vices, because someone who plucks all the strings at the same time makes his melody confused and inept, and seems to play as it were a children's prank, so in preaching, someone who touches all [the strings] at the same time in a general manner and speaks against vices in general, saying 'You will not be proud: avaricious: given to carnal desires' is not an effective preacher. Therefore he ought to touch, in a specific way, first one string then another, expounding the kinds and the dangers of pride, of avarice and of carnal desires: since according to S. Gregorius[2] 'Who gave understanding to a cock?' The minds of the listeners are intent, rather like the tightened tensions of the strings on a guitar, which the expert touches with his plectrum, to render the appropriate modulation, even though they are not struck at one go… So, specifically, the conditions and dangers of sin should be spelled out, and specific denunciations and teachings are to be applied to counter those frailties in plain words which can be understood by the people/laity: not by way of far-fetched oddities and declarations and philosophical reasonings[3] and dubious natures of animals[4] all of which caress the ears of literary types or which have as their goal the reputation of the preachers: yet fail to heal the wounds of the sick, but blind: fail to fulfil God's precept, by which they are commanded to declare to the people their sins: for which, since the time for preaching is too short, it is stupid to go hunting for so many circumlocutions and [to spend] a large part of the preaching-time more on the commendation of saints about whom he is preaching – they don't need our commendation – than in castigating the vices which he should be preaching against.'[5]

Bromyard emphasizes the need for the preacher's wholeness of character, his integrity, not just to exist but to be apparent:
'..in preaching it's not the voice alone of the teacher which is trusted, but the testimony of his dress, his bearing, his look, his devotion, his prayer, his humility, how he spends his time, his private conversation, his self-denial in eating and drinking: in the face of these witnesses let his word stand..'[6] He has met, it seems, fellow-mendicants who fell short of these values through a wish to be popular:
'..however, where people hear that they have no words of edification or morality but rather speak as letter-carriers and messengers in that there they pass on all the rumours of the countryside: and if there is some contest or armed conflict[7] they support one party and damn the other: then people despise both the individual [preachers] and their preaching. And often, when they [the preachers] are telling the tale and engaging in frivolity people smile at them to their face, deride them when they're gone and judge them to be fools..'[8]
Picking up on his stricture on 'self-denial in eating and drinking' he wryly comments: 'It's rather unsuitable for a man to preach for the church when he proclaims the poverty-stricken Christ with a corpulent belly and rubicund cheeks.'[9]

The weight of experience encapsulated in these few words of P.12.18 is all the more impressive for its simplicity. They come from a man who had trudged the rough roads of England,[10] summer and winter alike, and addressed gatherings of men and women in villages and towns: many of whom will have been shrewd and perceptive judges of character and demeanour. Bromyard himself admits it could be hard going to drum up a quorum, and then to hold their attention (especially, one imagines, in the open-air): a lengthy passage in A26 AUDIRE reveals to us several of the pretexts for avoiding a sermon which he had encountered:
'Others excuse themselves saying 'Why should I listen? God bless you and prosper you: what more do we need to hear?' This is a commonplace saying which crops up when someone wants to hinder another hearing the word of God.. When they want to go to sorceresses a thought of *this* kind doesn't stop them, so it shouldn't stop them going to God and hearing Him.. Others excuse themselves on account of their business: to these the response can be made that no business gets in the way of their corporeal food nor even in autumn when they will perhaps say they have the daily food of the soul in their houses: that is the pater noster, and mass in church.. There are few indeed whose business keeps them away from the latest spectacles such as the so-called miracle plays[11]: on account of which they are kept away from hearing about the miracles of stupid clerics.. [Bromyard links a quotation from Chrysostomus on time spent at theatres and horse-races

with]..tournaments and suchlike.. Others excuse themselves by reason of remoteness, saying that's why they can not come to church or the word of God. To these the response is that they know how to go to market and to fairs, where distance is no barrier: it's in *preaching*, however, that God's fairs are held. In defiance of these folk there will rise in judgement the Queen of Sheba who came from the ends of the earth to hear the wisdom of Solomon: not only the Queen of Sheba but all the nations of Christendom in this cause can rise in defiance of the English: since there is scarcely to be found a single Christian nation which hears the word of God so rarely and so unwillingly.[12] I know: believe me, I know.'[13]

This sense of failure in his preaching mission played on Bromyard's mind. 'One of the apostles,' he ruefully comments, 'if he were here now could preach and batter his head in raising a clamour: and still have difficulty in bringing one single person to God.'[14]

There will have been irritating distractions for the preacher to combat: he admits the power, even quantifying it, of a coquettish or a beautiful woman and the allure of her voice. 'For a single silly woman, made up to the eyes, by her looks and her talk will sooner turn a hundred men to wicked lust than the very best man by his preaching [will turn] twenty to a yearning for good and abandonment of evil.'[15]

An account of one preacher's extreme reaction against what seems to have been the gaiety of a popular festival has an Italian provenance. What is notable is that Bromyard's sympathies lie entirely with the preacher, despite his ill-timed attempt to deliver an open-air sermon:

'The enormity of the madness of the spectators of and listeners to this kind of women dancers and women singers is clear from the preceding passage..
And yet they listen to such people more eagerly than to the men who praise and preach God, as is evident at A.13.3 and 4.[16] And they are hotter for such an actor and debaucher than for a preacher of God, as was shown in Italy. There, when an adherent of God, as the story was told, was being hindered from his preaching because of some dancing, accompanied by a drum-beat, under the impetus of the Spirit he ran and punctured the drum with a knife. Whereupon the countryfolk, on witnessing this, taking the side of the devil's disciple, manhandled God's champion and gave him a severe beating.'[17]

Preaching before a congregation composed of the rich and powerful may often have been unrewarding too. '..the great tyrants: the rich and the mighty ones, and the great sinners: they either don't come to a sermon: or if they *do* come they sleep or they chatter..'[18]

On English reluctance to attend church to hear the gospel Bromyard observes 'These people are unwilling, even from the nearby house or street where they sit taking their ease, to come to listen to Christ: instead, they leave the church when He calls to them..'[19] He even contrasts the stolid determination of a sanctuary-seeking homicide to remain in church for forty unbroken days – merely to escape a physical death – with the disinclination of his fellow countrymen to stay for *one* sermon, when the reward could be the avoidance of both a temporal and an eternal death.[20]

But most conscientious preachers will feel at times that they could have done better. Dominicans took enormous pains over the training and preparation of their preachers: only successful men were sent into the field.[21] From the negativity of the reasons for *not* engaging with the world in the exercise of a Dominican's calling – reasons he must have heard from colleagues – we may credit Bromyard with possession of the opposing, dynamic attributes: 'But, more's the pity, many take up the weapons of the sciences and virtues as if they were arms to protect oneself with and not to be used combatively, in that they don't bestir themselves, acting like men in their preaching and in their work. Instead they want to lead the quiet life… Such men..say 'I want to live in peace in the convent: to read and to chant [the offices]. I *don't* want to tear along through the world: it's a wearisome place. Moreover, hearing confessions brings unease to my conscience: and so on. And there are embarrassments and hard work in begging..' '[22] A preacher with John Bromyard's wide experience of the world, powerful and well-organized intellect and a skilful command of the resources of his language[23] and a range of engrossing material allied, above all, to a fervent desire to transform the men and women who stood before him and guide them to a more wholesome and godlier life: such a fascinating and patently virtuous man will undoubtedly have fulfilled the tasks God had led him to.

A representation of Blackfriars' Cross 'in Widemarsh Suburb' Hereford, where Bromyard will have preached, is given in Duncumb.[24] Pevsner notes that all that remains of the Dominican house is the range west of the cloister and the preaching cross.[25] It is 'of the C14 and the only surviving example in England of a friars' preaching cross. It stood in the cemetery of the friars..'[26] It has been much restored. Hinnebusch confirms the Dominican practice of using their cemeteries and churchyards for preaching.[27] The house itself adjoined Frog Lane and the buildings of the Knights Hospitallers of S.John,[28] and ran along Widemarsh Street.[29]

[1] Only the third occurrence in the *Summa* - the first was at F.4.1, the second at O.6.18 and this at P.12.25 - of *quiditas*: a word associated more with philosophical texts of the Scholastics.

[2] Moralia in Iob on Iob xxxviii [Bromyard's own reference.]

[3] Scholastic philosophy is also targeted in A24 ARMA and S4 SCIENTIA.

[4] Bromyard *does* cite fables (I counted 55 in the *Summa* but may have missed some). These citations, however, are brief references performing the function of pegs on which to hang a step in an argument: they are not developed for their own sake.

[5] Predica inquit longa themata vitando: quia sicut tediosum est quod citharedus in aula diu citharam preparat: Ita etc. Et statim ad quiditatem descendendo invectiones contra vitia in speciali faciendo: quia qui cithare omnes chordas simul tangit confusam et ineptam facit melodiam et quasi ludum videtur facere puerorum. Sic in predicatione qui generaliter omnes simul tangit et vitia dissuadet in generali dicens Non eritis superbi: non cupidi: non carnales: non efficacem facit predicationem. Oportet ergo in speciali modo ut nunc unam nunc aliam tangat chordam, exponendo superbie et cupiditatis et carnalitatis species et pericula: quia secundum beatum Gregorium. iii. moralium super illo Iob. xxxviii. Quis dedit gallo intelligentiam. Intente mentes auditorum sunt quasi quedam tentiones chordarum stricte in cithara quas tangit artifex cum plectro ut reddant consonam modulationem: licet non uno impulsu feriantur... Ita in speciali conditiones peccati et pericula sunt recitanda, et speciales invectiones et doctrine sunt contra illas infirmitates adhibende per plana

verba et laicis intelligibilia, non per curiositates et declarationes et rationes philosophorum et dubias naturas animalium que omnia litteratorum aures demulcent vel predicantium gloriam querunt et infirmorum plagas non curant: sed cecant, nec preceptum dei implent, quo precipiuntur annunciare populo peccata eorum, ad quod cum tempus predicandi non sufficiat fatuum est tot querere ambages et magnam predicationis partem potius in sanctorum de quibus predicat commendatione, qui commendationibus nostris non indigent quam in vitiorum contra que predicare deberet reprehensione. (P.12.25).

6   (..sicut in iudicio unius non creditur testimonio sed duorum vel trium) Ita nec in predicatione voci tantum creditur doctoris sed testimonio vestitus gestus aspectus devotionis orationis humilitatis occupationis private locutionis et parcitatis in esculentis et poculentis: in ore isto testium stet omne verbum.. (P.12.18).

7   aliqua briga vel guerra: the words could refer to any or all of the conflicts which plagued England during Edward II's reign.

8   ..ubi vero audiunt eos verba habere non edificationis nec morum, sed potius cursorum vel nunciorum quia ibi narrant omnes rumores patrie: et si sit aliqua briga vel guerrra defendunt unam partem et damnant aliam: et personas contemnunt et predicationes. Et frequenter qui eis narrantibus et trufantibus arrident in presentia eos derident in absentia et fatuos eos esse iudicant.. (P.12.18).

9   Ecclesie inconvenienter predicat qui pauperem christum pingui ventre et rubentibus buccis annunciat. (P.12.18). This is a pithier version of the text he cites from the Decretum, Distinctio XXXV [cap.iiii] where Gratianus uses the words of Hieronymus in Micham ii: Annon confusio et ignominia est iesum crucifixum pauperem et esurientem fartis predicare corporibus, et ieiuniorum doctrinam rubentes buccas tumentiaque ora proferre?

10   Evidence for this comes, for example, from the encounter with 'a rich man' from whom his older companion and himself (Dominicans travelled in pairs when on a preaching mission (Hinnebusch EEFP p.285)) sought a bed for the night. They were told to go instead to the clergy, secular or regular: 'We have to take in the king's bailiffs and agents in case [if we refuse] they do us harm.' (A.20.9).
   Quasi simile accidit alteri religioso me presente. Cum peteret hospicium a quodam divite: Respondit oportet nos accipere balivos et ministros regis, ne nobis noceant: vos debetis recipi a viris ecclesiasticis. (A.20.9). The younger Bromyard recalled the older Dominican's reply: a cautionary tale set in Italy.
   He will also have been passed many a time by wealthy prelates and other senior clerics on horseback, attended by members of their households: Ralph Baldock, bishop of London, was to be accompanied to the Council of Vienne by six men (CPR 1307-1313 p.380): while Henry Woodlock, bishop of the opulent see of Winchester, was content with a retinue of no fewer than sixteen men for his journey to Vienne in 1311 (ibid.p.382). The contrast between place-seekers in the Church and footsloggers such as Bromyard he brings out more than once: '..as those in Holy Church or under religious vows who look for luxuries and ease and chambers and *horses*, and shun the labours of preaching men..' (A.24.15).
   Ita in sancta ecclesia vel religione qui delicias et requiem et cameras querunt et *equos* et labores hominum predicantium fugiunt.

11   *The Harrowing of Hell*, the earliest extant miracle play in English – based on the apocryphal *Gospel of Nicodemus* – is dated to 1295 (Chronology p.371): the Chester Cycle of miracle plays to 1327 (ibid.p.405).

12   This contrast implies a reasonable knowledge of preaching success in other countries.

13   Alii se excusant dicentes quare audiam, bene facias et bene habeas: quid debemus plura audire. Et istud dictum frequenter contingit quando unus vult alium impedire ne verbum dei audiat.. Quando enim volunt ire ad sortilegas huiusmodi cogitatio eos non impedit: ergo non impediat ire ad deum et audire eum.. Alii se excusant societate que retrahit multos ab audientia verbi dei et operibus penitentie.. Alii se excusant occupationibus, quibus dici potest quod nulla occupatio eos impedit a

cibo corporali nec etiam in autumpno qui forte dicent quotidianum cibum anime habent in domo sua: scilicet pater noster, et missam in ecclesia..pauci sunt quos occupatio impedit a novis spectaculis sicut in ludis quos miracula vocant: quare ergo impediuntur ab audiencia miraculorum clericorum fatuorum.. [He quotes Chrysostomus who berates people for spending their whole day at the theatre and at horse-races: Bromyard adds] sicut in hastiludiis et huiusmodi.. Alii se excusant loci distantia dicentes se non posse venire ad ecclesiam vel verbum dei: quibus respondetur quod ad mercatum et ad nundinas sciunt ire ad magnam distantiam, in predicatione vero sunt nundine dei. Contra illos surget in iudicio Regina saba que venit a finibus mundi audire sapientiam Salomonis, et non solum regina saba, sed omnes nationes cristianitatis in causa ista possunt surgere contra anglicos quia vix invenitur natio cristiana que, ita raro et invite audit verbum dei. Experto crede magistro. (A.26.27, 28, 29). [The sourcing of the last three words to Innocentius III I owe to Mr Ian J. Andrews].

14   unus apostolus si presens esset posset tota die predicare et frangendo caput suum clamare: et vix unum ad deum converteret. (L.7.21).

15   Una nanque fatua mulier decorata suo aspectu et loquela citius centum ad concupiscentiam malam convertet: quam optimus homo sua predicatione viginti ad concupiscentiam bonam et desertionem mali. (S.10.7).

16   In A.13.3 and 4 Bromyard is urging Christians to campaign *actively* to ensure the triumph of good: reminding us that we have weapons for defence but also weapons for attack: 'non solum..arma defensiva: sed..etiam arma invasiva.'* It is a foreshadowing of the tenet that all that is necessary for evil to triumph is for good men to do nothing. As an example of the difference an individual can make – and the harm he can suffer by the simple execution of his duty – he instances the court official known as the summoner. The example is given extra poignancy by being placed immediately after a reference to the Passion of Christ 'qui verborum sagittas sustinuit..et postea verbera usque ad mortem.' 'This is what all martyrs sustained, like the summoners of our times: who, if they faithfully performed their office by summoning men would sustain, for their part [or, in part], such treatment.' (A.13.3). [Sic martires omnes sustinuerunt ad modum apparitorum modernorum: qui si fideliter officium facerent, homines citando: talia in parte sustinerent.]
         *Bromyard makes use of the same polarity, in the same words, at A.24.12
         (see note 22).

17   Ex his apparet quanta est insania spectantium et audientium tales choreatrices et cantatrices.. Et tamen libentius tales audiunt quam deum laudantes et predicantes sicut patet. A.xiii.iii.iiii. Et plus fervent pro tali mimo et corruptore quam pro dei predicatore: sicut patuit in ytalia. Ubi cum quidam dei cultor ut narrabant a predicatione sua propter tympanum et choream impediretur in impetu spiritus currens cum cultello tympanum fregit. Et rustici videntes, dyaboli cultorem defendentes, dei cultorem male tractantes verberaverunt. (C.15.9, 10).

18   ..magni tyranni: divites et potentes: et magni peccatores: vel ad predicationem non veniunt: vel si venerint dormiunt: vel garrulant.. (P.12.6).

19   Isti nolunt de proxima domo vel vico ubi sedent ociosi venire ut audiant christum, immo de ecclesia exeunt qui eos invitat.. (A.26.29)

20   Sed heu homicida stat per quadraginta dies in ecclesia ut mortem evadat temporalem, et vos non libenter statis in uno sermone ut temporalem et eternam evadatis. (A.26.36). The abjuration of the realm by a 'brigand, homicide, or other malefactor' is to be followed by his departure from the port assigned him by the coroner: 'Cum latro, homicida, aut alius malefactor ad ecclesiam diffugerit..' 'Et nisi hoc potero infra quadraginta dies continuos mittam me iterum ad ecclesiam..' (Statutes of the Realm, vol.I p.250).

21   Hinnebusch, EEFP pp.282-287.

22   Sed heu multi apprehendunt arma scientiarum et virtutum quasi arma defensiva non invasiva quia nec exurgunt, viriliter agendo predicando et laborando: sed volunt vitam quietam ducere… Tales..dicentes: Volo vivere in pace in conventu et legere et cantare, nolo per mundum currere:

multa tedia sunt ibi: et scrupulus conscientie in confessionibus audiendis: et huiusmodi: et verecundie et labores in mendicando.* (A.24.12)

> *The compositor will have misread 'mēdicando' for 'medicando'.

23 The language in which Bromyard and his confrères addressed gatherings of their fellow-countrymen was, naturally, English: presumably their own west-midlands dialect of Middle English. Within the convent Latin will have been the sole language used: obviously so in the liturgy of worship but also in conversation and in internal sermons. One such sermon is embedded in the structure of the *Summa* in V8, VISITATIO: easily discernible by such markers as 'Charissimi' (V.8.7), 'et specialiter *vos sacerdotes* et *curati*' (V.8.14) and *vos* coram deo de damno *respondebitis*' (V.8.15). At social occasions outside the convent, such as that recalled at N.3.13 (see Appendix II) where Bromyard was in the company of learned men, Latin will have been the language spoken. Not all clergymen, however, could manage that: even a bishop is known to have struggled over 'Metropoliticae' and had recourse, after a pause, to French: 'Seit pur dite'. This was Louis de Beaumont (bishop of Durham 1318-1333) at his consecration (DNB vol.II p.64), a notorious exception on a bench of erudite prelates.

The easy, fluid Latin Bromyard wrote and spoke will also have enriched contemporary English by adding to its pool of vocabulary. Its syntax had been influenced by that of Italian and French, most notably in the replacement of the accusative and infinitive construction after verbs of statement by the use of *quod* and a dependent clause, and by a word-order partly matching that of the vernacular. (For a general description of the orthography and syntax of the language Bromyard inherited see the brief account in Hector pp.23-25). There is also found the intermittent placing of *se* just after its governing verb in the manner of *vestirsi* (though not of *si veste*). An example of this is found in Bromyard's comparison of unfaithful judges to the cock used as a weather vane: 'Tales enim sunt sicut gallus super campanili qui *vertit se* ad omnem ventum: et illi se vertunt ad omne argentum.' (A.12.42). Higden's testimony to the status of French in the schools is apposite in this context of depicting the linguistic mix operating in the England of the mid-1320s: 'This corruption of the indigenous language stems today largely from two factors: that is, that boys at school, contrary to the practice of the other nations, from the first arrival of the Normans, abandoning their own native tongue, are compelled to construe [from and into Latin] in French: furthermore, that the sons of the nobility, from the very songs sung over the cradle, are taught in the French speech. Country men, in their desire to be likened to them, so as to appear, by this means, more respectable, strive with every effort to emulate the French.. (..quod videlicet pueri in scholis contra morem caeterarum nationum..derelicto proprio vulgari, construere Gallice compelluntur..) (Higden vol.II pp.158, 160).

24 Vol.I facing p.387. Duncumb adds, on p.403, 'This cross was probably surrounded by cloysters, in which a large audience might, under shelter, attend to the sermons of these friars..'

25 Pevsner, Herefordshire plate 40(b) has a photograph of the cross. See also Hinnebusch EEFP plate XXIII. Its restoration clearly postdates Duncumb (1804).

26 Pevsner, Herefordshire p.183.

27 Hinnebusch EEFP p.314.

28 The Knights Hospitaller had taken possession of Rhodes in 1309/1310: I suggest that Bromyard's informant of events 'in transmarinis partibus', the anonymous 'quedam religiosa persona' of A.12.34, who may also have spoken to Bromyard about the game of stailes – 'qui ludus communior est in transmarinis partibus' (A.15.23) – will have been one of the Dominicans' valiant neighbours. (Atlas pp.106, 136-137).

29 ..que iacent inter tenementa Prioris sancti Johannis Jerusolimitani in Anglia ex parte una, et venellam que vocatur Vroggelone ex altera, et extendunt se in longitudine a vico qui vocatur Wydemarstrete usque ad burgagium quod fuit quondam Nicholai Yweyn.. (Orleton pp.220-221).

22

BROMYARD ON BISHOPS AND THE LOWER CLERGY

Prelati (prelates) is one of the 321 headwords in Bromyard's *Tabula realis* (which precedes his primary text). This entry directs the reader, under no fewer than 84 headings, to 109 articuli of the *Summa* found in 29 different capitula. As if this were not enough a note at the end of this entry bids the assiduous reader consult 14 other entries whose headwords range from 'ambition' to 'simony'. This heavy concentration upon the higher ranks of churchmen reveals his concern over the health of the contemporary Church. If all were well therein that attention could be focused elsewhere.

Adumbrating, then, his views on the episcopacy – including the papacy – and the beneficed clergy in general these 84 brief abstracts alone are breath-taking in the audacity of their open, specific and well-directed assault upon both the shortcomings of, and the abuses committed by, the higher clergy. Taken in their entirety the passages to which the reader is referred constitute a major part of the *Summa*. The 84 headings are:

TABLE 22.1: THE ENTRY ON PRELATES IN THE *TABULA REALIS*

1. When prelates are negligent in their duties their subordinates are imperilled. A.8.15
2. Against prelates who forbear to reprimand in return for gifts. M.14.8
3. They change their churches just as others change wives. A.17.30 and P.13.39
4. They mortgage their soul for a return for which they wouldn't mortgage their shoe. A.23.23
5. They climb like ivy. A.25.27
6. The resentment harboured by prelates against the preachers. P.12.8
7. Those who conduct a good defence of souls: and those who do not. B.2.4, 5
8. The more they receive from their stipends the less they engage in combat. B.2.15
9. The ingratitude of such men. B.2.17
10. Such men are like the village dog. B.2.33
11. The concordat of prelates with the emissaries of the devil. C.4.15
12. Many are unfit for their task: the reason why. C.5.18, 19
13. Against non-residents. C.16.6 with following sections: and E.2.13 (especially valuable): and C.18.7 and V.2.3
14. Such men are guardians who are deaf and dumb: contrary to the provisions of the civil law. F.3.31
15. One day they will have to answer for the total damage. F.3.32, 33, 34
16. How they extort the licence of non-residence with false depositions. F.3.34
17. Item Christ on the cross in His own person *resided* for them. G.4.3
18. And by His own efforts raised the dead and healed the sick. P.13.22
19. Item against those who dispense and those who successfully importune a licence of non-residence. I.4.8, 9
20. Item non-residents are acting contrary to the examples of the prophets and saints. P.3.23
21. Also in defiance of ecclesiastical, that is, canon law. P.13.24
22. Against those who abuse their dispensation and against those who make excuses for themselves by reason of the meagreness of their benefice. P.13.25 and I.4.8

23. How they are bound by the oath they swore, [their hands] in the hands of their bishops, on undertaking the cure [of souls]. P.13.26, 50

24. The danger of the non-residents is illustrated by an *exemplum* from [the text of] Beda. P.13.27

25. Also by the authority of the blessed Gregorius. P.13.28

26. The peril of the Supreme Pontiff or Pastor in not bridling the power of those under him: in their hands the potential to grant dispensations is a double iniquity. P.13.29

27. Against negligent prelates. C.16.9

28. The danger of those failing to protect their flock. C.16.9

29. How they uphold merely the legislation regarding incomes which is lucrative for them. C.16.48 and P.13.16.

30. The peril for unrighteous prelates. C.18.4 with its sequence: and P.13.16

31. That those of more noble birth are often worse. C.18.6

32. Against [clerical] huntsmen. C.18.9

33. That they pursue their own interests and not those of Jesus Christ. D.2.12 and P.13.5, 8, 19

34. Such men are effigies on the walls of a besieged city. D.12.36

35. Also counsellors of prelates are held to account for harm if they do not point them the right way. F.3.35

36. That they expend greater efforts in resisting those who [would] make off with their sheaves and their moneys than souls [in their care]. H.4.13 with the sequence, and especially article 18.

37. On the one who said 'If I hadn't been one of the prelates I wouldn't be one of the damned.' I.11.24

38. Item they are watchmen. M.8.5

39. Against those who repudiate Christ – but not their benefice. M.9.15

40. Against those who do not uphold [the laws of] hospitality. M.9.15 and P.13.2

41. Against those who celebrate [mass] only once in a while. M.10.10

42. How they are chess-bishops. M.13.12

43. Through which gates they enter their church benefices. O.6.8

44. How they ought to partition their revenues into four parts. O.6.15

45. How they are in their houses only at the season of gathering in their harvests. O.6.22, 23

46. Immoral men given preferment are like the donkey [of a fable]. O.6.50

47. How they ought to be in their work. P.13.1

48. How they are obliged to nurture by means of food, doctrines and examples. P.13.2, 3

49. How they are passionate with regard to their own interest and *not* in the interest of Christ. P.13.5

50. How they should be the lion of Samson and the Ark of the Covenant: and that nothing is more perilous than their office if it is carried out negligently. P.13.6

51. That they should first put in order their own household. P.13.7

52. That because of their evil way of life and negligence the agents of the devil saluted them. P.13.9

53. Item the whole of Christendom is endangered because of this. P.13.10, 20

54. Against those in pursuit of benefices while nurturing worldly intent. P.13.11

55. Such men will not earn the reward of heaven. P.13.12

56. Against those holding or yearning for a plurality of benefices and in what way they resemble the devil. P.13.13

57. And against those holding the Church's property in conjunction with their own endowment. P.13.14
58. How they are an 'accidental', not a 'substantial' form. P.13.15
59. By allowing buying and selling in their churches they are acting in defiance of the commandment. P.13.16
60. How all their possessions are richer and more ornate than those of Christ and the Church. P.13.17
61. That each sin in them is weightier: and that they inflict more damage on the Church than do tyrants. P.13.30
62. Those who fervently pursue church benefices are like the thorn-bush [of Judges 9.8-15]. P.13.32
63. Also neglecting their duties they are likened to a scarecrow and effigy. P.13.33, 34
64. How they are likened to wolves in respect to their ingress and progress. P.13.35
65. And to a cat guarding cheese and to Hieronymus' lion. P.13.36
66. Those who exchange benefices and offices are like a stork. P.13.38
67. What other traders do openly they do secretly. P.13.39
68. How among the bishops greater/older thieves introduce lesser/younger [thieves], and how they are likened to the guards over Christ's tomb. P.13.40
69. All that they buy from church property is acquired for the church. P.13.41
70. That they are obliged to the restitution of what has been wrongly used up. P.13.42, 43, 45
71. It is difficult to see how they will be able to be saved. P.13.44
72. They want to have the profit from but not the care of their bride [the Church]. P.13.45
73. The men who receive the goods of the Church and make no restitution end badly. P.13.46
74. How many perils bishops are exposed to. P.13.47. (On the authority of S.Gregorius).
75. Those who fail to protect their flock will be damned. P.13.48, 50
76. So too those who live ungodly lives. P.13.49
77. They will be punished in chastisements more grievously than others [will]. P.13.51
78. The greater prelates, by their gifts of benefices to the undeserving, cause many to stumble. P.13.53, 54
79. What kind of purpose they should have in mind on receipt of a benefice. P.13.55
80. The difference between a mercenary shepherd and a thief. P.13.57
81. That one should not disparage prelates or one's superiors: and how a certain man said that the Church was not worthy of being governed except by scoundrels. P.13.58
82. That the concern of prelates should be the protection of their flock. S.3.9
83. Item prelates are the dilapidated wall of the Church. S.9.4
84. Item they should practise both a contemplative and an active life. V.7.4

Look up: ambition, dispensation, bishops, clerics, hospitality, almsgiving, mercy, pope, patrons, kings, priesthood, churchmen, [holy] orders, simony.

An analysis of the content of the passages the reader is directed to yields results which cannot be exactly quantified. They can, however, be roughly assigned to a score or so of areas of concern to Bromyard. The two most prominent of these are

(1) negligence over the performance of duties:

(2) non-residence and the abuse of 'Cum ex eo' dispensations.

Abuses such as place-seeking, pluralism, avarice, laxity in celebrating mass, lack of hospitality, misuse of church property, exchange of churches, allowing buying and selling within church: all of these have links to other failings, including the general charge of negligence, and are specifically addressed by Bromyard. Other broadsides are discharged against abuses such as the preferment of unsuitable and ill-equipped candidates for office: bribery: rivalry: the cavalier attitude to oath-taking: to reliance on nobility of birth: and to hunting as a distraction from duty. Nor does the papacy escape adverse criticism. He warns too of the consequences of sin: at least nine articuli remind clergy of the coming Day of Judgement. In a dozen articuli he seeks to point his fellow-churchmen to the right way.

The following pages will present some of Bromyard's views on church issues to which he gives less space but equal concern: but will begin with the controversy arising from *Cum ex eo*.[85]

Bromyard's eighth of 18 sections in the capitulum PRELATIO deals with the issue of clerical non-residence. This eighth articulus is itself divided into six sub-sections. This sixth sub-section is notable for an adverse criticism of 'the pope'.

'Sixthly there is demonstrated the remissness of the supreme shepherd on earth who is failing to compel his subordinates to residence [in their cures].'[86]

But which pope? It was Bonifacius VIII who in 1298 by his bull *Cum ex eo* authorized clerics to leave their cures for the purpose of study, thus regularizing a practice already informally accepted.[87] Boyle clarifies this measure. 'It should be understood, however, that this licensing system was not designed to allow rectors who were priests already to attend university, though some such availed themselves of it. Rather, its purpose was to attract young and promising clerics to parish work who were not yet subdeacons (or, at least, who were not yet priests.)'[88] The income from the parish was to pay for the university expenses of the holders of the livings, who were obliged to pay a vicar to perform their parochial duties. Boyle uses published episcopal registers to estimate the extent of this practice in the early fourteenth century.[89]

TABLE 22.2: *CUM EX EO* STUDY LICENCES IN THE EARLY 14TH CENTURY

Dioceses	Years	Grants	No. per year
Ghent of Salisbury	1297-1315	308	17.80
Woodlock of Winchester	1305-1316	105	9.55
Stapledon of Exeter	1308-1326	400+	c.22.23
Cobham of Worcester	1317-1327	147	14.70

Haines produces rather different figures for the Worcester diocese 1308-1349. He lists only five bishops for this period omitting the 3½ years of Maidstone's administration and the 1¾ years of Hempnall's. His starting year is 1302. I give his figures[90] (which do not cover complete episcopates) in tabular form:

TABLE 22.3: ABSENCE FOR STUDY FROM PAROCHIAL BENEFICES 1302-1349

BISHOP	YEARS	NO. OF LICENCES	YEARLY AVERAGE	BENEFICES AFFECTED
Gainsborough	1303-1307	85	23.2	59
Reynolds	1308-1313	79	15.8	54
Cobham	1317-1326	156	17.4	93
Orleton	1328-1332	55	11.5	47
Montacute	1334-1337	54	18.0	41
Bransford	1339-1348	43	4.7	39

Total of no. of *Cum ex eo* licences

1308-1349	387	9.44	274
1303-1332	375	12.93	253

Bonifacius VIII's honourable intention was to produce a more highly educated parochial clergy[91] and this was doubtlessly, on the whole, the result. One of the drawbacks was that the men replacing these beneficed clergy would not always be of a calibre adequate to their duties: another, that there were abuses of the licence, of which the two most obvious were that (1) the holder of the benefice was being paid by his parishioners out of their tithes for non-performance of his duties (2) some of these clerics studied in order to advance their own careers in the Church[92] rather than to devote the remainder of their lives for the betterment of their parishioners' Christian lives. It is on this side of the debate on 'Cum ex eo', hostile to it and its consequences, that Bromyard stands. It is in the capitulum CUSTODIA, which has as its theme the guardianship of God's people, that Bromyard makes one of his sternest, most telling and most sustained attacks on dereliction of duties. Of these he concentrates his fiercest denunciations on absentee priests and by implication on the church governance which permits this.

'The greatest possible distance between them and their flock – that's what they seek: allowing their ewes in the abandoned waste land to be eaten up by the wolves of hell, in as much as they appear to have made a pact and indenture between themselves and the demons, the terms being that *they* take the wool and the milk, i.e. the temporal benefits: and the demons the souls – they hanker for those and nothing else.

Just as the so-called noble hounds – greyhounds and suchlike – normally don't act as guard-dogs but as devourers..so the nobility and those buoyed up by their blood-lineage and arrogance..themselves elect, after abandoning their flock, to pass their time in the courts of the great to consume the flesh of the fat of the land. It is ordinary village dogs, you see, that are chosen for protecting a house and a flock: in the same way it is humble and simple men who should be chosen for the protection of God's flock.. And Christ chose fishermen for the protection of His Church and ever chose weakness to confound strength: and for *this* reason while God [God the Son?] had the responsibility and choice of the shepherds the flocks were well guarded. Now, however, simony and the king and ties of blood have control of elections and confirmations of this kind, and all is perverted, and the flock is eaten up by wolves. No wonder: for two reasons. First, because he [the beneficed rector] absents himself from his flock… But they [the beneficed rectors] will say, or will be able to say, two things to excuse themselves. First, they have a good vicar or priest to carry out [the duties of] the cure of the souls placed under their [the rectors'] care: to whom the response is to be made that a good many of them [the rectors] care little about the quality of their deputies or how they guard their flock: the one thing they *do* care about is that they [the rectors] cream off the profits. This is crystal-clear from day-to-day examples and our experience.. What response is the man going to make who is absent for a year or for several years if he were to say 'the cure [of souls] is the business of my deputy': he has to be asked whether that deputy is up to the task.. Even suppose that he *is* quite competent he cannot practise as great a hospitality even in welcoming the penniless nor can he exercise as great an authority in his teaching and rebuking as his master and lord.. Secondly they [(wealthier) parishioners] will be able to excuse themselves in formulating their excuses in their sins in that because they know that they [the rectors] and their replacements were excessively indolent and not up to the task of guardianship of souls and the freeing of booty from the jaws of the devil…for this reason they have provided them [the rectors] with a selection from the fastest hounds on the face of the earth.. So they [the rectors] take care of their hounds and falcons and the wealthy who bring presents and produce: while they have no affection for the penniless who bring nothing but their souls.. The bishops, however, and church dignitaries who guard those placed under their authority neither from themselves nor from others but instead draw and allow to draw them towards sins – they are within *no* law.'[93]

For Bromyard both the pope accused at P.13.22 of remissness (undoubtedly Iohannes XXII (1316-1334)) and the prelates who grant dispensations of non-residence betray their calling and deserve his harsh rebukes.[94]

Bromyard acknowledges that the Church has need of educated men and that she suffers a heavy loss by lack of them: his charge is that there is abuse of the licence to study in that a number of these licensees are not fulfilling their part of the agreement: that is they are not devoting themselves to their studies. He cites several biblical texts, and civil law texts on the law of contract, in O.4.15 and 16 (bolstering these with a cross-reference to R.5.60: which in turn sends the reader to other legal citations at M.9.15: and to P.13.43 which itself gives four further cross-references): the cumulative effect is similar to that of a lengthy charge-sheet in a court of law and indicates the gravity with which Bromyard views these derelictions of duty.

'And note that all the foresaid allegations seem to mount a heavy case against those awarded dispensations by their bishops*, in that it is for the sake of their education that they will be able to attend the schools for a seven-year period or other term less than seven years: after, that is, they have been preferred to churches which carry the care of souls, before they are ordained to the priesthood: this being in accord with the 'Liber Sextus' [1.6.34] De electione et electi potestate, Cum ex eo: *if they do *not* study with might and main in the schools, since that is the purposive reason for which the licence and privilege of non-residence and of non-ordination was given them, as is expressly made clear from the tenor of that constitution in which earlier he [Bonifacius VIII] shows how the Church is in need of educated men and that she suffers a heavy loss from lack of them..' Bromyard goes on to warn that those who fail to use the dispensation as it was intended will not be excused when they face God: 'si tamen viriliter non studuerint coram deo excusati non sunt.'[95]

[*Bromyard's long parenthesis interrupts the sentence structure, which runs '..by their bishops..if they do not study..']

Bishops, it is sometimes said, fall into one of three categories: scholars, saints or administrators. Bromyard perhaps takes administrative competence as a 'given', simply to be expected. In his bishops he certainly looks for a deep knowledge of Holy Scripture and a spiritual life developed in prayerful conversation with God. The dependence of English kings on educated men to conduct royal business in Paris, Avignon and other European courts, as well as to handle domestic affairs of state: and their plucking ecclesiastics from their church offices to do their bidding, or appointing able bureaucrats to wealthy benefices which then furnished their salaries: this need, this practice is not addressed head-on by Bromyard. What he seizes on is one of the consequences of this convention as it affected, for the worse in his eyes, the English Church in the reign of Edward II.

In a remarkable passage of the capitulum MUNDUS which launches a ferocious denunciation of the episcopacy he takes as a starting point the image – which only a minority of Englishmen will have seen – of the protuberances in the carved figures of bishops in the game of chess, which he develops in a series of dualities and polarities. The progress of his thesis is inexorable. Those bishops and lesser prelates (deans and archdeacons, one supposes) who lack both knowledge of the Bible and godly rectitude are unsuitable for their office. How were they appointed to their key positions? By payment, i.e. bribery: by importuning: by royal dictate: by threats from magnates: through family connections: or through 'certain letters' (papal?).

Such men are unfit to mediate God's message to the laity and the consequences are calamitous. They neglect their duty to protect the Christians under their care: instead it is the corrupt they defend and the *real* guardians of the Christian laity they muzzle: they lead an assault upon God, take bribes for condoning sin and while concentrating upon their own enrichment become agents of the devil and promoters of vice.

It is difficult to imagine graver charges. Directed at *specific* targets their thrust would carry a sharper edge but danger for an assailant.

'Horned chess-bishops, however, stand for bishops and other lesser prelates. If they be good, and spiritually horned from study of holy writ and conversation with God in prayers, as Moses (Exodus 24), then their horns signify that they have what they should have and what they do in fact have, such that in them is the sign and the impress: the knowledge, that is, of the New and the Old Testament, and that with those horns they will make an assault upon those going astray and will destroy the errors which are rising in rebellion against those two Testaments. But if they have turned bad, promoted to office through simony or while being unsuitable, by importuning, that is, or by handing over a bribe, or by royal command, or through the threats of magnates, or by certain letters or through fleshly favour – then they are not horned from godly eloquence of prayer or of reading: rather, their horns can mean two things, which are literally found in these men: [1] that is, that they have neither knowledge of the Testaments nor moral goodness: that, moreover, they neither attack the wolves nor drive them off from their flocks but instead *protect* them, and the guard-dogs, namely the preachers, they muzzle and expel so that they cannot guard the flock: or [2] they [the horns] can signify their own worldly power or cleverness by means of which they have, despite their unsuitability, been promoted and in their perverted morality and in their own bodies make their assault upon God. And chess-bishops such as these cross over three squares, diagonally: in that a triple evil perverts their operations: affection – that is, hatred – and greed: because if they promote someone they do this from fleshly rather than spiritual affection. But if they sharply correct or punish a man they do this rather from hatred of the person than of the

159

sin. As a result it frequently happens that they punish those who do not deserve punishment: or punish those who do deserve punishment beyond what is fair: and men who do deserve punishment they let off, unpunished. If moreover there is someone they should punish corporally, led astray by their greed for bribes they punish him in his purse. In consequence it comes about that they apportion sins to a fixed payment on the basis of an annual fee so as to acquire money they have not yet had: or that they, like hirelings, back away from the wolf who needs putting right so as not to lose the goods they have already got their hands on. And so, while they are concentrating on their own enrichment by piling up their moneys they also enrich the devil by letting souls slip from their grasp. The men who, by their office, should be leading the assault on the devil and the vices are now become proctors for the devil and promoters of vice.'[96]

Bromyard gives praise where praise is due. Among 'a few doughty warriors', now dead, who shielded the Church he will have numbered Richard Swinfield of Hereford (d.1317), John of Monmouth of Llandaff (d.1323): we need, however, at least a third: and if this section was written after August 1327 he might have considered Thomas Cobham of Worcester worthy of inclusion.

'..while the City of the Church..had a few doughty warriors it held its position well in defiance of all assaults of infernal agents and dictators and all kinds of unprincipled men. But with these [warriors] now dead, and others not of the former calibre, but like lifeless effigies in clerical dress arrayed on the ramparts of the Church...demons[97] and minions of demons invade and destroy the City of the Church without fear, and with none to resist them: this from the failure of David – i.e. pope, archbishop, bishop: because *this* lies at the door of any one of them..'[98]

Bromyard goes on to compare the stealthy, cunning approach of wolves towards a sheep-fold, upwind so that their scent should not carry to guard-dogs, to that of ecclesiastical place-seekers:

'On this theme this is how educated men coming to, or approaching in aspiration, church benefices, i.e. to the ewes and the cure of souls cover up, as far as they can, their evil reputation: simulating total humility and mature readiness they march forward to that goal: to *be fed* from Christ's flock, not to *feed* Christ's flock..'[99]

Bromyard uses elsewhere in the *Summa* the image of the preacher/Dominican as a guard-dog defending Christians against the malice of the enemies of virtue (depicted as wolves): while the men paid handsomely to stand up for moral values against the inroads of greed and its accompanying vices neglect their office and devote themselves to the enjoyment of their generous stipends. So he uses a text from Ecclesiastes to develop his metaphor:

'..that verse of Ecclesiastes xi: 'Better a live dog than a dead lion': i.e. an insignificant preacher or priest barking against vices than such a great prelate who, whether from fear, or a bribe, or through laziness, like a dead lion fails to roar against the vices of the wicked.'[100]

Bromyard's cruel comparison of the current crop of bishops to 'lifeless effigies in clerical dress arrayed on the ramparts of the Church' perhaps derives ultimately from a writer on siege warfare unknown to him, Aineias Taktikos (fl.367 BC), but may have been prompted by the stone defenders apparently resolute, though immobile, such as those on the Bars of York. It is a telling image. It follows a cruder likening, to a scarecrow, which will have rooted itself in the minds of countrymen and women.

'First they are compared and likened to a scarecrow or effigy positioned among the corn, with a fake bow and arrow in its hand and the shape of a live man. On seeing this, with such devices, the birds are at first frightened and fly away. Then, when they see no signs of life in it and suppose it to be a dead statue, they gradually approach: and in the end, perching on its head, befoul it with their excrement and gobble up the corn with no worry and it becomes a resting-place and refuge for the birds as they feed rather than something to scare them and protect [the crop]..their servants serve some bishops and churchmen in whom works of a spiritual life are lacking: and seeing them holding the place, the status and office of jurisdiction and correction at first are apprehensive: but after a time, seeing them to be statues, spiritually dead – for they neither live spiritual lives in themselves nor correct others effectively – approach and spiritually dishonour both them and their deputies, without fear.'[101] He then compares these prelates to a candle, snuffed out, and smoking.

Linked to the issue of non-residence is that of pluralism in that here too a parish will be deprived of its spiritual guide: the cleric enjoying the revenues of three parishes (or the prebend of a distant cathedral office)[102] will be absent from at least two of his benefices. 'A plurality of benefices is sought after not without sin nor held without peril.'[103] Pluralism in turn is another face of avarice and place-seeking: evils owing their genesis to an unhealthy love of money. 'Money conquers: money rules: money controls everyone.'[104] Since the Church may be exploited as a milch cow it follows that men unfitted from several considerations to the task of saving souls are appointed to richer benefices. 'But for guarding souls they [sc. bishops] appear to care little what manner of guardians they have except those presented to them by blood-ties or marriage alliances, or simony or a good bargain: even though they [sc. the men preferred] are neither chaste nor prudent nor godly nor literate.'[105] Bromyard also knows of the intolerable pressure applied to bishops or disposers of advowsons to prefer to benefices unsuitable candidates. 'If a prelate, cleric or layman has shown himself unwilling to bow to the requests of powerful bullies which they write to get their own clerics promoted: or for any other matters dear to their hearts: they immediately write off to their agents or friends [instructing them] to hurt them [sc. the prelates] in every single way they can.'[106]

But it is to the poisonous rôle played by money and its power to elevate the unworthy to positions both in Church and in state for which they are inadequate that Bromyard returns, time and again, throughout the *Summa*. In a passage wherein he reflects on the changeability of human affairs – 'So the world despatches to death and a poor grave now a pope now an emperor now a king and puts in his place a successor or heir'[107] – Bromyard mordantly observes '..just as he obtained that status by importuning and bribing, so nowadays they obtain almost all offices and places, both secular and church.'[108] The presence in the Church of huge numbers of unsuitable priests is acknowledged by a senior lecturer in theology whom Bromyard once heard declare that he would rather have one good priest celebrating mass on his behalf than a thousand bad priests.[109] The urge to acquire prebend after prebend is not merely a literary topos – 'so the greedy pile up estate after estate: prebend on prebend'[110] - as many a church career demonstrates in the early fourteenth century. The image of ivy's indefatigable climb up masonry reminds Bromyard of the determined ascent up the walls of the Church of men avid for high place, using every fingerhold available to secure their advance. '..Hypocrites who in their talk despise everything of the flesh, i.e. they put on an act of flying into the cerulean of sanctity. Their aim is to acquire church benefices, preferments, gifts, favours and popular acclaim… Others climb to the place of their desire and vanity like ivy or other shrubs clutching the masonry of inappropriate favour. For ivy, in its ascent, does not rely on its own vigour or strength but on the wall's. In the same way the men yearning to climb to the position of their ambition in the Church organization, having nothing, or very little of spiritual or churchly vigour and strength of learning and morality – these men rely on a wall, i.e. some prelate or patron or man of influence: and bind themselves to him by bribes, by blandishments, by ties of blood or by service.'[111]

That money is the driving force behind decisions to enter the priesthood Bromyard maintains, asserting that if such men could enjoy their income without taking holy orders and without celebrating mass scarcely one in a hundred would be ordained. This seems a harsh claim with more than a whiff of exaggeration to it. He stands by it: '..the evidence is this, that when they are poor [i.e. in a thinly endowed benefice: or as unbeneficed priests] they frequently celebrate: but when they've got their promotion scarcely once a year: or never.'[112]

Clerical concubinage is denounced by Bromyard surprisingly not so much for its moral but its social and economic consequences. 'But these men [sc. simoniac priests] feed wives out of Christ's patrimony and clothe other men's adulterers and concubines, maintain bastard sons, brigands of the future, and copiers of their fathers' crime. Remaining in the world, through poverty they would not be able to provide for their own, legitimate wives: and so they have themselves ordained so that, out of Christ's property, they may provide for other men's wives – and themselves.'[113]

In so many words does Bromyard assign temporal motives to their decision to take orders. Perhaps some or a good number of these concubinary priests would see themselves as pious men combining their parish duties with a decent family life, not unlike the position of their contemporaries, Orthodox parish priests in southern Italy and Sicily, and the major Greek-speaking lands. One might expect as well that some at least of these denounced Catholic priests would ensure a sound upbringing for their children. But Bromyard has a nose for corruption. 'For this is the merry boast of some, that their benefice is free from cure of souls.'[114] 'And the first question, when there is a mention of a benefice offered to them or awarded to friends: 'Is it with cure or without?' Then 'How much is it worth?' '[115]

In his travels Bromyard has heard complaints from priests living on reasonable incomes. A *family* can thrive on *one* carrucate worth less than ten marks a year, he writes: but has listened to priests [i.e. single men] saying that they cannot manage on an annual income of the same ten marks.[116]

It is some relief to turn away from money and its allure. The conduct of the liturgy also attracts Bromyard's censure. As to the frequency of the celebration of the mass he has much to say in reproach of lazy, negligent priests. He cites the *Decretales* [3.41.9] on priests who barely manage four masses a year.[117] He also has a stern view of priests who gabble their way through mass: 'So these men join together the beginning and the end of the verse: and they're in such a hurry, jumping over the middle, that I don't know whether God or man can follow it.'[118]

The hunting clergyman is such a well-loved figure in the novels of Robert Surtees and Anthony Trollope that we must put such characters from our minds. What might seem like healthy recreation for countrymen is to Bromyard a distraction from their duty to their parishioners. 'For some of them more willingly take hounds and falcons to the hunt than Christians to devotion.'[119] Such a priest, one imagines, would have few qualms over accepting a goose from a parishioner who offered the gift before making confession: the unstated contract being that a lighter penance be imposed for a heavier sin.[120]

Iohannes XXII is not named in the occasional criticisms Bromyard makes of the papacy: his first readers, however, (his Hereford fellow-Dominicans) will have understood who was singled out in this cutting attack. 'Do you really think, if Peter, or any of the pastors of the early Church, were now walking the earth, that they would have cognizance of these men who now claim to be their successors? And the same goes for all the founders of religious orders. For if they were now led before them on earth in their life, their clothes and the rest of what they use, and if the question were put to them 'Whose image and superscription is this?' [Matthew 22.20] any one of them for his part would answer 'Not mine: because I was poor in possessions and outer display.' *These men however* [pope and bishops] *are such in neither one nor the other.*' The image on the silver denarius handled by Jesus is appropriate for pope and bishops bearing the impress, not of Christ, but of Caesar.[121]

A similar note is sounded in Bromyard's criticism of the Avignon cardinalate which he encases, in an exhibition of his contempt for showy display and needless extravagance, in deliberately euphuistic language, such as 'cardinalium onerosa numerositate.'

'..for if you take away the burdensome aggregate of cardinals and horses and the excessive multitude of their households and the inordinate affection of their kin and the vain pride of all their appurtenances the need for huge contributions will cease. They must put an end to these to avoid scandalizing the frail body of the faithful who believe in Christ and have been ransomed by His blood: even though they can receive, without great sin, from those consecrated in the papal court, in accordance with the abuse or custom, the yearly value of the church: even though [they can receive] from the churches which are vacant the fruits of the first year: even though [they can receive] a tenth from the Church when they please:[122] *yet*, for avoidance of a scandal they should rein themselves in from such practices lest the fountain of life is turned into a fountain of poison. For if those who preside over that holiest of seats knew how, not just the infidels – Muslims, Jews, schismatics and heretics – but the faithful too are I don't say scandalized but full of reproaches concerning their appurtenances, which they judge to be pompous and deviating from the path which Christ followed, how the Christian population speaks belittlingly about that percentage which is kept back for the papal chamber from the men who are consecrated or from what is given: saying 'That bishopric he bought, he paid too much for it' – who will be able to stay clear of the simony pervading our system..?'[123]

The consequences for the individual churchmen who take out loans with which to purchase their bishoprics are next explored:

'..the very men who have been consecrated, whom they [sc. creditors] bind for a huge sum of money before they take anything from the church for the acceptance of which, through a loan, they at times hand over or promise in simoniacal fashion their churches or prebends to their creditors, at times mortgage their *pallium* or other valuable objects.. and find guarantors, and for the original sum perhaps commit themselves to double that: and that double, through interest, sometimes grows to tenfold the amount. To settle this debt they either exercise a tyrannical regime over their subordinates and enforce a contribution from their clergy to pay off the amount owing to the papal court..or they lead a miserable and frugal life..dwelling outside their diocese..'[124]

Bromyard next makes a triple proposal to reform the permanent government of the Church:

i   reduce the size of the cardinalate

ii   make its composition representative of the whole of Christendom (to replace the then existing French cabal[125])

iii   provide a secure investment-base from which its expenses can be met (to obviate the need for squeezing out money from the national churches).

'..It would be more consistent with sanctity therefore, both for themselves and for others, to have fewer cardinals: and *those* chosen from the whole world, in view of the fact that they are to rule the whole world: in whom consideration would be given rather for the Church than for the person or for his family connections. Such men would then

163

live, free from any scandal, off the estates of the Templars[126] or from some fixed investment assigned to them. 'Contributions' and exactions would then be ruled out for ever, instead of their constantly living from a quasi-uncertainty, off property wrongly acquired, and with the curses of thousands ringing in their ears..'[127]

Bromyard's literary register does not easily admit humour, and such few examples as are found are characterized by some bitterness. One such looks back to an earlier *exemplum* of an unduly lenient confessor to 'a certain powerful man' who ended by being scalped by the corpse rising from its coffin after being damned to hell.[128] The resultant 'red hat' gives Bromyard the chance of his wry comment on compliant counsellors: 'If all men of this kind had such hats there'd be a host of remarkable cardinals.'[129] Another instance of bitter humour comes out of the style in which bishops conventionally began or ended their letters. 'When they write 'By the grace of God bishop of such and such a place' they would more truly title their letters 'By the grace of Money' or 'By the grace of Power' or 'By the grace of Malice'.'[130] A longer extract does end with a joke, mixed with bitterness but still a joke, and at the expense of a bishop:
'Secondly on the matter of holding back church property: they are so blinded that they don't divide up the goods of the Church as they are required to do[131] (as is demonstrated at O.6.15), nor do they give the due alms to the poor nor show themselves in any way liberal to the poor – except just by lifting up their hand and blessing them: God knows with what feelings in their heart. This courtliness was mocked by one old woman in a jocular manner. The story goes that when she was begging a [silver] penny from a certain bishop but couldn't obtain one she sought a blessing. When, with no delay, she got *that* the woman replied 'If thy blessing had been worth a halfpenny I wouldn't have got it.' '[132]
And a mellower humour comes through in this quip from a cleric with a ready wit: 'And so when a certain bishop, as the story goes, kept calling his underling 'Brother' he replied 'Whatever the position is with brotherhood, one thing I know: thy tunic and thy scutcheon and mine aren't sisters!' '[133]

What may seem a rather wearisome catalogue of denunciations must be seen in the light of Bromyard's analysis of the woes of the contemporary Church within which his was not a lone voice expressing such views.[134] His mission in this task was surgical: to cut out each of the many abuses[135] choking the healthy life of the corporate body of believers. It was not to make specific proposals to ameliorate that life. To take one aspect of Church governance which perturbed him, the commandeering of the services of talented bishops – men such as Adam Orleton and Thomas Charlton, successive bishops of Hereford – for royal service as diplomats and administrators, he does not see his rôle to be that of an adviser on secular affairs. Within the Church he is harsh on failings of parish priests: his Spanish contemporary Guido de Monte Rocherii, in contrast, was devoting his thoughts and energy to the writing of a simple guide to aid simple priests, the *Manipulus curatorum*, which he published in 1333. One more specific proposal, however, which he puts forward is that 'it is essential for bishops making visitations in their dioceses to have the assistance of chosen men, chosen, as better and more faithful men, from each single parish, so that through their help sinners be visited, displayed, converted to good, and put right.'[136] Church wardens, in fact. But, greater than the accidentals, the substantial purpose which he never forgets from first to last in the *Summa* is that reforms of abuses and shortcomings within the Church serve one purpose: that it be enabled to discharge fully and with a pure heart and mind its double function of worshipping God and saving souls.

1   Prelatis negligenter agentibus subditi periclitantur. A.8.15.

2   Contra prelatos dissimulantes correctionem propter munera. M.14.8.

3   Mutant ecclesias suas sicut alii mutant uxores. A.17.30 et P.13.39.

4   Pro quo non obligarent sotularem obligant animam. A.23.23.

5   Sicut edera ascendunt. A.25.27.

6. Prelatorum invidia contra predicantes. P.12.8.

7   Qui bene defendunt animas: et qui non. B.2.4, 5.

8   Plus recipunt de stipendio et minus pugnant. B.2.15.

9   Talium ingratitudo. B.2.17.

10 Tales sunt sicut canis ruralis. B.2.33.

11. Prelatorum confederatio cum demonibus. C.4.15.

12 Multi sunt insufficientes et causa quare. C.5.18, 19.

13 Contra non residentes. C.16.6 cum sequentibus et E.2.13, bene, et C.18.7 et V.2.3.

14 Tales sunt tutores surdi et muti contra legem. F.3.31.

15 Respondebunt de toto damno. F.3.32 et 33 et 34.

16 Quomodo licentiam non residendi extorquent falsis allegationibus. F.3.34.

17 Item christus in cruce personaliter resedit pro eis. G.4.3.

18 Et per seipsum mortuos suscitavit et infirmos curavit. P.13.22.

19 Item contra dispensantes et impetrantes licentiam non residendi. I.4.8, 9.

20 Item non residentes faciunt contra exempla prophetarum et sanctorum. P.13.23.

21 Et contra iura ecclesiastica seu canonica. P.13.24.

22 Contra abutentes dispensatione et contra excusantes se beneficii exilitate. P.13.25 et I.4.8.

23 Quomodo sunt iurati in manibus episcoporum de cura habenda. P.13.26 et 50.

24 Periculum non residentium ostenditur exemplo Bede. P.13.27.

25 Et per auctoritates beati gregorii. P.13.28.

26. Periculum summi pontificis vel pastoris non refrenantis inferiorum potestatem, apud quos posse dispensare est duplex iniquitas. P.13.29.

27. Contra prelatos negligentes. C.16.9.

28. Periculum non custodientium gregem suum. C.16. arti.9.

29. Quomodo tantum tenent leges lucrativas pecuniarum. C.16.48 et P.13.16.

30. Malorum prelatorum periculum. C.18.4 cum sequentibus et E.7.4 et 5.

31. Quod nobiliores sepius sunt peiores. C.18.6.

32. Contra venatores. C.18.9.

33. Quod querunt que sua sunt et non que iesu christi. D.2.12 et P.13.5, 8, 19.

34. Tales sunt statue super muros civitatis obsesse. D.12.36.

35. Et consiliarii prelatorum tenentur de damno nisi eos informent. F.3.35.

36. Quod maiori conamine resistunt ablatoribus guerbarum et pecuniarum quam animarum. H.4.13 cum sequentibus, et specialiter 18.

37. De dicente si non fuissem de numero prelatorum non essem de numero damnatorum. I.11.24.

38. Item sunt speculatores. M.8.5.

39. Contra repudiantes christum sed non beneficium. M.9.15.

40. Contra non tenentes hospitalitatem. M.9.15 et P.13.2.

41. Contra raro celebrantes. M.10.10.

42. Quomodo sunt alphini in scacario. M.13.12.

43. Per quas portas intrant ad ecclesiastica beneficia. O.6.8.

44. Quomodo deberent dividere bona sua in quattuor partes. O.6.15.

45. Qualiter sunt in domibus suis tempore fructuum colligendorum tantum. O.6.22, 23.

46. Mali promoti sunt quasi asinus. O.6.50.

47. Quales esse deberent in opere. P.13.1.

48. Quomodo tenentur pascere alimentis documentis exemplis. P.13.2 et 3.

49. Quomodo sunt ferventes circa propriam partem et non circa partem christi. P.13.5.

50. Quomodo esse deberent leo samsonis et arca testamenti, et quod nihil est periculosius officio illorum si negligenter agatur. P.13.6.

51. Quod prius corrigant familiam propriam. P.13.7.

52. Quod propter illorum malam vitam et negligentiam demones illos salutaverunt. P.13.9.

53. Item tota christianitas periclitatur etiam propter hoc. P.13.10, 20.

54. Contra appetentes beneficia et habentes intentionem terrenam. P.13.11.

⁵⁵ Tales non habebunt mercedem celi. P.13.12.

⁵⁶ Contra habentes vel optantes plura beneficia quomodo sunt similes diabolo. P.13.13.

⁵⁷ Et contra habentes cum patrimonio suo bona ecclesie. P.13.14.

⁵⁸ Quomodo sunt forma accidentalis non substantialis. P.13.15.

⁵⁹ Permittentes mercationes in ecclesiis faciunt contra preceptum. P.13.16.

⁶⁰ Quomodo omnia sua habent ditiora et ornatiora quam christi et ecclesie. P.13.17.

⁶¹ Quod omne peccatum in eis gravius et quod plus nocent ecclesie quam tyranni. P.13.30.

⁶² Multum appetentes beneficia ecclesie sunt sicut rhamnus. P.13.32.

⁶³ Et negligentes assimilantur formidini et statue. P.13.33, 34.

⁶⁴ Qualiter assimilantur lupis quo ad ingressum et progressum. P.13.35.

⁶⁵ Et cate custodienti caseum et leoni Hieronymi. P.13.36.

⁶⁶ Beneficiorum et officiorum permutatores sunt quasi ciconia. P.13.38.

⁶⁷ Quod alii mercatores faciunt aperte ipsi faciunt clam. P.13.39.

⁶⁸ Qualiter inter prelatos maiores fures intromittunt minores, et quomodo assimilantur custodibus sepulcri christi. P.13.40.

⁶⁹ Omnia que emunt de bonis ecclesie acquiruntur ecclesie. P.13.41.

⁷⁰ Quod tenentur ad restitutionem male consumptorum. P.13.42, 43, 45.

⁷¹ Difficile est videre quomodo poterunt salvari. P.13.44.

⁷² Volunt habere commodum sed non curam sponse. P.13.45.

⁷³ Qui ab eis recipiunt bona ecclesie et non restituunt male finiunt. P.13.46.

⁷⁴ Quot periculis prelati exponuntur. P.13.47 per beatum Gregorium.

⁷⁵ Non custodientes gregem damnabuntur. P.13.48 et 50.

⁷⁶ Et male viventes. P.13.49.

⁷⁷ In penis gravius aliis punientur. P.13.51.

⁷⁸ Maiores prelati dando beneficia indignis multos scandalisant. P.13.53 et 54.

⁷⁹ Qualem intentionem habere deberent in beneficii susceptione. P.13.55.

⁸⁰ Differentia inter pastorem mercennarium et furem. P.13.57.

⁸¹ Quod non est prelatis vel maioribus quibuscumque detrahendum et quomodo quidam dixit quod ecclesia non esset digna regi nisi a reprobis. P.13.58.

⁸² Quod studium prelatorum deberet esse gregem suum custodire. S.3.9.

⁸³ Item prelati sunt murus ecclesie dirutus. S.9.4.

84 Item debent habere vitam contemplativam et activam. V.7.4.

Quere: ambitio, dispensatio, episcopi, clerici, hospitalitas, elemosyna, misericordia, papa, patroni, reges, sacerdotium, ecclesiastici, ordo [clericalis], symonia.

85 Liber Sextus 1.6.34 Cum ex eo: full text also in Boyle, Cum ex eo pp.271-272. The constitution's main provisions may be thus summarized:
1. men preferred to a cure of souls to proceed to the subdiaconate within one year of their preferment:
2. to be given leave of non-residence for study purposes for up to seven years:
3. during their period of study to enjoy the revenue from their benefices:
4. their bishops and superiors to ensure that the cure of souls be diligently exercised through good and adequate deputies who are to be deputed by them [the bishops] to the churches concerned*:
5. these deputies to be adequately remunerated:
6. within one year of the completion of their studies the beneficed men to proceed to be ordained as deacons and priests.
* '..ut per bonos et sufficientes vicarios ab eis in huiusmodi ecclesiis deputandos animarum cura diligenter exerceatur..'

86 Sexto ostenditur negligentia summi pastoris in terra qui inferiores ad residendum non compellit. (P.13.22)

87 Dispensation for non-residency for the purpose of study was not uncommon before *Cum ex eo*. Richard Swinfield as bishop of Hereford had, from 19 March 1283 to 13 October 1287, released 13 holders of benefices within his diocese for such study: eight for 2 years or less, three for 3 years, one for 5 and one for 7 years. (Swinfield pp.545-546). And Boyle Cum ex eo pp.267-268, citing Liber Sextus 1.6.14 and the clause Swinfield used: 'Super residentia vero (ut praemittitur) facienda, possit ordinarius gratiam dispensationis ad tempus facere, prout causa rationabilis id exposcit.'

88 Boyle, Cum ex eo, especially pp.263-268: and Boyle, Clerical Education, especially pp.22-26.

89 Boyle, Cum ex eo pp.297-298.

90 Haines, Orleton p.209.

91 Bromyard too recognized this need: ecclesia viris indiget litteratis [The church needs educated men] (O.4.17).

92 Judging that a degree in the civil law would further their careers in either Church or State better than a theological course would some clerics made such a choice. See Boyle, Cum ex eo pp.279-280, where he cites Iohannes Andreae, who took a permissive stance on this issue: 'sive in grammatica, sive in iure canonico, vel civili, vel scientia theologiae studeat.' Bromyard vigorously objected to clerics following a course of civil law while on this dispensation but noted 'Pro magna namque parte non residentes sunt iuriste', citing Hostiensis in denunciation of this practice. (P.13.24). He inveighs against the greed which draws men to the study of the civil law in ADVOCATI: 'quasi omnes volunt leges audire lucrativas..' (A.14.30).

93 Absentari a grege quantum possunt querunt: permittentes oves in deserto a lupis inferni devorari: intantum quod videntur pactum et indenturam inter eos et demones fecisse. Ita quod ipsi recipiant de ovibus lanam et lac id est temporalia commoda: et demones animas qui illas et nihil aliud petunt..
Sicut enim canes qui nobiles vocantur sicut leporarii et huiusmodi gregem communiter non custodiunt sed potius devorant.. Ita nobiles et elati sanguine vel superbia.. ipsi eligunt derelicto grege esse in curiis magnorum ut carnes pinguium comedant. Sicut enim canes rurales et simplices ad domus et gregis custodiam eliguntur Ita ad custodiam gregis dei humilitate simplices eligendi sunt.. Et cristus elegit ad custodiam ecclesie piscatores et semper infirma elegit ut confundat forcia. Et ideo dum deus habuit curam et electionem* pastorum greges bene

custodiebantur.   Sed modo Symon et cesar et sanguis habent huiusmodi electiones et confirmationes [et]** totum pervertitur, et grex a lupis devoratur. Nec mirum..

Propter duo. Primo quia absentat se a grege..   Sed dicent vel dicere poterunt duo ad sui excusationem. Primo habent bonum vicarium vel sacerdotem qui curam habent† animarum sibi subiectarum: quibus respondendum est quod multi eorum parum curant quales sint illi, vel qualiter gregem custodiant nisi quod ipsi lucrum reportent.   Quod quottidiano patet exemplo et experimento..quid ergo dicturus est qui per annum vel plures annos absens est si dicat ad locum meum tenentem cura pertinet: querendum est ab eo si ille est sufficiens.. Ponatur quod sit valde sufficiens non potest esse tante hospitalitatis etiam pauperes recipiendo nec tante auctoritatis in docendo et corripiendo sicut magister et dominus suus..   Secundo se excusare poterunt ad excusandas excusationes in peccatis: quod quia sciverunt quod ipsi et loca sua tenentes fuerunt nimis pigri et insufficientes ad animarum custodiam et ad predam de ore dyaboli liberandam.. Ideo providerunt eis de velocissimis canibus super terram currentibus.. Ita ipsi canes et

falcones et divites exenia et fructus afferentes custodiunt: et pauperes non afferentes nisi animas non diligunt..prelati vero et viri ecclesiastici qui subditos suos nec a se nec ab aliis custodiunt sed ad peccata trahunt et trahere permittunt†† nullius legis sunt. (C.18.5-10)

       * omitting the compositor's *et*
      **I supply *et*
      † *qui..habent* makes good sense: but I suspect that Bromyard may have written
       qui..habeat.
      †† my reading for *premittunt* of text

94

Sexto ostenditur negligentia summi pastoris in terra qui inferiores ad residendum non compellit. (P.13.22)

95

Et nota quod omnes predicte allegationes multum esse videntur contra illos cum quibus episcopi dispensant: quod causa eruditionis scolas exercere poterunt per septennium vel alium terminum infra septennium contentum: postquam ad ecclesias curam animarum habentes promoti fuerint antequam ad sacerdotium promoveantur Sicut patet libro. vi. decre. ti. de elec. c. cum ex eo. nisi in scolis viriliter addiscant, quia illa est finalis causa quare eis licentia et privilegium de non residendo et ad ordines non promovendo datum est: sicut expresse patet ex illius capituli tenore in quo prius ostendit quomodo ecclesia viris indiget literatis: et quod magnum damnum ex talium patitur defectu.   Deinde dat episcopis auctoritatem quod cum volentibus in scientia proficere dispensare poterunt: ut fructum in dei ecclesia suo tempore afferre valeant oportunum [sic].

Ex quo patet quod profectus in scolis causa est quare papa cum eis dispensare voluit de non residentia. Nec aliter eis talem dedit licentiam. Illa ergo causa cessante coram deo iudicantur sine licentia non residere et non ordinari: malo titulo iudicantur beneficia sua possidere per

Decretalem in. vi. de elec. c. licet. In qua privantur omnes non ordinati ad ordinem sacerdotalem infra annum, licet ergo non ordinati coram mundo titulo dispensationis excusentur: si tamen viriliter non studuerint coram deo excusati non sunt. (O.4.17).

96

Alfini vero cornuti episcopos significant: et alios inferiores prelatos qui si boni sint et cornuti spiritualiter ex studio sacre scripture et colloquio cum deo in orationibus sicut Moyses. Exo.xxxiiii. tunc eorum cornua significant ipsos habere quod habere deberent et quod de facto habent ita quod in eis est signum et signatum: scientia videlicet novi et veteris testamenti et quod illis cornibus expugnabunt errantes et destruent errores contra illa duo testamenta insurgentes. Si vero mali fuerint, symoniace vel indigne promoti, prece videlicet vel precio vel regio imperio vel magnorum minis vel litteris seu carnali favore non sunt cornuti ex divino eloquio orationis vel lectionis: sed potius illorum cornua significare possunt duo: que ad literam in eis inveniuntur: quod videlicet nec scientiam habent testamentorum nec bonitatem morum: quod insuper nec lupos expugnant vel a gregibus arcent sed potius defendunt, et canes id est predicatores expugnant artant* et expellunt ne gregem custodiant: vel significare possunt potestatem seu astutiam propriam et secularem per quas indigne promoti sunt, et deum in moribus perversis et membris suis expugnant. Et tales Alfini tria puncta obliquando pertranseunt: quia illorum opera triplex malum pervertit, amor videlicet odium, et cupiditas, quia si quem promovent hoc potius amore faciunt carnali quam spirituali. Si quem vero aspere corrigunt vel puniunt hoc potius faciunt propter odium persone quam peccati: ex quo accidit frequenter quod non puniendos puniunt: vel puniendos ultra condignum puniunt: et puniendos impunitos dimittunt. Si quem insuper in corpore punire deberent: munerum cupiditate seducti, in bursa puniunt, ex quo accidit quod peccata sub annuo censu ad firmam tradunt: ut pecuniam non habitam acquirant: vel quod quasi mercennarii lupum corrigendum fugiant[†] ne bona possessa amittant. Et sic dum proprie student ditationi pecunias colligendo diabolum etiam ditant, animas perdendo. Et qui ex officio deberent esse diaboli et viciorum expugnatores iam per cupiditatem sunt diaboli procuratores et viciorum promotores. (M.13.12).

> * Bromyard uses the same word (artare, artatio) at C.4.17, P.13.8, 9 and
> V.1.8, in the same context and with the same anger: in each case to
> protest against the muzzling of preachers (predicatores) by negligent
> bishops. 'On the contrary they would rather wish that they [preachers]
> kept quiet about other matters especially in which they themselves
> [prelates] are involved, against which they neither preach themselves nor
> would want others to preach..' (P.13.8). '..They don't resist, they don't
> destroy sins: instead, they *muzzle* those who would want to resist and
> make a defence [against sins] through advice and preaching..' (P.13.9)
> 'Si..non resistunt nec peccata destruunt sed potius illos qui consiliis et
> predicationibus resistere et defendere vellent *artant*: quis eos a proditionis
> periculo poterit excusare?'
> [†] in a parallel construction with 'tradunt' but perhaps attracted into the
> subjunctive by the proximity of 'acquirant'. This is a tenuous thread
> to build a conclusion on but since this 'attraction' is occasionally found
> in the *Summa* it is likelier to be Bromyard's own practice than a compositor's:
> and *may* indicate that Bromyard was a rapid writer who may not always
> have had the time, amid his other duties, to read through his work.

97 It is difficult for us to know to what extent 'demons' should be treated as a literary device in the *Summa* or considered as having a physical presence when we realize the several accounts which narrate their interference in human affairs. One of the 29 charges brought by Guillaume de Plaisans (a legal adviser to Philip IV) against Bonifacius VIII was that he kept a private demon. (Boase p.333). The charge must have been thought to command some level of plausibility. Depictions of demons abound in contemporary paintings in several media: one such, in a 14th century German manuscript, shows Virgil smashing open a barrel or huge bottle from which three demons emerge. (Kieckhefer pp.113, 115, figure 12b).

98 ...dum civitas ecclesie..paucos haubuit fortes bellatores statum suum contra omnes insultus demonum et tyrannorum et quorumcumque malorum tenuit bonum. Sed ipsis nunc mortuis, et aliis non quales ipsi fuerunt: sed quasi statuis mortuis in habitu clericali super muros ecclesie positis...demones atque demonum ministri absque timore vel resistentia civitatem ecclesie invadunt et destruunt: Sed hoc in defectu David id est pape, archiepiscopi, episcopi: quia ad quemlibet illorum pertinet.. (P.13.34).

99 Sic in proposito litterati venientes vel sperantes et appropinquantes ad beneficia ecclesiastica id est ad oves et ad curam animarum famam malam quantum possunt abscondunt: et omnem simulantes humilitatem et maturitatem incedunt ad illum tamen finem ut de ovibus christi pascantur: non ut oves christi pascant.. (P.13.35).

100 ..illud Eccl'es.ix.Melior est canis vivus leone mortuo id est parvus predicator vel sacerdos: qui contra vitia latrat tali magno prelato qui timore munere vel negligentia contra vitia quasi leo mortuus non rugit delinquentium. (P.13.36).

101 ...primo comparantur et assimilantur formidini seu statue posite in blado, habenti[*] arcum fictum et sagittam in manu et formam hominis vivi, quam volucres cum talibus signis videntes primo timent et fugiunt: deinde opera vite in illo non percipientes sed ipsam statuam mortuam imaginantes paulatim appropinquant, et in fine super caput eius sedentes ipsum permerdant bladumque absque timore comedunt, fitque avium bladum comedentium potius requies et refugium quam timor vel custodia... eorum ministri aliquibus ministrant prelatis et viris ecclesiasticis in quibus non sunt opera vite spiritualis, videntes namque illos locum, statum et officium tenere regiminis et correctionis primo timent, sed postea videntes illos esse statuas spiritualiter mortuas: quia nec spiritualiter in seipsis vivunt nec efficaciter alios corrigunt..appropinquant et tam ipsos quam subditos absque timore spiritualiter deturpant. (P.13.33)

* for 'habente' of text.

Of a multitude of such men two examples suffice: John de Aquablanca, dean of Hereford 1262-1320 and prebendary of Bullinghope at least from c.1291 to 1320 (Le Neve/Horn pp.3, 15): and Aymo de Savoy, archdeacon of York 1300-1307, provided by Bonifacius VIII. 'Aymo was under age, not in holy orders and held benefices to the value of 1000 marks..' (Gill pp.13-14)

..pluralitas beneficiorum nec sine peccato appetitur nec sine periculo possidetur. (P.13.13)

Nummus vincit, nummus regnat, nummus imperat universis.. (M.14.11). This quotation comes towards the end of an 'aria' on the power of bribes: 'For 'gifts' award honours to the undeserving and lack of a 'gift' pushes the deserving to the back.' 'Munera namque indignos honorant, et dignos muneris defectus postponit.' This observation chimes with the tenor of the magnificent poem 'In terra summus   rex est hoc tempore Nummus' (Carmina Burana 11) in which 'Nummus' occurs 47 times.

Pro animabus vero custodiendis parum curare videntur quales habeant custodes: nisi quos consanguinitas vel affinitas vel symonia vel bonum forum eis presentat: licet nec sint casti nec cauti nec sani nec litterati. (P.13.19) Bromyard's contemporary, the author of the Vita Edwardi secundi, concurs with the Dominican's damning judgement: 'Erubescat doleatque prelatus preesse populo nec prodesse , docentis officium assumpsisse et in doctrina populi mutum esse. Talem siquidem non prefert honestas set cupiditas, non moralitas set uenalitas, non sciencia set pecunia, non meritum set precium, non eleccio set ambicio..' (Vita p.180, of the year – and probably written in the year – 1320.) Wendy R. Childs' translation (of a slightly larger passage) is: 'Men completely ignorant of Holy Scripture usurp the burden of an office they cannot uphold, drawing on other people's knowledge rather than their own. May a prelate blush and grieve to find himself in command of the people without being of use, to have taken upon himself the duty of teaching, and to be dumb in instructing the people. It is indeed not honour but greed which promotes such a man [Henry Burghersh], not morality but venality, not knowledge but money, not merit but a bribe, not free choice but soliciting votes..' (Vita p.181).

..si quis prelatus clericus vel laicus noluerit tyrannorum audire preces quas scribunt pro clericis suis promovendis vel pro quibuscunque aliis negociis que cordi habent, statim scribunt ministris suis vel amicis ut illis noceant omnibus quibus possunt modis. (M.8.20)

Ita mundus nunc papam nunc imperatorem nunc regem et quemcunque potentem ad mortem et terram pauperem mittit et successorem vel heredem loco eius substituit. (M.11.112)

..sicut ille prece et precio statum illum obtinuit: ita nunc quasi omnia obtinent officia et loca, tam secularia quam ecclesiastica. (M.11.113)

..quidam valens sacre theologie professor in cathedra sua legens dixit quod maluit unum bonum sacerdotem pro ipso celebrantem quam mille malos. (M.10.3) ..Tali ergo [a bad priest] obolum non darem ut pro anima mea vel patris mei per annum celebraret.. (M.10.4)

Sic avari cumulant terram super terram: prebendam super prebendam.. (A.25.24)

Assimilantur eis [backsliders after the austerities of Lent] hypocrite qui ideo ore omnia carnalia contemnunt idest fingunt se in altum sanctitatis volare ut beneficia ecclesiastica promotiones munera et gratias et laudes hominum adipiscantur... Alii ascendunt ad locum cupiditatis vel vanitatis ad modum edere vel veprium per maceriam inordinati favoris. Edera enim in ascensu suo non innititur virtuti vel fortitudini proprie, sed parietis. Ita volentes ascendere locum cupiditatis in statu ecclesiastico, cum de virtute et fortitudine spirituali seu ecclesiastica et litteratura et moribus nihil aut parum habeant innituntur parieti idest alicui prelato vel patrono seu potenti: eique muneribus et precibus vel sanguine vel servicio ligantur. (A.25.25, 27)

112   ..quia sil illud beneficium quod promoti vel salarium quod sacerdotes cum ordine vel sacerdotio recipiunt possent sine ordine recipere et sacerdotio et missarum celebratione vix centesimus illorum ordinaretur. Quod per hoc patet quod quando sunt pauperes frequenter: promoti vero vix semel vel nunquam in anno celebrant.. (O.6.10)

113   Isti vero de patrimonio christi uxores nutriuunt et vesciunt aliorum adulteras et focarias: et filios sustenant spurios, futuros latrones et paterni criminis imitatores. In seculo enim remanentes pre paupertate uxores proprias et legitimas non possent sustentare: ideo se ordinari faciunt ut de bonis christi sustentent alienas et seipsos. (O.6.11)

114   Hec namque est aliquorum iocunda iactatio, quod beneficium habent non curatum. (P.13.44).

115   Et prima aliquorum questio quando de beneficio eis oblato vel amicis dato mentio fit: utrum sit curatum vel non, et quantum valeat. (P.13.45)

116   ..illud male pretendunt post beneficium obtentum: quia si habes unam carrucatam terre vel minus vel parum ultra sicut frequenter contingit: se et uxorem et familiam exhibet in domo, et filios duos vel tres in scolis, et filias nuptui tradit: pro cuius terra vel redditibus vix inveniret qui ei daret. x. marcas per annum, quis ei crederet, qui nec habent ex parte dei uxorem vel filios aut filias, qui dicunt quod cum beneficio ecclesiastico. x. marcarum vel amplius domum tenere non possunt sed domum ecclesie cadere permittunt. (P.13.25)

117   ..statuto ecclesiastico in quo reputatur inconveniens quod sacerdos vix quater in anno missarum celebret sollemnia.. (M.10.10) vix quater in anno celebrando.. (O.6.26)

118   Ita isti principium versus et finem simul coniungunt, et medium ita festinando saltant, quod nescio si deus illud intelligat vel homo.. (O.6.26)

119   ..nonnulli namque illorum libentius ducunt canes et falcones ad venationem quam cristianos ad devotionem. (O.6.18)

120   Sicut faciunt nonnulli vulpinam facientes confessionem, quia ad modum vulpis qui antequam confiteretur sacerdoti aucam portasse legitur.. (P.7.30)

121   Numquid si Petrus in terris nunc existens: vel aliqui prime ecclesie pastores noticiam haberent de his qui nunc se fatentur illorum esse successores: sic de omnibus religiosorum fundatoribus. Si enim in tali vita, habitu et ceteris que in usu sunt nunc coram eis in terris ducerentur et quereretur ab eis: cuius est imago hec et superscriptio: quilibet pro parte sua responderet: non mea: quia ego fui pauper in re et exteriori ostensione: Isti vero nec sunt in uno nec in alio. (P.3.23)

122   Kelly neatly sums up Iohannes XXII's financial changes: '..he created a new fiscal system, extending to all countries the payment to the holy see of annates, i.e. the first year's revenue of a benefice, reserving (1319) all minor benefices for three years to the papacy, and levying special subsidies..' (ODP p.214)

123   ..subtractis namque cardinalium onerosa numerositate et equorum et familie nimia multitudine et parentele inordinata affectione et totius apparatus superba vanitate tantarum necessitas cessabit collectarum. A quibus ideo cessare deberent ne gregem pusillum qui in cristum credit eiusque sanguine redemptus est scandalisarent: licet de consecratis in curia iuxta abusum vel consuetudinem annuum ecclesie valorem: licetque de ecclesiis vacantibus primi anni fructus: licet etiam quando eis placet ecclesie decimam sine magno peccato recipere possent: tamen propter vitandum scandalum a talibus se refrenare deberent: ne fons vite fons efficiatur veneni. Si enim illius sanctissime sedis presidentes scirent quomodo non solum infideles saraceni, iudei, scismatici, et heretici, sed etiam fideles de illorum non dico scandalisantur sed obloquuntur apparatu quem superbum et a cristi tramite deviantem iudicant, quomodo de illa retentione quam a consecratis vel datis in curia pro camera retinent pape populus detrahit cristianus dicens Non tam bene tanti illum emit episcopatum, quis nostram symoniam vitabit..
(H.4.16)

124 ..ipsos consecratos: quos ad magnam pecunie summam obligant antequam aliquid de ecclesia sumant pro qua mutuo accipienda ecclesias aut prebendas creditoribus symoniace quandoque dant vel promittunt quandoque palium vel alia preciosa obligant.. et fideiussores inveniunt et pro simplo forte se obligant ad duplum: et duplum ratione interesse quandoque crescit in decuplum. Pro quo solvendo vel tyrannidem in subditos exercent et collectam de clero faciunt pro debito curie solvendo..vel miseram vitam et parcam..extra dyocesim morando ducunt.. (H.4.17)

125 Guillemain provides figures (pp.183-192) which amply justify Bromyard's call for reform both of numbers and of the unbalanced national representation in the cardinalate. The change from Italian dominance under Benedictus XI to French under Clemens V and Iohannes XXII is marked. In 1304 the Sacred College was made up of 19 cardinals of whom 15 were Italian, 2 French, 1 English and 1 Castilian. Clemens V in his pontificate chose 24 cardinals, of whom one was English, 23 French (twenty of these from the Midi). Iohannes XXII elevated 28 men to the College, of whom 4 were Italians, 1 Castilian and 23 French (of whom twenty came from the Midi). Iohannes had awarded 26 of his 28 scarlet hats in four promotions: 1316 (8), 1317 (1), 1320 (7) and 1327 (10).
In short, from 1305 to 1331, in nine promotions Clemens V and Iohannes XXII chose 52 cardinals, of whom 46 were French: of these 46 forty came from the Midi. Guillemain drily comments, of Iohannes' appointments, 'Jean XXII jugea bon de ne pas oublier les Italiens: il en nomma quatre..'! (p.185)

126 The question of what to do with the estates of the recently suppressed Order of Templars was one of the main subjects for debate at the Council of Vienne of 1311-1312. The Hospitallers were, eventually, the main beneficiaries.

127 ..Sanctius ergo et pro se ipsis et pro aliis esset: pauciores et de toto mundo electos habere cardinales: utpote qui totum mundum sunt recturi: in quibus ecclesie potius quam persone vel parentele esset provisum: qui de terris templariorum vel de aliqua certa et eis assignata portione sine scandalo viverent: muneribus et exactionibus in sempiternum exclusis: quam semper quasi de incerto et de male acquisito et cum multorum vivere maledictionibus non diis sed peccatis detraho: nec pono os in celum sed in scenum eo modo quo paulus petrum reprehendit. Gal.ii. (H.4.17)

128 ..propter meam negligentiam quia tales dilexi sum damnatus..et accipiens eum per caput totam pellem cum pilis inde extraxit.. (A.7.20)

129 Si nunc omnes tales huiusmodi haberent capellos essent multi mirabiles cardinales. (M.13.9)

130 ..quando scribunt: dei gratia espiscopus talis loci: veratius litteras suas intitularent pecunie vel potentie vel malicie gratia.. (P.13.19)

131 Instead, they misuse Church revenues to buy themselves large estates and marry their kin into the gentry and nobility. '..quod prelati magni et alii iudices de parvo statu et parentela exaltati de bonis ecclesie et aliis male perquisitis magnas emunt terras, pulchra construunt maneria: consanguineas vel filias suas magnorum maritant filiis..' (P.13.46)

132 Secundo circa rerum ecclesie detentionem intantum excecantur quod bona ecclesie non dividunt ut tenentur sicut ostensum est O.vi.xv. nec elemosynas debitas dant pauperibus nec in aliquo erga pauperes se liberales ostendunt, nisi tantum manum elevando et ipsos deus scit quo corde benedicendo. Quam curialitatem quedam vetula iocunde derisit: de qua fertur quod cum importune denarium a quodam episcopo peteret, nec obtinere potuit petivit benedictionem, quam cum statim daret Respondit mulier: Si benedictio tua obolum valuisset illam non obtinuissem. (P.13.20)

133 Unde cum quidam prelatus subditum suum, ut fertur, fratrem vocaret Respondit Quomodocunque sit de fraternitate, unum scio, quod tunica tua et scutella tua et mea non sunt sorores.. (E.4.4)

134 Trenchant criticism of the governance of the Church and its hierarchy had long antecedents. Just over a century before Bromyard was writing his *Summa* the Carmina Burana received their final form. ('Die meisten Carmina Burana sind in zwölften und im frühen dreizehnten Jahrhundert

enstanden': Carmina Burana p.837). Among the more memorable strictures in this collection is 131[a]:

> Bulla fulminante
> sub iudice tonante,
> reo appellante,
> sententia gravante
> Veritas supprimitur,
> distrahitur
> et venditur
> Iustitia prostante;
> itur et recurritur
> ad Curiam, nec ante
> quid consequitur
> quam exuitur quadrante.

The pope's gatekeepers are deafer than Cerberus: the one way to make them hear is to strike their doors with 'a *silver* hammer' (malleus argenteus).

Disapproval of corrupt practices continued to be voiced, often stridently, well into Bromyard's time. Of the year 1313 the author of the 'Vita' writes: 'What shall I say of the clerks who beset the Curia these days, and buy dignities and prebends with a great profusion of cash as if in the marketplace? If we say that simony is committed, the pope himself [Clemens V] cannot be excused, because simony is mutually binding; for just as it binds the purchaser so also it condemns the seller.' ('Vita' p.83: Childs' translation). On other levels too controversy raged, namely the pastoral, political, administrative and theological. The question of the poverty of Christ was one of these. Salvatorelli writes: 'John XXII, who had the gift of embittering and carrying to extremes all conflicts, was now involved in a struggle not only with the Spirituals, but with the regular oganization of the Order, the Community (or Conventuals), and so with all the Franciscans. We see the existence in Italy at the beginning of the 14th century of a radical opposition to the pontificate which considered the contemporary papacy as a manifestation of the Antichrist and an institution of the devil [..una opposizione radicale al pontificato che considerava il papato attuale come una manifestazione dell' Anticristo e un istituto diabolico.]. The most representative figure of this opposition was Fra Dolcino.. Raniero bishop of Vercelli preached the crusade against him in 1305.. and on 1 June 1307 he was burnt alive in Vercelli.' (Salvatorelli p.793). Opposition to the wordliness of the papacy is assocated too with Iacopone da Todi (d.1306) and Ubertino da Casale (d.c.1330)

One extreme in the political debate on the extent and validity of papal secular power was upheld by Marsiglio of Padua and Jean de Jandun in their *Defensor Pacis* of 1324 (presented to Ludwig of Bavaria in summer 1326 in Nuremberg) [see chapter 30 note 79]: but even an ardent supporter of absolute papal power such as Agostino Trionfo, in his *Summa de potestate papae* of 1320 affirmed that a heretical pope should be deposed.

The controversy over Iohannes XXII's four winter sermons of 1331-32 , on whether the souls of the saints already enjoy the full vision of God, condemned as heretical in 1333 by the University of Paris, came too late for the *Summa*: nor was it a matter, one suspects, apt to engage Bromyard's attention. He was essentially a man concerned with a more momentous issue, the saving of souls of those he could reach. For him the administration of the Church had importance chiefly as it rendered that primary goal more attainable: and abstract theorizing he dismissed with scorn.

[135] On one such abuse, the unhealthy veneration of saintly relics, he quotes Prosper, *De vita contemplativa*: and continues: 'bene volunt colligere fragmenta et reliquias sanctorum eis dimissas sed non mores: Sicut illi qui vadunt cum indulgentiis: qui omnia predicant et sustinent propter lucrum temporale..' (R.5.5) 'They eagerly yearn to collect the fragments and relics of saints left them – but not their moral standards: just like those who go about with indulgences: all their preaching, everything they put up with is for the sake of reward in *this* life..'

[136] Ita prelatis dioceses suas visitantibus necessarium est adiutorium electorum virorum qui ad hoc de singulis parrochiis eliguntur* fideliores et meliores: ut per eorum auxilium peccatores visitentur ostendantur et ad bonum convertantur et corrigantur. (V.8.4)
    * Did Bromyard write 'eligantur'?

23

SOME OBSERVATIONS ON *EXEMPLA*

The nature of the 13th and 14th century *exemplum* has been the subject of much recent investigation, following Welter's initial survey. One such study, Les *Exempla* Médiévaux: Nouvelles Perspectives[1], incorporates illuminating essays by a score of scholars, among them, Peter von Moos.[2] He writes:

'This reference [to human deeds recorded in history] is quite frequently accompanied by a short passage of dialogue, by a spiritual response, by a pointed saying (*dictum*, fable, maxim). Even if the lesson is conveyed by fables or parables, the fictive element is integrated into a scene of real life. The facts which are related come from the day-to-day narrative of the lives of ordinary people or from the events comprising the history of the great; they may take their origin from "news items", from tittle-tattle of a recent scandal in the news, or from heroic deeds of a distant past and of a near-mythical source. It has often been said, and rightly, that the *exempla* found in homilies prefer the former to the latter. The people in these stories are for the greater part anonymous, designated, usually, by a *quidam*; the historical reality of these vague anecdotes is confirmed – to make up for the vagueness – by oral witnesses or by the personal experience of the speaker, who becomes, in this way, the authenticator of the past event. The preacher who was addressing a crowd or, at all events, an audience made up of ordinary people of diverse backgrounds, had in essence an interest in presenting the story of a normal everyday man, to minimize the difference between the man in the story and the people listening...'[3]

Von Moos fastens upon the tendency of many medieval preachers to use the camouflage of *rex quidam* or *sapiens quidam* to hide the identity of mighty persons known to him: and, conversely, to replace a hero of the past with a contemporary king of France[4]. Bromyard follows the first practice many times, perhaps, when referring to his contemporaries, as a protective device (as he assuredly does in his allusions to the powerful men of the England of his day): but evidence of the latter convention would be difficult to assemble.

Of the nature of Bromyard's *exempla* it is fair to conclude that he eschews anything that partakes of von Moos' 'tittle-tattle of a recent scandal in the news'[5] but incorporates the other elements of the German scholar's description.

In her study of a collection of 252 *exempla* dating from the third quarter of the thirteenth century[6] Isabella Rava-Cordier[7] points to the anonymous preacher's use of geographic social and cultural references as a means of bridging the gap between pulpit and congregation: the nearer the better for the preacher's task of persuasion.[8]

Subjective interpretations render social and cultural linkages harder to quantify than geographic or topographic references, which she illustrates in her Figure 2.[9] This reveals the proximity of the principal houses of the Penitential Order of Jesus Christ in the south of France to 17 towns, among them Montpellier, Orange, Nîmes, Marseille and Toulon, all of which are named in this collection. This firm siting of the content of the *exempla* in the region of the audience is in marked contrast to Bromyard's practice, who avoids any mention of Herefordshire, Shropshire, Worcestershire or other nearby counties in *his exempla*: for him, it seems, remoteness of location strengthens authenticity.

'There are others who for the purpose of persuading people of the validity of their message make use of, at times, *exempla* only, at other times of authorities only: but it is better to make use of any one of these in the task of persuading the audience to your point of view, so that those not moved by one may be moved by another, since there are large numbers of people moved more by one than by another.'[10]   In his frequency and in his numbers of both *exempla* and citations of authorities Bromyard fulfils Humbertus' advice in unstinting measure.

Bromyard's 189 capitula are divided into exactly 1200 articuli. If one assumes that a good deal of planning was expended in preparation for the writing of the *Summa* – an assumption I believe one must make – then a scheduling of the articuli for each capitulum would have given him a framework to adhere to which would have then freed his thoughts from recurring decisions on the development of each capitulum. This freedom would have been a merciful boon for a writer in his situation: a religious subjected to the frequent interruptions to his writing, his adding of referenced citations and his adding and checking of cross-references.   These interruptions, of course, are mainly those instanced by Hinnebusch in his detailed account of the Dominican's daily routine.[11]

If one accepts that Bromyard may well have sketched out his 1200 articuli in advance of beginning his text it becomes easier to understand the advantages for him of composing the *Summa* in a series of smaller units: freed, moreover, from the tyranny of alphabetic order in that he could add at will to any articulus regardless of sequence.

One unit shaping his writing will have been the paper[12] or parchment he wrote on: folded in two, one imagines, giving him four pages. These two leaves and four pages may have been passed to fellow friars for immediate copying, or perhaps only in larger units of gatherings of eight or ten leaves.

This, I admit, is speculation. One point which may readily be conceded is that he will have needed an efficient filing system and remarkably retentive memory.

In an attempt to test Boyle's implicit theory that Bromyard wrote the 189 capitula in alphabetic order[13] I undertook an analysis of the distribution of *exempla* throughout the *Summa* to see whether their distribution and frequency could be a pointer to confirming or refuting Boyle's belief. In so doing, one essential preliminary was measuring the length of each capitulum (the measuring of *fractions* of columns in my text was done by eye). The tables and graph accompanying this examination set out the data thus obtained.

The distribution and frequency of *exempla* throughout the *Summa* fall within a not unusual pattern, except within the grouping which I isolated as V1 to V12 and X1, the final thirteen capitula. Whether this aberration was due to the nature of these capitula or whether it reveals clues as to the order of Bromyard's composing may call for closer study: though resolution of the question may remain elusive.

Another of my arbitrary groupings, A1-11, also displays aberration from the norm in that those eleven capitula are noticeably shorter, at an average of some 1650 words, than any other group: which may be evidence that they mark a tentative beginning to the *Summa*. But I submit that no inference may safely be drawn as to Bromyard's order of composition of the 165 capitula betweeen A11 and V1.

Before the presentation of the data given in the three tables and graph come, randomly chosen, four of Bromyard's *exempla* as a tiny sample of his use of the device.

1.   In his capitulum ANGELUS Bromyard asserts that angels take delight in the spiritual progress of good men, and stay with them: but shun the society of evil men.

'On this point there may be adduced the story of two men travelling by road together, so the tale goes, while a third man followed them some way back. The man following at times saw a young man with these religious ahead of him: and at times he seemed suddenly to disappear. This happened several times, to his astonishment. So when they'd arrived at the entrance to the town he asked these religious who that very handsome young man was, and where he'd got to. They assured him they'd had no such companion with them: so he told them what he'd seen. They realized, from what their follower recounted, that in the places where their conversation had been on honourable matters the young man was seen with them: but when their talk had strayed on to other themes he'd vanished...'[14]

The three men understood that the mysterious companion had been either Christ or an angel.

2.   In DECIME (Tithes) comes this moral tale.

'First, the story of a man who, it is said, on entering his grange after autumn and surprised at the unusual meagreness of his store [of grain] caught sight of the devil squatting on the heap. He realized that this was the consequence of a deceitful tithing and ordered the whole lot to be tithed again. This done, the grange was refilled..'[15]

So, tithing is accompanied by abundance: failure to tithe by penury.

3.   Those envious of and wishing ill to others so as to benefit from their deaths may not always get what they intend. (From INVIDIA).

'They are compared to a certain man incarcerated in the clerics' prison owned by the archbishop of Reims. This man killed his two companions and fellow-prisoners in order to get their food supply which was lowered by rope into the well. They [the two] had been in the habit of giving proof that they were alive by shouting: he then, for several days, imitated their voices, and so, after their deaths, he, in their names, got hold of their ration of bread.' A woeful and evil man, in everyone's judgement: for a short prolongation of the miserable life he was enduring in prison to kill two men: almost certain to die anyway, since no one survived in that jail longer than a year: 'and yet in reality some men consumed by envy are more wretched and in a worse state than this creature', Bromyard concludes.[16]

4.   The folly of people who say to others [presumably to religious] 'You are to pray and fast for us' is exemplified by this story in PENITENTIA, of 'a certain man' (quidam) who'd been moved to exercise penitence.

'Returning from confession, as the story has it, he had fallen into the habit of putting on a melancholy face and wouldn't accept the consolation offered by his wife, saying 'How could I put on a cheerful face when I call to mind that I'm burdened with so many fastings through my confessor?' She kept on promising him that she was willing to undergo the whole of the fasting on his behalf. And so, comforted by this, he got in the habit of eating and drinking, and putting on a pleasant face. But God, wanting him to pull back from this mistake, showed him through a vision his approach, with his wife, to the gate of heaven: and Peter, the keeper of the gate of heaven, taking by hand his wife and admitting her: but, as he attempted, in his eagerness, to enter, thrusting him back, saying 'Because she performed the works of penitence on your behalf, so she will receive the reward on your behalf, and the prizes of her merits.' After this courteous warning by means of the vision he then performed his own penitence. He understood that each person will receive his or her own reward in accordance with individual effort. I Corinthians iii.[17]

The four *exempla* selected here, and one or two others occurring in passages of the *Summa* presented for other purposes, cannot adequately indicate the variety found within the whole 1217: moreover the main units of composition, the capitula, are not sermons. Within the capitula, however, there are sub-units, usually the articuli, or even sections of the longer articuli, which approximate to sermons, not least in their urgent desire to persuade to a point of view or to action or to abandonment of an action. In these Bromyard certainly uses his *exempla*, not as diversionary and diverting tales, but as instruments enlisted for the task of persuasion.

The data in table 23.1 and in the two succeeding tables reveal so many deviations from the mean in the density of *exempla* within individual capitula that no safe conclusion may be drawn as to the order in which Bromyard wrote these capitula.
N1, Nativitas, has only one *exemplum* for its 15.75 columns whereas O7, Ornatus, has
16 *exempla* in its 13.25 columns. Obviously the differing natures of the capitula led Bromyard to suit his employment of the device to their content.
Certain anomalies, however, do stand out: the most notable being observed in the ten capitula V2 to V11 inclusive which muster between them only 4 *exempla* in their 119½ columns. By contrast the nine capitula E1 to E9 in their 120 columns contain 110 *exempla*. Other startling polarities are seen between G3, Gratia, with one *exemplum* to its 18.75 columns and G4, Gratitudo, with 7 in 14: and between I3, Infirmitas, with 16 in 11½ columns and I6, Invidia, with only 4 in 18½ columns.
As to length of capitula the group A1-11 stands out as markedly shorter than the mean of just over 13½ columns: but this is not the only grouping to diverge from the mean. Other shorter groups are A16-19: C1-3: C12-15: D2-5: S5-7. There are also groups of longer capitula.

TABLE 23.1: LENGTH OF GROUPS OF CAPITULA : THEIR MEAN LENGTH:
THE NUMBER OF EXEMPLA : THEIR FREQUENCY OF
OCCURRENCE AND PERCENTAGE DEVIATION FROM THE MEAN

	COLUMNS	MEAN LENGTH OF CAPITULUM	NO. OF EXEMPLA	NO. OF COLUMNS PER EXEMPLUM	% OF EXEMPLUM DEVIATION FROM MEAN
A1-11	43.3	3.94	12	3.61	+ 71.09
A12-27	224.33	14.02	124	1.81	- 14.22
B1-4	43.58	10.90	28	1.56	- 26.07
C1-18	194.5	10.81	97	2.01	- 4.74
D1-12	125.33	10.44	65	1.93	- 8.53
E1-9	120.08	13.34	110	1.09	- 48.34
F1-8	126.5	15.81	43	2.94	+ 39.34
G1-5	91.5	18.30	25	3.66	+ 73.46
H1-6	61.17	10.20	29	2.11	0.00
I1-13	173.83	13.37	88	1.98	- 6.16
L1-7	85.33	12.19	55	1.55	- 26.55
M1-14	254.5	18.18	148	1.72	- 18.48
N1-4	37.42	9.36	9	4.16	+ 97.16
O1-8	135.67	16.96	58	2.34	+ 10.90
P1-14	313.42	22.39	128	2.45	+ 16.11
Q1 + R1-7	147.08	18.39	60	2.45	+ 16.11
S1-14	138.5	9.89	68	2.04	- 3.31
T1-5	90.75	18.19	49	1.86	- 11.85
V1-12 + X1	167.17	12.86	21	7.96	+277.25
A1-X1	2574	13.62	1217	2.11	

The figures for the columns of text given in these tables are keyed to the first printed
edition of the *Summa*, Goff J-260 [Basel, not after 1484].

TABLE 23.2: GROUPS RANKED IN DESCENDING ORDER OF DENSITY OF
EXEMPLA TO TEXT (HIGHEST DENSITY FIRST, LOWEST LAST)

1.   E 1-9

2.   L 1-7

3.   B 1-4

4.   M 1-14

5.   A 12-27

6.   T 1-5

7.   D 1-12

8.   I 1-13

9.   C 1-18

10.   S 1-14

11.   H 1-6

12.   O 1-8

13. =   P 1-14

14. =   Q 1 + R 1-7

15.   F 1-8

16.   A 1-12

17.   G 1-5

18.   N 1-4

19.   V 1-12 + X1

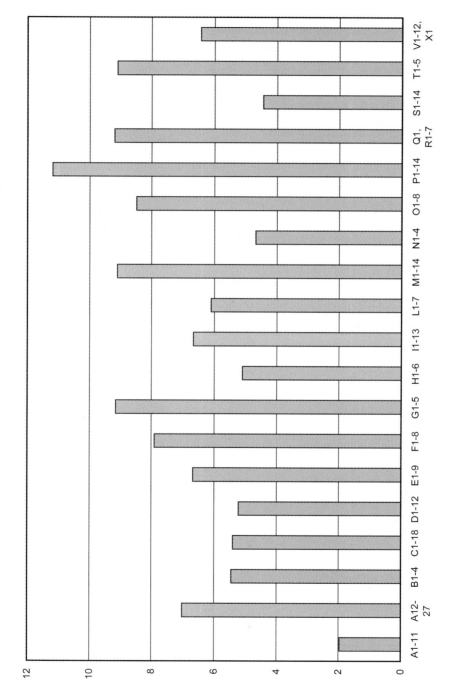

GRAPH : THE RELATIVE LENGTH OF GROUPS OF CAPITULA

TABLE 23.3: THE LENGTH OF EACH CAPITULUM : AND THE NUMBERS OF
ARTICULI AND EXEMPLA IN EACH

		COLUMNS	ARTICULI	EXEMPLA	EXEMPLA PER COLUMN OF 25 HIGHEST DENSITIES
A 1	ABIECTIO	2.33	3	-	
2	ABIICERE	2.25	2	-	
3	AB INFANTIA	6.67	2	2	
4	ABSTINENTIA	3.75	2	2	
5	ABSCONSIO	2.66	4	-	
6	ABUSIO	2.50	4	-	
7	ABSOLUTIO	7.25	4	2	
8	ACCIDIA	6.12	6	3	
9	ACCEDERE	1.13	4	-	
10	ACCIPERE	3.50	4	1	
11	ACCUSATIO	5.12	3	2	
12	ACQUISITIO	27.50	6	22	
13	ADVENTUS	16.50	8	3	
14	ADVOCATI	22.50	5	17	
15	ADULATIO	13.50	4	7	
16	ADORATIO	3.25	3	1	
17	ADULTERIUM	6.25	2	6	0.96
18	ADVERSITAS	3.67	2	-	
19	AMBULATIO	5.33	9	1	
20	AMOR	10.50	9	5	
21	AMICITIA	18.67	10	11	
22	ANGELUS	8.50	7	2	
23	ANIMA	11.67	8	5	
24	ARMA	8.00	5	6	
25	ASCENDERE	16.33	8	3	
26	AUDIRE	18.67	13	12	
27	AVARICIA	33.50	15	23	
B 1	BEATITUDO	6.50	5	2	
2	BELLUM	27.50	11	17	
3	BENEFACERE	1.33	2	1	
4	BONITAS	8.25	6	8	

		COLUMNS	ARTICULI	EXEMPLA	
C 1	CARITAS	7.67	4	-	
2	CARO	6.25	5	4	
3	CASTITAS	2.25	4	2	
4	CIVITAS	13.00	6	3	
5	CONTRITIO	12.50	7	6	
6	CONFESSIO	29.50	14	26	0.88
7	CONSCIENTIA	11.00	6	4	
8	CONSUETUDO	13.67	7	4	
9	CONCORDIA	2.50	3	2	
10	COGITATIO	8.75	7	8	0.91
11	CONSILIUM	19.50	12	10	
12	COMPASSIO	5.00	3	3	
13	CONVERSATIO	3.67	3	-	
14	COR	9.50	8	3	
15	CHOREA	4.75	6	3	
16	CORRECTIO	22.00	9	3	
17	CRUX	17.50	3	16	0.91
18	CUSTODIA	5.50	3	-	
D 1	DAMNATIO	13.75	7	9	
2	DESPERATIO	7.67	3	11	1.44
3	DECIME	6.33	9	3	
4	DEDICATIO	7.75	5	8	1.03
5	DELECTATIO	4.50	5	2	
6	DETRACTIO	20.25	12	7	
7	DISCRETIO	1.67	2	1	
8	DISCORDIA	4.50	3	2	
9	DILECTIO	13.67	6	4	
10	DIMITTERE	8.00	5	4	
11	DIVICIE	16.25	10	5	
12	DOMINATIO	21.00	14	9	
E 1	EBRIETAS	5.50	9	6	1.09
2	ELECTIO	9.75	6	1	
3	ELEMOSINA	27.50	11	30	1.09
4	EQUITAS	2.00	1	2	
5	ERUBESCENTIA	3.00	3	2	
6	EUCHARISTIA	32.00	14	38	1.19
7	EXEMPLUM	14.50	8	5	
8	EXECUTOR	20.33	10	22	1.08
9	EXCOMMUNICATIO	5.50	4	4	

		COLUMNS	ARTICULI	EXEMPLA	
F 1	FALSITAS	32.75	8	11	
2	FAMA	6.33	4	1	
3	FERIE	24.75	8	5	
4	FIDES	31.33	13	14	
5	FILIATIO	14.75	9	8	
6	FORTITUDO	2.00	3	-	
7	FRATERNITAS	4.33	3	1	
8	FURTUM	10.25	3	3	
G 1	GAUDIUM	20.75	6	6	
2	GLORIA	26.00	7	6	
3	GRATIA	18.75	7	1	
4	GRATITUDO	14.00	9	7	
5	GULA	12.00	10	5	
H 1	HOMO	16.00	9	2	
2	HOMICIDIUM	7.50	7	2	
3	HONESTAS	2.67	4	-	
4	HONOR	12.00	3	5	
5	HOSPITALITAS	7.50	6	7	0.93
6	HUMILITAS	15.50	6	13	0.84
I 1	IEIUNIUM	6.33	6	3	
2	INCONSTANTIA	7.50	6	4	
3	INFIRMITAS	11.50	9	16	1.39
4	INOBEDIENTIA	6.75	3	4	
5	INTENTIO	5.33	3	-	
6	INVIDIA	18.50	7	4	
7	YPOCRISIS	7.33	3	4	
8	IRA	7.33	6	3	
9	IUDICES	23.00	7	15	
10	IUDICIUM HUM.	15.50	5	6	
11	IUDICIUM DIV.	16.25	5	3	
12	IURAMENTUM	22.25	11	17	
13	IUSTICIA	26.25	10	9	
L 1	LABOR	10.50	7	4	
2	LAUS	3.25	3	1	
3	LEX	10.50	5	4	
4	LIBER	9.67	5	1	
5	LOCUTIO	16.67	7	15	0.90
6	LUDUS	5.25	7	1	
7	LUXURIA	29.50	9	29	0.98

		COLUMNS	ARTICULI	EXEMPLA	
M 1	MALEDICTIO	2.67	3	2	
2	MANDATA	10.25	7	3	
3	MARIA	22.50	5	14	
4	MATRIMONIUM	7.00	4	4	
5	MENDACIUM	3.00	2	1	
6	MERCATIO	12.50	3	5	
7	MILITIA	6.75	4	-	
8	MINISTRATIO	22.33	8	19	0.85
9	MISERICORDIA	26.50	9	13	
10	MISSA	4.67	4	2	
11	MORS	98.00	24	69	
12	MUNDICIA	9.00	8	1	
13	MUNDUS	18.33	8	9	
14	MUNUS	11.00	6	6	
N 1	NATIVITAS	15.75	6	1	
2	NEGLIGENTIA	2.67	3	-	
3	NOBILITAS	12.00	5	4	
4	NOCUMENTUM	7.00	4	4	
O 1	OBEDIENTIA	14.67	5	6	
2	OCIUM	3.67	3	5	
3	ODIUM	4.50	2	-	
4	OPERATIO	10.00	4	-	
5	ORATIO	24.00	8	16	
6	ORDO CLERIC.	61.33	9	15	
7	ORNATUS	13.25	9	16	1.21
8	OSTENSIO	4.25	3	-	
P 1	PATIENTIA	11.75	6	12	1.02
2	PASSIO CHRISTI	31.75	9	10	
3	PAUPERTAS	24.25	7	14	
4	PAX	21.50	10	6	
5	PECCATUM	20.50	7	4	
6	PECCATOR	12.50	9	-	
7	PENITENTIA	54.33	20	34	
8	PENA	22.50	9	9	
9	PERSEVERANTIA	8.00	5	2	
10	PIETAS	2.67	2	2	
11	PREDESTINATIO	18.50	6	1	
12	PREDICATIO	28.50	12	10	
13	PRELATIO	49.33	18	17	
14	PULCHRITUDO	7.33	4	7	0.95

		COLUMNS	ARTICULI	EXEMPLA	
Q 1	QUERERE	5.00	3	1	
R 1	RAPINA	29.25	8	20	
2	RECIDIVUM	13.00	5	3	
3	REDDITIO	4.25	2	4	
4	REGIMEN	10.33	8	4	
5	RELIGIO	59.00	24	20	
6	RESTITUTIO	14.00	7	8	
7	RESURRECTIO	12.25	6	-	
S 1	SACERDOTIUM	9.50	4	-	
2	SANCTITAS	4.67	3	-	
3	SAPIENTIA	14.33	7	6	
4	SCIENTIA	15.50	8	8	
5	SENECTUS	4.75	4	-	
6	SENSUS	3.33	4	3	
7	SEQUI	5.33	3	4	
8	SERVIRE	17.75	9	6	
9	SYMONIA	6.67	4	3	
10	SOCIETAS	6.75	7	3	
11	SORTILEGIUM	14.75	8	14	0.95
12	SPES	4.67	4	1	
13	SPIRITUSSANC.	13.75	7	5	
14	SUPERBIA	16.75	6	15	0.89
T 1	TEMPTATIO	20.67	9	20	0.97
2	TESTIMONIUM	5.00	3	5	
3	TIMOR	6.33	4	6	0.95
4	TRINITAS	11.75	3	4	
5	TRIBULATIO	47.00	13	14	
V 1	VERITAS	9.33	6	8	0.86
2	VERBUM	5.67	5	1	
3	VIA	8.00	4	3	
4	VISUS	9.50	6	-	
5	VINDICTA	9.67	7	-	
6	VIRTUS	4.50	4	-	
7	VITA	9.50	6	-	
8	VISITATIO	37.25	3	-	
9	VOCATIO	14.25	7	-	
10	VOLUNTAS	11.75	5	-	
11	VOTUM	9.50	4	-	
12	USURA	18.00	9	8	
X 1	CHRISTUS	20.25	3	-	

[1] Edited by Jacques Berlioz and Marie Anne Polo de Beaulieu: see under von Moos.

[2] Op. cit. pp.67-82.

[3] Cette référence est le plus souvent accompagnée d'une petite scène de dialogue, d'une réponse spirituelle, d'une pointe (*dictum*, apologue, apophtegme). Même si la leçon est véhiculée par des fables ou paraboles, l'élément fictive est intégré dans une scène de la vie réelle. Les faits rapportés proviennent de l'histoire quotidienne des petites gens ou de la grande histoire; ils peuvent être des «faits divers», des racontars de la «chronique scandaleuse» récente, ou des faits héroïques d'un passé lointain et d'origine presque mythique. On a souvent dit, et à juste titre, que les *exempla* homilétiques préfèrent les premiers aux seconds. Leur [sic] personnages sont plutôt anonymes, désignés par un habituel *quidam*; la réalité historique de ces obscures anecdotes est, en revanche, assurée par des témoins oraux ou par l'expérience personnelle de celui qui parle et qui devient ainsi autorité historique. Le prédicateur qui s'adressait à une foule ou du moins à un auditoire laïque de diverses conditions, avait en effet intérêt à présenter l'histoire d'un homme ordinaire, à minimiser la différence entre le personnage de l'histoire et son public... (Von Moos p.76)

[4] Au besoin le prédicateur remplaçait un héros du passé par un roi de France contemporain, ou le camouflait par l'anonymat, en le désignant par *rex quidam* ou *sapiens quidam*, bien qu'il ait connu son vrai nom. (Von Moos p.77)

[5] des racontars de la "chronique scandaleuse" récente.

[6] Bibliothèque d'Arras MS 1019 (formerly 425).

[7] Rava-Cordier pp.25-248.

[8] L'indication de cette proximité [between the preacher, the place of composition and the audience]
- proximité entendue comme voisinage dans l'espace, rapprochement dans le temps et parenté – n'est
- elle pas là précisément pour aider le prédicateur à persuader, à convaincre en donnant authenticité et vraisemblance au récit? (ibid. p.225).

[9] ibid. p.233.

[10] Humbertus vol.II p.395, from his *Liber de eruditione praedicatorum* written, according to Berthier, before 1240 (p.xxi).

[11] EEFP pp.209-226.

[12] It is much likelier that Bromyard used parchment rather than paper. Paper manufacture came to south-east Spain by 1150 when a mill was set up at Játiva: to north-east Italy, at Fabriano, in 1276: and to France, at Troyes, as late as 1348. (Encyclopedia Americana volume 21 p.259). Bromyard mentions parchment in INVIDIA: '..parchment–makers who are glad to see sheep dying off: and bad priests, glad when their parishioners need funerals..' (I.6.2): a macabre observation, all the more pointed for the large-scale animal (and even human) mortality of the late 1310s.

[13] Boyle, Date p.535: 'He may have begun the *Summa* a year or two after his return to Hereford..for by 1330 he had reached the letter I of the *Summa*..': p.537: '..it seems likely that he was composing the article *Tribulatio* [T5] during those summer months of 1348.. Not many articles remained to be written after *Tribulatio*..'

[14] Ad hoc potest adduci hystoria de duobus ut fertur euntibus simul per viam quos tercius alonge sequebatur. Is vero qui sequebatur aliquando vidit iuvenem cum precedentibus religiosis illis, aliquando ut videbatur subito ab eis discessit, et cum hoc pluries accideret admirabatur. Cum ergo ad introitum ville venirent quesivit a religiosis illis ubi et quis esset iuvenis ille pulcerrimus: qui cum respondissent se nullum talem socium habuisse et ipse narrasset quid vidisset Invenerunt per verba eius quod in loco ubi loquebantur de honestis fuit iuvenis visus cum eis: ubi vero de aliis loquebantur*, disparuit. Intelligentes per hec eum fuisse cristum qui discipulis de eo loquentibus affuit, vel angelum eius.. (A.22.9)
    *for 'loquebatur' of text

187

15 Primo hystoria de illo qui ut fertur intrans grangiam suam post autumnum et admirans insolitam[†] cumuli parvitatem vidit dyabolum sedentem super cumulum et intelligens hoc esse propter malam decimationem iussit totum iterum decimari: quod cum factum fuisset grangia repleta fuit de residuo.. (D.3.6)

       [†] for 'insoliti' of text.

16 Cuidam incarcerato assimilantur in carcere clericorum archiepiscopi remensis qui duos quos secum habebat in carcere socios occidit: ut ipsorum occuparet annonam: que per cordam eis in puteum deponebatur ipsis prius de vita per vocem emissam fidem facientibus quorum voces per aliquos finxit dies. Et sic ipsis mortuis illorum nomine panis illorum portionem accepit. iste ab omnibus miser iudicabatur et malus qui propter parvam prolongationem tam miserabilis quam gerebat in carcere vitam in quo ad mortem positus erat: duos occidit homines ipse in brevi de morte sua quasi certus: quia nullus in carcere illo ultra annum vivere dicitur, et tamen in rei veritate nonnulli invidi isto sunt miserabiliores peiorisque existunt conditionis. (I.6.2)

17 Ipse namque sicut historia illa continet de confessione rediens tristem vultum facere consueverat nec uxoris recipere voluit consolationem dicens: Quomodo vultum hilarem facere possem cum me per confessorem meum tot ieiuniis oneratum cogito: Cui illa promittere solebat quod totum pro illo ieiunare vellet. Qui sic confortatus comedere et bibere et bonum vultum facere solebat. Deus enim illum ab hoc retrahere volens errore: ei per visionem ostendit quod ipse cum uxore sua partem[‡] appropinquabat celi et quod Petrus celi ianitor uxorem eius manu capiens ipsam introduxit: Ipsum vero intrare volentem et nitentem repulit dicens: Quia hec pro te opera penitentie egit: ideo hec pro te mercedem accipiet et premia meritorum: Qua visione curialiter ammonitus deinceps propriam egit penitentiam: intelligens quod unusquisque propriam mercedem recipiet secundum proprium laborem. i.Cor.iii. (P.7.17)

       [‡] Perhaps a compositor's misreading for 'portam'.

24

BOYLE'S DATING OF THE *SUMMA*

Boyle's influential study on the date of the *Summa* was published in 1973. Already in his 1962 contribution on the 'Cum ex eo' of Bonifacius VIII he had dated at least part of the *Summa* (O.4.17) to the onset of the Black Death in England[1]: and in his 1974 article on the *Summa Confessorum* of John of Freiburg he assigns an even later date of 1330-1348 to Bromyard's *Summa* and dates his *Opus Trivium* to about 1330.[2]

Boyle writes: 'Bromyard had been licensed to hear confessions in the diocese of Hereford in early 1326, though he was actually absent from the Dominican house at Hereford when his fellow-penitentiary, Hugh Ledebury, was admitted to this office on 1 February 1326.'[3] Bannister, who edited Orleton's register (the source of the information), makes it clear that Bromyard was *not* licensed on that day: 'Feb. 1 [1326]. John [de Bristol], Provincial Prior of the Preaching Friars, presents to the Bishop Hugh de Ledbury and John de Bromyard, to be admitted to hear Confessions, etc. Hugh de Ledbury is admitted, but John de Bromyard's admission is postponed owing to his absence.'[4]

Boyle continues: 'He may have begun the *Summa* a year or two after his return to Hereford and his assumption of a penitentiary's duties,[5] for by 1330 he had reached the letter I of the *Summa*..' He then quotes the 1330 sentence.

Although he does not propose a year for Bromyard's return, after linking Bromyard to February 1326 Boyle seems to place his beginning the *Summa* to 1328 ('a year or two after his return to Hereford') and wedded to his assumption of Bromyard's following an alphabetic order of composition, implies that a period of two years took him to I.11.3 and the mention of the year 1330.[6] Boyle concludes 'it seems likely that he was composing the article *Tribulatio* during those summer months of 1348, some eighteen years after he had written the *Iudicium [Divinum]* entry noted earlier. Perhaps the *Summa* as a whole was complete by the end of that year.'[7] [1348]

The Basel edition, the first to be printed, has 688 folio leaves including 5 blanks. The first Tabula vocalis (listing the 189 capitula), the Tabula realis and the second Tabula vocalis occupy 35 leaves. From the Prologus to I.11.3 there are 289 leaves: from there to the end of the text at X.1.27 there are 359 leaves. Boyle therefore invites us to contemplate a heroic fervour of creation in which Bromyard wrote 144.5 leaves per year: whereas in the eighteen years from 1330 to 1348 his average dropped to a pedestrian 19.9 leaves per year. His wordage for the 289 leaves, at an average of 1510 per leaf,[8] is approximately 436,000 (written, one should remember, in a language other than his native tongue): which would demand 218,000 words per year in the two years 1328 to 1330: a rate of composition more than *seven* times faster than the annual 30,000 words (for the remaining c.542,000 words of I.11.3 to X.1.27) which Boyle's 1330 to 1348 thesis implies. An additional labour for Bromyard in those two hectic years of 1328 to 1330 would have been the furnishing and checking of the roughly 6,500 citations (some 44.6% of the total citations) supplied to that huge section from the Prologus to I.11.3.

The dating of the compilation of the Tabula realis will depend on one's view of how Bromyard approached his endeavour: did he pre-plan his 189 capitula with their articuli? Did he index the work as he went from one capitulum to the next? Did he read through the completed *Summa* and only then produce his guide? Did he enlist the help of his fellow-Dominicans in Hereford to index the book, a sheaf of leaves at a time, or only when completed? (It seems likely, as Binkley suggests, that the copy of the *Summa* made from Bromyard's autograph was made by his colleagues at Hereford.)[9]

We should remember too the restrictions upon Bromyard's time available for writing imposed upon him by his religious duties. Hinnebusch describes in detail a régime which many of us would find extremely taxing.[10] In 'The Daily Schedule' he writes: 'The liturgy was the framework into which all the other activities of the priory were fitted.' He goes on to specify the times and demands of the liturgical hours of prime, terce, sext, none, vespers, compline, matins and lauds through winter and summer seasons.[11] Bromyard may well have received some concessions for extra study and writing time[12], but short winter days, poor artificial lighting, periods spent on preparing inks, pens and writing surfaces will have taken up precious hours.

Also taking him away from his dormitory cell[13] were his active duties as both preacher and confessor, duties for the saving of souls which, quite properly, he saw as his prime task and reward.[14]

The final sentence of the 1330 passage quoted by Boyle merits closer inspection. 'Quod utrum verum sit et tempus illud ab incarnatione Christi computetur, quinquennii expectatio ostendet, cum nunc annus currat millesimus trecentesimus tricesimus.' (I.11.3) [Whether this is true, and that period is reckoned from Christ's incarnation, the waiting time of five years will reveal, since now we are in the year 1330.] [The reference is to Daniel 12.12: 'Happy the man who waits and lives to see the completion of one thousand three hundred and thirty-five days!'[15]] If Bromyard had been engaged on the *Summa* till 1348 he would have had all of thirteen years after the end of 1335 to return to I.11.3 and observe that Daniel's prophecy could *not* be interpreted as he alleges Jewish rabbis wished – one may imagine that he would not have been averse from pointing out their error – but he did not. Boyle does not comment on what would have been an omission.

Another text Boyle employs comes at O.6.39: 'Magister Joannes de Monumuta episcopus Landavensis habuit responsum de curia romana per suum archidiaconum *qui adhuc vivit* et haec mihi retulit. [Boyle's italics]. He comments: 'The archdeacon in question is M. Alexander of Monmouth. He became archdeacon of Llandaff in 1323, under bishop John of Monmouth, and was still alive in 1337, the last date we have for him. Since Bromyard refers to the archdeacon as "still living," then it seems reasonable to suggest that *Ordo clericalis* may have been written sometime between 1330 and 1337 plus.'[16]

The known predecessor of M. Alexander in office was M. Henry de Cranborne. He was provided to the archidiaconate on 13 December 1289 and was still in possession on 24 April 1306.[17] The date of his vacating office is unknown. M. Alexander is known to have been the archdeacon on 15 July 1323[18]. His entry into the office will therefore have been at some time from April 1306 to July 1323. He was, moreover, despatched by his bishop to Avignon to seek clarification on a point of canon law arising out of the promulgation of the *Clementinae* of 1317.[19] Bishop John of Monmouth had died on 8 April 1323[20]. One cannot safely assert, as Boyle does, that it was in 1323 he became archdeacon: on the CPR evidence alone[21] one could not state that he became archdeacon under John of Monmouth: it is only Bromyard's evidence (*per suum archidiaconum*) which proves that he did. Furthermore, he was sufficiently well thought of by the chapter to be elected by it as bishop, on 25 June 1323,[22] with royal assent being granted on 15 July.[23] (Papal provision of John de Eglescliffe, a Dominican, blocked Alexander's rise)[24]. He was still archdeacon on 8 March 1337.[25]

Boyle again relies on his assumption of Bromyard's alphabetic progression and makes clear his belief that ORDO CLERICALIS was written after IUDICIUM DIVINUM. In fact, Bromyard's sentence can not in certainty be interpreted as implying bishop John's death: though weight must be given to 'qui adhuc vivit.' If we do assume John of Monmouth's death the only safe inference as to dating is that it refers to a time after 8 April 1323.

Dr Boyle compared a sentence of Bromyard's at P.3.26 to a constitution of the Augustinian Canons issued at Leicester in 1346.[26] From this comparison he concluded that Bromyard had this constitution in mind when he wrote the capitulum PAUPERTAS and that consequently this capitulum can be placed 'definitely after 1346.'

The constitution runs thus: [the italics are mine]:

Item quod *canonici regulares* dicti ordinis quicumque de cetero tunicis nimis strictis vel botonatis, *capis*, clocheis seu rotundellis, et aliis quibuscumque vestibus aut capellis, serico aut sindone alterius coloris quam sit ipsum indumentum sive capella apparatis seu botis rostratis, de cetero penitus non utantur.

Bromyard wrote:

Canonici etiam *regulares* nuper in actis et ordinationibus capituli sui statuerunt quod canonici tales *cappas* non portarent de burneto rugosas quales portant aliqui predicatores.

Boyle noted that the constitution does not correspond exactly to that cited by Bromyard. Indeed it does not. Apart from 'canonici regulares' only one noun verb or adjective is shared between the two extracts: 'capis' and 'cappas'. Nor is it merely a matter of vocabulary. The sense too differs markedly. I offer translations:

(a)   The constitution:

Also that the canons regular of the said order – no matter who – in future should on no account use tunics which are too tight or buttoned capes,[27] cloaks or riding-capes or any other vestments or hoods furnished with silk or muslin of a colour other than is [that of] the garment itself or the hood: [nor should they use] boots with pointed toes.

(b)   Bromyard:

Furthermore the canons regular recently decreed in the acts and ordinances of their chapter that the canons should not wear such pleated capes[27 bis] of burnet [brown cloth] as some preachers wear.

I am not persuaded, then, that Bromyard, consistently punctilious in his citations of documents, had seen or heard of this constitution of 1346. Pleated capes of burnet seem far removed from tight tunics, buttons, riding capes, silk and muslin, and boots with pointed toes.

Boyle's selection of the extract from the Acta of the united chapter of the Augustinian canons meeting at Leicester in 1346[28] should be placed in the context of the other surviving Acta of the period 1234 to 1350 and of the Constitutions of Benedictus XII promulgated on 15 May 1339[29].

Fundamental to our understanding of these Acta and their potential for aiding us to date Bromyard's reference to the Augustinian Canons at P.3.26 is that only *some* of the Acta of their Chapters are extant. Salter remarks: 'Of the Chapters which in the natural course would fall in 1261, 1264, 1267, 1270 and 1273 we know nothing..'[30] and 'Nothing is known of the Chapters in 1300, 1303, 1306 and 1309..'[31] Furthermore, even when one or two details are known from extraneous sources of what transpired at Chapters, the Acta of those Chapters have not survived.[32] We are faced with a gap between the surviving Acta of the Leicester Chapter of 1276 and the Northampton Chapter of 1325: that is a loss of the Acta of fifteen triennial Chapters. It is not unreasonable to suppose that among those lost Acta would have been at least one passage which would have a closer correspondence with Bromyard's sentence than the one accord (capis – cappas) of the 1346 text cited by Dr Boyle. It is notable that of the surviving Acta of the Province of Canterbury of 1234, 1237, 1276, 1325, 1328, 1331, 1334, 1337 and 1340: and of the united Provinces of Canterbury and York of 1341, 1343, 1346 and 1350 six have comments to make on clothing and dress.[33] Then there are the Constitutions of Benedictus XII. In 1337 he had issued his directives for the Black Monks, following these in 1339 with a bull of thirty-nine chapters for the Black Canons (the Augustinians), *De forma & honestate habitus & vestimentorum* being the 19th.[34]

As an example of the fastidious attention bestowed upon dress in the surviving Acta this translation must suffice:

'Following the example of the Levites under Moses the canons should use linen tunics. On a journey and in carrying out their vows of obedience they are to have narrower sleeves, in the cloister and in the church and in other places of their rule wider [sleeves], and both in the cloister and on a journey they are to have black capes. The canons are also to have linen shirts or, if their prior consents, shirts of linsey-woolsey, a pelisse of lamb, a white tunic, white hose, rounded boots reaching up to the mid-calf, coverings[35] of white or black or of russet: the fur of squirrel and miniver and rabbits being totally forbidden: and both canons and lay brethren are to have no garment in any point remarkable contrary to the rule. Blankets are to be removed from the dormitory and are to be allowed for journeys.'[36] [From the Acta of the Chapter of 1234 at St Frideswide's Oxford].

Exactly a century later, in the Acta of the Dunstable Chapter of 1334, we meet the same concern for propriety of dress:

'Furthermore we charge all superiors of our Order to forbid their brothers the use of surcoats with broad and dangling sleeves and also of any kind of buttoned sleeves, and also the use of capes of blue cloth.'[37]

The Huntingdon Chapter of 1328 had previously forbidden the use of surcoat or tunic slashed in front, or of any garment whatever whose refinement or non-conformity was so eye-catching as to deserve censure. These strictures, however – and their repetition seems to denote some lack of success in their enforcement – are as nothing compared with the 900 words Benedictus XII devoted to the topic in his bull of 1339. One or two extracts only may convey the tenor of his regard for minute detail:

'Hoods, however, should they happen to be donned outside the aforesaid places [cloister, chapter-house, refectory and dormitory] should be decent, and those which are worn with capes, mantles, cloaks or riding-capes should be of one and the same colour with these.' He too bans miniver - and squirrel-fur. Surplices should be 'large and ample according to the reasonable custom of whatever church, extending in the length of the sleeves roughly four fingers' width, and reaching roughly beyond mid-shin in length.' Sleeves should not be 'tongued' [slashed] or buttoned.[38]

All these provisions, laid down over scores of years, reveal a continuing campaign to outlaw among the (younger?) canons a taste for cutting a dash and aping fashion. The two texts, the Leicester extract and Bromyard's reference can not be used to date Bromyard's PAUPERTAS sentence at or after 1346.

The one indisputable point in time we have for dating the *Summa* is the one Bromyard gives us at I.11.3, namely 1330. The *Summa*, of course, is an enormous compilation, almost three times the length of the Vulgate Bible, and must have occupied him for several years. We have no means of knowing the order in which he wrote his 189 capitula. Boyle, however, sought to date the capitula I.12 to X.1 from 1330 onwards on the basis of alphabetical order and used three elements in this construct.

The first is the reference to M. Alexander of Monmouth at O.6.39. If 'qui adhuc vivit' implies the death of the bishop of Llandaff, which occurred on 8 April 1323, any date from 8 April 1323 to 8 March 1337 may be deduced: i.e. a date *before* 1330 or *after* 1330.

His second is his reliance on the item from the Acta of the Leicester Chapter of 1346, and the correspondence of one word, capis, with one word, cappas, in Bromyard's PAUPERTAS.

The third is his linking of the multiple allusions to the catastrophic and unprecedented flooding which destroyed the harvests both of grain crops and of hay over a series of years from 1314 onwards, which brought in its wake dearth, sky-high food prices, starvation, animal disease and human mortality: all catalogued and analysed in chilling detail by Kershaw and by Jordan: with the very heavy rains of one season, namely midsummer to Christmas 1348. Bromyard's TRIBULATIO is simply one witness among a multitude of witnesses testifying to the cataclysmic weather and suffering of the people of England during the years 1314 to 1318.

Also to be considered is negative evidence: the absence of references to events in the 1330s and 1340s which Bromyard might be expected to have made (if that is, we were to accept Boyle's dating). The young Edward III's daring coup against Mortimer on the night of 19 October 1330 at Nottingham, followed by his declaration of 20 October, to be published by the sheriff of York and all other sheriffs of England,[39] roundly dissociating himself from the damage and dishonour and impoverishment wreaked upon the realm and the people of England is but the first, and most dramatic, of a series of developments to which Bromyard makes not even an oblique allusion. Most telling of all is the lack of any reference to the large-scale hostilities between England and France which broke out in 1337 and of any hint of anti-French sentiment in the *Summa*. The French raids on the south coast of England in 1338: the Flanders and Picardy campaigns of 1341 led by John de Montfort and of 1342 by Edward III: and the victory at Crécy in 1346: all these military conflicts would inevitably have coloured Bromyard's depiction of English feats of arms[40] in a strikingly different way than the portrayal he *does* give us, that is of a poorly led, badly disciplined and unsuccessful army, evidenced in the extracts presented from P.8.6, P.13.10, N.3.15, R.4.11 and B.2.24.
A further point to remember is that this is not Bromyard's final work.[41] Boyle's dating of the *Summa* to c.1328 to 1348 does not stand up.

[1] Boyle, Cum ex eo p.283.

[2] Boyle, Freiburg p.265.

[3] Boyle, Date p.535.

[4] Orleton pp.350-351.

[5] which *must* have been *after* 1 February 1326: for Boyle, therefore, Bromyard's starting date was 'a year or two after.. his assumption of a penitentiary's duties.'

[6] Boyle, Date p.535.

[7] ibid. p.537.

[8] based on a count of five separate leaves.

[9] Binkley, Hereford pp.257-258. He may well have had 19 confrères in the Hereford Convent. Binkley applies the *prima facie* general comment at C.4.17 (mentioning 'viginti fratres') to the specific case of the hostility directed by 'the bishop, the dean and chapter, and the secular clergy' towards the Dominicans' attempts firmly to establish their priory in Hereford. Since this hostility pre-dates the settlement of 1322 the 'magnus custos' would seem to be Adam Orleton, bishop of Hereford 1317-1327.

[10] Hinnebusch, History pp.349-366 (4 - the Daily Schedule; 5 - The Daily Life of the Friar 6 -Silence and Recreation; 7 - Religious Life Outside the Priory; 8 - Conclusion).

[11] ibid. pp.349-353.

[12] ibid. p.352: ' advanced students were dispensed from choir and recited their office alone or in groups': and see note 108 on p.371. A judicious prior may well have spared Bromyard some of the tasks of preparation described by Hector in his chapter (pp.15-20) on parchment, paper, pens and inks.

[13] ibid. pp.356-358.

[14] *Summa*, passim: and Boyle, Fratres communes pp.254-255 quoting from the prologue to the first Dominican constitutions of 1220: 'Studium nostrum ad hoc principaliter ardenterque summo opere debeat intendere ut proximorum animabus possimus utiles esse.' (Our energies should be directed principally, enthusiastieally and totally to this end, namely our ability to be of use to/for the souls of our neighbours.) [My translation].

[15] The revelation by Bromyard that he was writing IUDICIUM DIVINUM in 1330 owes its origin to his reflections on the Last Judgement and the End-time. He states that the divine judgement is both individual, at one's death: and general, at the End [..divinum iudicium est duplex, unum particulare quod singulariter de quocumque fit quando moritur.. Aliud generale quod in fine erit omnibus simul congregatis.. (I.11.1)]. He goes on to cite the fifteen signs assembled by Hieronymus which indicate the approach of the End. He then points out that Christ was unwilling to disclose to His disciples the time of the Second Coming [Tempus vero cristus discipulis indicare noluit.. (I.11.3)]. Some, Bromyard writes, compute the time adducing Daniel's prophecy 'Beatus qui expectat et pervenit ad dies mille trecentos triginta quinque' (Daniel 12.12). Jewish scholars, he asserts, interpret this text with regard to their Messiah, extrapolating the extent of a year from that of a day by using Ezekiel 4.[6] 'diem pro anno diem inquam pro anno dedi tibi..': after which the Messiah Who is to bring them consolation will come: [..iudeorum magistri hanc litteram exponunt de messia illorum per hunc modum inter *vos* iudeos.. post quos [sc. annos] messyas qui eos consolabitur veniet. (I.11.3).] 'Whether this is true, and that period is reckoned from Christ's incarnation, the waiting time of five years will reveal, since now we are in the year 1330.'

Bromyard is thus a witness to Jewish messianic expectations perhaps similar to those recounted by Joshua Prawer. 'By the middle of the eleventh century a tremor of great approaching events was felt in the Jewish world.' The awaited year was 1068, a thousand years after the traditional date of the Roman destruction of the Temple. An alternative date was postulated, falling within the 19 Metonic years of the greater cycle of 256 years, that is, between 1085 and 1104 (Prawer pp.10-11). By some means Bromyard had learnt of such Jewish hopes for 1335. Dismissing these hopes, however, he concludes that Christians, basing themselves on the truth, and not expecting the coming of the Messiah, Whom they had already received, say that if anyone *does* come then, it will not be the Christ but the Antichrist: '..si quis tunc venerit, non cristus sed antichristus erit.' (I.11.3).

The importance of this passage for the status of Boyle's thesis is that Bromyard did *not* add a comment in 1335 on the non-appearance of the Jews' Messiah.

16   Boyle, Date p.535.

17   Le Neve/Jones p.23.

18   ibid. p.23.

19   *Summa* O.6.39.

20   Le Neve/Jones p.21.

21   CPR 1321-1324 p.326 (of *15 July* 1323): 'Signification to W. [Walter Reynolds] archbishop of Canterbury of the royal assent to the election of Master Alexander de Monemuth, archdeacon of Llandaff, to be bishop of Llandaff.'

22   Le Neve/Jones p.21.

23   ibid. p.21.

24   ibid. p.21.

25   ibid. p.23.

26   Boyle, Date pp.535-536.

27   Perhaps 'mantle' would be a closer translation. Hinnebusch, EEFP p.340, on the Dominican habit writes: 'A black mantle, called the cappa, completed the habit.'

28   Boyle, Date pp.535-536.

29   Salter pp.xii-xiii, 4-59, 247-249.

30   ibid. p.xii.

31   ibid. p.xiii.

32   ibid. pp.xiv, xv.

33   ibid. pp.4-20, 49-59.

34   ibid. pp.214-267 and especially pp.247-249.

35   coopertoria.

36   Salter p.4.

37   ibid. p.17.

[38]   ibid. pp.247-248.

[39]   CCR Edward III 1330-1333 pp.158-159. Besides 'the earl of La Marche' Edward arrested Sir Oliver de Ingham and Sir Simon de Bereford.

[40]   Warfare pp.116-120, including good maps at pp.117 and 118.

[41]   See Binkley's evidence for the order of composition of Bromyard's works presented above in chapter one.

25

THE DEPICTION OF JEWS IN THE *SUMMA*

Bromyard embraces the medieval judgement which attributes the blame for the execution of Jesus to 'the Jews': influenced, undoubtedly, by their portrayal in the fourth gospel as a uniform mass hostile to Jesus.[1] He also accepts at face value one or two tales showing Jews in a poor light: though these tales are penetrated by mythic elements such as the conversion of Jews who had defaced an image of Christ, which then bled.[2]

The unbridgeable gulf separating medieval Christians from Judaists lay principally in the latter's inability to accept Jesus as the Messiah, the Son of God, and God. Bromyard's interpretation of Isaiah 53 (which includes the words 'He is despised and rejected of men; a man of sorrows and acquainted with grief..'), seeing here, rather than the nation of Israel, a prophecy of Christ, leads him to criticize what he considers a failure by Jewish theologians to discern inner meanings in the Hebrew Scriptures which would then have the potential to open their eyes to the truths of Christianity. Instead of such illumination they are content, he maintains, with the surface readings of the texts. 'In the knowledge..of the Jews: who are satisfied merely with the outer husk and chaff of knowledge, i.e. the historical interpretation and not the inner core, i.e. the spiritual understanding..'[3] This is a viewpoint Bromyard has inherited from Augustinus: 'For what is what is called the Old Testament but a concealment of the New? And what else is what is called the New but an unveiling of the Old?'[4]

To set against this adverse stance there are, sprinkled throughout the bulk of the *Summa*, many occasions when he chooses to praise the social virtues and active practice of compassion which permeate Jewish groups and which elevate them above the host Christian populations. To illustrate Bromyard's admiration for their knowledge of and keeping of the Hebrew scriptures, for the wise and responsible leadership of Jewish elders and for their charity I append six passages. It is noteworthy too that Bromyard is aware of the disadvantages under which they lived.

Usury does not feature in these six extracts. Bromyard knows that some Jews lent money at interest, as did some Christians.[5] He knows also that Jews did not charge interest on loans to fellow-Jews.[6] He gives his views on usury in the capitulum V12, near the end of which he delivers this analysis, which sees the need for borrowing large sums of money as stemming from the practice by clerics of bribing senior clerics – he does not name Iohannes XXII but assuredly has the papal court at Avignon in his sights – in order to obtain lucrative preferment: in a word, simony. Cut that out and usury will, to a very large extent, wither away.

'Let them tremble in fear, therefore, those who preside at the supreme court of Christendom and all others who, for whose gifts, incomes and demands and greeds and extortions considerable numbers of men take loans at interest from Jews and others: who, by a name favoured within court circles, style themselves *facilitators*... since take away from the Curia simony and greed, and to the greatest extent usury will cease in the state.'[7]

Bromyard's commendations of Jewish uprightness and kindness raises the question of where he observed such behaviour. One difficulty in answering is that we do not know when he was born. If he was born between 1270 and 1275 he *might* have seen Jews in Oxford or Gloucester: much likelier would be stories told him by his father or uncles:[8] for in 1290 Edward I ordered the expulsion of all Jews from England.[9] In his travels in France and Italy, however, lies a greater probability of contacts[10] enabling him to form his approving comments. It will be apparent that he uses his observations as a yard-stick against which to measure Christian shortcomings. Visual reminders of the Judaic alternative had an architectural presence on or within churches in the portrayal of the triumphant *Ecclesia* opposing a defeated *Synagoga*, blindfolded, her spear broken.[11]

'For the Jews, infidels as they are, who have not received as many gifts from God as have Christians: basing themselves on God's teaching at Deuteronomy 15[.4] Who declares 'By no means shall there be a needy man or a beggar among you' do not suffer the poor among them to beg from door to door: but among their own people make collections and obligatory contributions for the sustenance of their poor: whereas Christians – Christians by name rather than by deed make collections with the result that they impoverish ordinary people [*or* with the intent of making paupers of the simple folk.]'[12]

'Otherwise there will be against us not only the examples and life of all the people I've mentioned [among these, the Rechabites] but also, in general terms, of all the Jews: among whom can scarcely be found one man so simple or plebeian but that he knows how to enumerate by heart God's commandments: which, moreover, they uphold to the letter in the strictest manner, as is made clear at F.4.10. Among us, however, few are found of the common people who have the capacity to recite them by heart: but fewer still both among clerics and ordinary folk who manifest them *in their actions..*'[13]

[Bromyard contrasts previous captivities of Jews, including the Babylonian exile, with that wrought by the Romans under Vespasianus and Titus, whose consequences endure to the present day (i.e. c.1330) – 'Hec vero a romanis facta durat usque in hodiernum diem.' From this centuries-long misery he draws the conclusion that their sin must have been great. He continues:] 'But the gravity of their sins can not be found in their undertakings. Therefore one is obliged to investigate the cause of their captivity in their *faith* – the minor [the minor proposition of the syllogism] is shown to be true – both as far as the enterprises they undertake and as far as the punishments they frequently undergo. For they perform works of devoutness and mutual support far better than Christians do, as is made clear at F.3.15. There it is shown that they help those who are stumbling and getting into difficulties: but Christians...' [There follows a charge-sheet of sins of omission and commission].[14]

'The great difference is that they [Jews] do not allow their own people to beg from door to door, as is made clear at E.3.28. Yet Christians allow their own to starve to death.[15] *Their* leaders make collections from the rich and levy contributions from the rich to feed the poor: *our* Christian leaders on the other hand take collections and taxes from the poor to feed the pride of the rich.'[16]

'One reads that a certain Jew had accepted the Christian faith. After his baptism he was asked – since he was so influential a figure in Jewish society – what had prompted him to take on our faith. He replied that the reason for his conversion was the virtue of our faith. But when people sought to discover how he knew this virtue he gave this reply: the people of Christendom could not still endure to the present day by the virtue of their actions alone, since their actions are disgraceful. Therefore it must be that it was by virtue of our faith that, quite rationally, he was motivated, since he could see that the actions Jews carry out were good in that they observe God's commandments most punctiliously.'[17]

'But *we*, at great price, hire false witnesses in matrimonial and other cases. *They* [Jews] neither blaspheme, nor willingly give hearing to those who blaspheme or utter depraved oaths: whereas we find it a laughing matter when we do this or hear this [*or** whereas we chuckle at people doing this or listening to this.]'[18]

* 'ridemus' could be transitive and 'facientes' and 'audientes' accusative: or intransitive, with 'facientes' and 'audientes' nominative, as in my first translation.

[1] The multi-essay volume 'Anti-Judaism and the Fourth Gospel: Papers of the Leuven Colloquium 2000' has as a broad motif the charge of anti-semitism which has been levelled against the author.

[2] His source is the *Speculum historiale* of Vincentius Bellovacensis and the account is dated to the reign of Constantinus IV (668-685). It reads:

..tempore constantini quarti quidam iudei locantes domum christiani: et invenientes in ea imaginem sancti* crucis et crucifixi: cum eam cultellis et huiusmodi percuterent non sine magna illorum admiratione sanguis recens exivit. Aliis dicentibus quod fuit ficticium et illusio: Aliis contrarium asserentibus: pro veritate comprobanda sanguis colligitur: et super omnes infirmos illorum positus: omnes sanavit: quo viso: omnes ad fidem conversi sunt: et festum istius miraculi annuatim in terra illa colitur. (C.17.19).

*'crux' is fem. but 'crucifixus' masc.

This *exemplum* predates the iconoclastic controversy which shook the Orthodox world from c.725 to 842, but may have acquired some impetus from it.

[3] In SCIENTIA Bromyard distinguishes between *knowledge* of virtues and the *possession* and *active employment* of virtues, to benefit oneself and others. This state is contrasted with that of the sophist: 'Non dicit scientiam vanitatis et obscuritatis ad modum sophiste..' (S.4.6) He has just read Isaiah 53, so influential for the development of Christian theology: 'He is despised and rejected of men; a man of sorrows and acquainted with grief.. he was wounded for our transgressions, he was bruised for our iniquities.. he is brought as a lamb to the slaughter, and as a sheep before her shearers is dumb..' What Bromyard cites is part of verse 11: 'by his knowledge shall my righteous servant justify many..' (In scientia sua iustificabit [ipse iustus servus meus] multos..) – relying on his readers' knowledge of the text he omits the words within square brackets. He then pointedly contrasts 'his knowledge' with 'the knowledge of the Jews' in order to denigrate their inability or unwillingness to penetrate the outer surface of texts – and Isaiah 53 is in the forefront of his mind – so as to understand the inner meaning, which would then open the eyes of the blindfolded Synagogue to the true nature of Jesus as Messiah, Son of God, and God.

..verificatur illud Esaie.liii. In scientia sua iustificabit multos. In scientia inquit sua non iudeorum: qui scientie tantum volunt corticem et paleam, idest intellectum historialem, et non medullam, idest intellectum spiritualem. Sed in scientia sua, idest dei, habent proprietatem: ut sit spiritualis et spiritualiter intellecta: sicut ipse spiritus est.. (S.4.6, 7)

In S.4.14 he writes as a trained theologian using the concepts which allow a Biblical text to be interpreted in four ways, namely: the literal (and this sense also incorporates the exegesis of parables) ii the moral iii the allegorical iv the anagogical or spiritual. It is in the third category of exegetical methods that he finds (contemporary?) Jewish scholars deficient: 'sensus allegoricus est quando aliquid veteris testamenti exponitur de his que accidunt in novo testamento.' ('The allegorical sense is when a text of the Old Testament is explained in the light of what happens in the New Testament.')

4   Quid est enim quod dicitur testamentum uetus nisi occultatio noui? et quid est quod dicitur nouum nisi ueteris revelatio? (PL XLI p.505).

5   William Cade of St Omer, 'a usurer who had agents in every part of western Europe', lent large sums to Henry II. (Saul p.142).

6   Exodus 22.25: Deuteronomy 15.1-9, 23.19-20.

7   Paveant igitur presidentes in suprema curia christianitatis et omnes alii pro quorum muneribus redditibus et questis, et cupiditatibus et exactionibus multi mutuum accipiunt ad usuras a iudeis et aliis: qui curiali nomine se vocant prestatores...quia aufer de curia symoniam et cupiditatem: et maxima ex parte usura cessabit in civitate. (V.12.29).

8   If Bromyard had been of an age, in or before 1290, to remember seeing Jews in England he would have seen on their outer garment the badge of yellow felt 'of the Length of Six Inches, and of the Breadth of Three Inches' to be worn by 'each Jew after he shall be Seven Years old.' This constant mark of humiliation, setting the carriers apart from Christians, he *may* have considered one of their punishments. (The Statutes of Jewry which contain this instruction have been attributed to 4 Edward I and to 18 Edward I: see Statutes of the Realm vol.I p.221).
Another mark of inferiority imposed on Jews, which was not only a humiliation but a powerful impediment to their ability to mount a successful legal action against Christians, was contained in canon 26 of Lateran III of 1179: 'Testimonium quoque christianorum adversus Iudaeos in omnibus causis, cum illi adversus christianos testibus suis utantur, recipiendum esse censemus.. cum eos subiacere christianis oporteat..' (COD p.200)

9   Prestwich pp.343-346.

10   Stow pp.6-7 with Table1.1 accepts Baron's figures for the Jewish population of France in the year 1300 of 100,000 out of a general population of 14 million. This state was followed by expulsions in 1306 and 1322. For Italy in 1300 Baron estimates Jewish numbers at 50,000 from a population of 11 million, after the near destruction of Jewish communities of southern Italy.

11   ibid. p.8. Stow cites the two statues adorning the central portals of Notre Dame in Paris. They are of the late twelfth century.

12   Infideles enim iudei qui non receperunt tot dona a deo quot receperunt cristiani innitentes doctrine dei. Deutro.xv.dicentis. Omnino indigens et mendicus non erit inter vos. Non paciuntur pauperes suos inter eos ostiatim mendicare: sed inter eos faciunt collectas et taxationes pro pauperum suorum sustentatione, cristiani vero nomine potius quam opere collectas faciunt ad simplicium depauperationem.. (E.3.28)

13   Aliter non solum erunt contra nos exempla et vita omnium predictorum [among these, the Rechabites]. Sed etiam generaliter omnium iudeorum: inter quos vix ita simplex vel laicus invenitur quin cordetenus sciat dei mandata computare: que etiam ad litteram strictissime tenent: sicut patet F.iiii.x. Inter nos vero pauci inveniuntur de laicis qui cordetenus illa sciant recitare: sed multo pauciores tam inter clericos quam laicos qui illa opere ostendant.. (M.2.10)

14   Sed illorum [sc. iudeorum] delicti gravitas in operibus illorum inveniri non potest. Ergo oportet quod in fide illorum investigetur causa captivitatis illorum. minor patet: et quantum ad opera que faciunt et quantum ad penas quas frequenter sustinent. Faciunt enim opera pietatis et mutue supportationis multo meliora quam cristiani, sicut patet. F.iii.xv. Ibi ostensum est quod iuvant cadentes et deficientes (F.4.9, 10): sed christiani... [There follows a charge-sheet of sins of omission and commission].

15   A reference to the devastating rains, poor harvests and animal and human mortality of 1314-1318.

Magna differentia illi [sc. iudei] ostiatim mendicare non permittunt suos: sicut patet E.iii.xxviii. Et cristiani suos mori fame permittunt: illorum [sc. iudeorum] principes a divitibus colligunt divitesque taxant ut pauperes nutriant: cristianorum vero principes econverso collectas et taxas faciunt a pauperibus ut divitum nutriant superbiam. (F.3.15)

..legitur quendam iudeum fidem recepisse cristianorum quo baptisato quesitum fuit ab eo postquam ita magnus fuit inter suos quid eum movit ad susceptionem fidei nostre Qui respondit causam conversionis esse virtutem fidei nostre: querentibus vero quomodo ipse sciret virtutem ipsemet respondit quasi sic: quia inquit gens cristiana virtute operum tantum durare non posset quia opera pessima sunt. Ergo oportet quod sic [for 'sit' of text] virtute fidei rationabiliter fuit motus: quia vidit quod iudeorum opera fuerunt bona: quia strictissime mandata dei observant. (F.4.10)

Nos vero falsos testes in causis matrimonialibus et aliis care conducimus Ipsi [sc. iudei] nec blasfemant nec blasfemantes aut turpiter iurantes libenter audiunt. Nos vero hec facientes vel audientes ridemus. (P.8.11)

26

BROMYARD'S STANCE VIS-À-VIS MUSLIMS

The fact that he cites no sura of the 114 in the Quran by number or by name strongly suggests, despite his remark at X.1.19 'as is clear to anyone examining the Quran'[1], that Bromyard's understanding of its teaching comes at some remove: and presumably dependent on the translation of Robertus de Ketton (completed by 1143).[2] The long account, some 1570 words inserted towards the end of the *Legenda sanctorum* within the narrative of Pelagius I (pope 556-561), is a fairly accurate and sober description of Islamic beliefs and practices, and not unfavourable[3]: but Bromyard seems not to have seen it. Of the 'five pillars' of Islam (the testimony that there is no God but God and Muhammad is his messenger: the five daily prayers: the Ramadhan fast: alms-giving: and pilgrimage) it is only alms-giving that he fastens upon. Even obvious markers of difference such as abstention from pork and wine are either unknown to him or too trivial to mention.

As to doctrine he is aware that Muslims believe in paradise which Muhammad has promised to the faithful[4]: and that they hold Jesus to have been a good prophet but not God[5]: 'But conceding the first, i.e. that he was a good man or prophet, they are forced to concede that he was God: proof: because he himself says [dicit] that he is God. John viii.'[6] Of pre-Islamic society he knows that the sun and moon were the objects of worship.[7] He does not conceive of the possible sameness of the God worshipped by Muslims and the God worshipped by Christians. A story of a Christian seeking in marriage a Muslim's daughter ends with the Dominican equating the Muslim's God with the devil.[8] Bromyard will have known that inter-faith marriage alliances were formed in the lands of conflict but chooses not to deal with these.[9]

It is in the sphere of morality, decency and the translation of compassion into practical help for others that Bromyard's admiration for Muslims is evinced.[10] It may be suspected that he emphasises their chaste conduct and charity so as to show up Christian frailties here: 'for in the law of the Muslims, that is in the Quran of Muhammad, adultery is forbidden.'[11] A cross-reference to this passage reinforces the statement at P.8.11 that Muslims and Jews detest and punish adultery: 'as was demonstrated at A.17.10.' He also pointedly contrasts Muslim loyalty towards Muhammad with the verbal abuse which, by oaths, Christians heap upon the Messiah: 'They display greater reverence to the condemned Muhammad than we do to Christ who reigns in heaven since not even for avoiding death would they castigate him [Muhammad] in such oaths as we do [Christ]'.[12]

It is possible to combine admiration for a moral code which censures and punishes adultery, and simultaneously to rebuke a society which permits its men to have four wives at the same time: and this is Bromyard's position. His statement at A.17.10 is to be set against his judgement on multiple sexual liaisons at X.1.19. They read thus:

'For in the law of the Muslims, that is in the Quran of Muhammad, adultery is forbidden: in as much that an adulteress is authorized to be killed or thrust out of sight in life-long imprisonment..'[13]

'..since if a daughter disinherited in her father's will on the grounds of unchastity of life in justice has no basis for complaint so, a fortiori, nor do the Muslims who, in accordance with their and Muhammad's law, lead an unchaste life in respect of their wives and concubines permitted them under their law: as is clear to anyone examining the Quran.'[14]

Bromyard again uses his approval of good works carried out by Muslims as a stick with which to beat bad Christians:

'Muslims too do good works in the in the field of personal conduct and the law of nature: both better and more, indeed, than bad Christians: for example in feeding the poor: in living honourably according to the law of nature, in not doing injury to one's neighbour, in giving each man his due. Jews and Muslims abound in such works: more so than many Christian lands.'[15]

Bromyard quotes here the fine words from the Institutiones of Iustinianus – 'Iuris praecepta sunt haec: honeste vivere, alterum non laedere, suum cuique tribuere.'[16] In the capitulum ELEMOSINA he adds to his praise:

'But not only the Jews, the Muslims too honour and assist their poor more than Christians do.[17] They are shocked, moreover, that our behaviour in this respect is so bad. One of them, the story goes, after being sent to Paris, when he'd diligently given thought to a multiplicity of facts of Christian life, and found much to admire, was asked what, in his view, was most remarkable of all he'd seen: he replied that there *was* one point among all the others, namely this: that those who were the better dressed and less in need had the seats nearer the fire: whereas the unclothed and the poor ate outside, or if inside, in the coldest part.'[18] This tale leads immediately to one from the Deeds of Charlemagne (ex gestis Karoli Magni) in which a Muslim prince called Goliandus comes, under a truce, to the king's quarters to discuss terms of peace and a possible conversion to Christianity. Seated at the king's side, however, dismayed at the contrast between the rich apparel, food and drink of Charlemagne's minions and the scarecrow vestments and meagre diet of the priests (servi dei vestri) he told the king 'People little love their Lord and God, it seems to me, who so little honour His servants. I do not want to be of the society of those who so little love their God.'[19] He walked out, in high dudgeon.

Another example of Christian wrong, the sin of simony, is depicted as all the more shameful in that it is shocking to Muslims.[20]

Writing only thirty years or so after the Muslim capture of Acre and the fall of the last Christian stronghold in the Holy Land: and as the *reconquista* continued of the occupied territories in the Iberian peninsula: Bromyard could not but address questions troubling so many Christians of his age. Why had God permitted Christians to be dominated by Muslims? Why had He allowed them to achieve such a territorial expansion?

Bromyard's answer is to list, one by one, Christian infractions of the Ten Commandments.[21]

'So, having respect to our actions, by transgressing God's commandments it is no surprise that we suffer the blows listed above in this same chapter: or that God has allowed the Muslims to expel us from many lands which we formerly occupied, such as the Holy Land, and others, about which some people are surprised that He even allowed those infidels in many regions to lord it over Christians and gain victories in war over them..'[22]

Our reverses, then, Bromyard concludes, are God's punishment – and he included a reference to the animal mortality and agricultural collapse of the recent dreadful years 1314 to 1318 – for our failure to keep His commandments. It was on condition of keeping those commandments that God had given Christians dominion over the Holy Land and over many lands occupied by the non-believers.[23]

204

This motif recurs at intervals throughout the *Summa*. In an age of conflict and untoward events Bromyard offers a similar explanation to that given by Augustinus in North Africa of the early fifth century. He fears that the catastrophe suffered by the Jews in the seventh decade of the first century may strike his own generation: 'And so it is reasonable to fear that the same fate may be visited upon Christians. We can see a mass of evidence to support this, in that a large part of the world which once was Christian is now occupied by Muslims.'[24]

He makes no reference to the Muslim assault on the Christian frontier in Asia Minor:[25] but he is aware of the wars in the Iberian peninsula (making the point that the fault-lines between two cultures are found at the line of demarcation marking different languages and different legal systems): 'For where there are two kings and territories and domains: and especially if they have different legal systems or languages – as have the Christians and Muslims – frequent wars break out and peace is a rare commodity, as in Spain, where Christians and Muslims plot against each other, the reason being that each of the parties is struggling to annex frontier lands to its own laws and control.'[26]

In the important capitulum CRUX he addresses several issues raised by the crusades against Muslims. His first of three articles is on the preaching of the cross: and this he will develop under five sections, viz.:
1. with what justice preaching against Muslims can take place
2. some sermon-texts suitable for preaching the cross
3. how those taking the cross and going to the Holy Land are helped by God
4. the benefit of going
5. the ingratitude and danger of those not going. (C.17.0)

On this first section he cites Innocentius III (1198-1216) from the *Decretales* dealing with the claim which we have to the Holy Land, from which it may be concluded that the pope can lawfully grant indulgences for the sake of the recovery of the Holy Land: the prime purpose being that the land which was made sacred by the birth, life and death of Christ should be cared for and lived in by Christ and Christians, not by Muhammad and the Muslims.[27]

Next Bromyard adduces the argument that the Holy Land was in Christian possession: was subjected then to a Muslim assault, and conquered: and that Christians have therefore a right to recover what is theirs. He names two heroes among the Christian emperors, Heraclius (610-641), famed for recapturing in 629 the Holy Cross which the Persians had removed from Jerusalem during their invasion of 614: and Constantinus I (Caesar 306-308: Augustus 308-337). 'Secondly, since it was once under the Christian emperors, as is evident from Heraclius and Constantinus and others: it therefore seems just that it should be brought back to the Roman domain since the present occupiers of the land are possessors of bad faith. The argument for this, A.12.8. 'He is said to be a possessor of bad faith who purchases contrary to the prohibitions of the laws. Codex book XI [title 47] On landless serfs and registered slaves statute 'Just as..' '[28] Bromyard's reference was to the capitulum ACQUISITIO and three citations of civil and canon law to back up his stance.

He next gives the counter-argument which the Muslims might put forward: 'Here it could be said that their land which was taken by the Christian emperors by the use of force they [the Muslims] have now recovered and presently occupy: and this was lawful for them.'[29] To this Bromyard responds that Constantinus, now a Christian, did not seize it by military force but simply continued the rule he had maintained before.[30]

The dominating figure of Innocentius III is again cited by Bromyard. 'In other lands, however, which the Roman emperors did not control, according to Innocentius in the previous citation, the pope has the power to impose a constitution to the effect that they should not harass Christians and furthermore has the power to exempt them [Christians] from their [Muslim] authority. If they do the opposite he has the power to deprive them of their dominion.' Bromyard then cites in support the Decretales *De iudeis et saracenis* and five other canon law texts. [31]

The ambitious claims of Innocentius III are once more cited. The Lord constituted his own viceroy (vicarium suum proprium) not only over Christians, according to Innocentius, above: but as a corrector of the Muslims, if they were to act contrary to the law of nature: and of the Jews, if they were to act contrary to the law of Moses. [32]

Since Christ bade us preach the gospel to all nations the pope can command that they [the nations] should admit the preachers of salvation to their territories. If they fail to comply they are to be compelled by war conducted by the secular arm. (..sunt compellendi bello et brachio seculari.) [33]

However, the pope and other preachers of the cross should not directly or expressly provoke anyone to the homicide of non-believers: but [should urge them] to liberate and defend church faith and fatherland: and to bring back the land occupied by the infidels to the worship of the Christian faith. [34]

In preparation for the dispatch of missionaries who would be expected to accompany or to follow the crusade to recover the Holy Land planned by the Council of Vienne for 1319 the Council ordered, in canon 11, that chairs be set up for the teaching of Hebrew, Arabic, Greek and Chaldean (i.e.Syriac) at the universities of Paris, Oxford, Bologna and Salamanca, and at the Roman Curia in Avignon. The Council also named the authorities who were to be responsible for the financing of these chairs. [35] The Council of Canterbury of February 1292 had also recommended sending Arabic-speaking 'spiritual warriors' to the East to work for the conversion of Muslims. [36] Acre had fallen on 18 May 1291. Nine months later the recovery of the Holy Land weighed heavily on the minds of those present at the New Temple on 13 February and at Lambeth on 16 February.

'Item, since every action of Christ is an instruction for us – for he told his disciples, sent to every land 'Go and teach all peoples' etc. – it would seem expedient that before the exercising of the material sword there should be sent in advance to the land of Syria suitable spiritual warriors, not ignorant of Arabic speech, efficaciously to move the hearts of the traitors to [i.e. to embrace] the Christian faith which, blinded by treachery, they have in manifold actions thus far assaulted. And if perhaps the warriors of this kind are led away to martyrdom as the infidels harden their hearts it is confidently to be hoped that through the operation of Christ's grace as miracles radiate their brilliance they will be moved to the Faith more efficaciously through the merit of the martyrs than by the urging of sermons.' [37]

Bromyard gives no indication of awareness of the career of the Franciscan tertiary Ramon Lull, who had helped to found the college of Miramar in Mallorca in 1276 for the study of Arabic. [38] Bromyard could not but have agreed with Lull's claim that 'imperium est propter hoc ut teneat iustitiam, et cum gladio defendat Romanam Ecclesiam..contra infideles qui possident Terram Sanctam'. [39] This assertion was made in 1314, one or two years before he was stoned to death by Muslims at Bougie in North Africa.

Bromyard also addresses this need for skilled linguists to preach to the unbelievers in the capitulum SCIENTIA.

'Secondly [Bromyard's *Primo* had contained a cross-reference to L.3.10, in which he deplored the neglect by lords temporal and spiritual of godly laws and their devotion to studies which brought worldly profit] [they are reproved] by Guilhelmus de Monte Lauduno in his gloss [of 1319] on the *Clementinae* [Book 5] titulus I *De Magistris* capitulum I at the end. For in that chapter it is ordained that in the universities there should be Catholic men equipped with a sufficient understanding of the Hebrew Greek Arabic and Syriac languages to instruct the studious how to preach in the foresaid languages against the infidels..'[40]

Guilhelmus had complained that the endowments called for by Clemens V at the Council of Vienne had not been adequately forthcoming from the appropriate churchmen, both bishops and abbots.[41]

There is, then, a chasm between Bromyard's earnest desire to convert Muslims to the Christian faith and the widely-held view of present-day Christians that such proselytization would be a hostile, or at least unfriendly, enterprise. Bromyard took at face value Jesus' instruction 'Go forth therefore and make all nations my disciples..'[42]

---

[1] sicut patet intuenti Alcoranum. (X.1.9.)

[2] Sharpe pp.559-560 s.v. Robert of Ketton. Robert was in Barcelona by July 1136 studying with Plato of Tivoli (who himself was a colleague of Abraham bar-Hiyya). In Toledo his chief interests were mathematics and astronomy[1]: but he put these on hold to undertake, at Peter the Venerable's inducement, the enormous task of the translation, from a manuscript which Peter managed to acquire, of the Quran.

It was Peter (c.1092-1156: abbot of Cluny) who commissioned and paid for the translation: not only of the Quran but of five other works which together form the Toledan Collection. Peter's aim was to make Islamic beliefs and practices known to his fellow Christians so that they could be countered and refuted.

In his prologue to his *Liber adversus nefandam haeresim sive sectam Saracenorum*[2] he declares his stance:

'So, whether Muhammad's error should be disparaged as heresy or is to be defamed as paganism, action and writing must be directed against it. But because the Latin-speakers and most especially the men of the present day, through the decline of the studiousness of former times, consonant with the speech of the Jews who long ago wondered at the diverse languages of the apostles, know only their mother tongue: they were not able to recognize the nature of such a huge error, let alone confront such a huge error.. I was aggrieved that the Latins were ignorant of the cause of such great perdition, and that no one could be stirred, through this very ignorance, to stand against it. There was no one to make a challenge, because there was no one who recognized the situation. So I took myself to those skilled in Arabic, from which a deadly virus has proceeded and infected more than half the globe. These men [i.e. Christians skilled in Arabic] both by urgent request and by payment I persuaded to the translation from Arabic into Latin of the origin, life, teaching and the very body of law which is called al-Quran. And to ensure the completest confidence in the translation, and that nothing by any deceit could be taken away from the understanding of our [translators: or fellow-Christians: (nostrorum)], I also added a Muslim to our Christian interpreters. The Christian interpreters were Robert of Ketton, Hermann of Dalmatia, Pedro of Toledo: Muhammad was the Muslim.'[3]

In the opening to book I he addresses the followers of Islam. 'It seems strange and perhaps it *is* strange, that a man geographically far removed from you, of a different language, separated in belief, alien in both customs and way of life, from the furthest west write to men of the east or south and attack in my speech people I have never seen, whom perhaps I will never see. I attack you, I repeat, not as our people often do, with weapons but with words, not with violence but with

207

rational argument, not with hate but with love: with such a love that ought to exist between Christians and men turned away from Christ: such as existed between our apostles and the gentiles/pagans of that time, whom they invited to the law of Christ..'[4]

[1] Kritzeck pp.62-65: and Migne PL CLXXXIX columns 659-660

[2] ibid. columns 663-720

[3] ibid. col.671

[4] ibid. col.673

[3]   Varazze vol.II pp.1261-1266.

[4]   in paradiso quem machometus in alcorano suis fidelibus promittit. (A.27.63)

[5]   Sura iv verse 171 is one of several texts Bromyard may have been guided by for his statement at F.4.18 of the Muslim rejection of the deity of Christ. 'Christ Jesus the son of Mary was (no more than) a Messenger of Allah.. Say not "Trinity": desist..for Allah is One God.. (far exalted is He) above having a son.' Sura v verse 17 declares: 'In blasphemy indeed are those that say Allah is Christ the son of Mary.' This is reinforced at 5.75. Bromyard does not mention two other cardinal rejections of fundamental Christian doctrine: one, that Jesus is son of God: two, that Jesus was crucified. The first belief is dismissed in sura ix (Tauba, Repentance: or Baraat, Immunity): 'The Jews call Uzair [Ezra] a son of God, and the Christians call Christ the Son of God..Allah's curse be on them: how they are deluded away from the Truth.' (9.30). The second is roundly rebuffed in 4.157: 'That they [Jews] said (in boast) "We killed Christ Jesus the son of Mary the Messenger of Allah", but they killed him not, nor crucified him, but so it was made to appear to them..'

The lack of any denunciation by Bromyard of these Quranic assertions may well indicate either that his opportunity to study the Latin Quran was severely limited, or that he had access to a compilation which featured only a handful of extracts from the Quran.

In his own lifetime the armies of Islam had driven Christians from their last strongholds in the Holy Land: the Christian-Muslim frontier in Spain remained fluid: in Asia Minor Osman I's Ottoman Turks seized Bursa in 1326 and Nikaia (Iznik) in 1331, under his successor, Orkhan. It was against this background that Bromyard adduced his arguments, especially in the capitula ACQUISITIO and CRUX, which envisaged the necessity of warfare to recover lands occupied in a series of armed aggressions by Muslims. Given this stance it would be remarkable if he had held back from commenting adversely on certain passages in the Quran such as those already cited (9.30 and 4.157) or others, such as

       'The punishment of those who wage war against Allah and His Messenger [Muhammad], and strive with might and main for mischief through the land is: execution, or crucifixion, or the cutting off of hands and feet from opposite sides..' (sura v verse 33).

The inference of silence must be that his acquaintance with the Quran was only partial.

[6]   Idem [i.e. that Jesus is God] probatur per concessa ab ipsis infidelibus: ipsi enim concedunt christum bonum fuisse prophetam: sed non deum: sicut patet in alcorano lege videlicet saracenorum. Sed concedentes primum: videlicet quod fuit bonus homo vel propheta concedere habent quod fuit deus: probatio: quia ipsemet dicit se esse deum. Jo.viii. (F.4.18)

[7]   Nam ipsi [Muslims] solem et lunam et alios planetas colere solebant.. (P.8.11)

[8]   quidam christianus petivit in uxorem filiam cuiusdam sarraceni quam carnaliter diligebat et carnaliter concupivit sed aliter habere non potuit quam per matrimonium: pater vero distulit usque responsum haberet a deo suo id est diabolo. (P.7.28)

[9]   Heer pp.143-144 quotes Fulcher of Chartres (1059-1127), Badouin I's chaplain, who died in Jerusalem. 'We who were once Westerners are now Easterners, a Roman or a Frenchman in this country becomes a Galilean or a Palestinian..

For we have forgotten the lands of our birth. A man here..may have taken to himself a wife, not a compatriot, but a Syrian or Armenian, or even a baptized Saracen, and live together, with all his wife's clan.. He who was once a stranger has become a native, the immigrant has become an inhabitant.'

10 See also Moran Cruz pp.67, 79: 'These intolerant attitudes [she cites, without being specific, three councils (Lateran IV, Lyon II and Vienne) and the Decretales]..contrast remarkably with the attitudes of some Christians who could appreciate Islamic virtues and argue that Muslims took their religion more seriously than the Christians did, or that Muslims fasted and gave to the poor more rigorously than the Christians did.' Her note 78 cites Larissa Taylor's *Soldiers of Christ: Preaching in Late Medieval and Reformation France* (Oxford 1992).

11 ..in lege enim saracenorum videlicet in alcorano machometi prohibetur adulterium. (A.17.10) Sura xvii (Bani Israil, The Children of Israel) and sura xxiv (Nur, Light) both contain verses condemnatory of adultery: 'Nor come nigh to adultery: for it is a shameful (deed) and an evil, opening the road (to other evils) (17.32): 'The woman and the man guilty of adultery or fornication, flog each of them with a hundred stripes..and let a party of the Believers witness their punishment.' (24.2)

12 ..ipsi exhibent reverentiam maiorem machometo damnato quia nec pro morte sustinenda sic eum iuramentis vituperarent quam nos ad christum in celo regnantem. (A.23.15)

13 In lege enim sarracenorum videlicet in alcorano machometi prohibetur adulterium, intantum quod adultera precipitur occidi *vel in carcere perpetuo retrudi*. (A.17.10)
For 'life-long imprisonment' Bromyard must have had in mind sura iv (Nisaa, The Women) verse 15: 'If any of your women are guilty of lewdness, take the evidence of four (reliable) witnesses from amongst you against them: and if they testify confine them to houses until death do claim them, or Allah ordain for them some (other) way.' The coda to this verse leaves open the possibility of other action. A. Y. Ali comments that 'lewdness' may well refer to female homosexuality.

14 ..quia si filia exheredata in testamento patris: eo quod impudice vixit: iuste non habet querelam ergo a fortiori nec sarraceni: qui secundum legem suam machometi impudicam ducunt vitam quantum ad uxores et concubinas quas secundum legem illorum habent: sicut patet intuenti Alcoranum. (X.1.19)

Sura iv verse 3 is the basis for Bromyard's condemnation of 'an unchaste life.'
The verse reads '..marry women of your choice, two, or three, or four; but if ye fear that ye shall not be able to deal justly (with them) then only one, or (a captive) that your right hands possess.' Verse 24 of the same sura adds: 'Also prohibited are women already married, except those whom your right hands possess.. ' On 'whom your right hands possess' the translator comments 'i.e. captives in a Jihad.' Verse 25 continues in the same vein: 'If any of you have not the means wherewith to wed free believing women, they may wed believing girls from among those whom your right hands possess.' The translator's gloss on the last five words is 'i.e. captives in a Jihad, or war under the orders of the righteous Imam against those who persecute Faith. In such cases formal hostility dissolves civil ties.' Also relevant are verses 1-6 of sura 23, Al Muminum (The Believers), especially verse 6:
1. The Believers must (eventually) win through - [i.e. prosper, succeed
    (note by translator)];
2. Those who humble themselves in their prayers;
3. Who avoid vain talk;
4. Who are active in deeds of charity;
5. Who abstain from sex,
6. Except with those joined to them in the marriage bond, or (the captives)
    whom their right hands possess – for (in their case) they are free from blame...

15 ..etiam saraceni opera de genere morum et de lege nature bona faciunt: et meliora et plura quam mali cristiani: sicut pascere pauperes: honeste secundum legem nature vivere: alterum non ledere. Ius suum unicuique tribuere, plus in talibus operibus habundant iudei et saraceni quam multe terre christianorum. (C.17.33)

16 So Bromyard associates both Muslims and Jews with the guiding principles of the Christian emperor Iustinianus I: 'The precepts of the law are these: to live honourably: to hurt no one: to render to each man his own.' (Institutiones I.1.3)

17   Non solum vero iudei sed etiam saraceni plus pauperes suos honorant et iuvant quam cristiani. (E.3.28, from the capitulum ELEMOSINA, alms-giving).

On alms-giving (zakat) a number of texts in the Quran urge Muslims to be charitable: indeed this duty is reckoned as one of the 'five pillars' of Islam. The important sura ii (Baqara, The Heifer) enjoins this in four separate verses in almost identical words: 'And be steadfast in prayer; practise regular charity' (2.43, 110, 177, 277). The message recurs at 4.77, 162: and in sura v (Maida, The Table Spread) at 5.58.

18   Et de hoc quod nos ita male habemus nos ad pauperes nostros: mirantur et scandalisantur. Quorum unus ut fertur parisius missus cum multa cristianorum facta diligenter cum admiratione considerasset: requisitus quod esset maius mirabile in oculis suis de omnibus que vidisset Respondit unum inter alia esse quod melius vestiti et qui minus indigent propinquius iuxta ignem sedent: et nudi et pauperes extra ostium vel intra ostia in frigore comedunt. (E.3.28)

19   Quod etiam de hoc scandalisentur patet ex gestis Karoli magni in quibus continetur quod cum circa expugnationem moraretur saracenorum quidam magnus princeps inter eos Goliandus nomine ad eum sub treuga venit de pace et cristianitate quam recipere intendebat* tractaturus. Iuxta regem ergo comedens et comedentium et ministrorum ordinem diligenter considerans et singulorum conditionem statum et diversitatem et officium inquirens, in fine quesivit qui essent illi qui in pauperrimo apparatu comederunt super terram. Rex vero respondit illos esse dei nostri servos quos pro eius amore pascimus. Princeps vero regi dixit: servi tui ita splendide vestiuntur et laute comedunt et bibunt: et servi dei vestri nudi et famelici derelinquentur parum videntur dominum et deum suum diligere qui ita parum servos suos honorant, nec volo de eorum esse societate qui ita parum deum suum diligunt, et cum indignatione recessit. (E.3.28, 29)

*An example of Muslims abjuring Islam and converting to Christianity which Bromyard may have remembered is found at the end of the ninth book of the *Gesta Francorum*:

Non post multos dies [after 28 June 1098] baptizatus est ammiralius cum illis qui Christum recognoscere maluerunt.

A few lines above the author had expressed the concept as 'Christianitatem recipere', the same words as Bromyard was to use. (Gesta Francorum p.71).

20   Si enim illius sanctissime sedis presidentes scirent quomodo non solum infideles saraceni, iudei, scismatici, et heretici, sed etiam fideles de illorum non dico scandalisantur sed obloquuntur apparatu quem superbum et a cristi tramite deviantem..quis nostrum symoniam vitabit. (H.4.16)

21   M.2.12 He extends the scope of the fifth commandment (Thou shalt not kill) to include allowing someone to die. 'The fifth however they transgress in many ways, both by actively killing and by standing aside, that is by allowing large numbers of people to die of starvation' – a reference to the recent famine years of 1314-1318.

Quintum [sc. mandatum] vero multipliciter transgrediuntur [sc. christiani] *tam occidendo active: quam permissive*, permittendo videlicet multos fame mori.. [my italics]. He also accuses Christians of the sin of usury (et usuras excercendo).

22   Habendo ergo respectum ad ea que facimus, mandata dei transgrediendo, non est mirabile quod mala sustinemus supra eodem capitulo enumerata: vel quod deus permisit saracenos de multis terris quas olim occupavimus nos eiicere: sicut de terra sancta et de aliis de quibus nonnulli mirantur quod etiam permisit illos infideles in multis partibus christianis dominari et de eis in bello victorias obtinere.. (M.2.12)

23   Ita sub eadem conditione dedit christianis dominium terre sancte: et multarum terrarum quas infideles occupant. (M.2.13)

24   Item timendum est ne christianis idem contingat. Cuius contingentie magna nunc cernitur evidentia, de hoc quod magna mundi pars que olim fuit christianorum nunc a saracenis occupata est. (O.6.21)

25   Vakalopoulos draws attention to the unremitting pressure of the several groupings of Turkish war-bands which engendered 'agony and terror in the souls of the inhabitants' [of Anatolia]:

(..gennousan tēn agonia kai ton tromo stis psyches tōn katoikōn..) (p.102). The Ottomans took Brousa/Bursa in 1326 and Nikaia in 1331. After the fall of Nikaia, Vakalopoulos continues, 'the few market-towns which still remained free, to avoid the horrors of siege and capture agreed to pay crippling taxes to the Turks.' The religious basis for justifying the imposition of a tax specifically upon non-Muslims living under Muslim rule was – and is – sura ix verse 29 of the Quran:

'Fight those who believe not in Allah nor the Last Day, nor hold that forbidden which hath been forbidden by Allah and His Messenger, nor acknowledge the Religion of Truth from among the People of the Book, until they pay the Jizyah with willing submission and feel themselves subdued.' (Quran 9.29). (On the *jzíah* or poll tax and its application to Christians and Jews see Cohen p.68-72 and notes 103 to 129 on pp.229-231.) Vakalopoulos writes too of the seizure of Christian churches and of coarse behaviour (..na probainoun sykhna stēn kataskhesē tōn ekklesiōn tōn khristianōn kai na pherōntai banausa..) (p.104). See also NCMH vol VI p.799: 'The countryside was rapidly brought under Turkish control, and one by one the cities were starved into submission..' (of the period after the battle of Bapheus in 1302).

That Bromyard had access, either direct or indirect, to reports of conditions in the eastern Mediterranean (Greece? Rhodes? Cyprus?) is evident from the story of a possessed woman at A.12.34: 'Unde retulit quedam religiosa persona que fuit inter fideles in transmarinis partibus quod vidit ibi quandam demoniacam per quam dyabolus loquebatur..' [On this point [unjust acquisition] a certain religious who'd lived with Catholics overseas reported that he'd seen there a possessed woman through whom the devil spoke..']

26 Ubi enim duo reges et terre et dominia: et specialiter si sint diversarum legum vel linguarum sicut christianorum et saracenorum frequenter fiunt ibi bella: et raro est ibi pax: sicut in hyspania ubi machinant ad invicem christiani et saraceni: et ratio est quia quilibet nititur contractam propinquam trahere ad leges et dominium suum (B.2.20 from the capitulum BELLUM).

Bromyard thus acknowledges that war is not unexpected between contiguous states, especially when there are major cultural differences between them: indeed, he instances several conflicts between Christian and Muslim powers. Nowhere, however, does he call Muslims 'enemies': his interest is rather to bring them to the love of Christ. Moreover, he punctures the vanity of boastful militants at C.17.12 (in a passage quoted in chapter 12). His stance, then, may be seen as different from some contemporary secular positions, as exemplified in the 'Statutum de Terris Templariorum' of 17° Edward II, 1323-24:

'..but since the lands and tenements aforesaid were given to the brothers of the said Order for the defence of Christians and the Holy Land against the pagans and Muslims, *and other enemies of Christ and Christians*, and of the universal sacrosanct Church..' [..contra paganos et Saracenos, et alios inimicos Christi et Chrstianorum..] (Statutes vol.I p.195).

27 Quantum ad primum [sc. qua iusticia predicari possit contra saracenos] est sciendum quod innocentius. Extra. li.iii.ti.xxxiiii. de voto et voti redemptione. c.quod super his*[1] questionem illam de iusticia quam habemus ad terram sanctam tractat. Ex qua questione aliqualiter elici potest quod papa pro terra sancta recuperanda iuste indulgentias dare potest. Primo ut terra que christi nativitate et inhabitatione et morte est consecrata: a christo et christianis et non a machometo et saracenis colatur et inhabitetur. (C.17.1)

*[1] Decretales, 3.34.8: Innocentius III to the archbishop of Canterbury [either Hubert Walter or Stephen Langton]: Quod super his..

'You raised the question about those who, after taking the sign of the cross, are unable usefully to fulfil their vow on account of infirmity or poverty or other just cause..'

Innocentius gives the reasonable decision that it serves no purpose for the weak and poor to go to the Holy Land to be a burden to others [..quod debiles et inopes magis illuc in defectum quam ad profectum accedunt: cum isti pugnare non possint et illi mendicare cogantur..].

The rich would be welcome, since they could bring soldiers with them: craftsmen and farm-workers would be useful too. The rest could redeem their vows: that is, make a monetary contribution to the Christian cause.

28 Secundo: quia sub imperatoribus christianis aliquando fuit: sicut patet de Eracleo et Constantino et aliis: ergo iustum videtur ut ad romanum imperium reducatur quia terram modo occupantes sunt possessores malefidei. Argumentum ad hoc A.xii.viii. Malefidei possessor dicitur: qui contra legum interdicta mercatur. C.li.xi.de agri.et ser.l.quemadmodum.*[2] (C.17.1)

*[2] Quemadmodum, Codicis Lib.XI [Titulus XLVII,] De agricolis
et censitis et colonis.
The seventh section of the titulus begins
'Quemadmodum originarios absque terra: ita rusticos censitosque
servos vendi omnifariam non licebit..'
[Just as in every way it will not be lawful for landless serfs or
peasants or registered slaves to be sold..]
The key judgement for which Bromyard cites this text comes in
the last sentence:
'malae fidei namque possessorem esse nullus ambigit, qui aliquid
contra legum interdicta mercatur.'
[For no one doubts that he who purchases anything contrary to the
prohibitions of the laws is a possessor of bad faith.]

29   Hic dici posset: quod terram suam a christianis imperatoribus violenter acceptam: ab eis
recuperaverunt et occupant. Et hoc fuit eis licitum. (C.17.1)

30   ..quia constantinus factus christianus non violenter illius terre dominium occupavit sed dominium
quod ante habuit continuavit. (C.17.1)

31   In aliis autem terris quas principes romani non habuerunt secundum innocentium ubi prius potest
papa constitutionem facere quod non molestent christianos et eximere eos ab eorum potestate, et si
contrarium fecerint potest eos dominio privare. Extra de iudeis et saracenis, cum sit.[1]   Et c.ex
speciali.[2] et c.i.et c.finali. Et dis.liiii. mancipia et c.sequenti. (C.17.1)

    [1] Innocentius III in eodem [concilio generali]:
    Cum sit nimis absurdum ut blasphemus christi in christianos vim potestatis exerceat
    quod super hoc toletanum concilium provide statuit: nos propter transgressorum
    audaciam in hoc generali concilio innovamus prohibentes ne iudei publicis officiis
    preferantur: quoniam sub tali pretextu christianis plurimum sunt infesti... Hoc idem
    extendimus ad paganos. (Decretales 5.6.16)
    [2] Gregoris IX astoricen. Et lucen. episcopis:
    Ex speciali quem erga illustrem regem portugalie gerimus charitatis affectu..Mandamus
    qua regem ipsum sollicite inducatis ne in officiis publicis iudeos christianis preficiat
    sicut in generali concilio continetur. Et si forte redditus suos iudeis vendiderit vel
    paganis: christianum tunc deputet de gravaminibus inferendis clericis et ecclesiis non
    suspectum per quem iudei sive saraceni sine christianorum iniuria iura regalia
    consequantur. (Decretales 5.6.18)
    [1] Innocentius III in the same [general Council]:
    Since it is too absurd that a blasphemer of Christ should exercise the force of authority
    against Christians which with foresight on this matter the Council of Toledo determined:
    we, on account of the temerity of transgressors make an innovation in this general
    Council [Lateran IV] forbidding Jews to be promoted to public offices, since under such a
    pretext they are extremely hostile to Christians... This same measure we extend to
    Muslims. (Decretales 5.6.16)
    [2] Gregorius IX to the bishops of Astorga and Lugo:
    Out of the special affection which we bear to the illustrious king of Portugal.. We
    command that you take trouble to induce the king in person not to promote in public
    offices Jews [in authority] over Christians just as is contained in [canons of] the general
    Council [Lateran IV]. And if it happens that he has sold his revenues to Jews or to
    Muslims: let him then depute a Christian of integrity in regard to damages brought on
    clerics and churches through whom Jews or Muslims should follow royal laws with no
    injury to Christians. (Decretales 5.6.18)

The texts Bromyard calls in support here have the general tenor that Christians should not be
placed in positions of inferiority to Jews or to Muslims. From Gregorius IX's letter to the bishops
of Astorga and Lugo it seems clear that king Sancho II (1223-1248) had farmed out to Jews or to
Muslims the collection of his revenues.

32   .universaliter constituit vicarium suum proprium non solum supra christianos secundum innocentium ubi prius sed ut corrigat saracenos si contra legem faciant nature: et iudeos si contra legem faciant moysi.. (C.17.2)

33   Insuper cum christus precepit evangelium omni creature idest omnium hominum nationibus predicare: et mandare potest papa quod admittant predicatores salutis sue in terris suis: si vero predictis non obdediant sunt compellendi bello et brachio seculari. (C.17.2). (In support of this view he cites the Decretum C.23.q.8 c.9 Omni timore: that if anyone dies for the truth of the faith and the saving of his country and the defence of Christians he will be rewarded with a heavenly prize.)

34   Papa vero et alii crucis predicatores non debent quoscunque directe provocare ad homicidium infidelium vel expresse: sed ut ecclesiam fidem ac patriam liberent et defendant: et terram ab infidelibus occupatam redigant ad cultum fidei christiane. (C.17.3)

35   Schein pp.246-247. Her eighth chapter assesses 'The Crusades at the Council of Vienne'.

36   ibid. p.138: Powicke & Cheney p.1110. The names of some of the preachers who undertook this perilous venture have survived. In a letter dated 27 August 1320 Edward II writes to the king of Cyprus [Henri II] requesting such help as they might need for three Dominicans, Robert de Braybroke, John de Scone and Robert de Hattecoumbe. They were going to the Levant 'ad praedicandum fidem catholicam Saracenis, zelo devotionis accensi.' (Foedera vol.I pars II p.433). Hattecoumbe had probably been a member of the Dominican convent in Oxford in 1318 (BRUO pp.844-845), and was granted safe-conduct on 8 October 1320 for 3 years on going overseas (CPR 1317-1321 p.506). He does not re-appear in the records.

37   Item, quod omnis Christi actio nostra est instructio, qui missis in omnem terram discipulis ait: Ite et docete omnes gentes etc., videretur expediens ut ante gladii materialis exercitium premittantur ad terram Syrie spirituales ydonei bellatores, ydiomatis arabici non ignari, qui corda perfidorum moveant efficaciter ad fidem christianam quam excecati perfidia multipliciter hactenus inpugnarunt. Et si forsitan bellatores huiusmodi obduratis infidelibus martirio abducantur, fiducialiter est sperandum quod operante Christi gratia coruscantibus miraculis ad fidem movebuntur efficacius merito martirum quam exhortatione sermonum. (Powicke & Cheney p.1110).

38   Abulafia p.98.

39   Schein p.248 and n.2.

40   Secundo a Guilhelmo de monte lauduno in glosa sua super constitutiones clementinas titulo de magistris capitulo.i.in fine. In illo nanque capitulo ordinatur quod in universitatibus deberent esse viri catholici sufficientem habentes hebraice grece arabice chaldee linguarum peritiam ut studiosos doceant quomodo in predictis linguis contra infideles predicent.. (S.4.2)

41   ..quibus [sc. the schools of the four languages] vult in stipendiis sufficientibus per ecclesiarum prelatos tam exemptos quam non exemptos sufficienter provideri.. Hec voluntas male producta est ad effectum.. (S.4.2)

42   euntes ergo docete omnes gentes baptizantes eos in nomine Patris et Filii et Spiritus Sancti.. (Secundum Matthaeum 28.19). The English version is that of NEB.

27

BROMYARD AND ADAM ORLETON

Few of Bromyard's first readers will have failed to hear in the title of capitulum C4, CIVITAS[1], an echo of Augustinus' *De civitate dei*. The two cities (or two states) are set out in the argument to Book Two of the *Retractationes* – '..two Cities: of which one is of God, the other of this world.'[2]

Bromyard begins his explosive attack on 'great bishops' with a fable: a fable which has four participants: wolves, dogs, shepherds, sheep.[3] In this fable the aim of the 'wolves' is to kill and eat the sheep. To achieve this their first step is to persuade the shepherds to rid themselves of the guard-dogs. They point out to the shepherds that the root of the quarrel between wolves and shepherds is the dogs. These once removed, the wolves take the sheep. 'Such a crafty scheme is used by the devil for the destruction of the City of the Church. For the devil sees that preachers, by their teaching and preaching and fending off wolves from the flock, in the manner of wise men in the State [civitate] and in the manner of guard-dogs [canum] protect the sheep-pen of the Church.'[4] Bromyard extends the analogy. 'And he reflects, and knows, that this is an enormous help in the defence of this City [civitatis] which he is striving to overturn. And in fact he *is* overturning it by influencing the more important bishops of this Church-State [civitatis ecclesiastice] to muzzle the preachers[5] so as to send them away: whereupon all will be at peace. And when they've been removed or muzzled by means of their laws and regulations they [sc. the wolves] invade and destroy the Church's flock with none to resist them: and these demons who are besieging the City of God [civitatem dei], through this influence of theirs in handing over the men of good sense and muzzling the guard-dogs have increased their power to such an extent that it is an event which *should* evoke astonishment that one powerful guardian of State and Church [or, of a city and a flock] would rather put up with a thousand usurers in a city, and a thousand prostitutes, than twenty friars..'[6]

This exaggeration of numbers to an impossible point is a rhetorical device laying bare the depth of hostility Bromyard felt for the 'magnus custos.' Binkley rightly assigns this outburst to the sense of grievance experienced by the Dominicans over the opposition, headed, it seems, by the bishop of Hereford, to their struggle firmly to establish their house in Hereford. In 1317 Iohannes XXII ordered the archbishop of Canterbury, Walter Reynolds, to resolve the dispute. Edward II in 1319 provided a new site, and in 1322 Adam Orleton confirmed the grant.[7]

This passage should, however, be mined for other conclusions and insights. The first of these is the light thrown upon the dating of this capitulum, which would not have been written *before* 15 March 1317 (when the saintly bishop Richard Swinfield died) nor after 25 September 1327, when Adam Orleton was translated to Worcester and a new bishop was provided to Hereford.[8] Bromyard would not have wished to insult Thomas Charleton gratuitously: furthermore the legal dispute had been settled on 23 February 1322: with an ill grace: Orleton's clause in his grant, referring to pressure from a king whom he considered unworthy of his high office, seems to have been dictated through gritted teeth: 'we unwilling to resist in anything contrary to that which has been done for the honour of God and Holy Church by our lord the aforementioned illustrious king of England..'[9] The unsaid element hangs in the air like a sword of Damocles.

The second is the extraordinary nature of the remark about the thousand usurers and the thousand prostitutes. Where on earth did these words come from? Bromyard's anger might have generated the charge: but a likelier source may well be an unguarded (or even deliberate) aphorism from the lips of Orleton himself: a man not afraid to make harsh public denunciations.[10] To usury Bromyard does devote a capitulum: but his rare references to prostitution[11] ensure these words a more damning impact.

A third significant feature of this excerpt is the accusation that the muzzling of (outspoken) preachers by their bishops is the work of the devil. In the capitulum VERITAS Bromyard gives free rein to his resentment against episcopal control. 'As are the pernicious servants for fear of whom the men condemned by them dare not unfold the truth to their lords. As are the bishops who have jurisdiction over religious, who mete out punishment and *impose silence*: or others who contrive that silence and a muzzling of his preaching be imposed on the man who speaks out against the arrogance and vanity of the powerful.'[12] Can anyone doubt but that Bromyard himself was so gagged? For a man so passionately devoted to upholding good and righting wrongs his forcibly repressed energies must have made the constraint a penalty scarcely bearable. Of the two men who sat on the bishop's throne in Hereford from 1317 to 1344 by far the likelier target for Bromyard's disgust is Adam Orleton.

Of 1324 Murimuth records,[13] as one of the measures of the parliament of 23 February to 18 March,[14] the setting up, at Edward's instigation, of a commission to investigate the charge levelled against Orleton 'that he adhered to the party of [Roger] Mortimer and other enemies of the king, as it was said, by providing the same enemies with men, horses and arms..'[15] Murimuth goes on to say that the bishop refused to plead: that the commission found against him: and that Edward ordered his temporalities to be seised and held, as of one who was a traitor to the king.[16]

There may have been a reluctance among shrewder lawyers to be drafted on to the commission[17]: some may not have wished to make an enemy of Orleton, a man suspected, after all, of links to powerful dissidents: others may even have foreseen the demise of Edward II's régime.

With Isabella's and Mortimer's invasion in September 1326 Orleton's influence on the forming of opinion and his closeness to the new régime revealed his formidable stature. This new situation may well be seen as a factor inducing us towards a dating of the 'magnus custos'[18] passage of C.4.16, 17 to the pre-September 1326 period: but some readers may feel that Bromyard's language is sufficiently guarded that the passage could equally have been written before or after Orleton's enhanced prominence in affairs of State, until his translation to Worcester.

Bromyard *may* have encountered Orleton well before his appointment to the bishopric. Haines considers that he was probably born in Hereford, where there were several Orletons.[19] He is styled doctor of canon law by 1310[20] and was also skilled in the Roman law, 'utriusque iuris peritus' in 1307,[21] and was a canon and prebendary of Hereford from 1311 to 1317.[22]

1   I use both 'city' and 'state' in translating this passage. Bromyard sets out in his introduction to the capitulum both the narrower and the broader scope of the word: three times writing 'civitas vel communitas.'

2   '..duarum civitatum, quarum est una Dei, altera huius mundi'.
Bromyard sharpens the antagonism: his beginning to C4 is
> Civitates sunt due: una dei altera diaboli.. Two cities there are: one of God
> the other of the devil.. (C.4.0)

3   This fable bears some resemblance to Halm 266 of the Teubner edition (Leipzig 1852).

4   Tali arte utitur dyabolus ad destructionem civitatis ecclesiastice. Videt enim quod predicatores docendo et predicando et lupos a grege arcendo ad modum sapientum in civitate et ad modum canum ovile ecclesie custodiunt. (C.4.16)

5   To preserve the equation of rôle between the guard-dogs of the fable and the preachers I translate the verb 'artare' and its abstract noun 'artatio' by 'muzzling'. The nickname 'Domini canes', the hounds of the Lord, given the Dominicans by their enemies Bromyard may here be embracing as a badge of honour.

6   Et cogitat et scit quod multum iuvat ad custodiam istius civitatis quam nititur evertere. Et de facto eam evertit: informando maiores prelatos istius civitatis ecclesiastice quod predicantes artent ut dimittant, et tunc erunt in pace, quibus per leges et statuta eorum vel emissis vel artatis sine resistentia gregem ecclesie invadunt et destruunt, et intantum isti demones civitatem dei obsidentes in ista informatione de sapientibus tradendis et canibus artandis invaluerunt: quod tamen mirabile est dictu quod unus magnus civitatis et gregis custos tollerabilius sustineret in civitate mille usurarios et totidem meretrices quam viginti fratres.. (C.4.16, 17)

7   Binkley, Hereford p.260.

8   Powicke and Fryde p.230.

9   ..nos nolentes in aliquo contra id quod in honorem Dei et sancte ecclesie actum est per dominum nostrum, illustrem regem Anglie prefatum resistere.. (Orleton p.221). Orleton's choice of adjective for Edward II, though conventional, shows him to have been not devoid of humour.

10   Haines' *Itinerary* of Adam Orleton dates his sermon at Oxford between 15 and 26 October 1326 (Haines, Orleton p.227). It was in this sermon, according to John Prickehare, that Orleton called Edward II 'a tyrant and a sodomite': and, Prickehare asserted, he repeated this charge at Wallingford at Christmas 1326 while with queen Isabella. (Mortimer pp.50-52). (Between these two dates, on 16 November, the king had been apprehended). The Lanercost chronicler attributed to Orleton a sermon at the deposition parliament on 13 January 1327 on the text *Rex insipiens perdet populum suum*, 'A foolish king shall ruin his people' (Haines, Orleton p.169: McKisack p.89). William Dene's *Historia Roffensis* assigned Orleton an exposition, at this parliament, of the text *Vae terrae cuius rex puer est* (Ecclesiastes 10.16): 'Woe to the land whose king is a boy': a text which Bromyard uses at R.4.11 to attack the misgovernment of England by Edward's régime.

11   In a passage beginning with a citation of the *Digest* (47.11.1.2 Qui puero stuprum, On procuring a boy for sexual intercourse: for which Roman law provided capital punishment for both instigator and associates if the assault took place) Bromyard warns those who rent houses to male or female sinners to beware of such a judgement –
> Et etiam peccatoribus vel peccatricibus, sicut meretricibus et huiusmodi locantes vel concedentes domos, sicut faciunt in magnis villis.. (P.8.23).

12   Sicut sunt iniuriosi ministri dominorum propter quorum timorem ab eis damnificati non audent veritatem dominis suis ostendere. Sicut sunt superiores religiosorum prelati qui puniunt et silentium imponunt: vel alii qui procurant quod silentium et predicationis artatio imponatur ei qui contra potentium loquitur superbiam et vanitatem. (V.1.8).

[13]   Murimuth pp.42-43.

[14]   Powicke and Fryde p.517.

[15]   Hoc anno, in Quadragesima, tenuit rex Angliae parliamentum Londoniis; in quo fecit inquiri contra Adam episcopum de Herefordia ex officio, per legales viros de comitatu Herefordiae super eo quod adhaesit illis de Mortuo mari et aliis inimicis regis, ut dicebatur, eisdem inimicis accommodando homines, equos et arma. (Murimuth pp.42-43)

[16]   Et licet ille episcopus noluit respondere, inquisitione faciente contra eum, rex mandavit omnia temporalia sua seysiri et teneri, sicut illius qui fuit proditor regis. (ibid. p.43). The charge was laid on 1 March 1324. Emden expands: 'As there was no precedent for a bishop being arraigned before a civil court, Orleton declined to plead unless the archbishop of Canterbury gave him leave, and was forthwith granted protection by the archbishop and bishops..' (BRUO p.1403).

[17]   However, known enemies of the bishop, such as Adam Halfnaked, Richard de Scholle and Walter de Brugge, would doubtless have accepted the duty with relish. (Haines, Edward II p.155). Halfnaked and de Scholle were later to be warned by Orleton against association with William de Irby, prior of St Guthlac's in Hereford, whose excommunication he called for on 2 August 1324 (Orleton pp.305-306). Bromyard presumably monitored these developments with close interest.

[18]   As an instance of the magnificent bearing he was not loath to maintain one may cite the size of his entourage for his diplomatic mission to Avignon which left London on 30 March 1327: he was accompanied by 70 men and 46 horses. (Haines, Orleton pp.27-28).

[19]   Haines, Orleton ODNB vol.41 p.934.

[20]   BRUO p.1402.

[21]   Haines, Orleton ODNB vol.41 p.935.

[22]   BRUO p.1402.

28

BROMYARD'S REFERENCES TO RECENT FRENCH HISTORY

John Bromyard belonged to an international order, which maintained good lines of communication among its many centres and oversaw a frequent interchange of personnel.[1] It is therefore perhaps surprising that his extra-literary references to events of recent or near-contemporary history in foreign lands are limited for the most part to France and to Italy. He has but a single reference to the Spain of his day:

'..And peace is a rarity, as in Spain where Christians and Muslims are plotting against each other: the reason being that each party is struggling to bring over to its own legal system and dominion the bordering territory.'[2]

There is also just one reference to a verbal account reaching Bromyard's ears, whether directly or indirectly he does not reveal, given by a religious who had lived among Catholics in the eastern Mediterranean.[3]

Bromyard's references to recent French history focus on three reigns: those of Louis IX (1226-1270), Philippe III (1270-1285) and Philippe IV (1285-1314).

Louis IX was only twelve when he inherited the French throne. Bromyard telescopes two and a half decades when he invokes the ordinance of 1254 (which followed on the inquests conducted within Louis' own domain in 1247), but his summary is just:

'This is how a noble king behaved on the death of his predecessor, who had acquired a great deal. He despatched throughout his realm one bishop and four religious, experts in both God's law and secular law, instructing them that if they discovered anything wrongly acquired they should restore it.'[4]

Louis' immediate predecessor was his father Louis VIII (1223-1226): but Bromyard will have had in mind the long reign of Philippe II (1180-1223). The great inquest of 1247 was headed by teams of *enquêteurs*, 'composed not of a cleric and a knight, as was customary, but of Dominicans and Franciscans: barely more than a couple of secular clerics can be traced among them.'[5] Richard details some of the abuses perpetrated by Philippe II's officials: stating that complaints were particularly numerous in Languedoc: 'nobles and, above all, widows and orphans reported unwarranted confiscations and arbitrary acts committed by the royal officers...the dark underside of the progress of royal power and monarchical administration was exposed.' He cites the findings of William C. Jordan that, in the case of the *bailliages* alone, of which there were no more than seventeen or eighteen, twenty changes of incumbent occurred between 1247 and 1249.. 'It appears that the king deprived of their posts officers who were compromised, had been extortionate or simply guilty of abuses of power, and replaced them..'[6]

Bromyard may have conflated the two great inquests: that of 1254 was again led largely by Dominicans and Franciscans.[7]

S.Louis' passion for equity is adduced to point a moral in IUDICIUM DIVINUM:

'So in this judgement God does for his chosen ones who have previously suffered hurt what a certain king used to do for his subjects. When he wished to remove from office bailiffs and men of high office he would detain them under guard while a herald proclaimed to those over whom they had presided that if they had injured anyone or done harm to anyone while in office that he who felt he had been injured should come and freely lay down his complaint. This blessed custom the kings of France used to observe with regard to the provosts of Paris, through which one of the said provosts was lately hanged.'[8]

Richard confirms Bromyard's point: '..it was laid down that on leaving office, the *bailli* or seneschal must continue to reside locally for forty (or fifty) days to answer any accusations which might be brought against him.'[9]

Again in DOMINATIO Bromyard praises S.Louis as exhibiting the qualities of the ideal king: his early readers will perhaps have compared and contrasted king Louis' devotion to justice with that of later kings:

'By the example of S.Louis the king.. Twice a week he used to sit in a public place to give personal audience to the complaints of the poor about his ministers or any others, so that he could dispense justice to all.'[10]

In his coy allusion to Philippe IV's shirking responsibility for injustices perpetrated by his ministers Bromyard includes a reference to S.Louis which serves as a contrast to and comment upon Philippe. The passage begins

'This is how a certain great king used to excuse himself whenever he was informed of injustices committed through the agency of some of his men.. It is to be feared that he would go with them [to hell] since he neither corrected nor dismissed them – as *did* S.Louis: see below in the chapter CONSILIUM section 47.'[11]

Bromyard's cross-reference to C.11.47 deals with good and bad counsellors, and S.Louis' refusal to place self-advantage before moral uprightness.

'And [the example of] S.Louis king of France in whose *Deeds*[12] it is stated that when his emissary, on his return from the Roman Curia, reported to him that he had been successful in his request for the vacancy of all the cathedral churches, i.e. the episcopal sees,[13] he [Louis] took the bull from him and hurled it into the fire. He said 'For the other matters with which We burdened thee We are grateful to thee: on *that* matter however which thou securedst on request, to the peril of Our souls We give thee ill thanks.' Note D.12.4. Furthermore one reads of him that he had one counsellor extremely shrewd in giving counsel and in the execution of affairs: however, he had one characteristic which was less just, namely that he consistently determined, right or wrong, to take the king's part and to gain an advantage for the king, whether it were fair or unfair. In this he is like many of the present day who would rather be excommunicated and separated from God and the Church than abandon carrying out the wishes and getting an advantage for their lords, as they say: since in very truth there *is* no advantage, as will be clear at the End: as is made clear at A.27.43. Well: this man he [Louis] warned, twice or three times, to give up that practice; when he refused to comply he summoned him before his Council and said 'In my behaviour to thee I have followed the Gospel by giving thee private warnings: but since thou hast not listened to me thou wilt be to me as the publican and wilt no more serve me...' This is how a lord has to examine and watch over and temper his counsellors and servants and to discharge those who will not be corrected: otherwise peril looms over both him and them.'[14]

Bromyard's cross-reference here to D.12.4 instances Louis IX's 'hands on' approach to his administration. The question he would put to potential officers on their incomes was to ascertain whether they could live off them: if they could not, the likelihood of their financial corruption was that much greater. He would also seek third-party opinion on their worth.

'..By the example of S.Louis the king about whom it is written that he would scrupulously examine potential officers on their life and reputation, and whether they had a sufficient income to live on.'[15]

His cross-reference to A.27.43 is to the question of the degree of responsibility borne by a lord whose officer commits a wrong resulting in a profit for his lord.

'The officer says 'The lord who gains the advantage should endure the peril' [to his soul]. The lord says 'I acted on his advice: he should endure the peril.' Each would want to shift the load on to the other: they cannot: each will bear his own burden.'[16]

The hanging of Pierre de la Brosse on 30 June 1278 is introduced by Bromyard as an example which noblemen – and the context here is a powerful denunciation of the *English* nobility for riding roughshod over the poor – should bear in mind, and fear. He links a striking inscription found over the door of Pierre la Flote's office –

pierre regna: et pierre regne: pierre pendi: et pierre pendera[17] –

with a predecesssor of la Flote, namely Pierre de la Brosse, who had been barber-surgeon to Louis IX and then chamberlain to Philippe III. Court intrigue[18] led to his downfall and hanging.

La Flote himself was one of a notorious cabal of close counsellors to Philippe IV, along with his chief financial adviser Enguerran de Marigny, Guillaume de Nogaret and Guillaume de Plaisians 'whose abilities were hampered by no scruples save loyalty to their master..all sordid makers of epoch–making history.'[19] It is of this king, and these men, that Bromyard comments in ACQUISITIO:

'This is how a certain great king used to excuse himself whenever he was informed of injustices committed through the agency of some of his men. 'What can I do?' he would say: 'I have three ministers who will go to hell for me.' He knew them to be unjust to give himself satisfaction.'[20]

La Flote was killed at the battle of Courtrai in July 1302. Bromyard does not specify who was responsible for the ominous superscription although the likeliest candidate is Philippe IV himself. Bromyard goes on to explain the link:

'For there was a certain great man in the kingdom of France before him [La Flote] called Pierre de la Brosse who in the end was hanged. He [Philippe?] therefore wanted to remind that second Pierre who was a great man in the kingdom after him that he should be apprehensive of the fall/fate of his predecessor.'[21]

---

[1] 'For instead of the parish the friar had an organization of his own: an international order. The order threw him together, often very closely, with a big, mobile professional brotherhood. [This] served among other things as a transcontinental information exchange..' Murray, p.285.

[2] ..et raro est pax: sicut in hyspania ubi machinant ad invicem christiani et saraceni: et ratio est: quia quilibet nititur contractam propinquam trahere ad leges et dominium suum. (B.2.20). See A.17.6 for a reference to the early Muslim conquests in Spain and Provence.

[3] Unde retulit quedam religiosa persona que fuit inter fideles *in transmarinis partibus*.. (A.12.34). In some manuscripts the title of William of Tyre's history appears as *Historia rerum in partibus transmarinis gestarum*. The title may well not be William's: but the location is certainly understood to be levantine. See Edbury & Rowe pp.2-3. Rhodes had fallen to the Knights Hospitaller of S.John in 1309/10. This person who had taken religious vows may have lived at

some time in the Hospitallers' house in Hereford, which neighboured the Dominican convent. (Orleton pp.220-221).

4

Sic fecit rex nobilis mortuo antecessore suo, qui multa acquisivit: misit enim per regnum suum unum episcopum et quatuor religiosos viros expertos in lege dei et mundi: precipiens: si qua* male acquisita invenirent: restituerent. (A.12.57-58).
     *as neuter accusative plural a correct alternative form to 'que'.

5

Richard/Lloyd p.106.

6

ibid. pp.106-107.

7

ibid. pp.163-164.

8

In hoc ergo iudicio deus facit electis suis iniuriam prius pacientibus: quod facere consuevit quidam rex subditis suis: quando enim ballivos et homines magni officii de officiis suis amovere voluit: illos in custodia detinere solebat precone clamante ad illos quibus prefuit: ut si quem leserit†: vel si cui iniuriam in officio suo fecerat veniat qui lesum se sentit et querimoniam suam libere deponat. Hanc benedictam consuetudinem solebant observare reges francie quo ad prepositos parisienses: per quam quidam dictorum prepositorum nuper suspensus fuit. (I.11.12).
     †Bromyard switches from the expected plural verb after 'ballivos' to the singular.

9

Richard/Lloyd p.157.

10

Exemplo s.Lodowici regis..bis in ebdomada sedere solebat in loco publico ad audiendum personaliter querelas pauperum de ministris suis vel quibuscumque aliis: ut omnibus iusticiam faceret. (D.12.4).

11

Sic se solebat excusare quidam rex magnus cum informaretur de iniuriis factis per aliquos de suis...timendum est quod ipse iret cum eis: quia eos non correxit: nec fugavit: sicut fecit sanctus Lodowicus infra c.de consiliis.xlvii. (A.12.43). Barber instances some of the harsh measures perpetrated at the king's behest by his agents. He quotes the bishop of Angers who in 1295 called them 'officials of hell.' (Templars pp.32-44).

12

de cuius gestis habetur.. This phrase, the 'de eo legitur' of the same passage and the 'de quo scribitur' of D.12.4 all confirm that Bromyard's source or sources for *these* accounts is/are literary. His source for other stories may well be oral.

13

The 'advantage' for Louis IX would have been the enjoyment of the temporalities of the bishoprics and archbishoprics for the time that the see was vacant. Richard notes that the kings of France of this age handed over the temporalities of abbeys and bishoprics after a vacancy was filled only when the new abbot or bishop had sworn an oath of loyalty to the king: the property in question being known as regalia. (Richard/Lloyd p.38). Of this oath Richard writes 'St Louis made little distinction between obedience owed by prelates and that owed by vassals. He said of the bishop of Chartres: 'He was my man, since he had placed his hands between mine.' (Richard/Lloyd p.222).
This is an extraordinary story. Of the seven men who occupied the throne of S.Peter during Louis' long reign it is difficult to suggest one who would have so cravenly yielded such a concession: certainly not Innocentius IV even though he settled in Lyon from December 1244 to 1251. Nor is it readily believable that Louis would have made such a demand, or that an emissary would have negotiated alone on a matter of such gravity. Yet Louis' hurling a papal bull into a fire seems oddly plausible!
This same story appears (as no.116) in the *Liber Exemplorum*, a collection dated by A. G. Little to 'between 1270 and 1279, probably between 1275 and 1279'. The author attributes the king's dramatic reaction to 'Lodowyco Christianissimo' – which should indicate Louis IX – but then adds 'qui quidem tempore beati Thome Cant[u]ariensi [sic] regnavit..' a clause which would reveal the king as Louis VII. The author states he found this material 'in eodem libro', which Little identifies as the *Gemma Ecclesiastica* of Giraldus Cambrensis (1146-1226). Bromyard *does*

source the story to the *Gesta* of Louis IX: his vocabulary, moreover, differs from that of the *Liber Exemplorum* which has

'..litteras a manu portitoris arreptas statim in ignem misit..'

whereas Bromyard has

'..bullam ab eo acceptam proiecit in ignem..'

It may well be that a story emanating from the reign of Louis VII was later fastened upon Louis IX.

14 Et sancti Lodovici regis francie de cuius gestis habetur quod cum nuncius suus de curia romana rediens ei nunciaret quod ei impetraverat vacationem omnium cathedralium ecclesiarum id est episcopatuum bullam ab eo acceptam proiecit in ignem dicens de aliis negociis de quibus te oneravimus scimus tibi grates: de illo autem negocio quod impetrasti in periculum animarum nostrarum scimus tibi malas grates. Nota D.xii.iiii. Item de eo legitur quod habuit unum consiliarium valde sapientem in consiliandis et agendis: sed tamen unam conditionem minus iustam habuit, quod videlicet semper voluit per phas et nephas partem regis defendere et facere regis avantagium sive esset iustum sive iniustum, sicut adhuc faciunt multi qui citius volunt excommunicari et a deo et ecclesia separari quam dimittere quia faciant voluntatem et avantagium dominorum suorum ut dicunt: quia in rei veritate avantagium non est quod in fine patebit, sicut patet A.xxvii.xliii. Hunc ergo bis aut ter ammonuit quod illam consuetudinem dimitteret: quam cum dimittere nollet vocato eo coram consilio suo ait feci tibi secundum evangelium te secretius ammonendo: sed quia me non audisti eris mihi sicut publicanus mihique amplius non servies...Ita dominus consiliarios et ministros examinare et custodire et pacificare et incorrigibiles expellere habet aliter periculum imminet sibi et ipsis. (C.11.46-48).

15 Exemplo sancti Lodowici regis de quo scribitur quod ponendos in officiis diligenter examinare solebat de vita et fama et si haberet unde viveret. (D.12.4).

16 Minister dicit: dominus qui habet avantagium: habeat ipse periculum. Dominus dicit: de consilio suo feci: habeat ipse periculum: quilibet vellet alteri fardellum imponere, et non possunt: quia unusquisque onus suum portabit. (A.27.43).

17 ..sicut scriptum fuit super ostium camere domini petri de laflote: pierre regna: et pierre regne: pierre pendi: et pierre pendera. (N.3.17). [..as was written over the door of Pierre de la Flote's chamber: Pierre ruled, and Pierre rules: Pierre paid, and Pierre will pay.]

18 Pierre de la Brosse received sympathetic treatment from Dante (Purgatorio 6.19-23):

Vidi Cont'Orso, e l'anima divisa
  Dal corpo suo per astio e per inveggia,
Come dicea, non per colpa commissa;

Pier dalla Broccia dico: e qui proveggia,
  Mentr' è di qua, la donna di Brabante..

Pierre had accused Philippe III's second wife, Marie daughter of Henri III of Brabant, of poisoning Louis, the first-born of his first wife Isabella of Aragon. Marie was cleared of this charge and turned upon Pierre (hence Dante's 'hatred and jealousy') who was sent to the gallows. Camerini entertained doubts on Marie's clearance: 'Purgata più o meno giustamente la regina della colpa..' (p.330).

19 Previté-Orton vol.II p.783.

20 Sic se solebat excusare quidam rex magnus cum informaretur de iniuriis factis per aliquos de suis: quid inquit iste possum ego: habeo enim tres ministros qui ibunt ad infernum pro me quia sciebat ipsos iniustos: ut ei placerent. Sed timendum est quod ipse iret cum eis: quia eos non correxit: nec fugavit: sicut fecit sanctus Lodowicus infra c.de consiliis. xlvii. Et notate quod parum curavit de animabus ministrorum.. (A.12.43). S.Louis is used here as a moral yardstick against which Philippe IV's turpitude is made evident.

223

Fuerat enim quidam magnus in regno francie ante eum petrus vocatus de labrose, qui finaliter suspendebatur: voluit ergo illum secundum petrum qui magnus fuerat in regno post illum commemorare quod casum predecessoris sui formidaret. (N.3.17).

29

BROMYARD ON ITALY

Anyone attempting to construct a chronological frame for Bromyard's life and writings has little to aid him or her beyond the books themselves. A mention of his name in February 1326[1] (in his absence): the granting of a licence in October 1352 to another friar in Bromyard's stead (from which his death has been surmised)[2]: and the one solid date to build on, given us by Bromyard himself, the year 1330 in which he wrote a sentence in the *Summa* at I.11.3: to these indicators Binkley adds the settlement of February 1322[3] when Adam Orleton made his grant of lands and tenements to the Hereford Dominicans.[4] Binkley cautiously pointed out 'He may have travelled in Italy at some time in his life, as has been suggested..'[5] In this writer's view the weight and scope of Bromyard's observations on Italy make this contention quite undeniable: the problem lies in deciding which period of his life to allocate them to.

Bromyard makes repeated references to the series of wars which scarred northern Italy during the first third of the fourteenth century.[6] Lombardy is his generic term for the area on which he seems best informed. He defines conflict in 'Lombardy' as being between Ghibellines and Guelfs, and in Genoa as between supporters in the Spinola and Doria clans. He knows of the crusade directed by Iohannes XXII against the Estensi marquises of Ferrara in late 1321. His four references to Guido da Montefeltro, who died in 1298 either at Assisi or at Ancona, appear to depend upon an oral tradition he somehow accessed. Further south, of Roman affairs he has at least heard of clashes between the Orsini and the Colonna. Another passage seems to indicate that he has himself visited Rome. He knows of prison conditions in Naples: and an interesting account of a conversation in the capitulum PAUPERTAS is difficult to interpret otherwise than as revealing that he spent some time in Brindisi and Puglia. One or two other asides reinforce this cumulative evidence that Bromyard travelled extensively in Italy.

When he travelled can not be proved beyond doubt: but a case, based on the extract from PENITENTIA, may be made for suggesting that he spent Easter of 1318 in Rome. There is no evidence that he learned any of the dialects of Italian: the *Summa* is peppered with French words and proverbs, but the single Italian quotation seems suspect. Latin will have been his means of communication.

The passages and comments which support the contention that he knew Italy from personal experience are the following:

1. '..that he walk in good company in the manner of those in Italy in the territories of wars who wait for company so as to travel in the safety of numbers.'[7]
2. '..just as is evident in Lombardy, where merchants and pilgrims hire mercenaries to protect themselves against robbers.'[8]
3. 'And just as the guides and armed bodyguards of pilgrims and businessmen are hired at great expense by travellers [to protect them] against enemies and brigands, as in Lombardy and the lands of war..'[9]
4. 'Just as a pilgrim in a foreign land full of wars and brigands enters it in dismay and worriedly racks his brain as to how he will be able to cross it in greater safety by hiring guides and mercenaries..'[10]

5.   '..and so, just as in time of war those passing through the territory of some lord strive to have some document of safe-conduct of that lord..'[11]

6.   '..as is clear in Lombardy where they do not have fixed and locally born lordships, and as a consequence the land is troubled by unceasing wars..'[12]

7.   'It's clear that to a great extent the wars that are taking place in Lombardy are unjust in that, as frequently happens, they are not started on the authority of the prince but of a more powerful man in the city/state [civitate], and not for an honourable cause but for hatred and partisanship of Ghibellines and Guelfs: also in that by these wars they put Christendom in turmoil.'[13]

8.   '..just like Italian acclamations: for in that land fights and encounters frequently occur between the leaders of the Ghibellines and Guelfs, under whom the ordinary inhabitants call out, when they have to assemble for the dominant party – however evil, unjust and odious it may be – crying 'Viva! Viva!' '[14]

9.   '..and for those who arrive late at cities whose gates are closed by day: just as happens in cities which are at war: as is apparent in Italy. Anyone coming too late to these does not get in: nor are there anywhere outside houses in which they can be put up, because of the wars. People arriving under these circumstances get poor lodgings and become figures of fun for the enemy.'[15]

10.   'Because just as those arriving too late at a city in Italy whose gate is fastened from night-fall: and on account of the wars no house outside the gate is to be found..'[16]

11.   'Literally the same thing [betrayal of the agents of betrayal by their employers] happened in Genoa a city-state of Italy in the dispute between the adherents of the Spinola and Doria families.'[17]

12.   Bromyard, in LEX, writes of the legal establishment dragging cases out in their courts over many years, to the detriment and impoverishment of the parties. 'In which act they are likened to the mercenaries of Italy in two aspects. First, in that just as the wars of those Italians would not be so damaging to their country and neighbouring peoples nor so protracted in the absence of mercenaries, in that without these so many villages [castra] and townships [villas] would not be destroyed or ravaged.. Secondly, just as these same mercenaries foster wars there for their own advantage and drag them out so, on this subject, in a lay court, over one piece of land…'[18]

13.   Bromyard invokes the image of the Wheel of Fortune, then speaks of the Roman populace 'in which from of old there used to be discord between two great clans: namely between the Colonna on the one side and the Orsini on the other. In one encounter between them the populace is reported to have shouted in support of the Colonna, whose success and power was reputed the greater, calling out 'Long live the Colonna! Death to the Orsini!' That same day the Colonna were defeated and the winners took it out on the populace. At another encounter, however, they shouted, on the contrary, for the Orsini who were then on top: change of fortune, you see, is followed by change of speech.
But on that day the Orsini were defeated: the people shouting out the name of the victors were suddenly embarrassed [erubuerunt] and became afraid. In a third conflict they called out 'Vive qui venke! Vive qui venke!' i.e. 'Long live the winner!'[19]

14.   'Again, such men [hypocrites] are likened to the Italians who habitually so conduct themselves that when the lord pope or cardinal or their [temporal] lord enters the city or village [castrum] they run to meet him calling out 'Viva!' 'Long live so-and-so!' Those who have no love for him, however, cry out, in a loud voice, with the rest 'Viva!' but, *sotto voce*, add 'for a short time.' '[20]

15.   In his capitulum LUXURIA Bromyard refers to one event which can be fairly precisely dated: namely the crusade which was declared by the papacy against the Estensi

of Ferrara in late 1321 and which was being preached at Parma in February 1322.[21] The passage is preceded by a judgement of Hieronymus found in the *Decretum* (xxxii.q.iiii. in eo) headed by the rubric 'Unusual pleasure and shameful acts of marriage are called lust and uncleanness.'[22]   Bromyard has already cited Exodus 20 and Deuteronomy 5 as witnesses that fornication is a criminal and mortal vice: Hieronymus is now called to witness that it is a greater offence for a Christian to commit fornication than for an unbeliever. 'If then in one [aspect] it is a greater crime: in both it is criminous and mortal.'[23]   'Pertinaciously to assert the contrary is held to be heretical by the church, which recently adjudged the marquises of Ferrara heretics and preached the cross against them for one cause, in that it was imputed to them that they had stated[24] that fornication is not a mortal sin.'[25]   Bromyard goes on to cite the *Clementinae*[26] (titulo de hereticis capitulo ad nostrum § vii) 'where numbered among heretics are those who said that the carnal act, since nature leans towards this, is not a sin, especially when the one exercising this is tempted.'[27]   It is notable that Bromyard omits here the first part of the seventh error, namely 'that to kiss a woman is a mortal sin since nature does not incline one to it,'[28] perhaps because he had mental reservations on the explanation. The proposition itself required a gloss of Iohannes Andreae stating that kisses are not mortal sins 'when they can take place without lust: or through local custom: or on account of peace or other necessary or reasonable cause.'[29]

Norman Housley traces the origin of the hostility between the papacy and the Estensi rulers of Ferrara. 'The death of Azzo VIII Este in 1308 led to a disputed succession; Venice supported Azzo's natural son, Fresco, while Azzo's brother, Francesco, appealed to and received the backing of Pope Clement V.'[30] After Venetian, then papal, administration 'an Estensi regime hostile to the popes was restored in 1317'[31], under three grandsons of Obizzo I, lord of Ferrara 1264-1293.

At the end of 1321 crusades were declared against both Matteo Visconti lord of Milan and the Estensi. In May 1324 Iohannes XXII renewed the crusade against the Este family and the Commune of Ferrara.[32]

Bromyard may be thought disingenuous in his contention that the papal crusade was launched against the Estensi for one reason only [una de causa], the heretical claim attributed to them. 'The popes had been suzerains of Ferrara since it had been given by the Countess Matilda to Gregory VII in 1077 and confirmed to Pascal II in 1102.'[33] The grandiose schemes of Iohannes XXII for a greater exercise of control over the affairs of northern Italy may well be considered to underlie this charge of heresy. It is instructive to remember that a like reason was adduced to justify the military operations against the Visconti directed by the papal legate Bertrand du Poujet. Mollat recounts the tale of the Milanese priest shown by Matteo a silver statuette engraved 'Jacobus [for Jacques Duèse], papa Johannes', its head pierced.[34] In September 1320 Matteo Visconti was accused of

	i	denying the resurrection of the body
	ii	denying divine providence
	iii	denying the existence of heaven and hell
	iv	partaking in a Black Mass
	v	bowing before the bones of Ezzelino da Romano[35].

There must therefore remain the powerful suspicion that a heresy charge was a useful tool for Iohannes for justifying military action against Ferrara's lords. Bromyard cannot have failed to discuss north-Italian affairs during his travels, was a sharp observer of the world around him, and unafraid to make pungent comments upon human frailty of both great and small: one must respect his integrity and conclude that he believed and accepted the papal view. One of the Estensi, after all, may have let slip such a remark, and the *Summa* may possibly be the sole source extant of a lost oral tradition. On the other hand this seventh of the eight errors of the Béghards and Béguines denounced by the council of Vienne of 1311-1312 Bromyard may have erroneously blamed on the three brothers, Rinaldo, Niccolò I and Obizzo II, who ruled Ferrara.

16.   'However, a sign that repentance made here [as opposed to that made in purgatory] according to rite is pleasing to God we can accept as sufficiently evident from the fortunes which are often seen. For often enough it is seen that in Lent when Christians perform works of repentance God bestows fine weather on them, and awards a hoped-for sun, as if showing himself placated by repentance. But, in contrast, when after Easter and in summer they return to their sins as dogs to their vomit He gives terrible weather and the worst kind of unseasonable rain and misery [maximasque pluviarum et miseriarum intemperies] openly displaying His anger at our sins. In the same way this is clearly demonstrated by the evidence of the work at Rome in which a procession was ordained, on account of such punishments by God, on the feast of S.Mark, which occurred soon after the celebration of Easter: and in Vienne too and in those areas in which rogation days were ordained for the cessation of the punishments which God accepted from those who, following the repentance of Lent, returned to their accustomed sins..'[36]

The feast of S.Mark falls on 25 April. Easter may fall from 22 March to 25 April inclusive. The years of the early fourteenth century in which S.Mark's 'occurred soon after Easter' [quod cito occurrit post festum pasce] are few, viz.:

Date of Easter
April   20   no year between 1264 and 1337
      21   no year between 1280 and 1359
      22   1302
      23   1318 and 1329
      24   no year between 1272 and 1356.[37]

The double mention of Rome and Vienne (which lies some 15 miles south of Lyon) seems to reveal a personal intimacy with the two cities.[38] 1302, if we accept 1352 as the year of Bromyard's death, appears too early for his travels in France and Italy. 1329 is close enough to Bromyard's own dating of 1330 for 'this year' given at I.11.3. But the coupling of his recitation of the tribulations generated by appalling and unseasonable rains and miseries *in summer* with his linking of the feast of S.Mark and Easter is strongly persuasive of acceptance of 1318.

17.   '..as is manifest with the people of Rome and of Vienne who, after converting during Lent to the army of God, which they had previously deserted, again after Easter deserting that army suffered such dreadfully heavy retribution: to allay which there was ordained in Rome a major litany shortly after Easter, and a minor in Vienne.'[39]

18.   '..they used to erect statues or triumphal arches as the material evidence still shows, since right up to the present day Rome displays, in memory of the honour done to them, many such effigies.'[40]

19.   On three occasions Bromyard writes of men travelling to *Rome* where one would expect *Avignon* to be the destination. Does this intimate that Bromyard had in mind the period before March 1309 when Clemens V initiated the papal residency at Avignon? Was it a slip of the pen? If so, it was a triple slip. The passages are these:

'By reason of this [a taste for high living among senior clergy, and a consequent recourse to money-lenders] secondly the money-lenders themselves incur fresh ruin: in consequence of which the guarantors [of the loans] are excommunicated, reduced to poverty, and rushing to *Rome* are subjected to vexation..'[41]

'Which commission [to be fishers of men – not of honours, bishoprics etc.] some exceed to an enormous extent by devoting their studies and their work, both in their studies and in travelling to *Rome*, more to worldly honours than to the fishing for souls..'[42]

'..as is clear about those who travel to *Rome* for petitioning for bishoprics and prebends and cures of souls..'[43]

20.   '..just as a pilgrim comes [came?] to the pope who gives a generous indulgence in the year of grace..'[44]

21.   '..just as men jailed in Naples, i.e. with one iron chain round the necks of all..'[45]

22.   '..wait till the physician goes to Salerno and furthers his studies..'[46]

23.   In RAPINA Bromyard sketches a brief *exemplum* whose subject is a nameless king. Larner describes the Guelf propaganda onslaught against Manfred, Frederick II's illegitimate son, who had been crowned king of Sicily in Palermo in August 1258.[47]
The campaign, led by Brunetto Latino, asserted that he had murdered his father, his half-brother and two nephews. Manfred – 'the monstrous son of a monstrous father'[48] – enjoyed hunting: and these three elements (royalty: murder of a nephew: and love of the chase) may be sufficient both to identify Bromyard's subject as the Manfred killed at Benevento in February 1266 and to illustrate the strength and reach of the papal party's hatred of the Hohenstaufen.

'Fourth: the fittingness of the punishment of freebooters and dictators. First, it is manifested by the story in which it is said that a certain great prince was triply punished for his triple tyranny. Firstly, he'd driven many poor people from their homes and lands and destroyed their cottages and taken possession of their lands so as to extend his private park and forest. Secondly, he'd shown his contempt for the pope's interdict by crowning a stag and addressing him as 'Your Holiness', then giving chase to him. Thirdly, he had killed his own nephew, a nobleman and heir to great estates, so as more freely to take over his lands.

Now the very night that he was dying a certain holy man had a vision in which he saw the forementioned king sitting crowned on a throne: and first, hounds hurled themselves against him, lacerating him terribly: second, the stag horribly wounded him with his horns: thirdly, the young man stuck him through with a lance..'[49]

24.   Bromyard also comments on the foreign or non-native dynasties of Italy with a striking domestic image: '..for them it's like the fire in winter. When you're too far away you're cold: when you go too near you're burned. That's the case of those whose rulers live far away, in that they have no home-grown ruler, as is the case for many Italians..'[50]

25.   'Recently, moreover, in Italy some dreamer of this sort dreamt that if he killed some hermit he would become king of Sicily..however, when he'd killed him, he was hanged.'[51]

26.   'From experience the same thing [i.e. impoverishment of convents, pawning of books, lack of maintenance of fabric] is evidenced in parts of a province of the Kingdom of Sicily, where the custom is that men ride, in which its inhabitants have been reduced to a very small number: as is apparent in Brindisi and other areas of Puglia, in which houses are falling down and the number of inhabitants is diminishing to such an extent, as I learnt from the account of the Prior of Brindisi – *whose narrative the evidence of eyes*

and ears confirmed – that from his own convent he had only five colleagues where there used to be forty: because the land is filled with horses. Isaiah 2.'[52]

27.   At widely separated points within the *Summa* (in the four capitula CIVITAS, INOBEDIENTIA, RELIGIO and VISUS) Bromyard turns upon the imposing figure of Guido da Montefeltro.   His treatment of Guido differs markedly from the not unsympathetic handling Dante accords him in Canto XXVII of the *Inferno* where the rôle of villain, understandably in the light of Dante's own exile, is filled by Bonifacius VIII.

Guido first appears at C.4.11: 'Deprime cor tuum. Ecclesiastici.ii. Non sic Guido. R.v.ii.' The same cross-reference to R.5.2 is given at I.4.5 after 'Nota de gydone': as at V.8.56, where Bromyard writes '..sicut Guido qui obedire voluit in prosperis, sed non in adversis.' His major notice of Guido (who died as a Franciscan in September 1298) comes in the capitulum RELIGIO at R.5.2:

'For those who want only to obey in prosperous circumstances .. are of the order and profession of Guido: of whom it is said that, on coming to religious vows from a great worldly state, if something was enjoined upon him which was burdensome, for example to attend to his sick brothers or something similar, he would excuse himself saying 'For the love of God think: in all such tasks and labours I used to have someone at my beck and call who would minister to me in matters like these: don't put me now so low that I'm forced to minister to someone who used to minister to me.' When, however, his superior imposed on him something comforting where he could expect fine feasts or wines and delights of this kind, with lowered head he would reply 'Willingly, Father: it was for this reason I shaved my head, to be obedient.'[53]

Bromyard cites no authority for this knowledge of Guido. His use of direct speech, which he twice awards to Guido in this rather long excursus, is also striking. It seems fair to conclude that the likeliest source of this vignette of the skilled commander of the Ghibelline forces turned mendicant will have been a conversation with a Franciscan, perhaps of the convent at Ancona where Benvenuto places him.[54] (Bromyard's usual practice is to signal his dependence on a personal contact for an anecdote such as this).[55]

Guido's appearance in the *Summa* is interesting in several ways. It is yet another Italian connection which adds a piece to the jigsaw of clues which may be assembled to build up a picture of Bromyard's life: it contradicts the portrayal of Guido presented in the accounts of his conduct as a religious by Angioli,[56] Benvenuto[57] and the Anonimo Fiorentino[58]: it seems to show, too, that either Bromyard knew nothing of the underhand trick employed in 1297 by Bonifacius VIII to gain control of the Colonna stronghold of Palestrina suggested by the ex-general under pressure from the pope[59] and memorably encapsulated in Dante's lines

'Lunga promessa con l'attender corto
Ti farà trionfar nell' alto seggio..'[60]

or that Bromyard *did* know of the story but was unwilling to use it as it would show a recently dead pope in a shabby light.

[1]   Orleton p.350-351.

[2]   Trillek p.20: BRUO p.278: Boyle, Date p.534.

[3]   Binkley, Hereford, p.260.

[4]   Orleton pp.220-222, 249-250.

[5]   Binkley, Hereford p.262.

[6]   The wars of this period in northern Italy are traditionally presented as conflicts between adherents of pope and emperor, for whom the shorthand of 'Guelfs' and 'Ghibellines' is used. Hyde's revealing analysis (pp.132-141, 'The Age of the Guelphs and the Ghibellines') makes clear that this polarity holds good for the Romagna, where those resisting the papal rectors were fairly styled Ghibellines, but fails to offer a narrative of sufficient complexity to encompass the shifting rivalries among the governments of the major northern city-states. Parma, Bologna, Modena, Ferrara, Padua and Florence were all known as Guelf cities: strife, both internal and external, resulted in wars where Guelf fought Guelf.

Whenever it was in the papacies of Clemens V and Iohannes XXII that Bromyard walked the roads of Italy's countryside and the streets of its towns conflict, and sizeable groups of armed men, will not have been far away. On the 6th of May 1312 as Heinrich VII crossed the Ponte Molle on his mission to be crowned emperor he was warned by the count of Savoy to cover his armour, so as not to attract enemy fire. 'My lord count,' was his reply, 'of the two thousand men who have crossed this bridge, have you heard that a single one was killed or mortally wounded?' 'No', said the count. 'Very well. God had them in his keeping; He will preserve me too.' (Mollat p.109). For anyone lacking the assurance of being held in God's hands one frightening aspect of such encounters must have been uncertainty as to the soldiers' identity. The variety of languages must also have been disconcerting: Bromyard would have heard German and Swiss dialects, Catalan, Provençal, French and a medley of Italian dialects: the papal crusaders' force besieging Ferrara in summer 1309 consisted of men from Ferrara, Bologna, Padua, Vicenza, Florence, Lucca, Siena and the Romagna. The involvement of Robert of Anjou king of Naples and James II of Aragon in the affairs of the North: the descent of the imperial militia into Italy: the campaigns undertaken for Iohannes XXII by Bertrand du Poujet: the blockade of Genoa: the expansionist ambitions of the Visconti and a dozen other potentates and *signori*: as well as intra-city clashes: all plunged northern Italy into a maelstrom of violence utterly perplexing to outsiders such as Bromyard. Although painted perhaps c.1500 the 'Assassination of S.Peter Martyr' – he was killed in 1252 – ascribed to Giovanni Bellini (National Gallery 812) does suggest, with its stark middle ground and the indifference of the woodmen, a random brutality intensified by the contrast between the woollen cloaks of the unarmed Dominicans and the steel helmet and cuirass of the first assassin: a peril justly feared by travellers from Como to Milan sixty years or so after S.Peter's murder.

[7]   ..quod ambulet in bona societate ad modum illorum in ytalia in terris guerrarum qui expectant societatem ut vadant in numerosa multitudine.. (A.19.9)

[8]   ..sicut patet in lumbardia: ubi mercatores et peregrini conducunt stipendiarios pro se tuendos contra spoliatores. (A.22.13). Perhaps 'tuendos' is compositorial for 'tuendo'.

[9]   Et sicut peregrinorum et negociatorum conductores et defensores contra inimicos et spoliatores sicut in lumbardia et terris guerrarum care conducuntur a transeuntibus armati.. (C.18.4)

[10]   Sicut peregrinus in extranea patria: plena guerris et latronibus contristatus ingreditur: et sollicite cogitat quomodo securius per ductores vel stipendiarios conductos transire poterit. (M.11.67)

[11]   ..sicut ergo tempore guerre transeuntes per terram alicuius domini nituntur aliquam habere domini illius protectoriam scripturam.. (L.4.15)

[12]   ..sicut patet in lumbardia ubi certa dominia et nativa non habent: et ideo terra continuis vexatur guerris. (D.12.30)

13 ..patet quod pro magna parte bella que sunt in lumbardia sunt iniusta quia ut frequenter non incipiuntur auctoritate principis sed potentioris in civitate nec pro honesta causa sed pro odio et affectione partium guibilinorum et guelforum. Et quia his bellis suis christianitatem turbant. (B.2.36)

14 ..sicut de ytalicorum clamore: in illa enim terra pugne et frequentes fiunt congressiones inter magnos partium gibilinorum et guelforum sub quibus populares habitantes clamant: quando congredi debent pro parte que dominatur quantumcumque mala iniusta et odiosa sit dicentes vivat vivat. (H.4.5)

15 ..et tarde de nocte ad civitates venientibus: quarum porte de die clauduntur: sicut accidit in civitatibus que sunt de guerra: sicut patet in italia: ad quas nimis tardus veniens non intrat: nec extra in aliquibus locis sunt domus in quibus hospitari possunt propter guerras. Sic venientes male hospitantur: et ab inimicis subsanantur. (P.7.67)

16 Quia sicut venientes nimis tarde ad civitatem italie: cuius porta de nocte clauditur: nec propter guerras invenitur domus extra portam.. (M.9.43)

17 Idem etiam ad litteram accidit in ianua quadam ytalie civitate in briga inter illos de spinolis et de aurea. (F.1.18)

18 In quo facto stipendiariis assimilantur ytalie in duobus. Primo quia sicut illorum ytalicorum guerre sine stipendiariis nec essent patrie et vicinis tam nocive nec tam prolixe: quia sine illis nec tot castra et villas destruerent nec tot spoliarent.. Secundo: quia sicut ipsi stipendiarii ibidem propter commodum proprium guerras nutriunt et in longum trahunt: ita in proposito in curia laycali pro una terra.. (L.3.13, 14)

19 ..populo assimilatur romano in quo ab antiquo discordia esse solebat inter duas magnas parentelas: videlicet inter columnenses ex una parte et ursinos ex alia parte: in quodam ergo congressu inter illos fertur populus clamasse pro columnensibus quorum prosperitas et potestas maior reputabatur, dicendo vivant columnenses vivant, et moriantur ursini. Columnensibus vero illo die victis victores se durius ad populum habuerunt. In alio vero congressu econverso clamaverunt pro ursinis tunc dominantibus: mutationem namque fortune mutatio sequitur vocis. Ursinis vero illo die victis: clamantes victores erubuerunt atque timuerunt. In tertio vero conflictu clamaverunt vive qui venke vive qui venke id est vivat qui vincit. (H.4.6). The modern Tuscan for 'vivat qui vincit' is 'Viva chi vence.' However, if the crowd had used the subjunctive to indicate uncertainty their cry would have been 'Viva chi venca', which would vindicate the k in Bromyard's 'venke'.

20 Iterum tales [hypocrites] assimilantur ytalicis: qui de consuetudine habent quod domino papa vel cardinali vel domino illorum civitatem vel castrum intrante occurrunt clamantes: vivat: vivat talis, non diligentes vero cum aliis alte clamant vivat: sed submisse dicunt pauco tempore. (A.16.7)

21 Housley pp.26-27.

22 Extraordinaria voluptas et inverecunda opera nuptiarum luxuria et immundicia appellantur.

23 Si ergo in uno maioris est criminis: in utroque criminosum est et mortale.

24 The text presents a problem. I have translated as the sense seems to demand. See note 25.

25 Cuius contrarium asserere pertinaciter hereticum tenet ecclesia: que nuper marchiones ferrarienses hereticos adiudicavit et contra eos crucem predicavit una de causa: quia eis imponebatur quod †debuerunt† dixisse fornicationem non esse peccatum mortale. (L.7.10)

   † '..in that it was imputed to them that they ought to have said that fornication was not a mortal sin' seems to be contrary to the expected meaning. An emendation of 'quod debuerunt dixisse' to 'quod dicti sunt dixisse' would salvage the sense, though a corruption of 'b' to 'c' is hard to envisage. Postulating the loss of 'non' before 'debuerunt' does not yield an easy solution.

26   Clementinae 5.3.3 § 7.

27   ..ubi inter hereticos numerantur qui dixerunt quod actus carnalis cum ad hoc inclinet natura peccatum non est maxime cum exercens temptatur. (L.7.10)

28   Tanner pp.383-384 (Concilium Viennense 1311-1312): Septimo [the seventh heretical tenet], quod mulieris osculum, cum ad hoc natura non inclinet, est mortale peccatum, actus autem carnalis, cum ad hoc natura inclinet, peccatum non est, maxime cum tentatur exercens.

29   The Béghards and Béguines are sternly denounced by Clemens V and the Council of Vienne [Clementinae 5.3.3].   In his commentary on this section Iohannes Andreae takes pains to distinguish between lustful and innocent kissing. So 'oscula amplexus vel tactus non sunt mortalia cum possunt absque libidine fieri, vel ex consuetudine regionis, vel propter pacem vel aliam necessariam vel rationabilem causam.' (Iohannes Andreae ad Clementinas 5.3.3 'Septimo quod mulieris osculum').

30   Housley p.24.

31   ibid. p.24.

32   ibid. pp.26, 27.

33   Mollat p.70.

34   ibid. pp.89-90.

35   ibid. p.90.

36   Sicut manifeste operis ostendit evidentia Rome: in qua processio propter tales dei vindictas fuit ordinata in festo sancti Marci: quod cito occurrit post festum pasce. Et in vienna et in partibus illis in quibus ordinati fuerunt dies rogationum pro vindictis cessandis. (P.7.7)

37   The dates are based on Cheney pp.83-158.

38   Besides the references to Vienne in notes 36 and 39 there is also the knowledge Bromyard displays (at S.13.2) of a miraculously preserved tongue in Vienne. The town lies by the Rhône on the route south from Lyon to Avignon.

39   ..sicut patet de romanis et de viennitis: qui in quadragesima ad dei militiam conversi quam prius deseruerant post pasca iterum militiam illam deserentes gravissimas adeo sustinuerunt vindictas propter quas sedendas lethania maior in Roma cito post pasca: et minor in vienna ordinata fuit. (O.5.22)

40   ..statuas vel arcus erigebant triumphales sicut adhuc rei docet evidentia, nam usque hodie in illorum honoris memoriam roma plures tales ostendit effigies. (H.4.1)

41   Quorum occasione secundo ipsi usurarii novam incurrunt ruinam: quorum occasione fideiussores excommunicantur, depauperantur, ad romam currentes vexantur.. (H.4.17)

42   Quam commissionem multum excedunt nonnulli qui plus student et plus laborant tam in studendo quam etiam romam eundo circa mundi honores quam circa piscationem animarum.. (P.12.5)

43   ..sicut patet de euntibus ad romam pro prelaturis et prebendis et curis animarum impetrandis. (V.9.18)

44   ..sicut venit peregrinus ad papam dantem largam indulgentiam in anno gratie.. (V.9.1) The year of grace is that of 1300, promulgated by Bonifacius VIII on 22 February. See Boase pp.231-239. He quotes Villani as stating that at any given time in that year there were some 200,000 strangers in Rome.

45 quemadmodum incarcerati in neapoli: videlicet cum una catena ferrea circa collum omnium. (A.12.26)

46 expecta quousque medicus vadat salernam et addiscat. (E.2.13)

47 Larner p.40.

48 ibid. p.40.

49 Quarto pene raptorum seu tyrannorum congruitas. Primo historia ostenditur qua fertur quemdam magnum principem contra triplicem tyrannidem tripliciter fuisse punitum. Primo namque multos pauperes de domibus et terris suis expulit et habitacula eorum destruxit et terras illorum occupavit ut parcum vel forestam suam ampliaret secundo interdictum pape in terra sua contempsit: cervum coronando et eum papam vocando venabatur. Tertio nepotem suum nobilem et heredem magnum occidit ut terram suam liberius occuparet.
Illa ergo nocte qua moriebatur cuidam sancto viro visum fuit quod regem predictum vidit sedere in cathedra coronatum: quem primo invaserunt canes eum male lacerantes. Secundo cervus cum cornubus ipsum horribiliter vulneravit. Tertio iuvenis cum lancea ipsum perforavit.. (R.1.31)

50 ..est de illis sicut de igne in hyeme, a quo qui nimis est remotus frigescit: qui vero nimis appropinquat comburitur. Ita illi a quibus reges nimis distant quia regem nativum non habent, sicut multi italici.. (R.4.11)

51 Nuper etiam in italia quidam somniator somniabat quod si quemdam occideret heremitam fieret rex cicilie..suspendebatur. (S.11.6)

52 Experimento idem satis ostenditur in partibus provincie regni Cecilie, ubi communiter equitare solent, in qua facti sunt numero brevi paucissimi et incole eius sicut patet in brandusio et aliis apulie partibus in quibus domus cadunt et numerus inhabitantium intantum diminuitur quod sicut priore brandusino referente didici cuius relationem evidentia visus et auditus confirmavit quod de conventu suo tantum quinque habuit socios ubi solent esse quadraginta: quia terra repleta est equis. Ysa.ii. (P.3.27). (That 'the land is filled with horses' – et repleta est terra eius equis – [Isaiah 2.8] is but one of the indicators which prompt the prophet to his gloomy analysis of the state of the Jewish people. Bromyard thus links Puglia to Judah.) His journey into Puglia and presence in Brindisi remains an intriguing mystery. G. G. Coulton's translation of this passage appears in his 'Five Centuries of Religion' (1936), volume III pp 487-488: '..as I learned from the prior of Brindisi (and his words were confirmed by my eyes and ears), he had now only five brethren in his convent..' See Appendix III for a speculative attempt to provide an explanation for Bromyard's presence in Puglia.

53 Illi enim qui tantum obedire volunt ubi prospera imponuntur vel iniunguntur sunt de ordine et professione Guidonis: de quo fertur quod de magno statu in seculo ad religionem veniens: si sibi aliquid iniungeretur quod erat oneris: sicut quod serviret fratribus suis infirmis, vel aliquid simile, se excusare solebat dicendo pro deo cogitetis quod in omnibus talibus officiis et laboribus solebam sub me habere qui mihi in talibus ministraret: non ponatis me nunc ita basse quod cogar ministrare cui solebat ministrari: quando vero superior ei aliquid imposuit quod erat solacii, ubi bona sperabat festa vel vina et huiusmodi delectabilia, capite inclinato respondere solebat libenter pater, nam propter hoc rasi caput ut essem obediens. (R.5.2)

54 This reference, and those to Angioli and the Anonimo Fiorentino, I owe to Toynbee's entry on Guido Montefeltrano (pp.298-300).

55 As he does, for example, at A.12.11, A.14.49, C.8.1, M.6.19, O.7.15 and P.3.27:
(..quod accidit cenonis in francia: sicut sancto viro mihi narrante didici:
[..as happened at Sens in France, as I learnt from the account of a holy man..]) (A.12.11, etc.)

56 ..in ordine pie ac umiliter vixit, errata lacrimis et jejuniis diluens.. (Toynbee p.299).

[57] Devote assumpsit habitum, humiliter servavit regulam, et patienter tulit paupertatem; unde saepe visus est ire publice mendicando panem per Anconam..

[58] ..andando una fiata verso Fano, increscendogli, montò in su una asina d'uno che andava per la via: egli era sprezzato, et non si curava..
[..walking on one occasion towards Fano [some 30 miles along the coast north from Ancona], as he was putting on some weight, he mounted an ass belonging to a man going in the same direction: he was looked down on, but it didn't trouble him..]

[59] Toynbee p.299: Boase pp.178-180.

[60] Inferno, Canto XXVII, 110-111.

30

THE STATE OF ENGLAND

John Bromyard's *Summa* is neither a chronicle nor a history. Nevertheless, as a member of a preaching order who would also have heard the confessions of hundreds of English men and women of various degrees[1] in a turbulent period of his country's fortunes, Bromyard had, among his other duties, the diagnosis and healing of the ills he saw before him. He plotted the frame of his greatest work not as a political, social, economic, legal or military commentator dissecting the fabric of contemporary England but as a disciple of Christ. As such he confronted both public and private immorality, directing his energies to guiding his compatriots away from that selfishness expressed in many forms of evil towards a better life, grounded upon the teachings of the Bible.

Drafting the outline of the *Summa* Bromyard was able to start from the analysis of England's maladies he had already made in preparation for writing the *Opus trivium*. Certain units naturally suggested themselves. Among the 189 capitula we find all seven of the deadly sins: SUPERBIA, AVARICIA, LUXURIA, INVIDIA, GULA, IRA, ACCIDIA. Deriving from Isaiah 11.2, 3 are the seven gifts of the Holy Spirit, six of which also form capitula, namely SAPIENTIA, CONSILIUM, FORTITUDO, SCIENTIA, PIETAS and TIMOR [DOMINI]: only *intellectus* is missing. We find treatments of four of the seven sacraments: EUCHARISTIA, MATRIMONIUM, ORDO CLERICALIS and, for penance, CONTRITIO and PENITENTIA. Of the four cardinal and three theological virtues Bromyard handles FORTITUDO and IUSTICIA, CARITAS, FIDES and SPES. All seven of the spiritual works of mercy are dealt with, namely COMPASSIO, CONSILIUM, CORRECTIO, DIMITTERE, ORATIO and PIETAS (praying for the living and the dead), PATIENTIA and PREDICATIO (converting the sinner). Of the seven corporal works of mercy[2] ELEMOSINA, MISERICORDIA and SERVIRE may be seen to address the first three, and HOSPITALITAS and INFIRMITAS two others. The two great commandments given by Jesus[3] are expounded in AMOR and DILECTIO. Other capitula are based on the Ten Commandments, such as FURTUM, HOMICIDIUM, MANDATA and MENDACIUM. His concern for the reform of the clergy impelled him to include chapters such as ORDO CLERICALIS, PRELATIO, SACERDOTIUM and SYMONIA. This base of 43 chapters provided Bromyard with points of entry, as a surgeon, into the body of English society: to probe its vital organs, to examine its spiritual, moral, social and intellectual condition, to diagnose which rotten members should be excised, and to propose the needful cures.

Apart from this nucleus of subjects long considered fitting for a divine's sermons and commentaries he also selected a group of issues largely concerned with secular society, over a variety of aspects of that society's life. They incorporate

i the administration and practice of law, treated of in ADVOCATI, EXECUTOR, IUDICES, IUDICIUM HUMANUM, IUSTICIA and LEX:

ii the justification for the crusade, in CRUX:

iii political theory and principles of government in REGIMEN:

iv commercial practice in MERCATIO:

v education in SCIENTIA:

vi the dealings of advisers and counsellors in CONSILIUM:

vii military matters and the tournament in BELLUM and NOBILITAS:

viii   the responsibilities and conduct of the aristocracy in NOBILITAS:

ix   the organization of the state and the consequences deriving therefrom in CIVITAS:

x   the principles and practices underlying the relations among the different classes of society – Bromyard's divisions are (a) 'divites' and 'nobiles' and 'potentes' (b) 'mediocres' (c) 'pauperes' and 'simplices' – and their economic, social and political consequences: dealt with in ACQUISITIO, DIVICIE, ELEMOSINA, PAUPERTAS and RAPINA.

In addition to these ten areas affecting public, secular life there are other capitula where Bromyard addresses issues not only of morality but which also exercise a powerful and widespread influence upon community life, such as ADULTERIUM, LUXURIA and MATRIMONIUM.

Standing somewhat apart from the other 188 capitula is T5, TRIBULATIO, the sixth longest. Much of this chapter is occupied by reflections on the catastrophic series of wet summers and autumns which ruined harvests from 1314 to 1318 and caused heavy livestock and some human mortality, and a steep rise in prices of basic foodstuffs. The royal imposition of tallage and, in the northern counties, the devastations of Scottish incursions, added to the natural disasters: all this led to a national discontent of which TRIBULATIO is a powerful and near-contemporary witness.

Finally, from a variety of capitula there may be gleaned an intriguing scattering of references to events of his time in the sphere of high politics. Presumably for his personal safety and that of those among his confrères who would use his material these references are guarded, sometimes couched in backgrounds drawn from the Old Testament, coyly avoiding fourteenth-century names. Nevertheless they may be carefully decoded to present one more witness to the stormy history of the 1320s.

In and just outside Hereford, on 24 November 1326, Hugh Despenser the younger was drawn, hanged, beheaded, eviscerated and quartered: the elder Hugh Despenser had been drawn, hanged and beheaded at Bristol on 27 October 1326.[4] It may well be the Hereford execution which Bromyard obliquely refers to in his exordium to MALEDICTIO:

'..people therefore are deceived if they scorn the curses which they deserve. This became clear in the case of a certain nobleman who just lately was sufficiently powerful. He wanted to impark a common pasture: it was put to him that a great number of poor people had animals grazing there who would all curse him. This he admitted: he had often brushed off curses like these, and scorned them.. Afterwards this same nobleman was drawn and hanged.'[5]

In the decade from 1315 to 1326 the greatest beneficiaries from the massive scale of confiscations of lands were Edward II and Hugh Despenser the younger. These are analysed in some detail by Natalie Fryde in her 1979 study. Especially valuable on this subject are her three chapters: 'The rise of the Despensers': 'The aftermath of the civil war: Confiscations and the territorial settlement': 'The Despensers' spoils of power, 1321-6.'

Bromyard may have had in mind either the king or his unprincipled confidant: he is too canny to name names. Certainly in Hereford he was close enough to the younger Despenser's depredations in the south-west and in south Wales: a peripatetic friar will have seen and heard plenty of shocking evidence of Despenser's aggressive acquisitiveness both before and after the civil war of 1321-22. The arrival of the king and his entourage in Hereford, where Edward stayed from 29 January to 4 February 1322, will have furnished an opportunity for Bromyard (assuming that he *was* in Hereford then) to pick up information on affairs of state: given piquancy by the harsh reprimand the king delivered to Adam Orleton the bishop who himself suffered the confiscation of many of his assets because of his support for the barons, as the 'Vita' records.[6]

Another cautious allusion to a rebel may be meant to call to mind Thomas earl of Lancaster, executed outside Pontefract on 22 March 1322:

'So evil men will experience fitting punishments, as was appropriately demonstrated in what happened in the matter of the possessions of a certain lord sufficiently well known who died recently... It transpired in his death that all the goods found under his hand or in his manors were confiscated to the king.'[7]

After March 1322 his opponents' huge estates fell into Edward's possession.[8] Fryde sums up the situation: 'The rebels were an entirely defeated party, their leaders with few exceptions imprisoned, executed or in exile abroad. They were also disinherited but had no formal right to buy back their lands which had escheated to the king.'

The brutal and large-scale executions, publicly carried out in several cities and towns throughout the kingdom, together with the upheaval of society occasioned by the far-reaching confiscations of landed estates, will have profoundly shocked a great many English men and women. Fryde continues:

'The judges sentencing the Contrariants shared, to some degree, the outlook of the writer of the passages in Bracton dealing with treason, including the dictum that the offence of treason was so atrocious that the traitor should suffer 'the last punishment of bodily pain, *the loss of all his goods* and the perpetual disinheritance of his heirs so that they be admitted neither to the paternal nor the maternal inheritance.'[9]

It may also be Lancaster whose words are recorded here by Bromyard in a probable reference to the executions which followed Boroughbridge:

'And so when it was announced to a certain nobleman in the morning that on that same day he was to die a shameful death: falling to the ground he cried out 'Alas, I never loved my wife..' '[10]

A reference, however, to the siege of Berwick of autumn 1319 is free from ambiguity.

'Since just as danger threatens the whole army from the negligence of those keeping watch: as was evident in the army of the king of England in Scotland when the enemy passed through the king's army by night, causing losses: the fault, according to professional soldiers, derives from the fact that men of valour who are ordered to keep watch take a nap, sending a groom on horseback and in armour making him out to be the commander..'[11]

Robert Bruce's diversionary tactic, which led to the Scottish victory at Myton on Swale in September 1319, caused Thomas earl of Lancaster and other captains to withdraw their forces from the siege: 'the earl was even suspected of allowing the Scots to pass unopposed through his lines.'[12]

There may be a tenuous allusion to either Piers Gaveston or to Hugh Despenser the younger in GLORIA: although the passage is free from censure of this courtly practice:

'Many come to the king's court by different routes, and for different reasons are welcomed there and promoted: for some are welcomed and come there in boyhood, as do sons of noblemen to provide company for the king's son. Others are welcomed there and promoted because of the special affection which the king has towards them: just as sometimes it happens that because of that beauty/handsomeness [pulcritudinem] or because they perhaps are loveable [amabiles] or important [sturdy? grossi] they find a more special favour in the eyes of the king..'[13]

The grievances harboured by the groups on whom the burden fell heaviest of the taxes levied by the crown to pay for the Scottish campaigns especially of the middle years of Edward II's reign are several times given voice in the *Summa*. The system too of paying for goods, foodstuffs and live animals by tallies was also a cause of bitter resentment. The coincidence of some of the campaigns in Scotland with the dreadful harvests of 1314 to 1318 undoubtedly created even greater hardship.

'But alas, the princes and knights and armies of this present age when going to war rather placate the devil, with their savagery and extortion, than God. They go not with prayers but with the curses of many people, since they go not at the king's expense or their own but at the expense of the churches and the poor whom on their journey they despoil: and if perchance they do buy anything they would pay nothing but tallies. Christ fed five thousand with five loaves: *they* perform a greater miracle in that *ten* thousand are fed with a few tallies, i.e. dice, not once only or twice, as Christ did, but over and over again: not just men, as Christ did, but both hounds and horses, etc.: not with bread and fish as Christ did, but with delicate fare. See T.5.17 and F.8.1.'[14]

Humour there is here: but the flavour is bitter. Bromyard's cross-references are to TRIBULATIO and FURTUM:

'..it would be better for them [the 'vendors'] to have sixpence paid on the spot than a tally for five shillings which will never be paid out.'[15]

'The poor commit theft fearfully. If they are caught in the action they are put in prison and punished. The rich, on the other hand, openly spend what belongs to others: they pay nothing for it and yet pass through this life unpenalized.. If now the ewes and oxen and hens and capons and all the animals the rich eat without paying for – we spoke of this at B.2.24, E.3.22 and T.5.17 – would set up a bellowing in their bellies there'd perhaps be a louder clamour than in Noah's ark..'[16]

Maddicott observes that from the 1290s onwards men had seen their carts, their livestock, and their grain taken for the king's use in exchange for payment which was usually inadequate and often long deferred. 'Tallies and wardrobe debentures given to peasants who had watched their animals being driven off by the king's officials were no substitute for hard cash.'[17] The dearth year 1316 saw 'purveyance on a vast scale', and Maddicott specifies the huge amounts of foodstuffs to be requisitioned from Yorkshire for a Scottish campaign planned for August 1316 and comments: 'Such quantities could hardly be raised without the most oppressive action from above..'[18] An instance of such bullying, seemingly by the use of a veiled threat implicit in the demand for a quasi-feudal service (which was perhaps not owed), is recorded by Bromyard. It may well be linked to preparations for one of the Scottish campaigns.

'In earlier times whenever powerful leaders stopped off from their journey for hospitality at a religious house it was the practice for the convent to be favoured and helped because of their arrival: they would give them lands or incomes or some consideration so that they would pray for them and keep their memory. But now it will long be the worse for the house and their granges when they pass by them. And what of the requests for rights of carriage? On this matter it was only recently that a certain abbot, on receiving a request of carriage for conveyance [of material] towards the war zone, sent a hundred English marks. These were turned down as being insufficient: and in their embarrassing return the abbot made redemption and avoided trouble, happy to give, at the king's prompting, *two* hundred marks. Moreover, because of what they take in both their granges and houses without permission – for which they have been excommunicated by a decision of a provincial council – and in all these practices they make the poor and churchmen hold their memory not for prayers but for curses.'[19]

Bromyard does not tell us whether this royal demand for carriage-rights was justified or not.

The clergy had petitioned the king against the burdens unfairly imposed upon them by the officers of the king himself and by the magnates of the realm, all of whom were demanding use of their horses and carts for the logistical needs of the Scottish campaigns. The king's answer was unsatisfactory: '..from henceforth they shall not be unduly charged.' (Placet domino Regi quod super contentis in peticione decetero indebite non onerentur.)[20] Elsewhere he mentions the tendency of Church lands to be alienated into mortmain so as to free them of the obligations of feudal incidents: '..for men who have taken religious vows, because they want their estates to be free from services have seen to it that they alienate them into mortmain..'[21] He does not refer to Edward I's Statute of Mortmain of 1279 prohibiting such action (though it could be circumvented, after an inquisition *ad quod dampnum*, by payment of an appropriate fine)[22] but his use of the present tense [volunt] indicates that he knew of such procedures happening locally. Fryde too points out 'The value of the goods [taken in purveyance] was supposed to be assessed at the current market price and usually no immediate payment took place. The owners were merely given tallies or other types of receipt.' These exactions continued after the partial recovery from the years of spoiled harvests. 'The purveyances for the Scottish campaign of 1322 were among the largest of the whole reign.'[23]

The open disregard displayed by many of the magnates of the realm in Edward II's reign for laws which would hamper the prosecution of their private interests is well documented. McKisack observes that the evidence makes it plain that 'fourteenth-century England, for all its multiplicity of courts, statutes and justices was not a law-abiding country and that those responsible for the maintenance of order were faced with obstacles beyond their power to surmount.'[24] Bromyard's anger at the betrayal of the duties imposed on the nobility and magnates by their privileged rank and power is openly declared in several passages of the *Summa*.

'..our nobles and great men should strenuously make onslaughts against the enemies of the commonwealth and brigands too: and strenuously punish and subject to torture[25] malefactors in high positions: and show mercy on their poor neighbours. But, more's the pity, it's the opposite that happens: the property of their poor neighbours they confiscate in a multitude of ways: for no reason at all sometimes, or for a slight one – for example, for one word that displeases them – they beat or kill them, or for a trivial misdemeanour amerce and ill-treat them. Yet faced with open enemies and foes of the realm and evildoers of eminent status and power they are so cowardly that not even for the upholding of justice and defence of the state dare they assault, capture, strip or maltreat them as they have deserved.' If reproved for shirking their duties in this way they might reply 'They [the lawbreakers] would strike back.' '[26]

This seems to be not a sketch of the England of the later years of Edward I nor of the 1330s, much less the 1340s, under Edward III: rather, Bromyard's fervent denunciation is of the parlous anarchy of the post-Bannockburn period, of this and other reverses, such as Myton, at the hands of the Scots: of rebellion by the great earls against the king, of Boroughbridge and its aftermath, and of the lawlessness scarring England during the Despenser years. Bromyard's portrayal of the dismal state of English military skill and readiness reveals poorly trained troops, badly supplied:

'..these who can fittingly be called in the English expression 'town beaters', i.e. village fighters: who only when drunk talk proudly and fight: who in war against the infidels or against an enemy army, enduring want for three days, are worth nothing more but to return to their homes: or if they stay, to be trampled on by their adversaries.'[27]

This is possibly a reference to the ad hoc force raised by the mayor of York, Nicolas Fleming, and the archbishop of York, William Melton, which took heavy losses – Fleming was among the c.3,500 dead – facing the Scots at Myton on Swale in September 1319.[28] Bromyard's 'enduring want for three days' (which may mean no more than 36 or 42 hours) suggests his hearing more details than he gives here, perhaps through the Dominican network.

A contemptuous observation on an English battalion made by a seasoned man of standing (a case almost certainly of oral transmission) is recorded by Bromyard. Its dismissive humour probably ensured its survival, through several tellings, into this written account:

'As a consequence, as the army of England was setting out with such a glamorous show to face the enemy, a certain man of proven worth remarked 'It seems more like a wedding procession than a war party.' '[29]

A passage from NOBILITAS continues the censure of military incompetence, singling out the aristocracy, and links this defect with other charges. These, in Bromyard's way, are general, not specific: and two of his adverbs ('*male* acquisitos' and '*iniuste* capiunt') lack forensic precision: yet the force of his invective is undeniable. His opposition to the holding of tournaments leads back to the motif of military inadequacy: and the paragraph ends with a development of a verse from Ecclesiastes which was seized upon in a telling sermon at the time of the régime-change crisis of 1326/7.

'..it is no wonder that where noblemen live as tyrants in defiance of their neighbour and as bad Christians in defiance of God through wars, conflicts and disputes they should have in their lands disturbances of the peace: indeed it would be a wonder if they had peace since they unceasingly make assaults on God by their sinning and on their limbs by living like tyrants. It would moreover be a miracle if they were unyielding in the defence of their fatherland and realm, these people who ride about on horses wickedly acquired or fed from the goods of the poor and the church: who unjustly seize from the poor and from churchmen the source of their purchasing and gilding of their arms and of their superfluous self-ornamentation: the source of their purchase and stabling of their horses and of their hiring of knights and mercenaries. It would again be a miracle if tyrants and extortioners such as these were not despoiled, in life or in death, by other tyrants and extortioners, so that they should lose in the same manner as they acquired: and just as it was for vanity they made and gilded their arms that thus for naked vanity and not for goodness they should rejoice and be lauded by those by whom the sinner is lauded in his desires, psalm ix. Are not many noblemen of this modern age so lauded? Who heard of any of them being praised or who could praise [them] for a vigorous assault of the enemy and the defence of fatherland and church as *are* commended and praised Charlemagne, Roland and Oliver and other paladins of old? Solely for this, that they possess a gilded helmet priced at £40 and shoulder-plates and other external insignia of the same order and worth even more: and that at the joust he carried a thick, squared lance such as no one else carried or could carry, and that he overthrew both horse and rider on to the ground: and that he rode so well and handled that lance with an agility which suggested it was light as a feather: and that he attended parliament or the tournament with such a great number of horses. And what is this praise but praise of [i.e. given by] godless men, wretched and fearful: on this see Job xx 'The praise of the ungodly is short-lived.' It *is* short-lived because they stretch only to places and times of peace, not of war, and only to friends and not to the enemy. What is the worth of gilded arms then: they only make the enemy more daring, as is clear as at A.24.2. When they run away they are glad to throw them down for the enemy so as to make a quicker escape, as happened recently. What praise is it to wield the strongest lance against a man of peace, and cast down both horse and rider to the ground yet not to touch the enemy with any kind of lance in that he refused even to approach him let alone touch him with even the longest [lance]? Or what praise is it to have ridden well and handled his lance with ease and conducted himself with agility when facing a friend and neighbour and with equal agility to have fled from an adversary of the realm? Or what praise is it that in forbidden feats of arms, such as in tournaments and suchlike – on which see L.6.2 and X.1.17 – they are renowned and seek acclaim yet in deeds of virtue, for example in just wars and in defence of the fatherland they are faint-hearted, cowardly and ready to run, giving free rein to the enemy to lay waste the land, to loot and carry off plunder, burn villages, destroy castles and lead away captives? In all this they show the truth of 'Woe to the land whose king is a boy' and whose great men – whose task is to defend and govern the land – live like boys: 'whose princes feast in the morning' before coming to council or parliament, with the consequence that having dined well, and drunk deep, they understand less what counsel to give.[30] And, on the contrary 'Blessed the land whose king is noble and whose princes break bread seasonably, that is for refreshment, not for excess.' Ecclesiastes x.'[31]

The *Summa* contains several passages which protest against corrupt processes in law, such as suborning and bribing witnesses, which can be amply paralleled in the writings of his contemporaries.[32] Juries too may either be bribed or threatened to acquit the guilty and condemn the innocent.

'..just as perjured foremen of a jury and jurymen are the cause of such numbers of robbers and criminals through whom loyal subjects are often disquieted, in the same way those whose duty it is to bring charges against others, or punish them, and fail to do so: and who give witness of good character to, or help or support, the guilty are the cause of there being such numbers of sinners, on account of whom God afflicts the whole community with diseases, rains and famine.'[33]

'It is correct to say that there exists such a friendship [as between Herodes and Pilatus] between the petty dictators – those who acquire property wrongfully, that is – and the twelve perjured men. One of them wants to get a manor: another, an income..'[34]

'In the secular community, of the world, that is, robbers, murderers and suchlike, on account of their nobility of blood, or because of 'gifts', are freed from the gallows: twelve robbers, you see, free a thirteenth right in front of the judge.. And the reason is exactly the same in the community of the church, why there are so many men who rob God: I mean the sexually debauched, adulterers, evil Christians: because the church guitarists* do not touch them as they should: instead, they accept 'gifts' – or they see the wolf and are afraid.'[35]

*Bromyard continues here an image introduced earlier of the leaders of society as musicians playing a stringed instrument: for a harmonious melody each of the cords (representing strands in society) should be plucked fairly.

'But some men..when burdened in visitations and inquisitions of sinners or assizes or jury duty in peril of their souls with telling the truth – to telling which they are bound by oath – say they dare not tell the truth in case they are beaten up or killed or have their house burnt down.'[36]

'As to why men accused by scoundrels don't come [to court] to prove their innocence and to refute the malice of their adversaries I state what *they* usually say: 'We've no wish to be harassed in court and all for nothing. They take care of the party bringing the case: better to sit at home, to let such matters go, to give in to *their* own law, and not to be worn out by such a long journey.'[37] The 'long journey' might indicate a reference to cases called before the King's Court in Westminster Hall: a weary journey from Herefordshire.

'In this way doomsters and foremen of juries and torturers of the poor terrify poor and simple folk with their pomposity coupled with threats... they say 'Sell me such-and-such a piece of land or such-and-such a business: it would be a quit-claim for me: or give me so much money for the marriage of my daughter, or for some other cause: or it will be the worse for thee, because thou hast done such-and-such': imputing to them what they have never done..'[38]

The capitulum ADVOCATI is a repository of Bromyard's trenchant comments on the practice of the courts.

'..The story is told of a certain advocate, an extremely gifted man, most successful in the cases he undertook, who pretty well always triumphed and won. Later on he took religious vows and, on being delegated to handle similar cases which involved his convent, he always failed. [Asked to explain his dismal record] he gave his answer: 'When I was in the world I'd no scruples of conscience about lying, contriving tricks, inventing falsehoods. So, with this technique, I always won my case..' '[39]

The anecdote may have gained something in the telling before it reached Bromyard's ears. Enough of them circulated, however, to leave their basic truth incontrovertible. Bromyard gives us another he'd heard with a verbatim conversation:

'It happened lately that someone was discussing the situation of a friend – in all conscience well worthy of the gallows – who was held in prison. His interlocutor quipped 'Don't worry: if he comes up before the judge with six oxen in hand I'll make sure he gets off.' '[40]

'..in Westminster Hall, as it were the head and fount of all falsity: for there the law is torn to shreds and the ungodly prevails against the just.'[41]

'..since, as the proverb has it, a lawyer's tongue can damn you – unless it's tied down, with *silver* ropes.'[42]

'..since if petitioners approaching the courts of this world sometimes send on 'gifts' ahead of their case, in the hope of gaining their objective more expeditiously – on which they more often lavish greater expenses than they can win..'[43]

Bromyard quotes Oseas 4[.1] – 'non est enim veritas [et] non est misericordia [et] non est scientia Dei in terra' – and concludes: 'and this is especially manifested in the courts and the [court of common] pleas, in which they pay regard rather to 'gifts' than to the truth.'[44]

A specific corrupt practice Bromyard points to is that of engrossing all available lawyers in order to deny legal representation to one's opponents:

'The withdrawal of the service of experts in the civil law and of advocates has rendered [this practice] more influential than the truth. For in the situation that a man of influence who is also crooked is involved in a case (however unjust) against an ordinary man (who is guiltless) he, with his resources of money will engage every single advocate in the court of christendom (so-called), or every single serjeant in the king's court with the result that the penniless man, and the truth, will find in those markets no one for hire, either because all of them are in the pay of the other party or because they say they dare not [be hired] through fear of the [other] party.'[45]   Bromyard makes another reference to this sly practice:

'In this way the worldly wise sometimes accept money to keep quiet, perhaps because they cannot be hired to speak against another party. And so, when someone was bragging that he'd received a bagful of money for one advocacy, someone else capped this with 'I earned more by holding my tongue.' '[46]

This power, wielded by money, influence and threats can and does override juries, laws and justice itself. Bromyard states his truth, in stark simplicity:

'..their laws and statutes and deeds are likened to spiders' webs: which catch flies, but not the big beasts.'[47]

The wider consequences for a society whose system and operation of justice is corrupt are spelled out, with one especially chilling conclusion:

'And just as in the land where there is neither fear nor justice robberies and murders will keep multiplying..'[48]

'Once more, peace in this guitar [cf.C.4.4] is held back for the reason that one string is plucked more often and harder than it should be. For example, a poor man committing a minor offence will be fined heavily and beyond what is just in the court of the world. And just as a small string is touched too hard, the peace [or, harmony] of the melody is broken. So hatreds and maledictions are generated. A great man will commit a more serious offence and will not be fined. Once more the poor and the middling sort are taxed: and the greater men are let off. Look – some strings are stretched too much, some are too relaxed. *And such a society will not be at peace, nor will it endure.* As Augustinus states, De civitate dei book 2 chapter 21, 'The supreme destroyer of a State is INJUSTICE.'[49]

In what seems to be a reference to manorial or local courts Bromyard picks on the bullying tactics he will have learnt of when visiting villages and towns in Herefordshire. He condemns those lords of a manor who consider themselves free from guilt over excesses carried out, to their knowledge, by their agents. 'But they are *not* free from blame, since they love such [agents]..stewards and bailiffs and advisers who for an offence of six pence know how to bring back five shillings.'[50]   The 'stewards and bailiffs [under-officers of the sheriff] and advisers' mentioned here are seen in the capitulum ADVOCATUS as positions to be aspired to in the progress of their careers by young lawyers of flexible morality who, basing themselves on a degree in civil law, have proved themselves useful to magnates prepared to push such tools into posts of influence. The glittering prospect of a steady rise from modest backgrounds – able to afford several years' legal training – to enticing pathways to economic and social advancement beckoned to many young men of parts.   Most of us now would see this desire as commendable ambition for self-improvement. Bromyard views this through S.Paul's lenses: 'cupiditas: radix omnium malorum'. It may be also that he sees changes in circumstances as fostering social division, mainly because of huge disparities in earning power between the vast majority of the populace and nouveaux riches lawyers: although the single example he cites is the difference between rewards reaped by advocates and those given to lower clerics – a difference of more than 24-fold.

'So youthful scholars in the civil law or on the [King's] Bench, in the first or second year when they return from their school, are gracious to everyone, affable, and arrayed with some care. They are blessed by all their neighbours.. But when he has gained some modest knowledge of how to plead and how to cause damage to his neighbours and become an attorney and advocate and suchlike: he accepts favours from magnates and so, from being a member of their council he is put in charge of others, becomes a steward, a bailiff..[51]

'I say that a yearning for wealth is the reason why advocates study the civil law and their stratagems. They see, that is, that advocates of worldly cases are retained for considerable fees, while men who plead the case for souls are rewarded with contempt. And where they [advocates of secular cases] earn forty shillings these [advocates of spiritual matters] don't earn forty halfpence. And those men ride good horses and dress well. They receive 'gifts' from a good number of people and are soon promoted: they acquire lands, they pile up fine manors: whereas the others go on foot and are downcast in worldly terms. And this is the reason why such huge numbers, pretty well everyone, want to become students of the lucrative laws: why family and friends send their sons and nephews* to the study of the civil law: why the school of civil lawyers has a hundred or two hundred students whereas the school of theology perhaps can't muster five.'[52]

*nepotes: 'grandsons' in classical, 'nephews' in medieval, Latin.

Maitland cites the Statute of Gloucester of 1278 'which has been construed to mean that no action for more than 40 shillings can be brought in those local courts.'[53] Another reference to the extraction of heavy fines links such malpractices to a non-military use of paying for food with tallies: and ends with a questioning of the economic division of society:

'..lords *say* they detest greed: however, they are fond of their greedy agents who know how to procure much and give back little, who also know about giving tallies for food and raising heavy fines. And so lords like these get rich from what belongs to others and would be poor if each man had his own.'[54]

There is a further reference to improper holding of land, established through falsification or forgery of documentation (see also the passage from N.3.15 above):

'Would that such a level of diligent scrutiny were applied to determine by what right these men hold what, by means of fictitious ancestors or by personal acquisition, they are in possession of. If this were to happen they would find that they hold the whole, or a large part [of their estate] in defiance of reason and of the laws of God.'[55]

The most striking feature on the reverse of the silver pennies of Edward I is the long cross extending to the edge of the coin (each of its four angles occupied by three pellets). This type was continued by Edward II, though the obverse was replaced by an unflattering portrait notable for its staring eyes. He did not recall his father's coins, which therefore still circulated.[56]

This numismatic cross will doubtlessly have furnished wits with ample material for puns and other jokes: perhaps 'He's taken the cross' will have been one such. In a remarkable and lengthy passage of the capitulum CRUX – much of which is devoted to discussing the practicalities, the history and the moral issues of the crusade – Bromyard takes the element of popular humour familiar to all and uses it, in elaborate word-play, to transform it into a damning indictment of the corruption people saw in the various English courts. It is, therefore, an assessment and a condemnation of the ruling élite – king, royal circle, earls barons and magnates – which allowed such dishonesty to flourish.

'..yet some men place greater trust in the silver cross of the rich and evil, in which their god was fixed on a cross – I am speaking of SILVER. And this god with his silver cross makes many more false miracles than the true God with His cross may make real [miracles] in that through the cross of Christ, our Lord, *some* lame and crippled are made straight: but not all. *This* [cross], however, in the courts makes *all* the law suits of the crooks straight, to whatever degree they are twisted and bent. And if it is held in copious quantity and reverence, as it should be, it makes the lame and the prisoners walk and go free: and deaf judges and lords in positions of power who present a deaf ear – well, however unjust the case you bring, it makes them listen. And so the deaf hear. And lawyers who are dumb it makes find their tongue. And so the dumb speak and the blind see.[57] To give you an instance: a son will come, for his mother, to the twelve jurymen or to others who have an interest, demonstrating his justice which he has regarding the matter he seeks. But he gives nothing. They will tell him 'I do not see that thou hast justice in this matter or petition, but thou makest an injury to such and such who has justice in this matter.' However, once they have been marked with the sign of this cross,[58] or at least one of them, that is the foreman of the jury, the ancient of (evil) days, who knows how to recount the times of kings of old, how such and such was enfeoffed and such and such accepted similar matters. Such a man has superior vision and makes his colleagues see more of justice than they ought, indeed, where there is total injustice they aver that they see his justice: as is made clear at I.10.6. And so the blind see. The true God, one reads, even healed ten lepers, and Elisha one.[59] *This* god with his cross in the courts and departments, and where crooks lord it, heals *every* leper, and so lepers are cleansed not by gold which they ingest[60] but by gold which is given, in that sinners are deemed upright and clean, and the dead come to life again because men who deserve death are allowed to walk away. And the poor have the gospel preached to them because the undeserving – in both personal morality and knowledge – are given preferment in return for gifts. And so, in the same way that the miracles Peter truly performed Simon the magician performed by trickery,[61] so all the miracles which Christ or His cross performed *this* cross performs deceitfully, with its god – MONEY.'[62]

In NOBILITAS Bromyard contrasts skill in jousting with cowardice shown in the face of the enemy: and in several passages of the *Summa* he makes clear his opposition to and detestation of the tournament, citing both canon law and canonists.[63] The Church had banned tournaments in a general Council as early as 1139, a stance confirmed by the *Decretales* of Gregorius IX in 1234:
    'Adhering to the footsteps of our predecessors of happy memory Innocentius [II, 1130-1143] and Eugenius [III, 1145-1153]: those detestable fairs or feasts which they commonly call 'tournaments': in which knights are accustomed to convene by appointment and recklessly approach [each other] in order to fight, for the display of their strengths and boldness: whence deaths of men and perils of souls frequently come about: [these] we forbid to take place. And if anyone of them shall die there: even though penitence is not to be denied to him if he seeks it he is, however to forfeit church burial.'[64]
    This is a citation of a decree of the Third Lateran Council, of 1179, called by Alexander III. The words 'penitence is not to be denied' were glossed by Bernardus Parmensis who asserted that nor should the last rites be denied.[65] For Bromyard this decree, together with the glosses of Bernardus, of Hostiensis, and of Willelmus de Monte Lauduno was the final word of the Church on tournaments as the issue was not touched on in the *Liber Sextus* of 1298 or in the *Clementinae* of 1317. The change of policy promulgated at Lyon on 16 September 1316 by Iohannes XXII appears to have been quite unknown to Bromyard as Iohannes' bull had some ten years to wait before its widespread circulation. The *Extravagantes Iohannis XXII* were collected between 1325 and 1327 by Zenzelinus de Cassanis, who also glossed the collection. The ninth titulus, *De Torneamentis*, reversed Clemens V's banning of tournaments. Iohannes links the practice of jousting to preparations for the 'generale passagium' or general crusade called for by the Council of Vienne on 3 April 1312. It is worth quoting at some length in that

Iohannes rehearses Clemens' reasons for his ban – reasons which Bromyard too upheld, adding others of his own – and judged that his predecessor's reasons were outweighed by the more cogent needs of the projected crusade of 1319.

'..Certainly pope Clemens V of happy memory our predecessor carefully considering that the general crusade beneficially ordained for the assistance of the Holy Land was not lightly hampered by tournaments and tilts or jousts both because they frequently thus weaken those about to undertake the very business of the crusade in that they are rendered powerless to carry it out and because they sometimes pull back considerable numbers from the assumption of the cross while they are embarrassed to abstain when others are participating in them: specifically forbade these very tournaments and tilts or jousts in the kingdoms of France, England and Germany and some other provinces in which they were accustomed more frequently to be exercised: for the help advice or consent of those undertaking these or displaying prowess in these, and of those also in whose estates or jurisdictions they took place and did not prohibit this when they were able to, and of those welcoming in their own homes men proceeding to these or of those exercising commerce in whatever way with the same men, by promulgating sentences of excommunication against persons and of interdict against lands, absolution from this kind of excommunication, except [for persons] at the point of death, being reserved to the apostolic see. But...because some hold back from the belt of knighthood and because through fear especially of this same sentence do not presume to be available for military service, on account of which it transpires that men suitable and willing for the aid of the foresaid land in these kingdoms are found in smaller numbers than usual We [the pope singles out the recently deceased Philip IV of France and very many magnates and nobles of France and elsewhere who pressed for the cancelling of the ban on tournaments] recall those who on account of the exercise of these very tournaments or tilts incurred sentences of this nature, in absolution.. [the pope also granted dispensation to priests from the breach of church law in conducting the divine office in lands under interdict]. Given at Lyon 16 September in our first year [1316].'[66]

For Bromyard, then, guided by the *Decretales* and other canon law texts, total opposition to tournaments put him at odds with contemporary attitudes held by many high-ranking men who regarded tournaments as an excellent training for knights who faced wars in Scotland, Ireland and Gascony. Only if they threatened to take precedence over military duties did Edward I's view turn to hostility: so, about Christmas in 1306 'the king had issued writs for the confiscation of the lands and goods of a number of knights who had deserted the army in order to engage in a tournament.' The general approval of either the single, one to one, joust and of the mêlée was signalled by royal and aristocratic presence and indeed participation in these lavishly prepared events which occasionally welcomed foreign competitors.[67] 'Contrary to the opinion of some scholars, tournaments were felt to be a useful form of practice for war. Pierre Dubois, when instructed by Philip IV to protest against a papal bull condemning them, declared "que tout le monde se plaignait de la bulle, et qui'il n'y avait pas de meilleure préparation à la croisade, dont le pape invoqua les intérêts, que le turnois." '[68]

One factor to be weighed by rulers who licensed[69] the holding of tournaments was the cost in trained horsemen who were either killed or badly wounded. The clash, at a combined speed of up to 40 miles per hour, of lances on cuirass or helmet, propelled by the weight of armoured horses and riders, each of a ton and a half is vividly depicted in several manuscript paintings (often of the fifteenth century). Barker's plates IV, VII and VIII illustrate jousts of the thirteenth and fourteenth centuries.[70] Far more dangerous, however, was the mêlée, closer to the cavalry charge of warfare. Murimuth, writing of the year 1341, describes two tournaments:

'And at once there was proclaimed a tournament at Dunstable on the Monday before the oncoming Lent: to which tournament there came virtually the whole youth of armoured men of England, but none born overseas, so that the total of helmeted knights came up to 250 and more.

Afterwards, in the fortnight after Easter, the king held a tournament at Northampton where many noblemen were seriously wounded and John de Beaumont was killed.'[71]

Barker points to the damage to growing crops caused by the spilling of the mêlée out into the surrounding countryside.[72]

It was not only an overspill from a mêlée which could damage crops. Oftener the damage was caused by the leisured classes who hunted with hounds – the breed and size depending upon the game in season – or with hawks and falcons.

'..not only do they [sc. the great men] deserve the curses of the common folk whose grain crop they destroy by riding over it with their falcons and hounds..'[73]

'..for a sport is not in accord with reason in which one party enjoys himself and another is dismayed: in which the rich man hunts with hounds and birds of prey, takes a hare or a bird and lays low the poor man's crops. *He* has no share in what is taken: and the rich man's tournament is the poor man's torment.'[74]

The divisions in English society created by differences in wealth prompted many comments in the *Summa*, as did those of kinship and descent. Another marker of separateness much less widely discussed was that of regional divergence of speech. Bromyard raises this issue in CIVITAS and then expands it in order to plead for tolerance towards strangers, foreigners.

'But evil citizens, i.e. of the City of the Devil, divide others from them by reason of country, ethnic origin or language, harbouring anger and strife against them and provoking them because they are from another part of the land, saying 'Thou art a northerner': 'Thou art a southerner' or 'Thou art of such and such a nation' like that accursed maid-servant and gate-keeper who called out to Peter saying 'Thou art a Galilean: thy tongue,'[75] etc., and like those accursed Jews of Judges 12. [5, 6] who strangled everyone who couldn't pronounce 'shibboleth'... And so the outstanding preacher of God [Paul] was so concerned to summon all to oneness no matter what region or land they were of..'[76]

The foreigners he will have had in mind, some of whom he may well have met in England, will probably include Welsh, French and Italian residents, as well as subjects of the Empire. He could not, however, have met Jews in England.

One strand running through the *Summa* is Bromyard's marked hostility to the English aristocracy and magnates. He singles out for repeated adverse criticism what he sees as their abuse of power, neglect of duty, absence of concern for the many men and women below them in economic and social status, their lust for money, their personal immorality and their harshness.

'..they [the powerful] cruelly take from people who hardly have enough bread made from beans, and water, and for half the year [i.e. the winter months] do not once eat well but live in labour and hardships which never cease..'[77]

The powerful denunciation of 'our nobles and great men' has already been cited [at P.8.6]. Another passage is more than a denunciation: it enters the sphere where philosophy and politics intermingle and poses a critique of the structure of society:

'..how can it stand or agree with reason that one man, in heavy labour and sweat day and night scrapes a meagre living: and another, who leads a lazy, lustful and luxurious life, lusting in bed till nine o'clock in the morning, sating his desire, can take away that living: that one man can live enjoying every pleasure and another – who is made in the image of God, and serves God – can scarcely scratch a miserable living..'[78]

Bromyard will not have heard of Marsiglio of Padua[79] or come across the political writings of his older contemporary, Dante:[80] but has found his own path, through his voracious reading and his work as a confessor and preacher, to a stern assessment of the manifold ills besetting Edward II's England and to a grasp of how his native land could and should be governed.

'..it is worth noting that in antiquity the republics/commonwealths were well governed because they were governed not by blood or noble lineage but by common sense and the man who merited this. The men chosen for government were those who were suitable, and not barons and earls.'[81]   He then states the contrast: 'But these days, for the administration of the commonwealth, both in Church, in the guidance of souls, and in the ruling of our bodily existence it is younger men, who know nothing, who are set over us because of their heredity or their connections or their titles..they don't rule, they drift.'[82]

Bromyard extends this critique of the ruling élite to the barons and earls, bishops, knights and burgesses who, as a corporate entity when summoned by the king, became 'the king in council in parliament'. He plays upon the word's etymology (from the Latin *parabolare* and French *parler*) and ends with a surprising accusation.

'Rightly is it called 'parliament', since there they talk a lot: but what is spoken and ordained there is later totally or in large part distorted. Part of the reason for this is laid open at E.1.4.'[83]   'Just as the men who hold their parliaments and councils and judgements: after they've been warmed up by wine, since wine, among them, is the dominating factor, rather than reason. On this, see C.11.5.'[84]

These words seem both unduly harsh and hyperbolic, presumably deriving from behaviour of at most relatively few individuals. Yet he makes this same accusation at N.3.15: it cannot be without substance.   When we read his preceding sentences Bromyard's contemptuous stance is shown to bear weightier substance than the charge of taking too many cups of wine. The gravamen of his complaint against the supreme legislators is directed at their failure to enforce compliance with statute law. He has been considering the rôle of counsellors: the rôle of 'the one advised', though not stated explicitly, falls to Edward II.

'But even if all the counsellors are good, the one advised is still unwilling to operate or be guided according to their counsels. Certainly he has good eyesight. But he suffers arthritis in the joints of both feet and hands: and this weakness commonly follows the train of present-day parliaments, where advice is given in abundance, *but is not translated into action*. So, rightly is it called 'parliament..'* '[83 bis]

Schooled as he was in both civil and canon law it was by the enduring principles enshrined in these legal systems that he judged the government of his day: '..all empires and kingdoms and emperors and kings should be governed by the laws, not by custom or personal whim.'[85]   Bromyard's commitment to justice was reinforced also by his reading of Augustinus' *De civitate dei*. He quotes, approvingly, from book 4, chapter 4: 'and so if justice is removed what are kingdoms but large-scale criminality?'[86]   He also knew the declaration in the *Codex* of Iustinianus by the emperors Theodosius I and Valentinianus: 'It is an utterance worthy of the majesty of the ruler that the prince profess himself bound by the laws.'[87]

The passage in NOBILITAS inveighing against the destruction of grain crops by riders with falcons and hounds is linked, rather oddly, with the failure of guardians to fulfil certain provisions contained in clauses of 'the new Charter' in respect of their wards:

'...not only do they [sc. the great men] deserve the curses of the common folk whose grain crop they destroy by riding over it with their falcons and hounds, but for which they will be able to fear an even greater excommunication carried in the new Charter: in which are contained [these clauses]: that they should not marry off a ward with disparagement: that they will faithfully administer the guardianship committed to them: that they would not permit their wards' estates to perish: but would be held wholly to restore these to them in houses and in other things when they shall have come to full age in the same condition in which they received them. Because they have not kept these [undertakings] and for other deeds of theirs which they have carried out in defiance of God and of reason his *noblemen* – who now are dead – *have toppled down into the earth* that is, *the very lowest*. Ezechiel xxvi.'[88]

The 'greater excommunication' is that referred to by McKechnie: 'Both charters' [sc. the parva carta and Magna Carta] 'were republished and on 13th May [1253] the sentence of excommunication, which had accompanied the reaffirmations of 1225 and 1237, was repeated in a peculiarly impressive manner.'[89] This was in answer to complaints of infractions. As late as January 1298, in York, the great earls, before joining Edward I's army at Newcastle, 'insisted on a public proclamation of the charters and of the sentence of excommunication against all who infringed them.'[90] The sentence of excommunication 'was repeated in connection with the confirmations of 1237, 1253, 1255, 1276, 1297 and 1300 and at other times during the century.'[91]

The last confirmation of the Great Charter under Edward I was of 14 February 1301: there were no confirmations by Edward II.[92] However, Bromyard may have had in mind documents supplementary to Magna Carta: McKechnie mentions those of 1297, 1300 and 1311.[93]

The three clauses introduced by *quod* are subsumed in McKechnie's clauses 6 and 5[6] of his text of the Great Charter of Henry III of 1225, viz.:

Heredes maritentur absque disparagatione

and

Custos..reddat heredi cum ad plenam etatem pervenerit, terram suam totam..ad minus secundum quod illam recepit.[94]

While addressing the subject of absentee priests Bromyard makes a tantalizing reference to a comet's appearance:

'..daily experience tells us that if at another time [than at the full moon] a poor man or a pilgrim/traveller were to come to the house of such [a priest] asking for alms the renter [of the land] or the steward will reply 'my master is not at home: lo the man is not in his house' [Proverbs 7.19]. The poor man says 'And where is thy master?' The steward replies 'At the king's court': or 'At the court of another prince or bishop': or 'At Oxford': or 'At Paris' or 'At Bologna'... So those who make their appearances only at that time [after harvest, to collect the produce] and are resplendent in their exotic garments and like a [the?] comet with its long beard and hair...'[95]

The comet which is most likely to have made an impression in the first quarter of the fourteenth century is that which was visible in European skies from December 1315.[96]

It was catalogued in Chinese astronomical records: 'In the 2ⁿᵈ year of the epoch Yen Yew, the 11ᵗʰ moon, day Ping Woo, a strange star appeared, which afterwards became a comet. It entered Tsze, Wei Yuen. It passed through the S.D. from Chin to Peih, being 15 of those divisions. The next year, 2ⁿᵈ moon, day Kang Yin, it disappeared.'
Williams explains the dates as being 28 November 1315 and 12 March 1316.[97]

Avicenna's recommendations for the proper ordering of the State lead Bromyard to evaluate statutes regulating English affairs, on which he reaches a gloomy conclusion. He focuses attention upon the practice of forestalling, the purchase of goods before they reach the open market, with the intention of selling them on at a higher price than they would otherwise fetch. It is therefore closely linked to another corrupt practice, regrating.

'He [sc. the legislator] should also prohibit, he [Avicenna] maintains, the presence in the city/state of the gamester or dice-player: he should prohibit, too, pursuits and enterprises inimical to the interests of the state such as theft, kidnap [and] fornication.
If Muslims in their states have ordained statutes of this kind how much more [should?] Christians. But, more's the pity, almost all statutes now answer greed rather than [public] interest, and [tend to] the destruction of the state. A contemporary instance of this is to be seen in almost all [our] seaside cities where foreign merchants arriving with their ships can not sell as they like to anyone at all but are coerced by accursed statutes to sell [only] to certain powerful men in [that] city who then will sell the goods on to others at will. This practice impoverishes the state on two counts. First, in that fewer merchants – and those, as it were, reluctantly - come to such cities, in as much as that where there used to come, in some cities, twenty ships now there scarcely come five. Second, in that the advantage to be gained from the arrival of the merchants will not accrue to the whole city – which would enjoy the profit coming therefrom if they could buy, freely in an open market – but to the original purchasers, in that they sell on to the ordinary population at a higher price than would the principal merchants.'[98]

The existence and persistence of the problems caused by forestalling are both well documented: and Bromyard's judgement that the practice impoverished the State is well founded. What is difficult to defend, however, is his view that foreign merchants 'are coerced by accursed statutes to sell [only] to certain powerful men..' Statutes of widely separated years state the problem, deplore the practice and provide penalties of increasing severity for those breaking the provisions of the statutes.[99] From the repetition of such stern prohibitions it is clear that the problem lay not in the wording of these statutes but in failure to enforce them – as Bromyard points out at C.11.5.

The studies by Kershaw and Jordan of the catastrophically adverse weather conditions which afflicted England (and other north-European countries) especially in the years 1315 to 1318 inclusive and which are recorded by contemporary chroniclers have graphically laid before us the dreadful impact which the heavy and unseasonable summer rains had on both crops and livestock: and the scale of the human mortality which consequently ravaged both town and country.[100]
Although 1315 is often taken as the first year of the onset of the disasters which befell England the troubles really began in 1314, the year of Bannockburn.[101] Haines summarizes neatly: 'Heavy rains during the summer of 1314, the spring of 1315, and much of 1316, brought flooding, a three-year failure of crops, scarcity of food, high prices, particularly those for grain and fuel and, as a consequence, starvation, disease, and murrain of cattle.'[102] The contemporary account in the 'Vita' attributes the crisis, as

does Bromyard, to the hand of God. 'For in the past year [1314] there was such plentiful rain that men could scarcely harvest the wheat or store it safely in the barn. In the present year [1315] worse has happened. For the floods of rain have rotted almost all the seed.. And in many places the hay lay so long under water that it could neither be mown or gathered. Sheep commonly died and other animals were killed by a sudden pestilence.'[103] The Bridlington chronicler writes of six years of shortage and failure of agricultural produce and consequent high prices, starting from approximately 20 July 1315 to (presumably) July 1321. 'Also in the same year [1315] there came about a great dearth of corn round the feast of saint Margaret the virgin and in the subsequent autumn, so that a quarter of wheat was being sold generally throughout England for 30 shillings and never less than 24 shillings: and a quarter of white salt at the same price: in a similar manner barley, beans and peas for 14 shillings, and malt for 16 shillings: oats for 10 shillings. And it is to be borne in mind that the condition of low yields from the land and the scarcity or failure of all produce, and also the dearth of all foodstuffs for sale – although not at these same prices – endured without respite for six years. In a similar fashion human mortality and murrain among cattle was on such a scale, of such a kind and continuity as has not been seen by this generation. Nor could the corpses of the dead, because of the stink, be kept but that, before dinner or after dinner, they had to be buried without waiting for the morrow.'[104]

It is in this context that Bromyard's lengthy capitulum TRIBULATIO (some 19,000 words) should be read. He animadverts to these calamities at M.9.25 and O.5.30: but it is in this capitulum that we can understand, in passage after passage, the effect made upon him by the suffering he will have witnessed, as an intelligent and compassionate man – not yet licensed to preach and hear confession – in Herefordshire and neighbouring counties.

The severely cold winters, the continuously wet summers, the high prices of foodstuffs, the difficulties of transport over sodden earth, the human diseases: these plagues were also attended by a 'devastating series of livestock epidemics which afflicted most areas of Britain in this period. The famine years themselves were accompanied by a widespread sheep murrain.. a new epidemic afflicting only cattle and oxen and wiping out very large numbers of them, began its dreadful passage through Britain in the county of Essex at Easter 1319... Even now the seemingly interminable hardships of the protracted agrarian crisis were not at an end. Corn prices had remained quite low in 1319 but rose considerably in the year following the mediocre harvest of the wet autumn of 1320. This was preparatory to another disastrous harvest in 1321 and a rise in corn prices to inflated levels approaching those of 1315-17.'[105] A story presented as an *exemplum* illustrates the greed which sought to make profits out of the desperate need for basic foodstuffs: a story doubtlessly replicated throughout England:

'...in the dearth which recently preceded the present time, since he [unnamed] held a large quantity of grain, and all the grain in other granges of that village had run out, huge numbers of mice flocked to his grange: his steward came to him with this advice:

'It's better to sell thy corn, for three reasons. First, it's already very dear: the whole lot would fetch 20 shillings. Second, the neighbouring poor are dying of hunger, and we can sell, and make loans under pledge so that they can survive. Third, it's being eaten by the mice.' The landowner said he'd hold out for 30 shillings. His chamberlain, on hearing a cry at night, found his master being lacerated and killed by demons in the form of dormice.'[106]

Sixteen extracts, all but two from TRIBULATIO, express Bromyard's reaction to the years of ruined harvests, appalling weather, and human and animal mortality.

'..because if these rains now destroying the world came from natural causes they would fall less in summer than in winter..'[107]

'So why should we wonder if now there are rains and tempest when the corruption caused by lust and the contemplation of malice is greater than in the days of Noah: since a thousand deceits and novelties and ways of committing sin have now been invented which did not exist then? Why should we be surprised if famine is afflicting the population when the harshness of the lords is greater now.. than in Saul's days? Since what is made plain by the past is the certain guide to the future it is evident that those planets which reigned then reign now, and are causing our sufferings.'[108]

'Why should we be surprised if God is in our days killing our livestock because of our sins, and the rains are destroying our possessions and crops with the storms?'[109]

'Why should we be surprised if – through our greater sins – in these times of ours bairns and innocent children are dying of hunger and are being drowned through rainfall which exceeds all bounds: and are subjugated in war because of evil men: and because of sinners who defect from God, they fare ill in every aspect of their lives and suffer in the grip of tribulation?'[110]

'So the loyal labouring folk and middling folk are here often being lashed with the scourge of famine and tribulation: while the wealthy and the worthless, untouched by famine and distress, spend their days with their plenty: but in the end, like traitors, they go down to the gallows of hell.'[111]

'They [sc. 'the greater part of mankind' (maior enim pars hominum) of some 90 words before] misuse their own status to such an extent that there is scarcely anyone content with his/her own status, either with respect to what they have acquired (as was shown at A.27.5) or with respect to their diet or dress, since clerics go about in clothing and tonsure – except that their cloth perhaps is of one colour – just like squires, bishops just like knights, the wives of burgesses or squires just like those of knights or kings..'[112] So these aforementioned innovations and abuses of affairs and distortions bring about new storms: these are the planets which with storms and rains and wars torment those inventors of innovations and others on account of society. Why should we be surprised either that God exercises justice if He afflicts those who abuse all bodily creatures and even their own souls and with those battle against God and assail Him with all his gifts.. [Bromyard now cites S.Gregorius from an unreferenced homily]. 'So their summer would turn into their winter, and vice versa: peacetime for this reason would turn into a time of wars: the earth too for this reason would turn into sterility, livestock into mortality', which in these times of ours we have especially seen with oxen on a greater scale than we have heard or read of ever happening before..'[113]

'..the middling folk impute the whole cause to the magnates and to the rich: they say 'They are such harsh, such hard lords that it's because of them God will destroy the land: but *they* [the ruling élite] on the other hand impute the cause to the others, saying 'Our subjects are so untrustworthy..so disdainful and haughty that they are unwilling to serve or to work: so that it's because of them God is destroying the land.' '[114]

'..while the religious and perhaps a few of the poor people and the middling sort are assembling to conduct a procession directed towards the unseasonableness of the atmosphere and to the chanting of masses and litanies and to hearing God's speech, the people who are the cause of the weather conditions pass their time lasciviously in their beds or gluttonously in taverns or on other worldly matters: they do not join a procession nor do they pray.. instead, they are *pleased* about the coming famine because they'll get a higher price when they sell the grain and other produce they've piled up from long ago: moreover, the lands and the property of others stricken by famine they'll buy up for a song..'[115]

'..whereas the leaders in the city or camp who ejected their lord from the camp are the cause whereby the city is besieged by the ejected king, the common folk in the city, who are never the cause of the siege, suffer greater hardships of the famine during the siege...those very people who had received God in their baptism and during Lent into the strongholds of their souls, and afterwards foully threw Him out: God is besieging these people with diseases. All the hailstorms or rains we see falling, or other misfortunes, are equalled by the number of assaults God is making on the strongholds so that the stronghold can be restored to Him..'[116]

'And this seems just, that the rainfall of vengeance should cease by the efficacy of the rainfalls of tears.'[117]

'Rightly therefore through the waters of rain, or rather, of vengeance, he restrains him [man] to rectitude.'[118]

Bromyard plays here with two senses of rectitude: physical straightness and moral uprightness.

'Our [punishment] however is excessive rainfall, which is more disgraceful and weightier and gloomier for human hearts. And just as they went to other cities for water so we to other realms for corn.'[119]

Bromyard has in mind Amos 4.8: 'et venerunt duae et tres civitates ad civitatem unam ut biberent aquam et non sunt satiatae': translated from Hebrew by NEB as 'From this city and that, men would stagger to another for water to drink, but would not find enough..'

'..it can be stated of many.. that they are not returning to God, abandoning their former sins, but are turning away from God even more and are distancing themselves [from Him] by augmenting their sins. With every kind of calamity – the sword, starvation and death – and on every rank of mankind God has rained down his triple hammer-blows: the great ones in diverse civil discords and conflicts among themselves: the poor, reduced to beggary through starvation – many thousands of them he has slain through starvation: the middling sort through deaths, both of themselves and of their livestock etc.'[120]

'..the solemn vow made at baptism we are now breaking, those promises we are not upholding: instead we are counterfeiting [the testimony of our] witnesses and it's for this reason [God] is baptizing us again with waters and inundations, drowning sowings, meadows and crops already sown.'[121]

'..some.. say that never has there been such bad weather or so many storms as [there have] since men who have taken vows of religion and who pray solely for [this] world were multiplied throughout the world.'[122]

Bromyard naturally defends the mendicant orders against this slur: this remark seems to be important primary evidence of the blaming of Franciscans and Dominicans for the catastrophic climatic conditions of the crisis years of 1314 to 1318.

'..just as dishonest jurymen and foremen of juries are the reason for there being so many robbers and wrongdoers, at whose hands loyal men are often harassed, in the same way those whose duty it is to bring charges against or punish others and who fail to do this: and the men who clear the guilty by compurgation, or help and support them, are the reason why there are so many contraveners of God's laws: and it's because of *these* men that God is afflicting the whole community through pestilence, rain and famine.'[123]

Bromyard concludes this grim capitulum TRIBULATIO with a quotation from 2 Maccabees 1.7. The whole verse, in NEB's translation from the Septuagint, reads

'In the reign of Demetrius,[124] in the year 169 [i.e. 143 BC] we the Jews wrote to you during the persecution and the crisis that came upon us in those years since the time when Jason and his partisans revolted from the holy land and the kingdom.'

Bromyard uses this text to draw a parallel between the persecution and crisis that befell the Jews and that currently savaging his England. He will have selected the text precisely because the tribulation which descended upon the Jews took its origin not from acts of Antiochos IV but from the *revolt* of Jewish leaders themselves. Bromyard saw the calamities harrowing his fellow-countrymen as deriving from their turning away from God and His word.

In his chapter 'The World' (MUNDUS) Bromyard cites 3 Kings 21 [1 Kings 21.25,26], the account of the death of Naboth at the instigation of king Ahab and queen Jezebel over Naboth's refusal to sell or to exchange the vineyard coveted by his king. The NEB translation from the Hebrew is 'Never was a man who sold himself to do what is wrong in the LORD'S eyes as Ahab did, and all at the prompting of Jezebel his wife. He committed gross abominations..'

The uncannily close resemblance in sound and appearance between 'Isabella' and 'Iesabella'/'Iezabela'/'Hiezabel' – variant spellings of Ahab's queen's name – was a gift for the enemies of Edward's queen. Another parallel was that both Jezebel and Isabella were foreigners: Jezebel the daughter of the Phoenician Ethbaal king of Sidon,[125] Isabella the daughter of the French king Philip IV.

Bromyard does not mention Isabella or Edward. His reference is oblique but easily recognized by his clerical readers: indeed by anyone who knew the Bible. Invoking the image of chess it runs:

'Secondly, just as in the game of chess the queen always makes her captures [by moving] diagonally:[126] so the cruel mistress: to understand this [sc. the analogy] it is to be noted that just as none is to be found of greater mercy and compassion than a good woman filled with mercy, since such a one always feels compassion for the afflicted and strives to bend the mind of her husband and of her ministers to piety..in the same way there is no beast crueller than she [when turned] bad. Just as among brigands she is said to be crueller than her companions, urging them on to acts of cruelty and murders, where, without her, they would simply strip [their victims of their possessions], in exactly the same way a woman like this urges on her lord[127] and her followers to greater cruelty through her powers of persuasion and instigation of worse evil. If her lord is determined to seize hold of the outer trappings *she* is determined to take away life, as is clear from a reading of III Kings 21, the account of Ahab and Jezebel his wife. *He* wanted Ahab's vineyard: *she* contrived Naboth's death. *And that very same thing I have seen happen in my time.* Furthermore, if her lord says 'You are to beat [him]' or 'Put [him] in prison' she says 'Kill him': this is demonstrated in Luke 3 where Herodias engineered the death of John the Baptist: Herodes had only imprisoned him. Nor is it only devious courses they follow in this way: they also, deviously and perniciously, grasp 'gifts' purposely to nourish their proud station in life, and levy massive tallies or 'contributions': for if her lord rakes in heavy fines from the fatherland she, taking what's left, leaves [people] without a shirt to their backs: when he confiscates the *cloak* she confiscates the *coat* for him.[128] This is demonstrated by the fact that when the fine imposed by her lord is fixed high enough according to God and reason, and perhaps beyond reason, the mistress has to have a little something for her gold collection: for every pound, that is, her lord receives she has to have a shilling.. So it is to be feared that a couple such as they will be assigned to fuel the everlasting fire, *because in her heart she says 'I sit [on my throne] as a queen and I am not a widow: and I shall not see grief.'*[129] *And so in one single day shall come her calamities: death and grief and famine and she shall be incinerated in the fire: since strong is God Who shall bring her to judgement.* *'* Apocalypse 18.'[130 and 131]

---

* The words italicized from 'because' to 'judgement' are translated from Bromyard's text of Apocalypse 18.7, 8. The Stuttgart third edition reads 'iudicavit' which Bromyard *may* have chosen to change to 'iudicabit', or may have worked from a text deriving from a strong body of manuscripts which reads the future form. In either case his reading would seem to indicate that this chapter was written before Edward III's seizure of Mortimer on 18/19 October 1330[132] and execution on 29 November, and before the allocation, in the parliament of 26 November, of an estate for Isabella worth 4,000 marks per annum.[133]

The Apocalypse text itself looks back to Isaiah 47, a terrible commination of Babylon: Bromyard will have found apposite to what he expected Isabella's fate to be other verses therein such as 'Descende sede in pulverem..quia ultra non vocaberis mollis et tenera..et dixisti in sempiternum ero domina..' (Come down and sit in the dust..for thou shalt no more be called tender and delicate..and thou saidst, I shall be a lady for ever..)

This important and contemporary comment on the Mortimer/Isabella usurpation of power is mediated through the citation of three biblical texts and the unstated use of a fourth: namely 3 Kings 21 [1 Kings 21], Luke 3, Apocalypse 18 and Isaiah 47. Bromyard's deft exploitation of these texts enables him to discharge his fusillade of indictments at his primary target: not Orleton, nor Mortimer, but Isabella. They are to be dated to the period between the murder of Edward of Caernarfon and the arrest of Mortimer at Nottingham: that is, between 22 September 1327[134] and 18 October 1330.

Bromyard here takes the account of the judicial murder of Naboth, contrived through the machinations of queen Jezebel for her husband king Ahab, and uses it to launch from this an astonishingly virulent attack upon queen Isabella. He was faced with two main difficulties in framing the biblical history to fit the situation of England in 1327. The first is the assignment of blame for Naboth's death to Ahab, in 2 Kings 9.26: this version he rejects. The second is that it was Isabella and Mortimer who were ultimately responsible for Edward's murder, not Isabella and Edward for another victim's death. This obstacle he surmounts by the device of changing the 'mariti sui' to 'dominum suum' whereby 'dominus' is the link by which Edward, her husband and lord, becomes her lord, Mortimer.[135] The guilt of the order to murder Edward is then attributed to Isabella: for whereas her lord (Mortimer) ordered imprisonment and beatings she enjoined death: 'occidatur'. This once established, Isabella's guilt is reinforced by the parallels between Herodes and Mortimer (who each ordered imprisonment) and Herodias and Isabella (who each secured death). The metaphor from chess is reintroduced: just as a queen in chess moves 'oblique' (diagonally, deviously) so does Isabella. The collective prompting of greed to feed the couple's pride drives them to impose heavy monetary fines on a nation-wide scale ('de patria').

Although Bromyard states in CHRISTUS that 'if a prince or king who is negligent on account of his negligence vis-à-vis the extirpation of heresy or even at times useless and dissolute and negligent towards his kingdom and the keeping of justice can be deposed from the kingdom he has acquired by the deputy of Christ on earth..'[136] and indeed cites two examples of this papal intervention, he certainly does not contemplate the assassination of a bad king: an idea given wide circulation by the huge popularity of the *Communiloquium* of Iohannes Wallensis.[137]

One of the most insistent notes heard through many of the 189 capitula forming this great work is the percussive assault on the cavalier and unscrupulous corruption and misrule exercised by the potentates and *mafiosi* of England, whom Bromyard lambasts time and time again. One passage from many such concludes this chapter.

'The methods by which the robbers and tyrants plunder what is not their own are many. Three of these are uncovered through that 'fork' with three teeth held by the extortioners – on which see I Kings 2.'... 'With this third prong they avidly expect gifts, payments, presents, donations and 'courtesies' – from everyone..speaking at times through 'middlemen' and stating 'You *have to* hand over something: a yearly payment, that is, of so many shillings': or they extract something of this sort by threats. If they [the victims] refuse they plan to 'touch' them whenever the time and place is right: and sometimes they openly tell their bailiffs and agents to keep an eye on so and so – a malicious eye which will bring their targets no good – seeking an occasion whereby they can do them harm.'[138]

1.   As a confessor for over two decades Bromyard will have heard the innermost thoughts of men and women of many different backgrounds. He lists the confessor's question-words designed to prompt the reluctant to open their hearts further: 'who? what? where? how often? through whom? why? how? when?' (Quis quid ubi quociens per quos cur quomodo quando) in a neat hexameter line. (C.6.11). He knows of the married state's slide into routine: '..because those who live together out of wedlock in the most passionate love after being joined in marriage cool off..' (A.17.5) And '..few men are contented with their *own* wives..' (A.17.6). He notes that 'wine and confession reveal everything' (vinum et confessio omnia revelant) (E.1.4). An indication that he may have confessed women of the nobility is a possible deduction from NOBILITAS where he writes: 'They [sc. noble women] see women of lower social status begging with young children in their arms: if they had lived chastely they would have led a peaceful life. However they do not fear the fate of these women as they should in that the noble women enmeshed in the same vices are not few in number. Acts 18.' [A puzzling reference]. (N.3.17) Other insights into inner lives came his way: '..just as an adulterous woman who has been beaten by her paramour does not leave him but if beaten by her husband she *does* leave him..' (M.13.23)

2.   Six derive from Matthew 25.35, 36.

3.   Matthew 22.37-40.

4.   Bridlington pp.87-89: Baker pp.311-312.

5.   ..decipiuntur ergo qui maledictiones quas merentur contemnunt: sicut patuit de quodam nobili nuper satis potenti: cui cum communem pasturam imparcare vellet dictum fuit quod multorum pauperum animalia ibi pascerentur: qui omnes ei maledicerent: quod cum ipse contemneret quia frequenter tales evasisset maledictiones fatebatur..postea idem nobilis tractus et suspensus fuit. (M.1.1)

6.   Coming to Hereford, the king sharply rebuked the bishop of the place for supporting the barons against their natural lord, and he confiscated many of his goods in revenge. (Vita p.203 in Childs' translation).

7.   ..ita mali penas convenientes experientur quod congrue ostensum fuit in accidenti circa res cuiusdam domini satis noti nuper defuncti.. Accidit in morte sua quod omnia bona inventa in manu sua vel in maneriis fuerunt regi confiscata. (D.12.40)

8.   Bromyard accepts the justice of confiscation of property from those rebelling against the crown: ..sicut rex a sibi rebellantibus et crimen lese maiestatis committentibus iuste punire et omnia auferre potest.. (T.5.61)

9.   Fryde p.78: and p.247 note 35.

10.   Unde cum cuidam nobili in anglia in strage nobilium nunciaretur in mane quod eodem die turpi morte moreretur cadens in terram clamavit dicens heu nunquam dilexi uxorem meam.. (A.17.7)
Dugdale quotes Sir Andrew de Harclay as using these same words '..that he should die a shameful death..' (p.781). Dugdale further remarks '..many there were, who taxed him for Adultery, in keeping of sundry Women, notwithstanding he had a Wife.' [Alice, daughter and heir to Henry de Lacy earl of Lincoln]. (p.782)
Lancaster's execution is depicted in the Luttrell Psalter (56 recto): the bloody gash on his neck an indication of the first, unsuccessful, stroke. The painting shows the earl kneeling, hands together in prayer: a stance which is in accord with the account in the 'Vita': 'Tunc comes quasi orando caput extendit, et spiculator bis vel ter percuciens caput amputavit.' (Vita p.214).

11.   Quia sicut ex negligentia illorum vigilantium imminet periculum toti exercitui sicut patuit in exercitu regis anglie in scotia quando inimici per exercitum regis de nocte transierunt et damna fecerunt, qui quidem defectus sicut dicunt qui usum habent armorum ex hoc contingit quod viri valoris qui ad vigilandum ordinantur dant se quieti mittentes unum ribaldum in equo et armis dominum suum effigientem. (P.13.10)

[12]   Vita pp.166, 168. Vulgariter enim dicitur quod comes ille recepit a Roberto de Brutz quadraginta milia librarum..
Haines, Edward II p.118.

[13]   Alii ibi acceptantur et promoventur propter specialem affectionem quam rex ad eos habet: sicut aliquando contingit quod propter eorum pulcritudinem vel quia forte amabiles sunt et grossi specialiorem gratiam in oculis regis inveniunt . (G.2.8)
Haines, Edward II pp.20-21: p.366 notes 113, 115.

[14]   Sed heu principes et milites et exercitus moderni temporis euntes ad bellum potius dyabolum placant crudelitatibus et spoliis quam deum: non cum orationibus sed cum multorum vadunt maledictionibus, quia non in expensis regis vel propriis vadunt, sed in expensis ecclesiarum et pauperum quos eundo spoliant et si forte emant nihil solvant nisi tallias: cristus pavit quinque milia quinque panibus: ipsi maius faciunt miraculum, quia decem milia pascuntur paucis talliis
id est dicis, non semel tantum vel bis sicut cristus sed frequenter: non solum homines sicut cristus sed et canes et equos etc., nec pane et piscibus sicut cristus sed delicatis cibariis. Nota T.v.xvii, Et F.viii.i. (B.2.24)

[15]   melius..esset pro eis [sc. vendentibus] habere sex denarios statim solutos quam talliam quinque solidorum qui nunquam solventur. (T.5.17)

[16]   ..pauperes timide furtum committunt, in quo si capiantur incarcerantur et puniuntur, divites vero aliena aperte expendunt: nihil pro eis solventes et tamen inulte in hac vita transeunt… Si nunc oves et boves et galline et capones et omnia animalia que divites comedunt et non solvunt, de quibus dictum est B.ii.xxiiii. et E.iii.xxii. et T.v.xvii. in ventribus eorum sic clamarent: maior forte clamor esset in ventribus eorum quam in archa Noe.. (F.8.1)

[17]   Maddicott p.106.

[18]   ibid. p.185.

[19]   Bromyard's account of Edward II's demands upon the abbey is from BELLUM.
Antiquitus enim quando potentes principes declinabant ad hospitandum inter religiosos solebat domus per adventum illorum promoveri et adiuvari: quia dabant eis terras vel redditus vel aliquid ut pro eis orarent eorumque memoriam haberent. Sed modo peius erit diu domui et grangiis illorum quando per illos transeunt. Et quid propter petitiones cariagii. Unde nuper quidam abbas requisitus de cariagio pro vectura versus bellum misit centum marcas anglicanas, quas refutaverunt nimis parum reputantes, et in confusibili reditu illorum abbas redimendo vexationem fugit, letus regis consilio dare ducentas marcas. Et quid propter illa que in grangiis et domibus eorum sine licentia accipiunt, pro quo sunt excommunicati per sententiam provincialem. Et in omnibus istis faciunt pauperes et ecclesiasticos habere eorum memoriam non ad orandum sed ad maledicendum. (B.2.44)

[20]   Statutes vol.I p.173: Anno 9° Edwardi II 1315-16.

[21]   ..viri enim religiosi quia volunt loca sua esse a servitutibus libera: ea fecerunt amortisare. (C.2.16)

[22]   An example from 7 March 1324 of such a transaction is this:
'Licence for the alienation in mortmain by John de Calverley to the abbot and convent of Kirkestall of the manor of Heddingleye, held in chief as of the honour of Pontefract, which is in the king's hands, although it appears by inquisition *ad quod damnum* made by Thomas de Burgh, king's clerk, escheator beyond Trent, that if the said John died leaving an heir under age the king would lose the custody of the said manor during the minority.
                                                  By fine of 10 marks.'
(CPR 1321-1324 p.396)

[23]   Fryde pp.125, 126. Bromyard comments on the agents of the rich 'who are skilled in giving tallies for food' (qui etiam sciant tallias pro cibo dare..) (A.23.16)

[24] McKisack p.203.

[25] At I.9.33 he quotes, approvingly, the Codex of Iustinianus against the use of torture on a *decurio* [a member of a city council] and continues: 'Si ergo non debet torqueri decurio..ergo a multo fortiori non debet torqueri cristianus..' (I.9.33)

[26] ..nobiles nostri et potentes hostes reipublice et latrones fortiter invadere et magnos delinquentes fortiter punire et torquere deberent: et pauperum vicinorum misereri. Sed heu contrarium accidit: nam bona pauperum vicinorum multis modis auferunt et illos nulla quandoque vel pro levi causa, utpote pro verbo displicentie verberant vel occidunt: et pro parvo forefacto amerciant et male tractant: et contra hostes apertos et regni inimicos et magnos et potentes malefactores ita vecordes sunt quod nec pro iusticie reipublice defensione audent invadere, capere spoliare vel ut meruerunt male tractare. Sane illi de ista vecordia reprehensi respondere possent...quia ipsi remorderent vel repercuterent. (P.8.6)

[27] ..isti qui convenienter lingua anglicana toun bithares*. i.pugnatores villarum appellari possunt, qui tantum ebrii superbe loquuntur et pugnant: qui in bello contra infideles, vel contra inimicorum exercitum per tres dies penuriam sustinentes ad nihilum valent ultra nisi ut ad propria redeant, vel remanentes ab hostibus conculcentur. (P.8.6)
        *so I read the compositor's *touubit hares*.

[28] Knight pp.216-217.

[29] Unde nuper exercitu anglie eunte cum tali superbia contra inimicos dixit quidam valens: quod magis videbantur ad nuptias quam ad bellum procedere. (B.2.24)

[30] This charge, of men attending parliament when they had drunk deep, Bromyard makes elsewhere in the *Summa*, at E.1.4, reinforced by a cross-reference to C.11.5. See notes 83 and 84.

[31] ..quod ubi nobiles sicut tyranni contra proximum et sicut mali christiani contra deum vivunt, per guerras, brigas et discordias, in terris suis pacis habeant turbationes mirum non est, immo mirum esset si pacem haberent: qui continue deum peccando et membra sua tyrannice vivendo expugnant. Mirabile insuper foret si in patrie et regni defensione essent validi qui super equos equitant male acquisitos: vel de bonis pauperum et ecclesie nutritos: qui illud de pauperibus et viris ecclesiasticis iniuste capiunt, unde arma sua emunt et deaurant et superflue se ornant, et unde equos emunt et nutriunt, et milites et stipendiarios conducunt.* Mirabile iterum foret si tales tyranni et spoliatores ab aliis tyrannis et spoliatoribus non essent in vita vel in morte spoliati, ut sicut acquisierunt ita perdant. Et sicut ad vanitatem arma sua fecerunt et deauraverunt: Ita de vanitate nuda et non de probitate gaudeant et laudentur ab his a quibus laudatur peccator in desideriis suis, ps ix. Nonne multi sic laudantur nobiles moderni temporis quis aliquem illorum laudare audivit vel laudare potuit de strennua inimicorum expugnatione et patrie et ecclesie defensione sicut commendantur et laudantur karolus magnus, Rolandus et Oliverus et alii antiqui milites: sed de hoc quod galeam habent deauratam precii. xl. librarum et alas et alia insignia exteriora eiusdem forme et maioris precii. Et quod hastiludio grossam et quadratam portavit lanceam qualem nullus alius portavit vel portare portuit, et quod equum et ascensorem proiecit in terram. Et quod ita bene equitavit et lanceam illam ita agiliter movit ac si levissima fuisset. Et quod cum tot equis venit ad perliamentum vel torneamentum. Et qualis est ista laus nisi laus impiorum et miserorum et timidorum, de qua Iob.xx. Laus impii brevis. Brevis namque est, quia tantum ad loca et tempora pacis et non belli se extendunt, et solum ad amicos et non ad hostes. Quid valent arma tunc deaurata que hostes audaciores faciunt, sicut patet. A.xxiiii.ii. Et que fugiendo hostibus leti proiiciunt ut velocius fugiant, sicut nuper accidit. Que laus est contra hominem pacis fortissimam portare lanceam, et equum et ascensorem ad terram deiicere, et hostem nec cum quacunque tangere lancea, quia nec ei tantum appropinquare voluit quod cum longissima illum tangere potuissent? Vel que laus est quod bene equitavit et faciliter lanceam movit et agiliter se habuit contra amicum et vicinum, et agiliter fugit inimicum regni? Vel que laus est quod in factis armorum prohibitis, sicut in torneamentis et huiusmodi, de quibus dictum est L.vi.ii et X.i.xvii. sint gloriosi et appetant laudari et in factis virtuosis, sicut in bellis iustis et in defensione patrie sint formidolosi et vecordes et fugitivi, et hostes sinant terram vastare spoliare, et predam auferre, et villas comburere et castra destruere et captivos abducere? In omnibus

ostendentes quoniam ve terre cuius rex puer est et cuius maiores qui terram defendere et regere haberent pueriliter vivunt. Et cuius principes mane comedunt antequam veniant ad consilium vel ad perliamentum, ut pransi et potati minus intelligant quid consulendum sit. Et quoniam a contrario sensu, beata terra cuius rex nobilis est et cuius principes vescuntur tempore suo, scilicet ad reficiendum et non ad luxuriam. Eccs.x. (N.3.15)

        *for *conducant* of the text.

32   'Indeed, we can truly say this of the lord king's officials, that from the lowest to the highest they all eagerly apply themselves to avarice; from the lord chief justice to the least petty judge no one rejects a bribe. Furthermore, although some may not demand or extort money, nevertheless none of them has refused what is offered.' (Vita p.157, in the translation of Wendy R. Childs, of the year 1318).

33   ..sicut falsi patrie ductores et duodenarii sunt causa tot latronum et etiam malefactorum per quos fideles frequenter inquietantur. Ita qui alios accusare deberent vel punire, et non faciunt, et qui reos purgant vel iuvant vel supportant sunt causa quare tot sunt peccatores propter quos deus totam communitatem pestilentiis pluvia et fame affligit.. (V.8.34)

34   Recto talis amicicia est inter tyrannos seu falsos acquisitores et duodecim periuros.. Ita quod unus faciat eum lucrari de patria sua et alius de sua in comitatibus et curiis, quorum unus vult habere equum. Alius vaccam. Alius terram aut pecuniam. (A.21.26)

35   In communitate seculari seu mundi latrones homicide et huiusmodi propter sanguinis nobilitatem vel propter munera a suspendio liberantur: duodecim enim latrones liberant coram iudice tredecimum. Ecce corda que deberet tangi non tangitur et hoc propter munerum perceptores. Et hec est causa quare tot sunt latrones et homicide, quia in terra ubi non est iusticia multiplicabuntur latrones et homicide. Sicut patet C.ii.xv. Et eadem est causa in communitate ecclesiastica quare tot sunt latrones dei, videlicet luxuriosi, adulteri et mali christiani: quia citharedi ecclesiastici eos non tangunt sicut deberent: sed accipiunt munera vel vident lupum et timent. (C.4.4)

36   Nonnulli vero..quando in visitationibus vel peccatorum inquisitionibus vel assisis vel duodenis onerantur in periculo animarum de veritate dicenda, ad quam dicendam iuramento astringuntur, dicunt quod non audent dicere veritatem ne verberentur vel occidantur vel ne domus illorum comburatur. (V.1.9)

37   Et cur ab iniquis appellati non veniunt ostensuri suam innocentiam adversariorumque maliciam convicturi. Dico quod dicere solent: nolumus vexari frustra in curia: fovent appellantes: melius esset domi sedere et talia deserere, iuri proprio cedere: ne longo et tanto itinere fatigarentur. (A.14.16)

38   Ita placitatores et patrie ductores et pauperum tortores pompis et minis pauperes et simplices terrent..dicendo: vende mihi talem terram vel tale negocium: quia esset mihi quietum: vel da mihi tantam pecuniam pro filia mea maritanda vel alia causa: vel male erit tibi: quia sic vel sic: vel talia fecisti: imponendo eis que nunquam fecerunt. (A.14.17)

39   Unde fertur de quodam advocato sapientissimo et in causis fortunatissimo: qui quasi semper triumphavit et vicit: post religiosus factus et ad huiusmodi causas domum* tangentes emissus semper succubuit. Cuius fortune causam cum ab eo quasi admirans quereret Respondit Cum essem secularis non habui conscienciam menciendi, cautelas fingendi, falsitates inveniendi. Et ideo semper per huiusmodi prevalui.. (A.14.22)

        *reading 'domum' for 'demum'.

40   Tarde accidit quod quidam[†] loqueretur cuidam pro amico digno satis suspendio: quem habuit in carcere: cui alius: non timeas: si veniret coram iudice cum sex bobus in manu sua: ego facerem quod liberaretur. (A.12.23)

        [†]reading 'quidam' for 'quidem'

41   ..in aula westmonasterii: tamquam caput et fontem totius falsitatis. Ibi enim lacerata est lex: et impius prevalet adversus iustum. (A.14.5)

42 Quia proverbium est: quod lingua causidica est damnifera: nisi funibus argenteis circumligetur. (A.14.21)

43 ..quia si ad curias mundi aliquid petituri accedentes dona aliquotiens premittunt ut citius quod petunt obtineant. In quibus sepius plus expendunt quam lucrentur.. (O.5.8)

44 Non est veritas non est misericordia non est scientia dei in terra..et specialiter ostenditur in curiis et placitis: in quibus potius ad dona respiciunt quam ad veritatem. (V.1.14, 15).
This is Bromyard's view of the pleaders too: a carpenter would turn down a commission to build if the materials didn't match the plan: but a lawyer will, for money, undertake any case, however unjust it be. Ibi enim nulla invenitur causa quantumcumque iniusta que non inveniet advocatum vel adiutorem qui velit eam pro salario defendere et promovere.. (A.14.22)

45 Facta est contradictio legistarum et advocatorum potentior quam veritas. Quia si potens et iniustus habeat ibi causam adversus simplicem et innocentem quantumcunque iniustam ipse cum pecunia sua habebit omnes advocatos in curia vocabulo christianitatis vel omnes sergantes in curia regis intantum quod pauper et veritas in nundinis illis nullum venalem invenient vel omnes ex alia parte conducuntur vel quia dicunt quia non audent timore partis. (A.14.21)

46 Ita mundi sapientes pecuniam aliquociens accipiunt ut taceant: quia forte conduci non possunt ut contra aliam partem loquantur. Unde cum quidam iactaret se multa pro una advocatione recepisse: Alius respondit ego plus accepi ut taceam. (A.14.13)

47 ..leges et statuta et facta illorum comparantur telis aranearum: que muscas et non animalia magna capiunt. (I.9.21)

48 Et sicut in terra ubi non est timor nec iusticia multiplicabuntur latrones et homicide*.. (C.2.14)
*The compositor's [†]homicidie[†] could be read as 'homicidia' too.

49 Iterum pax in ista cithara impeditur ex hoc, quod una corda plus stringitur et durius tangitur quam deberet. Verbi gracia, unus pauper modicum delinquens in curia mundi graviter et ultra iusticiam amerciabitur. Et sic corda parva nimis dure tangitur, pax etiam melodie rumpitur. Quia inde odia et maledictiones generantur. Magnus faciet maius delictum et non amerciabitur. Iterum pauperes et mediocres taxantur: et maiores dimittuntur. Ecce corde quedam nimis trahuntur quedam nimis laxantur. Et talis communitas non erit pacifica nec durabilis. Quia secundum Augustinum de ci.dei.li.ii.c.xxi. Iniusticia maxime destruxit civitatem. De illis vero malis citharedis qui sic cordas non situando et non tangendo vel inordinate tangendo civitatem tam mundi quam ecclesie dissipant. (C.4.5)

50 Sed non excusantur: quia tales diligunt..sic senescallos et ballivos et consilarios: qui sciant pro offensa sex denariorum reportare quinque solidos. (A.12.43)
The stewards, bailiffs and counsellors are the agents of unscrupulous lords, characterized earlier in these terms: 'This saying, 'We have the law' is [the remark] of tyrants who declare 'We gained that by our sword and the law of war: whatever we have ridden over will be ours.' ' (..hec vox nos legem habemus tyrannorum est dicentium: lucrati sumus illud gladio nostro et lege belli et quicquid equitavimus: nostrum erit..) (A.12.40)

51 Sic iuvenes scolares in iure civili vel in banco primo vel secundo anno de scola redeuntes sunt omnibus graciosi, sociales, curiose ornati. Ab omnibus benedicuntur.. Sed cum sciverit modicum placitare et nocere vicinis suis et esse attorniatus et advocatus et huiusmodi accipit propinas a magnatibus sic de eorum consilio aliis preponitur, fit senescallus balivus.. (A.14.19)
The initial 'sic' links the youthful scholars to the nature of monkeys explored in the preceding lines: sociable and pleasant in youth, spiteful and hurtful in old age.

52 Dico quod amor diviciarum est causa quare advocati leges et cautelas addiscunt. Vident enim quod advocati causarum terrenarum care conducuntur ubi advocati animarum contemnuntur. Et ubi ipsi reportant quadraginta solidos isti non reportant quadraginta obulos. Et quod illi equitant bonos equos et bene vestiuntur: Accipiunt munera a multis: et cito promoventur, acquirant terras

edificant pulchra maneria: ubi alii peditant et sunt miseri quantum ad mundum. Et cogitant quam felices et fortunati essent qui talem statum attingere possent. Et hec causa est quare tanta multitudo et quasi omnes volunt leges audire lucrativas, quare parentes et amici filios et nepotes suos ad legum mittunt audienciam. Quare scola legistarum habet centum vel ducentos auditores: ubi scola theologorum non habet forte quinque. (A.14.30)

53   Maitland p.132. He goes on to qualify this interpretation.

54   ..domini cupiditatem ore detestantur: sed tamen cupidos diligunt ministros: qui multum sciunt procurare: et modicum reddere, qui etiam sciant tallias pro cibo dare: et graves emendas levare. Et sic domini tales sunt divites de alieno et essent pauperes si quilibet haberet suum. (A.23.16)

55   Utinam ita diligenter scrutarentur quo iure ipsi tenent que a falsis antecessoribus vel ab acquisitione propria possident: quod si facerent vel totum vel magnam partem invenirent se contra rationem et dei iura tenere. (C.16.42)

56   Oman pp.156-168, and Plates XVII and XVIII.

57   This rather daring play on infirmities being healed by the power of the cross on the silver pennies of Edward I and Edward II is keyed to the identical texts in Matthew and Luke which give Jesus' reply to the two disciples of John the Baptist. From his mountain prison of Makhairous (Josephus, Antiquities XVIII.119) he had sent the disciples across the Jordan to ask Jesus 'Art thou the one who is to come?' Jesus' reply was brief and memorable: 'The blind see, the lame walk, lepers are cleansed, the deaf hear, the dead come to life, the poor hear the gospel..' (Matthew 11.5, Luke 7.22).

58   The 'signati..cruce' is an example of Bromyard's play on words. It plays against the common meaning, applied to men who have taken the cross to go on crusade and who wear a red cross on their tunics. In such a sense it was used by Bromyard ('cruce signatorum') in the *exemplum* he quotes at C.17.7 taken from Iacobus de Vitriaco (see chapter 8 footnote 7).

59   Jesus' healing is recorded at Luke 17.12-14: Elisha's at 2 Kings 5.14 (IV Regum 5.14).

60   Was the ingesting of (dissolved) gold considered a cure, or at least a palliative, in Bromyard's day? Iohannes de Gaddesden [d. before 1349] 'prescribed gold daily for rich patients with *lepra*, considering it 'the best medicine.' ' (Rawcliffe p.224 note 104). She adds that potable gold was recommended as a supplement to be taken with theriac for the treatment of all four types of leprosy.

61   Acts 8.9-24.

62   ..tamen nonnulli plus confidunt in cruce divitum et malorum argentea: in qua deus illorum crucifixus est scilicet argentum et iste deus cum cruce sua argentea multo plura falsa miracula facit quam deus verus cum cruce sua faciat vera, quia per crucem christi et domini nostri aliqui claudi et contracti leguntur rectificati: sed non omnes: hec autem in curiis falsorum omnes causas rectificat, quantumcunque sint tortuose et curve. Et si in copia et reverentia ut debet habeatur omnes claudos et incarceratos ire et abire facit: et surdos iudices et dominos et in potestate positos qui quantumcunque iniustam causam habeas surdam prebent aurem audire facit. Et sic surdi audiunt. Mutos etiam advocatos loqui facit. Et sic muti loquuntur et ceci vident. Verbi gratia. Veniet filius matris sue ad duodecim iuratos vel ad alios quibus interest: iusticiam suam quam habet ad rem quam petit ostendens: nihil tamen dans, cui dicent non video quod iusticiam habeas in re ista seu petitione: sed tali iniuriam facis qui iusticiam habet ad rem illam, signati vero postmodum ista cruce, vel ad minus unus illorum, videlicet ductor patrie inveteratus dierum malorum qui scit narrare tempora antiquorum regum quomodo talis fuit feoffeffatus: et talis accepit similia. Talis plus videt et socios videre facit plus iusticie quam deberent, imo ubi omnino est iniusticia eius iusticiam se videre dicunt: et econverso, sicut patet I.x.vi. Et sic ceci vident. Verus deus etiam decem leprosos et Heliseus unum sanasse leguntur. Iste deus cum cruce sua in curiis et officiis et ubi falsi dominantur omnes leprosos mundat et sic leprosi mundantur non per aurum comestum sed per aurum datum, quia peccatores iusti et mundi reputantur et mortui resurgunt quia morte

digni abire permittuntur. Et pauperes evangelisantur, quia indigni in moribus et scientia pro muneribus promoventur. Et sic sicut miracula que Petrus vere fecit Symon magus fecit ficte. Ita omnia mirarcula que christus vel crux eius fecit hec crux cum deo suo denario facit false.. (C.17.36, 37)

63   e.g. at A.23.15, A.24.1, A.26.35, D.11.3, L.6.2 and N.3.15.

64   Ex concilio lateranensi. Felicis memorie innocentii et eugenii predecessorum nostrorum vestigiis inherentes detestabiles illas nundinas vel ferias quas vulgo torneamenta vocant in quibus milites ex condicto convenire solent: et ad ostentationem virium suarum et audacie temere congredi: unde mortes hominum et animarum pericula sepe proveniunt: fieri prohibemus. Quod si quis eorum ibi mortuus fuerit quamvis ei poscenti penitentia non negetur ecclesiastica tamen careat sepultura. (Decretales 5.13.1, De torneamentis: Lateran II canon 14 (COD p.176)).

65   Non negetur. nec etiam viaticum. xxvi.q.vi. si quis de corpore. l. di. penitentes. quia et per penitentiam viaticum intelligitur: quod decedentibus penitentibus non negatur..

66   ..Sane felicis recordationis Clemens papa quintus praedecessor noster attente considerans generale passagium in concilio Viennensi pro terrae sanctae subsidio salubriter ordinatum per torneamenta et hastiludia sive iuxtas non leviter impediri tum quia frequenter sic ipsum passagii negocium prosecuturos exinaniunt quod ad eius executionem efficiuntur impotentes tum quia interdum quamplures a crucis assumptione retrahunt dum ab illis abstinere (aliis ea exercentibus) erubescunt: torneamenta ipsa et hastiludia sive iuxtas in regnis Franciae, Angliae et Almaniae et aliis nonnullis provinciis in quibus ea consuevere frequentius exerceri specialiter interdixit: in facientium ea vel in eis praestantium opem, consilium vel consensum et illorum etiam in quorum locis vel districtibus fierent non prohibentium hoc cum possent et illorum procedentes ad illa in domibus suis recipientium vel commercium quomodolibet exercentium cum eisdem [in]* personas excommunicationis et in terras interdicti sententias promulgando, absolutione ab excommunicatione huiusmodi praeterquam in mortis articulo sedi apostolicae reservata. Verum quoniam (ut intelleximus) per sententiam huiusmodi periculum animabus ingeritur et pro eo maxime negocio dicti passagii derogatur: quia nonnulli militari cingulo abstinent, et quia vacare militiae metu praesertim ipsius sententiae non praesumunt, propter quod idoneos et voluntarios ad terrae praedictae subsidium in regnis eisdem contingit pauciores solito reperiri Nos...revocamus eos qui propter exercitium torneamentorum seu hastiludiorum ipsorum huiusmodi sententias incurrerunt, absolventes ab illis et cum eis qui sic ligati vel in locis propterea interdictis divina celebrarunt officia, super irregularitate inde contracta auctoritate apostolica dispensantes. Datum Lugduni xvi. Kalend. Octobris Anno primo. (Extravagantes Iohannis XXII Tit.IX cap.I in Corpus Iuris Canonici p.839).
      *My insertion

67   One such is recorded partly for the fact of the collapse of a wooden contraption built like an upper room. Edward III's queen Philippa and other ladies of the court were present. Some spectators were injured (..dominus rex habuit hastiludium..in vico qui le Chepe [vocatur?] ubi quaedam machina lignea, in modum solarii facta, pro regina et aliis regni dominabus, corruit et laesit plurimos in cadendo.) The year was 1331. (Bridlington p.102).

68   Haines, Edward II p.362 note 74.

69   Monarchs jealously guarded their right to license tournaments. So Edward II instructed the sheriff of Leicester, in a letter of 7 June 1320, to arrest and imprison anyone who dared to take part in a planned and unlicensed tournament 'this coming Monday' and to give him names of anyone so offending. (Foedera vol.II part I p.426).

70   Barker, J. and Luttrell Psalter 82 recto. The representations of the riders' posture are conventional, bearing little relation to reality. To avoid being unseated by the terrific forces felt on impact the rider had to lean forward, holding his lance, his legs straight. The force of the collision was then transferred from his shoulder to his buttocks – which were firmly planted against the cantle of his saddle – and to his stirrups, and thus to his horse. The high cantle enclosing the riders' hips is clearly depicted in the three saddles seen in the Luttrell Psalter at 82 recto and 83 verso.

71   Murimuth p.223.

72   Barker, J., pp.51, 52.

73   ..non solum maledictiones merentur simplicium, quorum blada cum avibus et canibus equitando destruunt.. (N.3.16)

74   Non enim est rationi conformis ludus in quo unus letatur et alius tristatur: in quo dives cum canibus et avibus venatur et leporem vel avem capit, et pauperis prosternit blada: qui de preda illa non participat: in quo divitum torneamentum est pauperum tormentum.. (L.6.3)

75   Matthew 26.69-73. Bromyard changes 'loquela' to 'lingua'. IIis 'tu borialis es: tu australis..' accords with Higden's statement that there existed a greater linguistic variation between northerners and southerners than between easterners and westerners.
        '..orientales cum occiduis tanquam sub eodem coeli climate lineati plus consonant in sermone quam boreales cum austrinis.' (Higden vol.II p.160), Higden goes on to report that southerners could barely understand northern speech: 'Tota lingua Northimbrorum, maxime in Eboraco, ita stridet incondita, quod nos australes eam vix intelligere possumus..' (ibid. p.162).

76   Mali vero cives videlicet civitatis dyaboli alios ab eis dividunt ratione patrie gentis vel lingue, iram et commotionem contra eos habentes et provocantes quia de alia parte terre sunt dicentes tu borialis es: tu australis vel talis nationis es: ad modum illius maledicte ancille hostiarie: que ad Petrum exclamavit dicens: tu galileus es, nam et lingua etc., et ad modum illorum maledictorum iudeorum. Iudicum.xii. qui iugulabant omnem qui nescivit dicere seboleth… Ex quo predicator dei egregius ita sollicitus fuit omnes vocare ad unitatem cuiuscunque plage vel terre essent.. (C.4.25, 26)

77   ..ab illis crudeliter accipiunt qui vix habent panem fabarum et aquam in copia nec per dimidium annum semel bene comedunt sed sunt in continuis laboribus.. (A.12.31)

78   ..quomodo cum ratione stare vel concordare posset quod unus in labore et sudore magno die ac nocte parcum acquirat victum, et alius qui ociosam et lascivam et delicatam vitam ducit, usque ad tertiam in lecto lasciviendo pro libitu suo illum victum auferat: quod unus voluptuose vivat et alius qui est ad imaginem dei et servit deo vix miserabiliter vivat..? (R.1.20)

79   Marsiglio of Padua (c.1275-1342) completed his *Defensor Pacis* in 1324. He had to take refuge with the emperor Ludwig of Bavaria: and in 1327 Iohannes XXII condemned five propositions, excommunicating him. The work's main points are:
    i   the Church must be completely subordinated to the State:
    ii   the State derives its authority from the people, who retain the right to depose the emperor:
    iii   the church has neither spiritual nor temporal inherent jurisdiction:
    iv   her hierarchy is of purely human, not divine, institution:
    v   S.Peter was never given the primacy:
    vi   the papacy owes its prerogatives chiefly to the Donation of Constantinus I:
    vii   the principal authority in all ecclesiastical matters is the General Council, which should be composed of both priests and laymen.
(ODCC[1] pp.862-863). Bromyard would have rejected every single assertion. Salvatorelli concludes:'It maintained..that the sole means of re-establishing peace in the world consisted of subordinating ecclesiastical authority to secular. The legislative and judicial power of the Church, for Marsiglio, lay originally in the hands of the people.. As regards the pontiffs, they could not lay claim to having received from Christ a supreme power over the Church since he had not constituted any clear head of the Church and Peter had held no greater authority than the other apostles, nor was it made evident that he had come to Rome. The papal primacy was a matter simply of opportunity, deriving from the community of the faithful and from the emperor with no implications beyond the right of convening and directing the ecumenical councils. Papal decrees had no binding force..it was not up to the pontiff to control the appointment of the emperor nor to require oaths of him nor to depose him nor to govern the empire during a vacancy; instead, the emperor could depose the pope.'

[Vi si sosteneva..che l'unico mezzo di ristabilire la pace nel mondo consisteva nel subordinare l'autorità ecclesiastica alla secolare. Il potere legislativo e giudiziario della Chiesa per Marsilio era originariamente nel popolo.. In quanto ai pontefici, essi non potevano pretendere di aver avuto da Cristo un potere supremo sulla Chiesa, perché egli non aveva costituito nessun capo visibile della Chiesa e Pietro non aveva avuto nessuna maggiore autorità degli altri apostoli né era dimostrato che fosse venuto a Roma. Il primato ponteficio era cosa puramente di opportunità derivante dalla comunità dei fedeli e dall' imperatore e non implicava se non il diritto di convocare e dirigere i concilii ecumenici. I decreti papali non avevano valore obbligatorio.. e al pontefice non spettava controllare la nomina dell' imperatore né richiedergli giuramenti né governare l'impero vacante; l'imperatore invece può deporre il papa.] (Salvatorelli p.799).

80   His *De Monarchia* (1312-1314?) was condemned as Averroist and heretical in 1329 (when Dante had been 8 years dead). It 'argued the need for a universal monarchy to achieve the temporal happiness of mankind and the independence of the Empire from the Pope and the Church, which should abandon all temporal authority and possessions and concentrate on happiness in the world to come.' (ODCC[3] p.450).

81   ..est advertendum quod antiquitus respublice bene regebantur: quia non sanguine nec genere nobiliori: sed a sensu et digniore regebantur, quando ad regimen aptiores eligebantur et non nobiliores. (R.4.10)

82   Sed nunc ad regimen reipublice tam in ecclesia in regimine animarum quam in regimine corporum iuvenes ignorantes causa sanguinis vel propinquitatis vel nobilitatis preponuntur..et ideo non regnant sed errant. (R.4.10)
      Bromyard's judgement supports that of the author of the 'Vita'. Of the year 1320 he writes (in Childs' translation): 'Men completely ignorant of Holy Scripture usurp the burden of an office they cannot uphold, drawing on other people's knowledge rather than their own.. It is indeed not honour but greed which promotes such a man, not morality but venality, not knowledge but money, not merit but a bribe, not free choice but soliciting votes [ambicio]..' (Vita p.181).

83   Si vero omnes consiliarii sint boni, consiliatus tamen secundum eorum consilia operari nec regi vult. Oculos quidem bonos habet. Sed podogram patitur atque cirogram, et ista infirmitas communiter sequitur parlamenta moderna: ubi multa dantur consilia: sed nulla fit in opere executio. Ideo merito vocatum est nomen eius parlamentum, quia ibi multa loquuntur: sed in toto vel magna parte est postmodum mentitum quod ibi fuit locutum et ordinatum. Cuius ratio in parte patet. E.i.iiii. Nota F.i.xliiii. Et O.vi.lxxi. optime. Et N.i.xxx. (C.11.4, 5)
      Knights of the shire had been summoned for the first time (joining the lords temporal and spiritual) in 1254: burgesses, representing towns, in 1264. Of eight parliaments held from 1300 to 1307 knights and burgesses were present at six. (Saul p.201).

84   ..multa facit [sc. ebrietas] hominem promittere dum ebrius est: que sobrius revocat... Sicut illi qui parlamenta et consilia et iudicia sua tenent: postquam sunt vino calefacti: quia vinum in eis dominatur plusquam ratio. De quibus C.xi.v. (E.1.4)

85   ..omnia imperia et regna et imperatores et reges legibus, et non ab usu vel propria voluntate deberent gubernari. (X.1.9)

86   Amo inquit iusticiam. Quid sunt magna regna nisi magna latrocinia? (D.12.33) This is another instance of Bromyard's quoting from memory: the received text has 'Remota itaque iustitia quid sunt magna regna nisi magna latrocinia?'

87   Digna vox est maiestate Regnantis legibus alligatum* se principem profiteri.. (Codex 1.14.4)
            *correcting 'alligatis'.

88   '..non solum maledictiones merentur simplicium, quorum blada cum avibus et canibus equitando destruunt, sed pro quibus etiam excommunicationem timere poterunt maiorem in nova charta latam. In qua continentur: quod wardam cum disperagio maritare non debent: quod tutelam eis commissam fideliter administrabunt: quod res pupillorum perire non permittant: sed in domibus et aliis in eodem statu in quo illa receperunt cum ad etatem venerint: eis integre restituere teneantur.

Que quia non tenuerunt, et propter alia facta sua que contra deum et rationem fecerunt *nobiles* eius qui iam mortui sunt *in terram corruerunt**, scilicet *novissimam.* Ezech.xxvi.' (N.3.16)

   *Ezechiel 26.11 has 'et statuae tuae nobiles in terram corruent': translated from
   the Hebrew by NEB as 'and your strong pillars will fall to the ground.' Bromyard
   seems to have interpreted 'nobiles' as a noun in apposition to 'statuae tuae.'

[89] McKechnie p.158.

[90] Powicke p.697.

[91] Thompson pp.98, 99.

[92] ibid. p.116.

[93] McKecknie p.158.

[94] ibid. p.500.

[95] ..quotidiana docet experientia, quia si alio tempore veniat pauper vel peregrinus ad domum talis elemosynam petiturus: Respondebit firmarius vel balivus dicens: dominus meus non est in domo. Ecce non est vir in domo eius. Cui pauper: et ubi est dominus tuus? Cui ille: In curia regis, vel alterius principis vel prelati vel oxonie vel parisius vel bononie… Sic isti qui tantum illo apparent tempore et vestibus splendent curiosis et ad modum stelle comate cum longa barba et capillatura… (O.6.22, 23)

[96] Jordan p.22.

[97] The previous observation of a comet recorded in the Chinese records was in April 1313: the next was in June 1337. (Williams pp.68, 69).

[98] Prohibeat [sc. legislator] etiam inquit [sc. Avicenna] quod non sit in civitate luctator vel aleator, prohibeat etiam studia et opera contraria utilitatibus civitatis sicut furtum rapinam fornicationem. Si talia statuta ordinaverunt in civitatibus suis saraceni: quanto magis christiani. Sed heu quasi omnia statuta modo sunt potius ad cupiditatem quam ad utilitatem et ad civitatis destructionem. Sicut patet modo quasi in omnibus civitatibus maritimis ubi mercatores extranei cum navibus venientes non possunt ad libitum vendere popularibus et omnibus sed coacti per maledicta statuta vendere aliquibus magnis de civitate qui illud aliis vendent sicut placet. Et istud depauperat civitatem propter duo. Primo quia mercatores pauciores et quasi inviti ad tales veniunt civitates intantum quod ubi solebant in aliquibus civitatibus venire viginti naves vix veniunt modo quinque. Secundo quia avantagium mercatorum veniencium non erit totius civitatis que inde avantagium haberet si libere in bono foro emere possent, sed illorum primo ementium, quia carius vendunt popularibus quam facerent principales mercatores. (C.4.12)

[99] The Statute concerning Bakers, Etc. (Statutes vol.I pp.203-204) is of uncertain date, but has been attributed to 51 Henry III and to 13 Edward I (1285). 'But especially be it commanded..that no Forestaller be suffered to dwell in any Town which is an open Oppressor of Poor People..which for Greediness of his private Gain doth prevent others in buying Grain, Fish, Herring..oppressing the Poor, and deceiving the Rich, [which carrieth away such Things, intending to sell them more dear]..' (..qui…multo carius vendere machinatur; qui mercatores extraneos cum rebus venalibus venientes circumvenit..)

Bromyard's observation about the reduction in the volume of shipping is given credence in the eleventh head of the Ordinances of 1311: 'Also, new Customs have been levied, and the old enhanced, as upon Wools, Cloths, Wines, Avoir de pois, and other Things, whereby the Merchants come more seldom, and bring fewer Goods into the Land..by which..things become more dear than they were wont to be.. We do ordain, that all manner of Customs and Imposts levied since the Coronation of King Edward, Son of King Henry, be entirely put out, and altogether extinguished for ever..' (Statutes vol.I p.159). The Ordinances as a whole were invalidated in 1322 (McKisack p.103). The persistence of forestalling, with its deleterious effects on the economy, is rehearsed in the first statute of the York parliament of 26 May 1335. 'Whereas before this time in many

Parliaments and now at this present Parliament..it was shewed to our said Lord the King, by the Knights of the Shires, Citizens of the Cities, and Burgesses of the Boroughs..that in divers Cities, Boroughs, and other places of his Realm, great Duress and grievous Damage have been done to him and his People by some people..which in long time past have not suffered, nor yet will suffer Merchant Strangers, nor other, which do carry and bring in by Sea or Land, Wines [Aver de pois,] and other Livings and Victuals, with divers other Things to be sold..other than to themselves..by reason whereof such stuff aforesaid is sold to the King and to his People..more dear than they should be..' Edward III is asked 'to provide Remedy..' (Statutes vol.I pp.269-270).

[100] The studies published by Ian Kershaw in 1973 ('The Great Famine and Agrarian Crisis in England 1315-1322') and by William C. Jordan in 1996 ('The Great Famine: Northern Europe in the Early Fourteenth Century') laid bare with a wealth of detail the unprecedented and devastating impact which the sustained and extraordinary bad weather had on the lives of the populations of England and of Northern Europe within the decade 1310-1320. Jordan observes (p.17): 'For reports of a continuous series of exceptionally cold winters there was nothing like the period 1310-1330..the years 1310-1320 appear to be the second worst period for severe, sustained summer downpours for the Middle Ages as a whole.' Of England Kershaw writes (pp.88-97) '..the harvest of 1314, only garnered with difficulty because of the wet conditions, was proving deficient and grain prices rose sharply in the summer months of 1315.. The harvest of 1315 was a disaster. Chroniclers and manorial records concur in attributing the trouble to the torrential rain which poured down throughout the summer months of 1315, producing widespread flooding and the ruin of hay and corn crops alike.' This inevitably led for corn to an 'even steeper rise in prices which during the spring and summer of 1316 reached unprecedented heights.' Livestock too was, naturally, adversely affected: Kershaw quotes the *Annales Londonienses* for February 1316: 'they ordained that the ordinance regarding livestock, fowl and eggs (*de bestiis et avibus et ovis*) should not stand because few were found on account of the dearth and lack of victuals.' The 'famine was accompanied, during the course of 1316, by a virulent and widespread epidemic of an enteric type – perhaps typhoid – which greatly increased mortalities. The epidemic spread across social boundaries, for it affected the aristocracy as well as the poor...the summer of 1316 brought renewed downpours of rain and a harvest worse, if anything, than that of the previous year.'

[101] Jordan p.18. This is confirmed by a source not cited by Jordan or by Kershaw, the chronicle of S.Mary's Abbey York. 'Eodem anno [1314] per Angliam periit maxima pars bladi et aliorum fructuum tempore colleccionis continuantibus pluviis et tempestatibus fere a mense Julii usque ad festum Sancti Michaelis Archangeli.' (S.Mary's p.65). (In the same year [1314] throughout England there perished the greatest part of the corn crop and of other produce at harvest-time as the rains and storms continued roughly from the month of July right up to the feast of S.Michael the Archangel [29 September.])

[102] Haines, Edward II p.97.

[103] Vita p.111 in Childs' translation.

[104] Bridlington p.48.

[105] Kershaw pp.96, 97.

[106] ..in caristia que nuper modernis precessit temporibus cum multa haberet blada et omnibus bladis in aliis grangiis illius ville deficientibus mures in maxima multitudine ad eius confluerunt grangiam: balivus suus ad eum venit dicens: melius est ut frumenta tua vendas propter tria. Primo quod iam valde charum est: summa enim venditur pro. xx. solidis. Secundo quod pauperes vicini fame moriuntur et possumus vendere et mutuare sub pignore ut vivant. Tertio quia comeduntur a muribus. (M.9.25).

[107] ..quia si iste pluvie mundum destruentes essent ex naturali causa minus caderent in estate quam in hyeme.. (T.5.1)

[108] Quod ergo mirabile si modo sit pluviarum tempestas quando maior est luxurie corruptio et malicie cogitatio quam in diebus Noe: quia mille falsitates et novitates et modi peccandi sunt modo inventi

qui tunc non erant. Quod mirabile si fames populum affligat quando maior est dominorum crudelitas..quam in diebus Saulis. Cum ergo preteritorum exhibitio sit futurorum certitudo patet quod illi planete qui tunc regnabant, nunc regnant et ista que patimur causant. (T.5.3)

109   Quod ergo mirum est si modernis temporibus deus animalia occidat propter nostra peccata et possessiones, et blada pluvia destruat tempestatibus. (T.5.5)

110   Quod ergo mirum si modernis temporibus infantes et pueri innocentes propter maiora peccata fame moriantur et nimiis pluviis submergantur, et propter malos in bello vincantur, et propter dei fugitivos peccatores in omnibus male prosperentur et tribulatione patiantur. (T.5.5)

111   Ita simplices et mediocres fideles virga famis et tribulationis hic frequenter verberantur. Sed divites et pessimi quos famis [sic] et tribulatio non attingit ducunt in bonis dies suos: sed finaliter tanquam proditores ad inferni patibulum descendunt. (T.5.9). The Benedictine chronicler of St Mary's Abbey York had a different experience to record.
         'In the year of the Lord 1316: the greatest dearth of corn in England with the result that on account of the starvation there came about an unmeasured human death-rate, *both of the wealthy and the poor.*' (Anno domini mᵒcccᵒxvi Maxima caristia bladum in Anglia ita quod pre Inedia immensa mortalitas hominum euenit, tam divitum quam pauperum.) (St Mary's p.69).

112   Statu etiam proprio intantum abutuntur quod vix est aliquis de statu suo contentus, vel quantum ad acquisitionem, sicut ostensum est. A.xxvii.v. Vel quantum ad victum vel vestitum quia clerici in habitu et tonsura excepto quod forte pannus est unius coloris vadunt sicut armigeri, prelati sicut milites, uxores civium vel armigerum sicut militum vel regum.. (T.5.18)

113   Iste ergo predicte novitates et rerum abusus et falsitates novas causant tempestates: isti sunt planete qui tempestatibus et pluviis et bellis illos novitatum inventores et alios ratione societatis torquent. Quod enim mirabile est vel quam iusticiam facit deus si illos qui omnibus creaturis corporalibus etiam et animabus propriis abutuntur et cum illis contra deum militant eumque suis expugnant donis omnibus affligat... Ita estas convertatur eis in hyemem et econverso. Tempus pacis hac de causa in tempus convertatur bellorum. Terra etiam predicta de causa convertatur in sterilitatem. Animalia in mortalitatem quam temporibus istis specialiter vidimus de bobus maiorem quam antea factam audierimus vel legerimus.. (T.5.19)

114   ..mediocres totam causam imponunt magnatibus et divitibus dicentes Ipsi sunt ita crudeles, ita duri domini quod propter eos deus terram destruet: Illi vero econverso istis causam imponunt dicentes: subditi nostri sunt ita falsi..ita dedignantes et superbi quod servire vel operari nolunt: ita quod propter eos deus terram destruit. (T.5.20)

115   ..dum religiosi et pauci forte pauperes de populo et mediocres ad processionem pro aeris intemperie faciendam et missas et letanias cantandum, et sermonem dei audiendum congregantur: Illi qui illius tempestatis causa sunt lascive in lectis vel gulose in tabernis aut circa alia mundialia morantur nec ad processionem veniunt nec orant..sed potius de fame gaudent futura, quia blada et alia ex antiquo congregata venalia charius vendent et terras et aliorum bona fame afflictorum quasi pro nihilo ement.. (T.5.21)

116   ..quandoque maiores in civitate vel castro qui dominum suum de castro eiecerunt sunt causa quare civitas est rege de castro suo eiecto obsessa: minores tamen in civitate, qui nunquam sunt obsidionis causa, dum obsidentur plus famis sustinent illis qui deum quem in baptismo et quadragesima receperunt in castris animarum suaram et eum postea turpiter eiecerunt, deus istos obsidet pestilentiis: quot enim grandines aut pluvias cadere videmus vel alias adversitates, tot insultus ad castra facit ut castrum ei reddatur.. (T.5.22)

117   Et hoc iustum videtur et pluvia vindictarum cesset per pluvias lachrymarum. (T.5.40)

118   Recte ergo per aquas pluviales imo vindicatrices eum ad rectitudinem restringit. (T.5.44)

119   Nostra vero [sc. vindicta] est nimis pluvia que turpior et ponderosior et tristior est pro cordibus humanis Et sicut illi iverunt ad alias civitates pro aqua ita nos ad alia regna pro frumento. (T.5.52)

[120] ..dici potest de multis..quod non revertuntur ad deum peccata priora deserendo, sed plus a deo avertuntur et elongantur peccata augmentando, quia dum omni genere plagarum gladio fame et mortalitate et omne genus hominum his tribus plagis percusserit, quia maiores in diversis brigis intrinsecis et discidionibus inter se et bellis extrinsecis, pauperes mendicantes fame, quia multa milia ex illis fame interemit: Mediocres mortalitate et quantum ad seipsos et quantum ad animalia etc. (T.5.52)

[121] ..votum enim solenne in baptismo factum frangimus et promissa non tenemus sed testes falsificamus et ideo aquis et inundationibus iterum nos baptizat: semina et prata et sata submergendo. (T.5.61)
Bromyard concludes this grim capitulum with a quotation from 2 Maccabees 1.7. The whole verse (with Bromyard's selection italicized) reads
regnante Demetrio anno centesimo sexagesimo nono nos Iudaei *scripsimus vobis in tribulatione et impetu qui supervenit nobis in istis annis* ex quo recessit Iason a sancta terra et a regno. (T.5.73)

[122] Sicut nonnulli..dicunt quod nunquam ita mala tempora nec tot fuerunt tempestates sicut postquam viri religiosi et orantes tantum pro mundo per mundum multiplicabantur. (O.5.30)

[123] ..sicut falsi patrie ductores et duodenarii sunt causa tot latronum et etiam malefactorum per quos fideles frequenter inquietantur: ita qui alios accusare et punire, et non faciunt: et qui reos purgant vel iuvant vel supportant sunt causa quare tot sunt peccatores: propter quos deus totam communitatem pestilentiis pluvia et fame affligit.. (V.8.24)

[124] Demetrios II (145-138 BC). See Bartlett p.221.

[125] I Kings 16.31. As if it were not enough for him to follow the sinful ways of Jeroboam son of Nebat, he contracted a marriage with Jezebel daughter of Ethbaal king of Sidon, and went and worshipped Baal; he prostrated himself before him.. (NEB I Kings 16.31). The Vulgate is: 'Nec suffecit ei ut ambularet in peccatis Hieroboam filii Nabath insuper duxit uxorem Hiezabel filiam Ethbaal regis Sidoniorum et abiit et servivit Baal et adoravit eum..' (III Regum 16.31).

[126] The rules of movement of chess pieces instanced by Bromyard are the same as today's. His 'oblique' (diagonally) might be read as a hint that the queen's moves were slightly underhand.

[127] The shift from 'mariti sui' to 'dominum suum' occurs here: Bromyard's device for marking Isabella's change of allegiance from Edward II to Mortimer.

[128] McKisack p.97 note 1 writes of Isabella's rapacity.

[129] Isabella herself, in her letter of 1325 to Edward as given in the 'Vita' (p.242), uses two of the key words from Apocalypse 18 ('widow' and 'grief'): 'uiduitatis' and 'luctus'.

[130] Secundo sicut in ludo scacarii regina semper capit oblique. Ita crudelis domina, Ad cuius intellectum advertendum est quod sicut non invenitur quis maioris misericordie et compassionis quam mulier bona et plena misercordia quia talis semper afflictis compatitur et animum mariti sui et ministrorum ad pietatem flectere nititur.. Ita non est bestia crudelior ipsa mala: que sicut inter latrones ipsis dicitur esse crudelior ipsos ad crudelitatem et homicidia excitando ubi sine ipsa tantum spoliarent: Ita etiam talis dominum suum et familiam ad crudelitatem excitat maiorem persuadendo et peiora procurando: quia si dominus vult exteriora rapere ipsa vult vitam auferre, sicut patet. iii. Regum. xxi. de Achab et Iezabel uxore sua. Ipse Achab voluit vineam et ipsa procuravit mortem Naboth. Et illud idem vidi temporibus meis fieri. Item si dominus dicit verberetis vel incarceretis ipsa dicit occidatur, sicut patet Luce. iii. ubi Herodias procuravit mortem Iohannis baptiste quem Herodes solum incarceravit. Nec sic tantum tractus obliquos habent: sed etiam oblique et iniuriose munera pro superbia sua nutrienda capiunt et tallias seu collectas graves levant: quia si dominus de patria capiat graves emendas: illa residuum capiendo nudos dimittit: quia ipsi auferenti pallium ipsa aufert tunicam. Quod in hoc ostenditur quod quando domini emenda satis alte taxatur secundum deum et rationem et forte ultra rationem

oportet quod domina aliquid habeat pro auro suo: pro libra videlicet quam dominus accipit oportet quod illa habeat solidum.. Ita timendum est quod tales deputabuntur ad ignem eternum sustinendum quia in corde suo dicit: sedeo regina et vidua non sum: et luctum non videbo. Ideo in una die venient plage eius, mors et luctus et fames et igni comburetur quia fortis est deus qui iudicabit illam. Apoc. xviii. (M.13.10)

131   It is noteworthy that Bromyard's implicit reference (by the mediation of Apocalypse 18) to the humbling of Babylonian pride threatened in Isaiah 47 is echoed by Geoffrey le Baker's 'Vita et Mors Edward Secundi' by his *iniquitas Babylonica*: and by his equation of Jezebel and Isabella. He furthermore underlines Jezebel's ancestry by the introduction of Baal – left unstated by Bromyard – and depicts Orleton and Burghersh as Isabella's sinister conspirators: 'hi, inquam, Baal sacerdotes, alumni Jesebellae, id est, Lincolniae et Herefordiae episcopi..' (p.308). While it is not impossible that a sermon of Bromyard's was disseminated as far as Oxfordshire it seems likelier that men brought up on close readings of biblical texts will have found their way to appropriate parallels independently.

132   Bridlington p.101: Murimuth p.62.

133   Bridlington p.102.

134   ibid. p.97.

135   Of 1325 Murimuth writes: '..statim post festum sancti Michaelis, voluit rex Angliae quod domina regina Angliae et filius suus praedictus, facto homagio, ut praemittitur, cito redirent. Sed..*propter nimiam familiaritatem contractam inter dictam reginam et R[ogerum] de Mortuo mari*, sine quo et aliis nobilibus de Anglia profugatis, noluit dicta regina redire, et maxime in odium illorum Dispensatorum..' (pp.45-46). In early and mid-1326 Edward's letters reveal his increasing anxiety about the consequences of this dangerous liaison. (CCR Edward II 1323-1327 pp.543, 576, 579: 'she..has drawn to her [Isabella] and retains in her company of her council the king's traitor and mortal enemy the Mortimer..' (p.579).

136   ..quia si princeps seu rex negligens..vel etiam..inutilis et dissolutus et negligens contra regnum et iusticiam observandam: de regno adepto deponi poterit per christi vicarium in terris.. (X.1.3)

137   John Waleys, O.F.M., (d.1285), completed his 'Communiloquium' by about 1272. It survives in some 147 manuscripts: (Swanson, Wales p.257 records 144, to which Sharpe p.338 adds three). In I.3.20 he writes, citing the book of Job, Gregorius I, John of Salisbury, Cicero and Augustinus: '..non est peccatum tyrannum occidere sed equum et iustum.' He adds: 'Unde et omnis princeps licet sit legittime institutus debet cavere tamen ab operibus tyrannicis, que sunt iniustis legibus populum subiectum opprimere..' (Communiloquium c5 recto).

138   ..modi quibus raptores et tyranni rapiunt non sua sunt plurimi: quorum tres ostenduntur per illam raptorum fuscinulam tridentem, de qua habetur.i.Regum.ii (R.I.1)... Tertio dente munera, pensiones, encenia, dona et curialitates ab omnibus cupide expectant..quandoque per mediatores loquentes et dicentes: oportet quod aliquid detis annuam videlicet pensionem tot solidorum, vel aliquid huiusmodi extorquent: quod si facere noluerint: cogitant eos tangere quando tempus viderint et locum: et hoc quandoque aperte suis balivis dicit atque ministris, ut videlicet oculum ad talem habeant in malum: et non in bonum: occasionem querentes quomodo ei nocere poterint. (R.1.3)

AFTERWORD

The enormous size of the *Summa* will always have presented a barrier to its being copied: Sharpe records four surviving complete manuscripts.[1] A few other copies are known to have existed,[2] a tiny number in comparison with more popular and accessible texts still with us in many scores of copies.

Some of the early readers will have plundered the book for its collection of *exempla*. One such reader was Thomas Brinton, who used Simon Bozoun's bequest to the Benedictine priory in Norwich: Devlin lists over forty occasions when those *exempla* were put under contribution, sometimes in multiple use.[3]

More discerning readers will have found the *Summa* easy to use. It is equipped with a superb index, the *Tabula realis*, which contains 321 headwords, each pointing the reader to entries in the texts: 'dyabolus', for example, is divided into 20 aspects leading to 32 specific references. Added to this is an admirable system of cross-referencing which guides the reader to precise sections of other chapters.

Concern for the reader's ease of access is a note sounded in the Prologue[4]: and is exemplified in his style, in that he employs a supple, fluid Latinity, easy to follow yet never stunted: bearing the influence of vernacular prose in word order and syntax yet still within the tradition of graceful and mature continental prose, markedly different from that of Aquinas or Duns Scotus.[5]

We should expect Bromyard to be of his time, as we are. Perhaps it is his earnestness which makes many of us rather uncomfortable, pervaded as we are by powerful forces advocating moral relativism. The needle of his ethical compass was securely seated in the teachings of the Bible, both Old Testament and New. It is worth remembering the count of his citations: 6,881 of the Old, and 3,624 of the New. (There is not the slightest hint of a rejection of any part of the Old Testament, as there *is* in canon 50 of Lateran IV.)[6]

His refusal to compromise, his utter rigour in adhering to moral certainties, which we saw in the deathbed scene of the man 'quem peroptime novi',[7] means that we are brought with a jolt to the recognition that we are *not* reading a modern liberal theologian or cleric when we come across a clause such as

'..just as fire indeed is good for burning wicked people and heretics..'[8]
a view probably heavily influenced by Exodus 22.18 'maleficos non patieris vivere'.

Bromyard's apparently casual assertion must, then, be placed in the context of his century's acceptance of the doctrine in an age accustomed to brutalities of judicial punishments. It is not, however, the imposition of a death penalty for a heinous crime such as murder which will shock a good many people who read Bromyard's aside but the barbarity of the mode of execution. A second element which shocks is his coupling of two distinct groups: the wicked: and heretics. Most of us will want to see the wicked punished: yet perhaps similar numbers will oppose the repression of dissent.[9]

A further striking contrast with much of modern thought is manifested in Bromyard's position on hell. For him the punishments of hell are eternal: there is no escape. He also shares a late-medieval pessimism on mankind's future chances of heaven, quoting, in illustration of this, from a *Life* of S. Thomas of Canterbury: '..on the day when saint [Thomas] died there died, in the whole world, three thousand and thirty three: of whom three thousand went to hell: thirty to purgatory: three to heaven.'[10]

It is noteworthy that apart from texts of canon law Bromyard does not quote from works of his contemporaries. The *Summa confessorum* of c.1300 is the latest non-legal text he cites – apart from his *own* writings. We find a remarkably dismissive judgement in VISITATIO: '..that truth in the writing of books is most signally diminished, in that modern books are not as truthful as the age-old ones..'[11]: a view which does imply acquaintance with the moderns. Perhaps we should not press the statement too far, given that he may not have come across the products of outstanding English coevals of the calibre of Walter Burley, William of Ockham, William of Paull, Robert Holcot, Nicholas Trevet and Thomas Bradwardine: even though Holcot and Trevet were fellow-Dominicans. There is, however, an even more contemptuous assessment in TRIBULATIO in a passage which begins by citing the excoriating assault in Isaiah I on the princes of Judah, from which Bromyard quotes verses 22 and 23, 'principes tui infideles..' His denunciation is aimed at the dominant members of Church, State and the legal profession: 'their exploits carried out in the modern fashion are to be likened to modern books, all of which are false.'[12] Such a manifestly erroneous judgement may indicate that Bromyard did not find the time to revise his work.

At intervals throughout the *Summa* recur words quoted approvingly from the *Institutiones* of Iustinianus: 'Iuris precepta sunt hec: honeste vivere: alterum non ledere: ius suum cuique tribuere.'[13] Each of these three concepts of the citizen's duty is handled and developed in chapter after chapter of the *Summa*: namely, the requirement to live one's life honourably and decently: to restrict one's desires and ambitions so that they do not impinge unfairly upon one's neighbours: and actively to ensure that each member of society is given his due. This is a node where the followers of the civil law and of the Gospel meet in perfect harmony. And as a student of the Roman law it is in the school of a 'broader' interpretation that Bromyard is established. 'The man who takes the *words* of any law rather than the *sense* fails to use that [law] well'[14] expresses the mind of a man prepared to be somewhat flexible, at least in the elucidation of law. Moreover, in matters where doubt exists, the kinder interpretation is to be adopted.[15]

The anger over injustice and yearning for fairness has as its concomitant a passionate support for oppressed sections of society. 'They [the powerful] cruelly take from people who hardly have enough bread made from beans, and water, and for half the year do not once eat well but live in labour and hardships which never cease..'[16] and 'How can it stand or agree with reason that one man, in heavy labour and sweat day and night, scrapes a meagre living: and another, who leads a lazy, lustful and luxurious life, lusting in bed till nine o'clock in the morning, sating his desire, can take away that living: that one man can live enjoying every pleasure and another – who is made in the image of God, and serves God – can scarcely scratch a miserable living?'[17] On this unfairness Bromyard concludes 'such a society will not be at peace, nor will it endure.'[18]

His passion for justice drove him to speak out against injustice: his frankness must have been, and seemed, subversive of the social order, more especially when his declamations were delivered in plain English to an English audience: and chapter 27 explores the probability that Bromyard, at some stage in his preaching career, was 'muzzled', presumably on the orders of bishop Adam Orleton. He makes the case for speaking out, rather than holding one's tongue, when what is seen as an error is propagated:

'Silence, when you are able to put your argument, is the same as consent.'[19]
'An error which is not resisted is given approval.'[20]
He had, also, doughty champions on his side, among them S.Augustinus. Psalm 84.11 reads
'iustitia et pax osculatae sunt'
and Bromyard quotes the bishop's comment: 'There is no one who doesn't want peace: but not everyone wants to bring about justice.'[21]
Bromyard was not overawed by the English aristocracy and launches several telling diatribes against their failure to live up to the responsibilities their huge estates and

revenues imposed on them. He tartly remarks, quoting Seneca, that nobility is nothing more than wealth acquired some generations back[22]: and stands out firmly against the hereditary principle underpinning the English power structure.[23]

Writing of those of his Order 'who journey through the world to preach and to hear confession' Bromyard admits that the task brings much weariness of the body: 'yet one must not cease from this.'[24] In his quieter England, whose population lay roughly midway between those of modern Latvia and Norway, where a red squirrel might traverse several counties without once going to ground, for roughly a quarter of a century he will have followed this path of duty, duty to God and to his fellow countrymen and women.

The rich canvas of the *Summa* is studied today mainly for its revelation of contemporary thought and life in the England of Edward II: but there will always be those who prize the book for its intrinsic values. These will include members of mendicant orders using the *Summa* in its primary function as a source of guidance and inspiration for their rôle as preachers. It has importance too as a literary text, as an outstanding example of the handling of a muscular yet supple prose which confidently displays its command of an impressive variety of forms. These include the pithy sound bite,[25] the brief direct speech,[26] the short anecdote,[27] the closely-argued paragraph-length proposition,[28] the 3,000 word essay,[29] and the forensic declamation.[30] Others will cherish the *Summa* for its openness and humanity, while some few will turn to it again and again, knowing that on any page they will engage, across the centuries, with a Christian of humility and distinction, who withstood the hardships and trials of his times with irreproachable courage and challenged his fellow countrymen to live their lives in the pattern of Christ.

---

[1] Sharpe p.221. The Bibliothèque municipale at Avignon has volumes 2 and 3 of a 3-volume set, lacking A-G.

[2] Among these are the copies bequeathed to the Benedictine priory of Evesham by Nicholas of Hereford (d.1392), valued at 9 marks: and to the Benedictines of Norwich by Simon Bozoun (d.1352), valued at 100 shillings (whereas the *Decretum* of Gratianus was appraised at 60 shillings and a two-tract volume, Eusebius' *Historia ecclesiastica* and Cassiodorus' *Historia tripartita* bore a valuation of 20 shillings.) The sheer size of the *Summa* meant that only men of means could afford to have it copied. One such was John Sheppey bishop of Rochester (d.1360). At Cambridge complete copies were bequeathed to the University library by John Thorpe (alive in 1430): and to Gonville Hall in 1497 by Robert Hayles. An *abbreviated* copy (valued at 20 shillings) was bequeathed to Corpus Christi by John Tittleshall in 1458. (Benedictines p.857: Cambridge p.837). The Oxford bookseller John Dorne in 1520 offered the *Decretum* for 10 shillings and the *Summa* for 8 shillings. (Madan pp.106, 112).

[3] Devlin pp.514-515. Bromyard's account of the execution of Thomas earl of Lancaster in 1322 is used by Brinton in four sermons in the 1370s: nos. 43, 48, 69 and 102.

[4] Bromyard states that he will give full references to civil law texts.

[5] Bromyard's rather discursive style is frequently punctuated by his references, which now would be relegated to notes.

[6] ..quoniam ipse Deus ex his quae in veteri testamento statuerat, nonnulla mutavit in novo. (COD p.233).

7   See Introduction note 58.

8   ..sicut ignis quidem bonus est ad malos et hereticos comburendum. (A.14.40)
The practice of burning unrepentant heretics had been instituted by Robert II of France in 1022. After initial opposition from the Church – a stance later maintained by S. Bernardus of Clairvaux ('Fides suadenda non imponenda') – her policy was changed in 1184 by Lucius III in his Bull 'Ad Extirpanda', which held that obdurate heretics should be delivered to the secular arm for this dreadful punishment. (ODCC^3 p.255).

9   Our own times are extremely familiar with the suppression of heretical views. The tyrannies of the Russian Gulag, the German concentration camps and the Chinese cultural revolution caused death and suffering on a scale unimaginable for the early fourteenth century. In this century even in liberal Britain candidacy for one political party resulted in a teacher's suspension: and the Association of Chief Police Officers has decided that even membership of the same party is a cause for dismissal from the Police Force. In Austria a historian was imprisoned on the grounds that he questioned the extent of the Shoah.

10   ..In qua [sc. Vita] habetur quod die quo sanctus predictus moriebatur in toto mundo moriebantur tria milia triginta et tres, de quibus tria milia iverunt ad infernum. xxx. ad purgatorium tres ad celum. (M.11.56). He counters the consolatory, defiant quip 'Wherever we end up we'll have company' by quoting the chilling comment of the *Decretum* (2.2.1.18) 'They will nonetheless burn because it's in the company of many that they will burn.' [His own text paraphrases Gratianus: 'non minus ardebit qui cum multis ardebit.']

11   ..illa veritas in scriptura librorum est multum notabiliter diminuta, quia novi libri non sunt ita veraces sicut antiqui. (V.8.12)

12   ..opera illorum novo modo facta libris novis assimilantur qui omnes sunt falsi. (T.5.18)

13   The quotation is briefly expounded at V.8.54: Cuius [sc. iuris] tria sunt precepta: Honeste vivere, quo ad seipsum: alterum non ledere, quo ad proximum: et ius suum unicuique tribuere, quo ad deum et hominem...

14   Ea [sc. lege] autem bene non utitur qui verba accipit cuiuscunque legis et non sensum. Sicut iudei legis moysi aut heretici legis christi. Et nonnulli legiste legis mundi seu Gratiani et iustiniani: qui nucis masticant testam et non nucleum.. (L.3.1)

15   Dubia vero potius sunt in meliorem partem interpretanda. (E.7.9)

16   See chapter 30 note 77.

17   See chapter 30 note 78.

18   Et talis communitas non erit pacifica nec durabilis. (C.4.5)

19   Tacere est consentire cum possis arguere. (O.6.14)

20   ..error qui non resistitur probatur. (P.13.50)

21   Nemo enim est qui non vult pacem: sed non omnes operari volunt iusticiam. (P.4.21)

22   ..nobilitas secundum Senecam nihil aliud est quam divicie antiquate. (G.2.36)

23   ..antiquitus respublice bene regebantur: quia non sanguine nec genere nobiliori sed a sensu et digniore regebantur quando ad regimen aptiores eligebantur et non nobiliores. (R.4.10)

24   Sed dicent in vita activa multe sunt temptationes et peccatorum occasiones que occurrunt ex visis et auditis in confessione, quantum ad illos qui per mundum discurrunt. Sunt etiam multa tedia corporalia.. Nec tamen est ab his cessandum. (V.7.2)

[25]   Introduction notes 110, 137: chapter 29 note 19: 30 note 47.

[26]   30 notes 39, 40.

[27]   22 note 132: 24 notes 16, 17, 30.

[28]   Introduction note 80: 21 note 5: 22 notes 111, 123.

[29]   A14, ADVOCATI.

[30]   Introduction note 97: 22 notes 93, 96: 30 note 31.

APPENDIX I : FROM HEREFORD TO AVIGNON

Travel in the fourteenth century was not to be undertaken lightly: travail indeed. But considerable numbers of people did take journeys requiring days, even weeks, of travel. One well-trodden path led from England to Avignon. Those riding on horses or mules will have been saddle-sore by the time they reached Provence: walkers will have been weary and blistered.

Even Bromyard's journey from Hereford to Dover will have been taxing, some 200 miles or more, which he might have covered in nine days. One possible route would have given him overnight stays in four Dominican convents, one house of Augustinian Canons and four Benedictine Abbeys, namely from Hereford to Gloucester (D.) – Cirencester (Aug.) – Oxford (D.) – Hurley (Ben.) – London (D.) – Rochester (Ben.) – Faversham (Ben.) – Canterbury (D.) – Dover (Ben.).[1] Then would come the wait for a boat willing to take a non-paying passenger.[2]

If Bromyard was fortunate enough to make the shortest crossing of the Channel, from Dover to Calais, we may guess at the approximate route he would have followed to reach Avignon. This will not have guaranteed him a bed every night in a religious house, and he may well have spent a night or two in a farmer's barn, but a plan – perhaps like the later coachman's pocket-book plan – will have listed and located the religious houses which lay on his way. Of the 23 mendicant houses on one possible route 20 are thirteenth-century foundations: 9 are Franciscan, 2 Carmelite, 1 Trinitarian and 11 Dominican. Benedictine and Cistercian houses were other possible sources of hospitality.

Nothing in the *Summa* indicates a personal knowledge of Paris: there are, however, references to Reims, Troyes, Metz and Mâcon which prompt one to suggest this more easterly route leading to Lyon from where he might have been lucky enough to secure river transport down the Rhône as far as Avignon.

His route, then, may have taken in many of the following towns, all with mendicant houses: Calais (C., by 1314): St Omer (F.): Béthune (F.): Douai (D.): Cambrai (F.): St Quentin (D.): Laon (F): Reims (D): Châlons-sur-Marne (D.): Troyes (D.): Bar-sur-Seine (Trin., 1303): Châtillon (F.): Dijon (D.): Beaune (F.): Chalon-sur-Saône (C., 1317): Mâcon (D.): Villefranche (F.): Lyon (D.): Vienne (F.): Valence (D.): Montélimar (F.): Orange (D.): Avignon (D.)[3]

---

[1] Knowles and Hadcock pp.64, 66, 68, 74, 134, 184, 185, 186.

[2] There is no internal evidence in the *Summa* to suggest that Bromyard took an emergency reserve of money for his travels: one must assume he begged his way. He *was* aware of money transfers offered by international organizations. Prompted by Matthew 6.19-20 ('nolite thesaurizare vobis thesauros in terra..') he writes:
'Following the example of people crossing from country to country, where they would be burdened by the weight of bullion, or where they are afraid of being ambushed, they hand over their money to some society or to someone from the society, taking a receipt from him, so that they may collect [the money] from the same society in the country they are going to.' (E.3.18) See chapter 6 note 2 for Moorman's account of the monks of Fécamp paying the fare for the first Franciscans to cross the Channel.

[3] Emery, passim.

APPENDIX II : BROMYARD'S ASSOCIATION WITH LLANDAFF

John of Monmouth, bishop of Llandaff for 26 years (consecrated 10 February 1297, died 8 April 1323)[1] is called by Bromyard 'saintly', 'sanctissimus'[2]. It seems clear from these five extracts that the Dominican was a welcome guest at at least one episcopal palace.

On the suborning of witnesses, especially in cases of fornication [ubi probanda est carnalis copula] Bromyard observes that lawyers tell witnesses that they should say they saw the couple together: adding place and false circumstances. 'And such providers of information within the diocese of Llandaff are to be excommunicated.'[3]

'And justice stands afar off, which of course was near at hand before an appeal. After an appeal one has to seek it [justice] at Llandaff or *Rome*[4] where at times perhaps it is not found, in that they lean on witnesses and they can be deceived.'[5]

'It seems therefore that lords who lay claim to the goods of the shipwrecked where no living thing escapes,[6] who even lay claim to the goods of those who have died intestate, as do the lords in the diocese of Llandaff…abuse the name of custom.'[7]

'Master John of Monmouth the bishop of Llandaff had a response from the Roman Curia through his archdeacon who is still alive[8] and reported this to me, that such a title[9] is false, and that those who are thus ordained need the dispensation of the Curia.'[10]

'To such an intention a certain saintly bishop master John of Monmouth formerly of Llandaff was accustomed to exhort them [sc. ordinands]. He used most strictly to forbid those approaching holy orders from approaching orders if their principal intention was the acquisition of temporal reward.'[11]

A man who knew his own countryside and the Welsh marches,[12] and had perhaps already travelled in both France and Italy: a scholar, moreover, of considerable erudition who commanded a formidable knowledge of the Bible, of canon and Roman law, with a preacher's resourcefulness and readiness of apt quotation and anecdote must have made a welcome addition to any dinner table or solarium, and especially to the company of learned men. It must also be a possibility that when he writes of hearing a certain saintly bishop recounting a story[13] this may be John of Monmouth or even Richard Swinfield, bishop of Hereford for 34 years (consecrated 7 March 1283, died 15 March 1317)[14]. Tout citing the 'Flores Historiarum' notes 'He is described as a man of notable goodness and holiness.'[15] The following passage is from CONSUETUDO:
'When someone begins to fast or to live according to religious rules it seems hard: with use it becomes easy. And so I learnt from the story told by a certain saintly bishop that a man known in his own country as a glutton of serious proportion, after becoming a prisoner of war and being held in jail for a lengthy period where he had only a small quantity of bread both in dimension and in weight, and after being freed from jail, became an expert in fasting and responsible diet..'[16]
Under MERCATIO and treating of commercial fraud Bromyard relates an *exemplum* he owes to 'an extremely saintly man'. 'One of these [examples] I heard from the account of an extremely truthful and saintly man..which he told of two merchants..'[17] The two merchants had made a lot of money by fraudulent means in the sale of wool: one

died suddenly: his partner, a fortnight after receiving the Host at Easter found it still lodged in his throat: taken to church by neighbours he could not bear to look at the crucifix and died, knowing he was damned. The extremely truthful and saintly man had witnessed these events.

In NOBILITAS he relates a conversation which took place at a nameless bishop's table. The talk had turned to sumptuous living: '..when at a certain bishop's table the question had been put as to which of the bodily parts caused the greatest expense: and when almost everyone had given as their answer 'the belly': a certain shrewd man in the gathering, asked his opinion, gave as his answer 'the eyes'...' This shrewd man went on to detail the six areas in which nobles and magnates go to extravagant expense, five of which are to gratify the eye, namely elaboration in their dress: elegance in their horses: attractive design in their houses: large expenditure on gold and silver plate: huge numbers of household servants: and a wide range of foodstuffs.[18]

What is certain is his acquaintance with and admiration for the bishop of Llandaff, John of Monmouth. John had become an Oxford M.A. by 1276 and in 1290 a doctor of theology.[19] He would have come into close contact with the Oxford Dominicans as one of the papal delegates appointed on 1 May 1313 to settle a dispute (over the qualifications requisite for graduation in theology) between the university and the friars.[20] Whenever it began, Bromyard's relationship with the bishop ended with John's death on 8 April 1323. It must have been of sufficient length for the evolution of the warmth Bromyard expresses for him. Since Llandaff lies some 50 miles south-west of Hereford – a journey on foot of two days – it is tempting to wonder whether Bromyard had served in some capacity in the diocese of Llandaff either as a Dominican or before taking religious vows. The time, also, to be allowed for the growth of an undoubtedly mutual affection has implications for our sketchy chronology of Bromyard's life.

The bishop's association with the magnates of Edward II's early years will have afforded Bromyard at least a second-hand knowledge of the dealings of high politics. Llandaff was elected to the Ordainers of March 1310 and so joined the earls of Gloucester, Lancaster, Lincoln, Hereford, Richmond, Pembroke, Warwick and Arundel: Robert Winchelsey of Canterbury, Langton of Chichester, Salmon of Norwich, Baldock of London, Simon of Ghent of Salisbury and Martin of St David's: and six barons, namely Hugh de Veer, William le Marshal, Robert FitzRoger, Hugh de Courtenay, William Martin and John de Gray[21].

John of Monmouth was also a member of the commission set up out of the Lincoln parliament of early 1316 to reform the realm and royal household which included Walter Reynolds of Canterbury, the earls of Pembroke, Hereford, Arundel and Richmond: the bishops of Chichester (Langton), Norwich (Baldock) and Salisbury (Martival): and Bartholomew Badlesmere[22]. John was still a close observer of power politics in June 1318, a member of the king's council which met at Westminster to deal with the tension rising out of Lancaster's rivalry with Edward[23].

There was another possible source of information on and insights into the stirring events of these middle years of Edward II. If N. Denholm-Young is correct in identifying the author of the 'Vita Edwardi Secundi' as John Walwayn, D.C.L., then Bromyard would have been in proximity in 1322 – provided we can place Bromyard in Hereford then – not only to a doctor of law but to a sharp observer of English politics with a detailed grasp of the tumultuous events of that age.[24]

Alexander of Monmouth was also an acquaintance of Bromyard's. He served as archdeacon of Llandaff under John of Monmouth. The date of his induction to this office is unknown: it was certainly after 24 April 1306 (when master Henry de Cranborne held that office[25]) and before 8 April 1323 when his bishop died[26], since Alexander had made the lengthy journey to and from Avignon to consult the Curia, on behalf of his bishop,[27] seeking clarification of the capitulum *Tua nos*[28] which deals with the issue of a gift by a potential prebendary to be conditional upon his retaining that gift if elected: i.e.,simony.

Alexander was sufficiently esteemed to be elected on 25 June 1323 by the chapter as the new bishop[29]: royal assent was granted by Edward II on 15 July 1323[30]: but a papal provision by Iohannes XXII placed John de Eglescliffe O.P., a Durham man, in the bishopric[31]. Alexander remained as archdeacon at least till 8 March 1337[32] and perhaps into 1338: by 9 October 1338 master Richard de Halton held the office[33].

[1]   Le Neve/Jones p.21.

[2]   O.6.49

[3]   Et tales informatores in epsicopatu landauensi* excommunicentur. (A.14.22)
        *correcting 'laudunensi' of text

[4]   The reference to Rome leads us back to some years before Clemens V finally established the papal court at Avignon in March 1309. Taken in conjunction with two other references to the Curia in Rome it might suggest that Bromyard's familiarity with John of Monmouth began nearer to 1300 than to 1320.

[5]   Et iusticia a longe stetit que scilicet ante appellationem erat prope: post appellationem oportet quod eam querat laudaue† vel rome ubi aliquando forte non invenitur quia innituntur testibus et possunt decipi. (A.14.27)
        †correcting 'laudune' of text.

[6]   Canon 24 of Lateran III declared excommunicate those who despoiled shipwrecked Christians of their goods: 'Illi etiam qui christianos nanfragia patientes..damnanda cupiditate rebus suis spoliare praesumunt..' (COD p.199).

[7]   Videtur ergo quod domini qui vendicant bona naufragorum ubi nullum vivum evadit qui etiam vendicant bona defunctorum intestatorum: sicut faciunt domini in episcopatu landauensi*…nomine consuetudinis abutuntur.
        *correcting 'laudunensi' of text.

[8]   Alexander of Monmouth. See notes 25 to 33.

[9]   The second of the nine articuli of ORDO CLERICALIS dealt with the requirements pertaining to proper ordination. A major bar to ordination was simony.

[10]   Magister Iohannes de monumuta episcopus landauensi† habuit responsum de curia Romana per suum Archidiaconum qui adhuc vivit et hec mihi retulit: talem titulum esse falsum et illos qui sic ordinantur indigere curie dispensatione. (O.6.39)
        †correcting 'laudunensis' of text.

[11]   Ad talem etiam eos hortari solebat intentionem quidam episcopus sanctissimus magister Iohannes de Monumuta quondam landauensis† qui accedentes ad ordines districtissime prohibere solebat ne quis ad ordines accederet principaliter in intentione habens alicuius rei temporalis emolimentum. (O.6.49)
        †correcting 'laudunensis' of text. The compositors had not heard of Llandaff and dubbed John bishop of Laon.

12   Whether Bromyard lived in Llandaff during the episcopate of John of Monmouth, perhaps as a member of his *familia*, or whether he simply made visits, cannot be determined from the evidence provided by the *Summa*. But he certainly spent time in Wales. There are other references to Wales and the Welsh at A.5.6., I.6.29, I.13.32, M.14.16 and T.2.6.

13   Unde quodam sanctissimo epsicopo narrante didici.. (C.8.1)

14   Le Neve/Horn p.1.

15   DNB vol.XIX p.234. 'Swinfield was a bountiful patron of learning, maintaining poor scholars at his expense at Oxford. He was particularly friendly to the mendicant friars..'

16   ..quando quis incipit ieiunare vel religiose vivere: videtur grave: quod tamen consuetudine fit leve. Unde quodam sanctissimo epsicopo narrante didici: quod quidam in patria sua maximus comestor, in bello captus et diu incarceratus, ubi non habuit nisi parvam panis quantitatem in mensura et pondere: hic postea a carcere liberatus: optime scivit ieiunare: et sobrie comedere.. (C.8.1)

17   Quorum unum cuiusdam valde veracis et sancti viri relatione didici..quod narravit de duobus mercatoribus.. (M.6.19)

18   ..cum in mensa cuiusdam prelati questio mota fuisset: quod[†] membrorum corporis magis sumptuosum esset[‡] et quasi omnes respondissent quod venter: quidam   sapiens inter eos quid ipse de hoc sentiebat requisitus dixit quod oculus fuit magis sumptuosum membrum.. (N.3.13)
               [†]See Kennedy para.98 for *quod* as an alternative to *quid* as an interrogative pronoun.
               [‡]For 'fuisset' of text. The compositor was influenced by 'fuisset' in the line above.

19   BRUO p.1295.

20   ibid. p.1295.

21   Haines, Edward II p.76.

22   ibid. p.102.

23   ibid. p.110.

24   See Childs in 'Vita' pp.xxiv-xxxii.

25   Le Neve/Jones p.23.

26   ibid. p.21.

27   *Summa* O.6.39.

28   Decretales 5.3.34. It ends '..sine dubio tam ille quam isti.. culpabiles iudicantur.'

29   Le Neve/Jones p.21.

30   CPR 1321-1324 p.326: 'Signification to W. archbishop of Canterbury at the royal assent to the election of Master Alexander de Monemuth, archdeacon of Llandaff, to be bishop of Llandaff.'

31   Le Neve/Jones p.21.

32   ibid. p.23.

33   ibid. p.24.

APPENDIX III : WHY DID BROMYARD TRAVEL TO BRINDISI?

The passage from P.3.27 cited as no.26 of Bromyard's references to Italy[1] seems to be evidence of a journey through Puglia as far as Brindisi. How are we to account for travel of such length? What could have impelled the Dominican to walk to the Adriatic port, knowing he had to face the roughly 900 miles of a return journey just to reach Avignon? (Sailing from Genoa to Naples, however, would have been an easier option.) Here is one, highly speculative, conjecture.

Interchange of personnel among Dominican houses was not uncommon: but a transfer from Hereford to Brindisi would have been a decision difficult for any provincial or prior to justify.[2] May one look to the field of diplomacy for an explanation?

Adam Murimuth, an Oxford D.C.L. by 1308,[3] will have met Dominicans of the Oxford convent at Avignon in 1312 in his rôle as proctor for the University in its dispute with the Dominicans over qualifications for graduation. He had a Hereford connection as a prebendary of Bullinghope 1320-1321.[4] An acquaintance with Bromyard *might* thus have been formed. In August 1323 he was commissioned by Edward II to execute a diplomatic mission to Robert of Anjou[5] king of Sicily.[6] Robert had been in his Provençal domains since April 1319,[7] where he would stay till April 1324,[8] which made Murimuth's task less arduous. Murimuth himself states that he reached Avignon about Michaelmas and had an audience with Iohannes XXII[9] (on a Scottish claim) in October 1323 but does not mention a meeting with king Robert. If Bromyard had accompanied Murimuth on his Sicilian matter[10] could it be that he was then entrusted with letters for Robert's chancery in Naples: and was then, for some reason, sent on to Brindisi?

---

[1]   In chapter 29.

[2]   The transfer of John Ergome in the 1380s from the house in York of the Austin Friars to the *studium generale Curie* in Naples required the greatest journey for the fourteenth century I am aware of for such a purpose. See 'Friars' (CBMLC 1) pp.xxix-xxx: BRUO p.644.

[3]   ibid. p.1329.

[4]   Le Neve/Horn p.15.

[5]   ODNB vol.39 p.825, Wendy R. Childs' article revising C. L. Kingsford's article in DNB vol.XIII. See Murimuth pp.40-41 for his own account of this commission: and CCR 1323-1327 p.136.

[6]   The 'Regno' rather than 'Trinacria' which was ruled by Federico II (1296-1337). (Morby p.103).

[7]   [1319]. Re Roberto partí allora per Avignone (aprile) ove rimase per cinque anni.. (Salvatorelli p.786).

[8]   Re Roberto tornò in Italia, dopo la lunga permanenza nei suoi domini provenzali, nell' aprile del 1324. (ibid. p.802).

[9]   ..dominus rex misit.. A[damum] Murimuth, ad curiam.. Qui similiter, circa festum sancti Michaelis, curiam Romanam intravit, et mense Octobris locutus fuit cum papa.. (Murimuth p.41)

[10] Aug. 17 [1323]. To R. king of Jerusalem and Sicily. The king reminds him that he lately wrote to him and requested him by his envoys to restore the portions of the counties of Provence and Forcalquier (*Folcatarii*) due to the king by inheritance.. he has therefore caused to be sent to the king of Jerusalem Master Adam Myrymouth, J.C.P., canon of Hereford.. and that he will send a suitable written answer by Master Adam.. (CCR 1323-1327 p.136).

ABBREVIATIONS

Abulafia   Abulafia, David: The Western Mediterranean Kingdoms 1200-1500: the Struggle for Dominion (London and New York 1997)

Albertus, Commentarii   Albertus Magnus: Commentarii super IV libris Meteororum (Venice 1494/95 [Goff A-278])

Atlas   The Atlas of the Crusades: edited by Jonathan Riley-Smith (London 1991)

Bartlett   Bartlett, John R.: The First and Second Books of the Maccabees: commentary (CUP 1973)

Baker   Baker, Geoffrey le: Vita et Mors Edwardi Secundi Regis Angliae: edited by William Stubbs (London 1883: Kraus reprint 1965) Rolls Series 76

Barker   Barker, Juliet R. V.: The Tournament in England 1100-1400 (Woodbridge 1986: reprinted 2003)

Benedictines   English Benedictine Libraries: the Shorter Catalogues: edited by R. Sharpe, J. P. Carley, R. M. Thomson, A. G. Watson: CBMLC 4 (London 1996)

Bernardus   Bernardus Clarevallensis:Sermones, Epistulae et opuscula (Paris 1513)

Berschin   Berschin, Walter: Greek Letters and the Latin Middle Ages: From Jerome to Nicholas of Cusa: revised and expanded edition: translated by Jerold C. Frakes (Washington D.C. 1988)

Biblia Vulgata   Biblia Sacra iuxta Vulgatam Versionem: adiuvantibus Bonifatio Fischer, Iohanne Gribomont, H. F. D. Sparks, W. Thiele: recensuit Robertus Weber: editio tertia (Stuttgart 1983)

Binkley, Hereford   Binkley, Peter: John Bromyard and the Hereford Dominicans: in 'Centres of Learning: Learning and Location in Pre-Modern Europe and the Near East: edited by J. W. Drijvers and A. A. MacDonald (Leiden, New York, Köln 1995)

Binkley, ODNB   Binkley, Peter: article on Bromyard, John in ODNB vol.7. (Oxford 2004)

Bloomfield   Bloomfield, M. W. and others: Incipits of Latin Works on the Virtues and Vices, 1100-1500 A.D. (Cambridge MA 1979)

Boase   Boase, T. S. R.: Boniface the Eighth (London 1933)

Bolgar	Bolgar, R. R.: The Classical Heritage and its Beneficiaries (Cambridge 1954)
Bologna	Università e studenti a Bologna nei secoli XIII e XIV: a cura di Carlo Dolcini, presentazione di Girolamo Arnaldi (Torino 1988)
Boyle, Clerical Edition	Boyle, L. E.: Aspects of Clerical Education in Fourteenth-Century England (Binghampton N.Y. 1977: reprinted in his 'Pastoral Care, Clerical Education and Canon Law 1200-1400' (London 1981)
Boyle, Cum ex eo	Boyle, L. E.: The Constitution "Cum ex eo" of Boniface VIII: Education of Parochial Clergy (Toronto 1962): reprinted in his 'Pastoral Care..'
Boyle, Date	Boyle, L. E.: The Date of the 'Summa Praedicantium' of John Bromyard (Speculum XLVIII, Cambridge, Mass., 1973): reprinted in his 'Pastoral Care..'
Boyle, Fratres Communes	Boyle, L. E.: Notes on the Education of the *Fratres Communes* in the Dominican Order in the Thirteenth Century (Rome 1978): reprinted in his 'Pastoral Care..'
Boyle, Freiburg	Boyle, L. E.: The *Summa Confessorum* of John of Freiburg and the Popularization of the Moral Teaching of St Thomas and Some of his Contemporaries (Toronto 1974): reprinted in his 'Pastoral Care..'
Boyle, Summa Summarum	The 'Summa Summarum' and Some Other English Works of Canon Law (Vatican City 1965): reprinted in his 'Pastoral Care..'
Breviarium	Breviarium ad usum insignis ecclesiae Sarum fasciculus I (Kalendarium et Temporale): edited by F. Procter and C. Wordsworth (Cambridge 1882)
Bridlington	Gesta Edwardi de Carnarvan Auctore Canonico Bridlingtoniensi: edited by W. Stubbs (Kraus reprint of 1965 of original London edition of 1883)
Brinton	The Sermons of Thomas Brinton, Bishop of Rochester (1373-1389): edited by Sister Mary Aquinas Devlin, O.P.: (Camden Third Series volumes LXXXV and LXXXVI (London 1954)
Brundage, LSCSME	Brundage, James A.: Law, Sex, and Christian Society in Medieval Europe (Chicago and London 1987)
Brundage, MCL	Brundage, James A.: Medieval Canon Law (London and New York 1995)
Brundage, Profession	Brundage, James A.: The Profession and Practice of Medieval Canon Law (Aldershot and Burlington VT 2004)

BRUO	Emden, A. B.: A Biographical Register of the University of Oxford to A.D. 1500: 3 volumes: (OUP 1957: reprinted 1989)
Cambridge	The University and College Libraries of Cambridge: edited by Peter D. Clarke: CBMLC 10 (London 2002)
Cambridge Illuminations	The Cambridge Illuminations: Ten Centuries of Book Production in the Medieval West: edited by Paul Binski and Stella Panayotova (London/Turnhout 2005)
Carmina Burana	Carmina Burana, Die Gedichte des Codex Buranus Lateinisch und Deutsch: Übertragen von Carl Fisher. Übersetzung der Mittelhochdeutschen Texte von Hugo Kuhn. Anmerkungen und Nachwort von Günter Bernt (Zürich und München 1974)
CBMLC	Corpus of British Medieval Library Catalogues
CCR	Calendar of Close Rolls (London 1893 to 1898 for the five volumes of the years 1313 to 1333)
CEHE II	The Cambridge Economic History of Europe: volume II: Trade and Industry in the Middle Ages: edited by M. M. Postan and Edward Miller, assisted by Cynthia Postan (CUP 1987)
Cheney	Handbook of Dates for Students of English History: edited by C. R. Cheney (London 1945: reprinted 1961)
Chevalier	Chevalier, Ulysse: Répertoire des Sources Historiques du Moyen Age: Bio-Bibliographie: Premier Volume A-I (Paris 1905): Deuxième Volume (Paris 1907)
Chronology	Storey, R. L.: Chronology of the Medieval World 800-1491 (Oxford 1973: reprinted 1995)
CIC	Corpus Iuris Civilis (Amsterdam 1681)
COD	Conciliorum Oecumenicorum Decreta edidit Centro di Documentazione, Istituto per le Scienze Religiose – Bologna: Curantibus Josephe Alberigo. Perikle – P. Joannou. Claudio Leonardi. Paulo Prodi: Consultante Huberto Jedin: Editio Altera (Basel, Barcelona, Freiburg im Breisgau, Roma, Wien 1962)
Cohen	Cohen, Mark R.: Under Crescent and Cross: The Jews in the Middle Ages (Princeton UP 1994)
Communi-loquium	Communiloquium sive summa collationum Iohannis gallensis (Strassburg 1489: facsimile edition Wakefield 1964)

Corpus Iuris Canonici	Corpus Iuris Canonici Gregorii XIII. Pont. Max. iussu editum (Paris 1618)
Courtenay	Courtenay, W. J.: Schools & Scholars in Fourteenth-Century England (Princeton 1987)
CPR	Calendar of Patent Rolls (London 1891 to 1904 for the six volumes of the years 1313 to 1334)
CUL	Cambridge University Library
Dante	Alighieri, Dante: La Divina Commedia..dichiarata con note tratte dai migliori commenti per cura di Eugenio Camerini (Milano 1889)
Daniel-Rops	Daniel-Rops, Henri: Cathedral and Crusade: Studies of the Medieval Church 1050-1350: translated by John Warrington (London 1957)
DDC	Dictionnaire de Droit Canonique..publié sous la direction de R. Naz: in 7 volumes (Paris 1935-1965)
De Hamel	De Hamel, Christopher: The Book. A History of the Bible (London 2001)
Dickinson	Dickinson, J. C.: The Later Middle Ages: From The Norman Conquest to the Eve of the Reformation (London 1979)
DML	Dictionary of Medieval Latin from British Sources Volume I A-L: prepared by R. E. Latham and D. R. Howlett et al. (OUP 1975-1997)
Dover	Dover Priory: edited by William P. Stoneman: CBMLC 5 (London 1999)
Dugdale	Dugdale, William: The Baronage of England or an Historical Account of the Lives and most Memorable Actions of Our English Nobility.. volume I (London 1675)
Duncumb	Duncumb, John: The History and Antiquities of the County of Hereford: volume I (Hereford 1804)
Dunelm	Catalogi Veteres Librorum Ecclesiae Cathedralis Dunelm.: Surtees Society 7 (London 1838)
Edbury & Rowe	Edbury, Peter and Rowe, John Gordon: William of Tyre, Historian of the Latin East (CUP 1988)
Emden, Survey	Emden, A. B.: A Survey of Dominicans in England based on the ordination lists in Episcopal Registers (1268-1358) (Rome 1967)
Emery	Emery, Richard W.: The Friars in Medieval France: a catalogue of French Mendicant Convents, 1200-1550 (New York and London 1962)

Encyclopedia Americana	The Encyclopedia Americana, International Edition (New York 1961)
Engels, Alexander	Engels, L. J.: article 'Alexander the Great' in Gerritsen, W. P. and van Melle, A. G., 'A Dictionary of Medieval Heroes': translated from Dutch by Tanis Guest (Boydell Press Woodbridge 1998)
Engels, Apollonius	Engels, L. J.: article 'Apollonius of Tyre' in Gerritsen, W. P. and van Melle, A. G., 'A Dictionary..'
Engels, Sages	Engels, L. J.: article 'Seven Sages of Rome' in Gerritsen, W. P. and van Melle, A. G., 'A Dictionary..'
Foedera	Foedera, Conventiones, Litterae et cuiuscunque generis Acta Publica.. Cura et studio Thomae Rymer et Roberti Sanderson..Vol.II Pars I Ab Anno M.CCCVII ad Annum M.CCCXXVII (London 1818)
Friars	The Friars' Libraries: edited by K. W. Humphreys: CBMLC I (London 1990)
Froelich, Karlfried	Froelich, Karlfried: An Extraordinary Achievement: the 'Glossa Ordinaria' in Print: in The Bible As Book: the First Printed Editions: edited by Paul Saenger and Kimberley Van Kampen (London 1999)
Fryde	Fryde, Natalie: The Tyranny and Fall of Edward II 1321-1326 (CUP 1979)
Gee & Hardy	Gee, Henry and Hardy, W. J.: Documents Illustrative of English Church History, compiled from original sources (London 1896)
GW	Gesamtkatalog der Wiegendrucke: volumes 1-8 part 1 (Leipzig 1925-1940)
Gesta Francorum	Gesta Francorum et Aliorum Hierosolimitanorum/The Deeds of the Franks and the Other Pilgrims to Jerusalem: edited by Rosalind Hill (OUP 1979)
Gill	Gill, A. R.: The Archdeacons of the Diocese of York (Market Weighton 1915)
Gilson	Gilson, Etienne: History of Christian Philosophy in the Middle Ages (London 1955)
Goff	Goff, Frederick R.: Incunabula in American Libraries (New York 1964): with A Supplement (New York 1972)
Grayzel	Grayzel, Solomon: The Church and the Jews in the XIIth Century, Volume II 1254-1314: edited and arranged, with additional notes, by Kenneth R. Stow (New York and Detroit 1989)

Guillemain	Guillemain, Bernard: La Cour Pontificale D'Avignon (1309-1376): Étude d'Une Société (Paris 1962)
Hain	Hain, Ludwig: Reptertorium Bibliographicum (Stuttgart and Paris 1826-1838: reprinted Berlin 1925)
Haines, Edward II	Haines, R. M.: King Edward II: Edward of Caernarfon: His Life, His Reign, and Its Aftermath 1284-1330 (McGill – Queen's UP 2003)
Haines, Orleton	Haines, R. M.: The Church and Politics in Fourteenth Century England: The Career of Adam Orleton c.1275-1345 (CUP 1978)
Haines, Orleton, ODNB	Haines, R. M.: article on Adam Orleton in ODNB vol.41
Hector	Hector, L. C. : The Handwriting of English Documents, 2nd edition (London 1966)
Heer	Heer, Friedrich: The Medieval World: Europe 1100-1350: translated from German by Janet Sondheimer (originally published as Mittelalter 1961: English edition New York 1963)
Hereford	Catalogue of the Manuscripts of Hereford Cathedral Library: R. A. B. Mynors and R. M. Thomson (Cambridge 1993)
Higden	Polychronicon Ranulphi Higden Monachi Cestrensis..edited by Churchill Babington: volume II (London 1869)
Hinnebusch, EEFP	Hinnebusch, W. A.: The Early English Friars Preachers (Vatican City 1951)
Hinnebusch, History	Hinnebusch, W. A.: The History of the Dominican Order: origins and growth to 1500 (New York 1965)
Honoré	Honoré Tony: articles on Roman Law in The Oxford Classical Dictionary, third edition, edited by S. Hornblower and A. Spawforth (OUP 1999)
Housley	Housley, Norman: The Italian Crusades; The Papal-Angevin Alliance and the Crusades against Christian Lay Powers, 1254-1343 (Oxford 1982, reprinted 1999)
Humbertus	B. Humberti de Romanis Opera De Vita Regulari edita curante Fr. Joachim Joseph Berthier OP (Torino 1956)
Humphreys	Humphreys K. W.: The Book Provisions of the Medieval Friars 1215-1400 (Amsterdam 1964)
Hyde	Hyde J. K.: Literacy and its uses: Studies on late medieval Italy (Manchester UP 1993)

Iohannes Andreae	Iohannes Andreae: Apparatus ad Librum Sextum: Apparatus ad Constitutiones Clementinas (Venice 1479)
Iohannes Wallensis	Iohannes Wallensis: Communiloquium: facsimile reprint of the Strassburg 1489 edition printed by Jordanes de Quedlinburg (Wakefield 1964)
James Apocryphal NT	James M. R.: The Apocryphal New Testament (Oxford 1966: corrected reprint of 1st edition of 1924)
James, Grey Friars	James M. R.: The Library of the Grey Friars of Hereford, pages 114-123 in Collectanea Franciscana I edited by A. G. Little, M. R. James, H. M. Bannister (Aberdeen 1914)
Ker	Ker, N. R.: Medieval Manuscripts in British Libraries (Oxford: vol.I 1969 vol.II 1977 vol.III 1983 vol.IV 1992)
Kerr	Kerr, Fergus: Thomas Aquinas: in The Medieval Theologians, edited by G. R. Evans (Oxford 2001)
Kershaw	Kershaw, Ian: The Great Famine and Agrarian Crisis in England 1315-1322: originally published in 'Past and Present' No.59, May 1973: republished in 'Peasants, Knights and Heretics: Studies in Medieval English Social History' edited by R. H. Hilton (Cambridge 1976)
Kennedy	Kennedy, B. H.: The Revised Latin Primer, edited and further revised by Sir James Mountford (London 1930, 1957)
Kieckhefer	Kieckhefer, Richard: Magic in the Middle Ages (CUP 1989)
Knight	Knight, C. B.: A History of the City of York (York 1944)
Knowles and Hadcock	Knowles, David and Hadcock, R. Neville, Medieval Religious Houses: England and Wales (London 1953)
Kritzeck	Kritzeck, James: Peter the Venerable and Islam (Princeton UP 1964)
Larner	Larner, John: Italy in the Age of Dante and Petrarch 1216-1380 (London 1980)
Langmuir & Lynton	The Yale Dictionary of Art and Artists: Erika Langmuir and Norbert Lynton (New Haven and London 2000)
Latham	Revised Medieval Latin Word-List from British and Irish Sources prepared by R. E. Latham, 2nd edition (London 1965)

Le Neve/ Horn	Le Neve, John: Fasti Ecclesiae Anglicanae 1300-1541: II, Hereford Diocese: compiled by Joyce M. Horn (London 1962)
Le Neve/ Jones	Le Neve, John: Fasti Ecclesiae Anglicanae 1300-1541: XI: The Welsh Dioceses: compiled by B. Jones (London 1965)
Le Neve/ Pearson	Le Neve, John: Fasti Ecclesiae Anglicanae 1066-1300: IX: The Welsh Cathedrals: compiled by M. J. Pearson (London 2003)
Lewis	Lewis, Bernard: The Ismāʻilites and the Assassins , chapter IV, pages 99-132, in A History of the Crusades Volume I, The First Hundred Years: edited by Marshall W. Baldwin, 2nd edition (University of Wisconsin Press 1969)
Liber Exemplorum	Liber Exemplorum ad usum Praedicantium saeculo XIII compositus a quodam Fratre Minore Anglico de Provincia Hiberniae secundum codicem Dunelmensem editus per A. G. Little (Aberdeen 1908)
Lincoln	Catalogue of the Manuscripts of Lincoln Cathedral Chapter Library: R. M. Thompson (Cambridge 1989)
Lintott	Lintott, A. W.: in the Oxford Classical Dictionary, 3rd edition, edited by S. Hornblower and A. Spawforth (OUP 1999)
Little	Little, Lester K.: Religious Poverty and the Profit Economy in Medieval Europe (London 1978)
Lloyd	Lloyd, T. H.: Alien Merchants in England in the High Middle Ages (Brighton 1982)
Lotario dei Segni	Lotario dei Segni (Pope Innocent III): De Miseria Condicionis Humane: edited by Robert E. Lewis (University of Georgia Press, Athens [GA] 1978)
Louda	Louda, Jiří and MacLagan, Michael: Lines of Succession: Heraldry of the Royal Families of Europe: Tables by Jiří Louda, text by Michael MacLagan (London 1981)
Louth	Louth, Andrew: Denys the Aereopagite (London 1989)
Loyn	Loyn, H. R.: The Middle Ages: a Concise Encyclopaedia (London 1989)
Luttrell Psalter	The Luttrell Psalter: a Facsimile: Commentary by Michelle P. Brown. (London 2006)
Madan	Madan, F.: The Daily Ledger of John Dorne, 1520: in Collectanea, First Series, edited by C. R. L. Fletcher (Oxford 1885)

Maddicott   Maddicott, J. R.: Thomas of Lancaster 1307-1322: a Study in the Reign of
                 Edward II (OUP 1970)

Maitland   Maitland, F. W.: The Constitutional History of England: edited by
                 H. A. L. Fisher (CUP 1963: reprinted from the 1st edition of 1908)

Makowski   Makowski, Elizabeth: "A Pernicious Sort of Woman": Quasi-religious
                 Women and Canon Lawyers in the Later Middle Ages (Catholic
                 University of America Press, Washington DC 2005)

Marrone   Marrone, Steven P.: Medieval Philosophy in Context in The Cambridge
                 Companion to Medieval Philosophy edited by A. S. McGrade (CUP 2003)

McKechnie   McKechnie, William S.: Magna Carta: A Commentary on the Great
                 Charter of King John: 2nd edition (Glasgow 1914)

McKisack   McKisack, May: The Oxford History of England: the Fourteenth Century
                 1307-1399 (Oxford 1959, reprinted 1997)

Menache   Menache, Sophia: Clement V (CUP 1998)

Mollat .   Mollat, G.: The Popes at Avignon, 1305-1378 translated from the 9th
                 French edition of 1949 by Janet Love (London 1963)

Moorman   Moorman, John: A History of the Franciscan Order (OUP 1968: reprinted
                 1998)

Moran Cruz   Moran Cruz, Jo Ann Hoeppner: Popular Attitudes Toward Islam in
                 Medieval Europe: in 'Western Views of Islam in Medieval and Early
                 Modern Europe: Perception of Other': edited by David R. Blanks and
                 Michael Frassette (New York 1999)

Morby   Morby, John E.: Handbook of Kings and Queens (Ware 1994: first
                 Published as 'Dynasties of the World' (OUP 1989))

Mortimer   Mortimer, Ian: Sermons of Sodomy: A Reconsideration of Edward II's
                 Sodomitical Reputation: in 'The Reign of Edward II: New Perspectives'
                 edited by Gwilym Dodd and Anthony Musson (York Medieval Press
                 2006)

Murimuth   Murimuth, Adae: Continuatio Chronicarum: Robertus de Avesbury: De
                 Gestis Mirabilibus Regis Edwardi Tertii: edited by E. M. Thompson
                 (London 1889)

Murray   Murray, A.: Confession as a historical source in the thirteenth century:
                 in the Writing of History in the Middle Ages: Essays presented to Richard
                 William Southern: edited by R. H. C. Davis and J. M. Wallace-Hadrill
                 (OUP 1981)

National Gallery	Illustrated General Catalogue, The National Gallery London (entries written by Cecil Gould and others) (London 1973)
NCMH	The New Cambridge Medieval History: volume VI (c.1300-1415): edited by Michael Jones (CUP 2000)
Nederman	Nederman, Cary J.: John of Salisbury: Policraticus (CUP 1990)
NEB	The New English Bible, with the Apocrypha: 2nd edition (OUP/CUP 1970)
Oates	A Catalogue of the Fifteenth-Century Printed Books in the University Library Cambridge compiled by J. C. T. Oates (Mansfield Centre CT 1986: reprinted from the original CUP edition)
OCD[3]	The Oxford Classical Dictionary, 3rd edition: edited by Simon Hornblower and Antony Spawforth (OUP 1999: first published 1996)
ODCC[1]	The Oxford Dictionary of the Christian Church: Edited by F. L. Cross (OUP 1958)
ODCC[3]	The Oxford Dictionary of the Christian Church: Edited by F. L. Cross: Third Edition edited by E. A. Livingstone (OUP 1997)
ODEP	The Oxford Dictionary of English Proverbs: compiled by W. G. Smith: Second Edition revised throughout by Sir Paul Harvey (Oxford 1952)
ODNB	The Oxford Dictionary of National Biography: Edited by H. C. G. Matthew and Brian Harrison (OUP 2004)
ODP	The Oxford Dictionary of Popes: J. N. D. Kelly (OUP 1986)
Ohler	Ohler, Norbert: The Medieval Traveller: translated from Reisen im Mittelalter (1986) by Caroline Hillier (Boydell Press Woodbridge 1989)
OLD	The Oxford Latin Dictionary: edited by P. G. W. Glare (OUP Fasc.1-8 1968-1982: Combined Edition 1982: reprinted 2005)
Oman	Oman, Charles: The Coinage of England (OUP 1931)
Origone	Origone, Sandra: Marriage Connections between Byzantium and the West in the Age of the Palaiologoi in Intercultural Contacts in the Medieval Mediterranean: Studies in Honour of David Jacoby, edited by Benjamin Arbel (London 1996)
Orleton	The Register of Adam de Orleton Bishop of Hereford (A.D.1317-1327), transcribed and edited with an introduction by the Rev. A. T. Bannister (Hereford 1907)

Orme	Orme, Nicholas: Medieval Schools: From Roman Britain to Renaissance England (Yale UP New Haven and London 2006)
Pantin	Pantin, W. A.: The English Church in the Fourteenth Century (Cambridge 1955)
PL	Patrologia Latina: edited by J.-P. Migne (Paris 1844-1864)
Petrus Venerabilis	Petri Venerabilis Abbatis Cluniacensis Noni Opera Omnia..accurante J.-P. Migne in Migne, PL CLXXXIX (Paris 1854)
Pevsner	Pevsner, Nikolaus: The Buildings of England: Herefordshire (Harmondsworth 1963: reprinted 1977)
Plöger	Plöger, Karsten: England and the Avignon Popes: the Practice of Diplomacy in Late Medieval Europe (Legenda 2005)
Powicke	Powicke, Maurice: The Thirteenth Century 1216-1307: 2nd edition (OUP 1962)
Powicke and Cheney	Councils and synods with other documents relating to the English Church II A.D. 1205-1313: edited by F. M. Powicke and C. R. Cheney: Part II 1265-1313 (Oxford 1964)
Powicke and Fryde	Handbook of British Chronology: edited by F. Maurice Powicke and E. B. Fryde: 2nd edition (London 1961)
Prawer	Prawer, Joshua: The History of the Jews in the Latin Kingdom of Jerusalem (OUP 1988)
Prestwich	Prestwich, Michael: Edward I (Yale UP 1988/1997)
Previté - Orton	Previté -Orton, C. W.: The Shorter Cambridge Medieval History: volume II, The Twelfth Century to the Renaissance (CUP 1952)
Quran	The Holy Quran: Text, Translation and Commentary by Abdulla Yusuf Ali (Beirut 1968)
Rashdall	Rashdall, Hastings: The Universities Of Europe in the Middle Ages: a new edition in three volumes edited by F. M. Powicke and A. B. Emden (OUP 1936)
Rava-Cordier	Rava-Cordier, Isabelle: La proximité comme élément de persuasion: les références géographiques, sociales et culturelles dans les *exempla* d'un Sachet provençal au XIIIe siècle: in Cahiers de Fanjeaux: La prédiction en Pays d'Oc (XIIe-début XVe siècle) (Toulouse, Fanjeaux 1997)

Rawcliffe	Rawcliffe, Carole: Leprosy in Medieval England (Boydell Press Woodbridge 2006)
Registrum	Registrum Anglie: edited by R. A. B. Mynors, R. H. and M. A. Rouse: CBMLC 2 (London 1991)
Richard/ Lloyd	Richard, Jean: Saint Louis, Crusader King of France: edited and abridged by Simon Lloyd: translated from French by Jean Birrell (CUP and EMSH Paris 1992: original French edition 1983)
Runciman	Runciman, Steven: A History of the Crusades volumes I-III (Cambridge 1951: reprinted 1988)
Saenger	Saenger, Paul: The Impact of the Early Printed Page: in The Bible as Book: the First Printed Editions: edited by Paul Saenger and Kimberley Van Kampen (London 1999)
St Mary's	The Chronicle of St Mary's Abbey, York from Bodley MS.39 edited by H. H. E. Craster and M. E. Thornton (Surtees Society volume 148, Durham 1934)
Saints[3]	The Oxford Dictionary of Saints: David Hugh Farmer, 3rd edition (OUP 1987)
Saints[5]	The Oxford Dictionary of Saints: David Hugh Farmer, 5th edition (OUP 2003)
Salter	Salter, H. E.: Chapters of the Augustinian Canons, edited by the Rev. H. E. Salter (London 1922)
Salvatorelli	Salvatorelli, Luigi: L'Italia Comunale Dal Secolo XI Alla Metà Del Secolo XIV (Milano 1940)
Saul	Saul, Nigel: The Batsford Companion to Medieval England (London 1983)
Sayers	Sayers, Jane: Innocent III: Leader of Europe 1198-1216 (London 1994)
Schein	Schein, Sylvia: Fideles Crucis: The Papacy, the West, and the Recovery of the Holy Land 1274-1314 (OUP 1991)
Sharpe	Sharpe, R.: A Handlist of the Latin Writers of Great Britain and Ireland before 1540 (Turnhout 1997)
Smalley	Smalley, Beryl: English Friars and Antiquity in the early Fourteenth Century (Oxford 1960)
Smith	Smith, Waldo E. L.: Episcopal Appointments and Patronage in the Reign of Edward II (Chicago Ill. 1938)

Statutes	The Statutes of The Realm..from Original Records and Authentic Manuscripts: Volume the First (London 1810)
Stephanus de Borbone	Stephani de Borbone: Tractatus De Diversis Materiis Predicabilibus: cura et studio Jacques Berlioz et Jean-Luc Eichenlaub: Corpus Christianorum Continuatio Mediaeualis CXXIV (Turnhout 2002)
Stow	Stow, Kenneth R.: Alienated Minority: The Jews of Medieval Latin Europe (Harvard University Press, Cambridge MASS 1992 and 1994)
Summa	Bromyard, Iohannes de: Summa Predicantium (Basel not after 1484)
Swanson	Swanson, Robert N.: Religion and Devotion in Europe c.1215-c.1515 (CUP 1995)
Swanson, Wales	Swanson, Jenny: John of Wales: A Study of the Works and Ideas of a Thirteenth-Century Friar (CUP 1989)
Swinfield	Registrum Ricardi de Swinfield, Episcopi Herefordensis A.D. MCCLXXXIII-MCCCXVII. Transcribed by William W. Capes (London 1909)
Tanner	Tanner, Norman P.: Decrees of the Ecumenical Councils: volume I: Nicaea I to Lateran V (Georgetown University Press 1990)
Templars	Barber, Malcolm: The Trial of the Templars (CUP 1978: Canto edition 1993)
Thompson	Thompson, Faith: The First Century of Magna Carta: Why It Persisted As a Document (University of Minnesota 1925: re-issued New York 1967)
Thorndike/ Kibre	Thorndike, L. and Kibre, P.: A Catalogue of Incipits of Mediaeval Scientific Writings in Latin: 2nd edition (London 1963)
Toynbee	Toynbee, Paget: A Dictionary of Proper Names and Notable Matters in the Works of Dante (Oxford 1898)
Trillek	Registrum, Joahnnis de Trillek Episcopi Herefordensis A.D.MCCCXLIV-MCCCLXI. Transcibed and edited with an introduction by J. H. Parry (London 1912)
Tritheim	Tritheim, Johann: De Scriptoribus Ecclesiasticis (Cologne 1546)
Tugwell	Tugwell, Simon: L'évolution des *vitae fratrum*: Resumé des conclusions provisoires: in L'ordre des Prêcheurs et son histoire en France méridionale (Toulouse, Fanjeaux 2001)
Vakalopoulos	Vakalopoulos, A. E.: Historia tou neou Hellenismou, volume I (Thessalonike 1961)

Vale Vale, Malcolm: England, France and the Origins of the Hundred Years War in 'England and her Neighbours 1066-1453, Essays in Honour of Pierre Chaplais', edited by M. Jones and M. Vale (London and Ronceverte 1989)

Vale, Vale, Juliet: Edward III and Chivalry: chapter 4, 'Ludi' and 'Hastiludia'
Chivalry at the Court of Edward III (Boydell Press Woodbridge 1982)

Varazze Varazze, Iacopo da: Legenda Aurea, edizione critica a cura di Giovanni P. Maggioni: 2nd, revised, edition (Firenze 1998)

Vauchez Vauchez, A., Dobson, B., Lapidge, M., editors, Encyclopedia of the Middle Ages, English edition (Cambridge 2000)

Vita Vita Edwardi Secundi: The Life of Edward the Second: re-edited text with new introduction, new historical notes, and revised translation based on that of N. Denholm-Young, by Wendy R. Childs (Oxford 2005)

Vitry Vitry, Jacques de: Histoire occidentale: traduction par Gaston Duchet-Suchaux: introduction et notes par Jean Longère (Paris 1997)

Von Moos Von Moos, Peter: L'exemplum et les exempla des prêcheurs in Les Exempla Médiévaux: Nouvelles Perspectives: Études réunies et présentées par Jacques Berlioz et Marie Anne Polo de Beaulieu (Paris 1998)

Ward Ward, Benedicta: Bede the Theologian: in The Medieval Theologians, edited by G. R. Evans (Oxford 2001)

Warfare Cambridge Illustrated Atlas: Warfare: the Middle Ages 768-1487: Nicholas Hooper and Matthew Bennett (CUP 1996)

Wenzel Wenzel, Siegfried: Latin Sermon Collections from Later Medieval England: Orthodox Preaching in the Age of Wyclif (CUP 2005)

Williams Williams, John: Observations of Comets from BC 611 to AD 1640, Extracted from the Chinese Annals: Translated.. (Arcturus Press 2000: reprinted from the London 1871 edition)

Witchcraft Robbins, Rossell Hope: The Encyclopedia of Witchcraft And Demonology (New York 1959)

WPH McEvedy, Colin and Jones, Richard: Atlas of World Population History (Harmondsworth 1978)

Wright Wright, J. Robert: The Church and the English Crown 1305-1334 (Toronto 1980)

LIST OF PASSAGES CITED FROM THE *SUMMA* IN THE INTRODUCTION

Prologus	A.13.14	L.7.42	O.6.48
Prologus	A.12.26	S.10.7	R.2.14
G.2.2	D.9.22	M.12.9	O.5.20
R.6.2	A.27.18	O.7.17	P.12.36
P.13.25	M.11.144	M.4.1	O.1.11, 12
L.4.15, 16	B.2.29	M.4.3	B.2.5
S.4.4	B.2.23	M.12.10	O.7.5
A.14.30	N.3.14	G.2.41	O.7.5
V.9.12	P.4.20	L.7.42	N.3.13
V.9.14	D.10.14	P.6.1	S.11.0
V.9.14	B.2.55	R.2.4	S.11.8
M.10.3, 4	D.9.11	V.9.2	S.13.5
F.3.6	R.5.48	P.13.12	V.9.9
M.11.149	R.5.50	O.6.54	G.1.13, 14
O.1.11	R.5.5	M.11.90	P.8.10
E.7.13	S.2.7	M.13.2	P.14.9
P.7.40	R.5.53	T.1.4	O.5.15
E.6.17	P.16.18	P.5.6	O.5.15
I.10.5	O.5.26	F.3.6	E.7.7.
D.4.11	P.12.6	I.6.9	M.13.3
M.11.93	S.8.9	F.3.21	P.2.20
I.11.21	R.5.52	O.4.10	C.6.11
P.9.11	R.5.29	E.1.4	E.1.4
F.3.5	S.4.10	I.7.3	A.17.5
X.1.8	V.8.50	E.6.20	M.13.23
Tabula realis	M.3.21	A.5.6	P.12.8
P.3.26	G.5.5	A.24.9	V.7.2
H.4.16	P.14.2	P.1.5	P.7.17
P.10.5	P.14.2	O.1.21	P.7.31
A.12.32	L.7.4	O.1.4	C.6.59

LIST OF PASSAGES CITED FROM THE *SUMMA* IN PART I

1	4	8	10	16
Prologus	Prologus	M.11.145	Prologus	P.7.51
S.1.1	S.3.8	C.17.7		N.3.16
S.1.2		C.17.7	12	
C.5.18, 19	6	M.4.12	B.2.41	17
C.18.4	I.5.8	P.11.2	B.2.50	S.3.5
D.2.12	B.2.10	Prologus	B.2.50	R.4.6
L.7.18	P.14.2	E.7.6	B.2.50	O.6.76
L.7.4, 5	S.3.11	A.8.18	C.17.12	
M.8.6	S.4.5	S.3.7	A.27.63	18
M.10.4	S.4.12	D.12.37	S.9.9	I.9.36
O.6.75, 76	A.27.6		C.17.18	
S.1.3	C.11.9	9		19
S.1.5	F.4.19	P.14.2	13	G.2.46
S.1.6	I.2.6	S.2.7	N.1.9	
S.1.4	I.13.12	I.7.1	S.3.5	
S.1.7	R.2.9	S.9.1	P.14.2	
S.1.8	S.5.4	A.24.12-15	G.5.22	
S.1.9	P.5.12	P.12.0	C.4.10, 11	
S.1.10	A.27.48	P.12.12	C.4.11, 12	
S.1.11	G.2.37	S.4.0		
S.1.12	G.2.37	S.4.3	14	
S.1.13	L.6.8	S.4.4	B.2.23	
	C.14.24	S.4.4	F.4.23	
2	B.2.51	S.4.12		
V.2.1	I.2.10	S.4.13	15	
S.4.8	Prologus	S.4.14	I.11.15	
	Prologus	S.4.15	G.4.21	
3	S.1.3	S.4.15	S.13.3	
C.11.10	S.3.5	S.4.15	X.1.3	
			X.1.9	

LIST OF PASSAGES CITED FROM THE *SUMMA* IN PART II

21

P.12.0	B.2.15	C.18.9	P.13.17	P.13.35
P.12.25	B.2.17	D.2.12	P.13.30	P.13.36
P.12.18	B.2.33	P.13.5, 8, 19	P.13.32	P.13.33
A.20.9	C.4.15	D.12.36	P.13.33,34	P.13.13
A.24.15	C.5.18, 19	F.3.35	P.13.35	M.14.11
A.26.27-29	C.16.6	H.4.13,18	P.13.36	P.13.19
L.7.21	E.2.13	I.11.24	P.13.38	M.8.20
S.10.7	C.18.7	M.8.5	P.13.39	M.11.112
A.13.3	V.2.3	M.9.15	P.13.40	M.11.113
C.15.9-10	F.3.31	M.9.15	P.13.41	M.10.3
P.12.6	F.3.32-34	P.13.2	P.13.42, 43,45	A.25.24
A.26.29	F.3.34	M.10.10	P.13.44	A.25.25, 27
A.26.36	G.4.3	M.13.12	P.13.45	O.6.10
A.24.12	P.13.22	O.6.8	P.13.46	O.6.11
V.8.7	I.4.8, 9	O.6.15	P.13.47	P.13.44
V.8.14	P.3.23	O.6.22, 23	P.13.48,50	P.13.45
V.8.15	P.13.24	O.6.50	P.13.49	P.13.25
A.12.42	P.13.25	P.13.1	P.13.51	M.10.10
A.12.34	I.4.8	P.13.2, 3	P.13.53,54	O.6.26
A.15.23	P.13.26,50	P.13.5	P.13.55	O.6.18
	P.13.27	P.13.6	P.13.57	P.7.30
	P.13.28	P.13.7	P.13.58	H.4.16
22	P.13.29	P.13.9	S.3.9	H.4.17
A.8.15	C.16.9	P.13.10, 20	S.9.4	H.4.17
M.14.8	C.16.9	P.13.11	V.7.4	A.7.20
A.17.30	C.16.48	P.13.12	P.13.22	M.13.9
P.13.39	P.13.16	P.13.13	C.18.5-10	P.13.19
A.23.23	C.18.4	P.13.14	O.4.17	P.13.20
A.25.27	P.13.16	P.13.15	M.13.2	E.4.4
P.12.8	C.18.6	P.13.16	P.13.34	V.8.4
B.2.4, 5				

303

23	26	27	29 (cont.)
A.22.9	X.I.9	C.4.0	H.4.5
D.3.6	A.27.63	C.4.16	P.7.67
I.6.2	P.8.11	C.4.16, 17	M.9.43
P.7.17	P.7.28	R.4.11	F.1.18
	A.17.10	P.8.23	L.3.13, 14
24	A.23.15	V.1.8	H.4.6
I.11.3	X.1.19		A.16.7
O.6.39	C.17.33	28	L.7.10
P.3.26	E.3.28	B.2.20	P.7.7
P.8.6	E.3.28, 29	A.12.34	S.13.2
P.13.10	H.4.16	A.12.57-58	O.5.22
N.3.15	M.2.12	I.11.12	H.4.1
R.4.11	M.2.13	D.12.4	H.4.17
B.2.24	O.6.21	A.12.43	P.12.5
	B.2.20	C.11.46-48	V.9.18
25	C.17.0	D.12.4	V.9.1
C.17.19	C.17.1	A.27.43	A.12.26
S.4.6, 7	A.12.8	N.3.17	E.2.13
S.4.14	C.17.1	A.12.43	R.1.31
V.12.29	C.17.2	N.3.17	R.4.11
E.3.28	C.17.3		S.11.6
M.2.10	L.3.10	29	P.3.27
F.4.9	S.4.2	A.19.9	C.4.11
F.4.10		A.22.13	I.4.5
F.3.15		C.18.4	V.8.56
F.4.10		M.11.67	R.5.2
P.8.11		L.4.15	
		D.12.30	
		B.2.36	

30

C.6.11	A.14.5	C.11.5	AFTERWORD
A.17.5	A.14.21	M.9.25	Prologus
A.17.6	O.5.8	T.5.1	A.14.40
E.1.4	V.1.14, 15	T.5.3	M.11.56
N.3.17	A.14.21	T.5.5	V.8.12
M.13.23	A.14.13	T.5.5	T.5.18
M.1.1	I.9.21	T.5.9	V.8.54
D.12.40	C.2.14	T.5.18	L.3.1
T.5.61	C.4.5	T.5.19	E.7.9
A.17.7	A.12.43	T.5.20	C.4.5
P.13.10	A.14.19	T.5.21	O.6.14
G.2.8	A.14.30	T.5.22	P.13.50
B.2.24	A.23.16	T.5.40	P.4.21
T.5.17	C.16.42	T.5.44	G.2.36
F.8.1	C.17.36, 37	T.5.52	R.4.10
B.2.44	N.3.16	T.5.52	V.7.2
C.2.16	L.6.3	T.5.61	
P.8.6	C.4.25, 26	O.5.30	APPENDIX I
P.8.6	A.12.31	V.8.34	E.3.18
B.2.24	R.1.20	T.5.73	
N.3.15	R.4.10	M.13.10	APPENDIX II
V.8.34	C.11.5	R.1.1	A.14.22
A.21.26	E.1.4	R.1.3	A.14.27
C.4.4	C.11.4, 5		O.6.39
V.1.9	X.1.9		O.6.49
A.14.16	D.12.33		C.8.1
A.14.17	N.3.16		C.8.1
A.14.22	O.6.22, 23		M.6.19
A.12.23	C.4.12		N.3.13
			O.6.39

INDEX

Most of the medievals are entered under their Christian names: so, 'Thomas Aquinas', 'Nicholas Donin', 'Iacobus de Vitriaco', 'Giraldus Cambrensis'. In other cases it seemed more natural to enter under 'surnames': so 'Trevet, Nicholas', 'Holcot, Robert', 'Higden, Ralph', 'Durandus, Willelmus', 'Orsini, Matteo'. Names of Englishmen are often given in their English form, but not always: so, 'Richard of Chichester' but 'Robertus de Ketton.'

'Bromyard' and '*Summa*' occur with such frequency that I have not listed their many scores of appearances.

Astorga, bishop of, 212
Athanasius, 56, 80, 81
attitude to Arabic writings, 122, 123
Augsburg, 122
Augustinian Canons, 191, 192
Augustinian Canons' vestments, 191
Augustinian Canons'*Acta*, 191-193
Augustinus, Ps., 57, 80
Augustinus, S., 12, 24, 51, 56, 57, 73, 74,
  76, 92, 98, 107, 197, 205, 215, 245, 250,
  272, 273
Augustus, emperor, 139
Aulus Gellius, 57, 87
Aurora, 94
Austin Friars of York, 89
Austria, 276
Authenticum, 98, 129
Autolycus, 13
Averroes, 57, 105, 121, 122, 123
Avianus, 94
Avicenna, 57, 105, 121, 122, 123, 252,
  268
Avignon, 5, 6, 20, 134, 159, 163, 190,
  197, 206, 218, 228, 233, 277, 281, 283
Aymon de Savoy, 171
Azo, 84
Azzo VIII Este, 227
Babylon, 257
Badlesmere, Bartholomew, 282
Baker, Geoffrey le, 272
Baldock, Ralph, bishop of London, 149
Balian of Ibelin, 118
Bannister, A. T., 189
Bannockburn, battle of, 241, 252
Bapheus, battle of, 211
Barcelona, 133, 207
Barker, J., 248, 265, 266
Baron, S. W., 200
Bar-sur-Seine, 279
Bartholomaei apparatus in Decretum, 115
Bartholomaeus Brixiensis, 58, 73, 74, 83,
  84, 92, 93, 115
Bartholomaeus, S., 113
Bartlett, John R., 271
Basel, v, 189
Basilius, S., 58, 80, 113
Baudouin I king of Jerusalem, 208
bear-baiting, 13, 25
Beatrix virgo, S., 113

Beaulieu, M. A. P. de, 187
Beaumont, John de, 249
Beaumont, Louis de, bishop of
  Durham, 151
Beaune, 279
Becket, Thomas, S., 21, 32, 43, 113, 122
Beda, 51, 58, 115
beggars, 5, 148
Béghards, 228, 233
Béguines, 228, 233
Beirut, 98
Bellini, Giovanni, 231
Bellum Catalinae, 92
Benardus Silvester, 94
Benedictines, 11, 192, 273, 275
Benedictus XI, 173
Benedictus XII, 191, 192
Benedictus XIV, 125
Benedictus, S., 58, 80
Benevento, 230
Bereford, Simon de, 196
Berlioz, J., 187
Bernardus Claraevallensis, S., 6, 11, 21,
  58, 59, 73, 74, 76, 79, 89, 99, 100, 113,
  141, 275
Bernardus Palpanista, 94
Bernardus Parmensis, 59, 73, 74, 83, 84,
  247
Bernardus, Ps., 59, 99
Berthier, J. J., 111, 187
Berwick, 239
Béthune, 279
Biblia sacra, 3, 29, 45-54, 81, 141
Binkley, Peter, xi, 17, 31, 32, 33, 43, 54,
  102, 103, 190, 194, 196, 215, 217, 225,
  231
Bisham, 279
Black Mass, celebration of a, 227
Boase, T. S. R., 28, 170, 233, 235
Boethium, commentator ad, 59, 87
Boethius, 5, 59, 81, 87, 88, 94
Boethius, Ps., 59, 87
Bolgar, R. R., 95
Bologna, 4, 18, 206, 231, 251
Bonifacius VIII, 15, 28, 59, 73, 74, 83,
  84, 114, 156, 157, 158, 170, 171, 189,
  230, 233
books, pawning of, 23, 229
Boroughbridge, 239, 241

Bosworth, A. B., 89, 95
Bougie, N. Africa, 206
Bourges, archbishop of, 134
Boyle, L. E., xi, 106, 110, 156, 168, 176, 187, 189, 190, 191, 193, 194, 195, 231
Bozoun, Simon, 273, 275
Brabant, 118
Bracton, 239
Bradwardine, Thomas, 274
Bransford, Wulstan, bishop of Worcester, 157
Braybroke, Robert de, 213
Brecon, 92
bribery, 243, 262
Bridlington chronicler, the, 253, 265, 269, 272
Brindisi, 225, 229, 234, 285
Brindisi, Prior of, 229
Brinton, Thomas, xi, 23, 273
Bristol, John de, 28, 189
Bromyard village, 4
Bromyard, John, passim
Bromyard's
absence on 1 February 1326 from the Lechlade licensing, 6, 21, 189, 194, 225, 231
access to books, 17, 55-77, 141
access to information from the Near East, 211, 219
admiration for Jewish translation of compassion into action, 197-201
advice for restraint of libido within marriage, 12, 24
attitude towards Muslims, 203-213
colleagues, 33, 194
comment on vineyards, 13, 26
comments on the family, 6, 8
concern for future generations, 1, 16
core texts, 3, 73-77, 88, 92, 93, 102
criticism of monasteries, 11, 23
criticism of parliaments, 243, 250
daily routine, 190
dependence on the Bible, 3, 29, 45-54, 273
distaste for musical flourishes, 14, 27
experience of sailing, 5, 19
exposure to foreign languages, 226, 231
fable of wolves, shepherds and guard-dogs, 215

familiarity with Avignon, 5, 19, 20
familiarity with canon law and Roman law, 3, 83-85, 97-98
indifference to images of saints, 9, 22
knowledge of chess, 271
knowledge of French, 20, 21, 225
knowledge of the Quran, 203, 204, 208
knowledge of universities, 4, 18, 19
lack of Greek, 88, 95
languages, 6, 151, 225, 231, 232
misattribution of sources, 137
'muzzling', 215, 216
opposition to the hereditary principle, 250, 275
preparation for writing, 33, 42, 43, 53, 141, 176
putative death, 28, 225, 231
qualities described by his superior, 15, 28
rate of composition of the *Summa* according to Boyle's thesis, 189
razor, 13, 26
reliance on his memory, 16, 17, 79, 88, 91, 141, 267
reproof of the 'magnus custos', 194, 215, 217
respect for Jewish acquaintance with the Scriptures, 197, 199, 200
respect for S.Louis, 219-223
schooling, 4, 17, 18
subject areas given the greatest emphasis in the *Summa,* 2
travels in Italy, 225-235, 285
understanding of Italian, 226, 232
use of Civil Law texts, 97, 98, 274, 276
use of florilegia, 91, 106
use of his own *Sermones*, 101, 102
use of sources, 55-77, 94, 222, 223
use of the account of Naboth's vineyard in his veiled attack on queen Isabella, 256-257
veneration for S.Gregorius, 114
view of a young woman's proper conduct, 12
view on the genitalia, 11, 24
warning on women's power to corrupt men, 11, 12
wordplay, 246, 247, 264
Brosse, Pierre de la, 221, 224
Bruce, Robert, 239, 260

Muhammad, reverence for, 203
Muslim rejection of Messianic status of Jesus, 208
Muslim assault on Christian lands in Asia Minor, 208
Muslim conversion to Christianity, 210
Muslim occupation of Christian territories, 205
Muslim rejection of divinity of Christ, 208
Muslim rejection of Jesus' crucifixion, 208
poll tax payable by Christians and Jews under Muslim rule, 22, 211
preachers to convert Muslims, 206, 213
pre-Islamic society, 203
reconquista in Spain, the, 205
translations of Islamic texts, 207
unchastity of women, 203
Myton on Swale, 239, 241, 242
Naboth, 256, 257, 271
Nadab, 134, 135
Naples, 135, 225, 229, 234, 285
National Gallery, London, 125
Navarre, 100
Neoplatonists, 81
Nero, emperor, 125
New Temple, the, 206
Newcastle, 251
Niccolò I brother of Rinaldo, 227, 228
Nicholas Donin, 133
Nicholas of Hereford, 275
Nicholaus Damascenus, 95
Nicolaus, S., 113
Nikaia/Iznik, 208, 211
Nîmes, 175
Noah, 240
Nogaret, Guillaume de, 221
North Africa, 205
Northampton, 21, 192, 249
Norway, 275
Norwich, 273, 275
Nottingham, 193, 257
Novellae, 97, 98, 129
Nuremberg, 174
Oates, J. C. T., 135
Obertus de Horto, 127
Obiectiones in dicta Talmud, 135
Obizzo I of Ferrara, 227

Obizzo II of Ferrara, 227, 228
Ockham, William of, 273
Odo de Soliaco, 99
Oliver, the paladin, 242
Oman, Charles, 264
Opus trivium Iohannis de Bromyard, 31, 32, 141
Orange, 175, 279
Ordainers, the, 282
Origenes, 66, 80
Orkhan, 208
Orleton, Adam, 6, 15, 21, 28, 151, 157, 164, 194, 215, 216, 217, 218, 222, 225, 231, 239, 257, 272, 274
Orme, Nicholas, 17, 18
Orosius, 67, 80
Orsini, G. Caetani, 20
Orsini, Giovanni, 20
Orsini, Matteo, 20
Orsini, the, 225, 226
Osman I, 208
Otto, 94
Ottobonus, 67, 83
Ottomans, 211
Ovidius, P., 67, 87, 94
Owst, G. R., xi
Oxford, 4, 5, 17, 18, 95, 192, 197, 206, 213, 217, 251, 277, 285
Pachomius, S., 82
Padua, 231
painting, 125
Palermo, 229
Palestrina, 230
Pamphilus, 94
Panaitios of Rhodes, 17
papal authority, views of, 29, 266, 267, 272
paper, 187
paper-mills, 187
Papias, 67, 115
paradise, 119
parchment, 187
Paris, 4, 5, 18, 21, 26, 102, 133, 134, 137, 159, 200, 204, 206, 251, 279
parliament, conduct in, 243, 250, 261
Parma, 227, 231
Parvum volumen, 128
Paschalis II, 227
Passionarium, 67, 139

Tritheim, Johann, 27, 51, 54, 93, 97
Trollope, Anthony, 162
Troy, 137
Troyes, 279
Tugwell, Simon, 125, 126
Turks, 119
Tusculum, 100
Ubertino da Casale, 174
Ulm, 125
Ulpianus, 128, 129
Ulrich de Argentorato, 106
university lectures, 4, 5, 18, 19, 107, 109
Urbanus II, 71, 83
Vakalopoulos, A. E., 210, 211
Valence, 279
Valentinianus II, emperor, 128, 250
Valerius Maximus, 71, 76, 87, 88, 93, 94, 137
Veer, Hugh de, 282
Vegetius, F., 71, 87
Venice, 118
Vergilius, P., 71, 87, 94, 170
Vespasianus, emperor, 198
Vicenza, 231
Victorinus, C. Marius, 71, 80, 82
Vienne, 209, 228, 233, 279
Vienne, Council of, 7, 206, 207, 228, 233, 248
Villani, Giovanni, 234
Villefranche, 279
Vincentius Bellovacensis, 71, 89, 99, 199
virginity and fecundity contrasted, 11, 24
virtues, the four cardinal, 237
virtues, the three theological, 237
Visconti, Matteo, 128, 129, 227
Visconti, the, 231
vision of God after death, 14, 27
visions, 14, 229
Vita Edwardi Secundi, 252, 267
Vita S. Iohannis Elemosynarii, 82
Vita S. Karoli, 125
Vita S. Mariae aegyptiacae, 82
Vitae Fratrum, 125
Vitae Sanctorum, 71, 101
Vitas Patrum, 12, 72, 79, 81
Wales, 284
Wallingford, 217
Walsingham, 21
Walter Map, 72, 99

Walter, Hubert, 211
Walwayn, John, 282
war and peace, 8, 9
Ward, Benedicta, 115
Warwick, earl of, 282
Wearmouth, 115
weather vane, oath-breaking judges are like a, 151
weather, the years of disastrous, 252-256, 269
Webber, Teresa, 51
Welsh, the, 249
Welter, J.-T., xi, 175
Wenzel, Siegfried, 32, 42, 300
Westminster Hall, 143, 244, 262
Westminster, 282
Wheel of Fortune, the, 27, 226
Whitby, 91
wigs, the vanity of, 14, 26
Willelmus de Alvernia, 105
Willelmus de Monte Lauduno, 72, 83, 84, 85, 207, 213, 247
William of Moerbeke, 88, 95
William of Rennes, 106
William of S. Pathus, 114
William of Tyre, 118, 221
Williams, John, 252, 268
Winchelsey, Robert, archbishop of Canterbury, 282
Woodlock, Henry, bishop of Winchester, 149, 156
Worcester, 4, 95, 215, 216
Wulfstan of Worcester, S., 42
Yolante of Hungary, 100
York, 89, 160, 193, 242, 251, 266, 268, 285
Yorkshire, 240
Zainer, Johann, 125
Zel, Ulrich, 32
Zenzelinus de Cassanis, 83, 85, 247
Zosimus, 94

322

VALEDICTORY

A sense of loss often accompanies the completion of a study, especially one such as this, rooted in a lengthy association with a writer and man one admires. Compounded with this is the well-founded fear that the prophecy of Q. Horatius has been fulfilled: 'The mountains will be in labour: the resultant birth a farcical mouse.'

Bromyard knew that charity in his day had become tighter[1]: I must hope for that open-handedness he steadfastly advocated[2], and console myself that my modest efforts have ended with no worse a case than that of the poor fellow 'who on falling and breaking his shin-bone found a needle, and quipped 'We always come out with a profit!''[3]

---

[1]   Sed heu sicut vestes modo sunt strictiores solito ita caritas..(C.1.15)

[2]   ..non sufficit vel corde egenis tantum compati: sed manus aperienda est. (B.1.11)

[3]   Sicut ille qui cadens et tibiam frangens invenit acum dicens: semper lucramur. (A.15.6)